EVIDENCE-BASED LEARNING AND TEACHING

Education has become a political, economic and social priority for Australia, with the success of schools (and teachers) being an integral part of the economic and social future of the country. As a result, quality assurance for learning and teaching has become increasingly debated among policy-makers and the broader public, with a call for more evidence, data and standards to ensure that schools and teachers are held accountable for students' learning outcomes.

In response, this book provides a snapshot of the types of evidence and data relating to learning outcomes that are being collected in our classrooms within Australia. The chapters in this book seek to interrogate current views of learning and teaching, beyond what is measured in external assessments that only capture a limited view of student learning outcomes. The chapters explore a range of fundamental topics within education, including positive learning environments, student voice and assessment. They explore and articulate the vital knowledge and skills needed for current and future teachers. In addition, these chapters make clear links between teaching, learning and the theories that frame, shape and inform these learning and teaching processes.

The research presented in this book provides practical and theoretical insights into learning and teaching in early years, primary, secondary and tertiary education.

Dr Melissa Barnes is a Lecturer in the Faculty of Education, Monash University, Australia.

Dr Maria Gindidis is a Lecturer in the Faculty of Education, Monash University, Australia.

Professor Sivanes Phillipson is a Professor of Education and Associate Dean International at the Faculty of Health, Arts and Design, Swinburne University of Technology, Australia.

EVIDENCE-BASED LEARNING AND TEACHING

A Look into Australian Classrooms

Edited by Melissa Barnes,
Maria Gindidis and Sivanes Phillipson

First published 2018
by Routledge
2 Park Square, Milton Park, Abingdon, Oxon OX14 4RN

and by Routledge
711 Third Avenue, New York, NY 10017

Routledge is an imprint of the Taylor & Francis Group, an informa business

© 2018 selection and editorial matter, Melissa Barnes, Maria Gindidis, and Sivanes Phillipson; individual chapters, the contributors.

The right of Melissa Barnes, Maria Gindidis, and Sivanes Phillipson to be identified as the authors of the editorial material, and of the authors for their individual chapters, has been asserted in accordance with sections 77 and 78 of the Copyright, Designs and Patents Act 1988.

All rights reserved. No part of this book may be reprinted or reproduced or utilised in any form or by any electronic, mechanical, or other means, now known or hereafter invented, including photocopying and recording, or in any information storage or retrieval system, without permission in writing from the publishers.

Trademark notice: Product or corporate names may be trademarks or registered trademarks, and are used only for identification and explanation without intent to infringe.

British Library Cataloguing-in-Publication Data
A catalogue record for this book is available from the British Library

Library of Congress Cataloging-in-Publication Data
A catalog record for this book has been requested

ISBN: 978-0-8153-5571-7 (hbk)
ISBN: 978-0-8153-5570-0 (pbk)
ISBN: 978-1-351-12936-7 (ebk)

Typeset in Interstate
by Deanta Global Publishing Services, Chennai, India

CONTENTS

List of figures		viii
List of tables		x
Foreword: The importance of evidence inteaching and learning		xi
Preface		xiv
Contributors		xvi
1	**Australian classrooms: Linking theory and practice** MELISSA BARNES, MARIA GINDIDIS AND SIVANES PHILLIPSON	1

SECTION I
Understanding learning and learners — 7

2	**Creating a learning environment that encourages mathematical thinking** JILL CHEESEMAN	9
3	**"Why do we have to do addition? I already know addition": A cultural-historical perspective of collaborative learning, teaching and assessment in early years mathematics** MEGAN ADAMS	25
4	**Encouraging language development through an online community: Lessons learnt from an action research project** MELISSA BARNES	35
5	**Neuroscepticism: Investigating teachers' experiences using a Whole Brain Teaching method** MARIA GINDIDIS	48
6	**Literacy in and for the 21st century: Considering the pedagogical place of social media within 21st-century Australian literacy classrooms through the lens of childhood** DAMIEN LYONS	60

7	**Listening to the voices of young children in educational settings** DEBORAH MOORE	71
8	**Student experiences of the career counselling process in secondary subject choices in Australia: A case for parent-school partnership** SARIKA KEWALRAMANI, SIVANES PHILLIPSON AND NISH BELFORD	82

SECTION II
Encouraging learning through pedagogy 97

9	**Hundreds of messages on a leaf: Inspirations from Reggio Emilia** JULIE RIMES, DAVID GILKES AND LOU THORPE	99
10	**Assessing student-generated representations to explore theory-practice connections** PETER SELLINGS	113
11	**Assessment to develop students' strategies and competence as learners** ANNA FLETCHER	123
12	**Groups in action: A closer look at how students respond to group work** KITTY JANSSEN, JUSTEN O'CONNOR AND SIVANES PHILLIPSON	138
13	**The Australian Curriculum, creativity and narrative accounts of the classroom** NARELLE WOOD	155
14	**Digital technology and learning** AMBER McLEOD	166

SECTION III
Navigating structures and tools 177

15	**Education for Sustainability (EfS): A priority or an "add on"?** MELISSA BARNES, DEBORAH MOORE AND SYLVIA ALMEIDA	179
16	**The changing landscape of early childhood curriculum: Empowering pre-service educators to engage in curriculum reform** LAUREN ARMSTRONG, CORINE RIVALLAND AND HILARY MONK	190
17	**Rights-based Indigenous education in Australia: Evidence-based policy to pedagogy** PETER JOSEPH ANDERSON AND ZANE MA RHEA	205

18 Collaboration in the classroom — 217
JANE McCORMACK AND MICHELLE SMITH-TAMARAY

19 Action research: A reflective tool for teaching — 229
LOUISE JENKINS AND RENÉE CRAWFORD

20 Personal practical knowledge: Artists/researcher/teachers reflecting on their engagement in an art practice and professional work — 239
NISH BELFORD

21 Evidence-based learning and teaching: Unlocking successful pedagogy — 257
MELISSA BARNES, SIVANES PHILLIPSON AND MARIA GINDIDIS

Index — 263

FIGURES

2.1	A diagram of complementary accounts methodology	12
2.2	Sequence of actions of Jessica weighing the dog	14
2.3	Jordan enjoying his success at counting by nines	16
2.4	Jordan had extended the problem beyond two groups of nine	17
2.5	Jordan's work sample – front of the sheet of paper	18
2.6	Jordan's work sample – back of the sheet of paper	19
2.7	Jordan's work sample and Mrs B's use of the pattern he had found	19
2.8	Timeline of Mrs B's interactions with Jordan	20
4.1	Action research plan	39
4.2	Number of posts per activity type	42
5.1	The research process	52
5.2	Overarching themes	54
7.1	Alice's drawing of her "secret place tree" in her kindergarten playground	76
7.2	Georgia's mapmaking of her "bush cubby" using the 3D materials for mapping, illustrating her knowledge of place and exclusion strategies	78
8.1	Ecological model showing nested relationships influencing student subject choice thinking	84
8.2	Cluster analysis with coding similarity with each student participant	87
9.1	Thinking about the brain – children's ideas and theories	104
9.2	Messages to the brain – representing theories in drawing	107
9.3	Sensory explorations of a leaf	108
9.4	The bushland provides another context for learning	108
9.5	A message from a body part to our brain – representing our thinking in different media	109
10.1	Abby's representation of the flame test	118
10.2	Bert's flame test representation	118
10.3	Carl's representation of the flame test experiment	119
10.4	Dana's depiction of the flame test experiment	119
11.1	The reciprocal influences of learning. Adapted from *Student-Directed Assessment as a learning process for primary students* (Fletcher, 2015, p. 349)	124
11.2	Forethought step 1: Engaging with the curriculum outcomes as learning intentions	128

11.3	Forethought step 2: Suggestions and strategies for the writer to set as goals when planning and monitoring learning	130
11.4	Forethought step 3: Determining text type and audience	130
11.5	Transition between forethought and performance: Ruby's assessment checklist of things to focus on	131
11.6	Transition between forethought and performance: Leon's assessment checklist of things to focus on	131
11.7	Self-evaluation phase	132
14.1	Adapted from Shulman (1986) and Mishra and Koehler's model (2006)	168
14.2	Experiential learning cycle (adapted from Kolb, 1984)	170
15.1	Four dimensions of sustainable development	181
15.2	Year levels taught by participating teachers	184
15.3	Roles of participating school leaders	184
16.1	Timeline illustrating some key EC reforms in Australia (correlating with their date of introduction)	192
16.2	An illustrative timeline that shows some of the key theories and approaches which have influenced the progression of ECE in Australia over time	193
16.3	The six stages of FDA – information adapted from Willig (2013)	197
16.4	Key coping strategies of curriculum change, as identified by participants of this study	198
18.1	The "iceberg": Elements of professional practice (based on Fish & Coles, 1998)	220
18.2	Factors that enable effective working relationships between speech pathologists and early childhood educators	223
19.1	Action research design principles – outlining two cycles	234
20.1	The Ultimate Cultural Icon, 2007, timber, acrylic, slide transparency mounts, archival photographic paper, 1240 x 55mm	243
20.2	Devi – acrylic on canvas, 3 x 5 feet	245
20.3	In the Pink, 2013-2014, watercolour, coloured pencil and pencil on paper, 198 x 268cm overall	246

TABLES

5.1	Overview of community teachers interviewed	53
8.1	Profile of student participants	86
10.1	Assessment rubric (total = 15 points)	117
11.1	Phases of the AaL process (Fletcher, 2017, adapted from Zimmerman, 2011)	127
11.2	Difference between SDA and TDA students' pre-test and post-test scores in vocabulary	133
11.3	Difference from pre-test to post-test in students' vocabulary scores	133
12.1	Dimensions and elements of the Productive Pedagogies framework considered particularly relevant for conceptual learning in small groups	139
12.2	Descriptions of group productivity using the Productive Pedagogies (PP) framework (Hayes et al., 2006)	143
14.1	Description of the task using Kolb's experiential learning cycle	171
18.1	Characteristics of a community of practice	219

FOREWORD
The importance of evidence in teaching and learning

As the research literature reinforces time and time again, teachers are crucial to enhancing quality in student learning. However, in these times of international testing, compliance regimes, standards and excessive accountability measures (Groundwater-Smith & Mockler, 2009), teaching can unfortunately be reduced to its simplest form in order to measure learning outcomes. The difficulty in so doing, as the contributors to this book more than make clear, is that the nature of evidence sought can also be quite limited (some might say, at times, superficial) and so impact both teaching and learning in unintended (and sometimes less than helpful) ways.

One of the most unrecognised and demanding aspects of teaching is the decision making teachers are constantly confronted by as they seek to ensure that their teaching actions align with their intentions for learning – the learning for all students in their classes. What may not be obvious to the casual observer is that in the very act of teaching, teachers are concurrently searching for evidence that what they are doing is positively impacting their students' learning. As they work with a diversity of learners in the same context at the same time, teaching is considerably more complex and sophisticated (Loughran, 2015) than encapsulated in the simple view of teaching as the transmission of information. Hence, the nature of the evidence that is compelling to teachers (especially in terms of the nature of quality) can be dramatically different to those who are not so familiar with the real demands, expectations and practices of the expert pedagogue (Berliner, 1986).

The structure of this book hints at the deeper layers of understanding necessary to not only make sense of some of the fundamental aspects of teaching, but also to link that with learning. In essence, pedagogy – the relationship between teaching and learning – means that as teachers seek evidence of their impact through practice, so too they seek evidence of quality learning that can further inform their practice. Therefore, to think about teaching in isolation from learning is to ignore the importance of the bonds that matter in shaping the search for meaningful evidence of impact of one on the other. As a relationship then, how teaching influences learning and how learning influences teaching matters.

It is not difficult to see why the manner in which the editors have organised and structured this book responds appropriately to richer understandings of pedagogy beyond teaching alone. Importantly, they have sought to share evidence of impact from across contexts, year levels and subject matter – to list but a few of the fields in which the studies have been conducted. But at the heart of the work is a deep desire to understand the classroom; whether that be in schools or teacher education programs.

In his return to high school teaching, Jeff Northfield as an experienced educational researcher and teacher educator noted that:

> Do those who try to influence practice (e.g., researchers, policy makers) really understand (or remember) the practice? The theories and the 'recommendations' seem to neglect the routine and contextual complexity of the classroom setting. Many of the 'theories' seem less useful from a teaching perspective. How do they apply to 7D on a Monday last period? Unpredictability is a factor – perhaps the theories come into play as I interpret the situation and respond to the way I see the situation unfolding. The best research in the world will have little impact until the conditions for teaching allow teachers time and opportunities to consider ideas in relation to the classroom contexts they experience.
>
> (Loughran & Northfield, 1996, pp. 22-23)

Northfield reminds us that teachers should not be viewed solely as implementers of others' knowledge and ideas. Teachers interpret ideas, opportunities and situations; review them through the lens of their knowledge and experience; and then respond in personal and idiosyncratic ways in relation to their students' needs, their particular pedagogical context and their appetite for turning difficulties into challenges for growth in knowledge and practice in teaching and learning. Teachers are, therefore, developers of knowledge and they do so in the very act of teaching whilst shaping, responding to and testing the gains in that knowledge through the quality of their students' learning, and the evidence on which that is based.

As has been noted many times across the years, quality matters. However, to understand quality, there is a great need for that understanding to be embedded in the reality of classrooms – thus encapsulating the views, understandings, practices and realities of what it means to be a teacher/teacher educator (Cochran-Smith, 2003; Hoban, 2004; Mitchell, 2010). Clearly then, those who do the teaching need to have a voice in shaping debates about quality and that means they are also central to the nature of the evidence that they find compelling.

Importantly, and again as the contributors to this volume demonstrate, just as teachers matter to any discussion about evidence, so too do students. In genuinely understanding the significance of pedagogy as a relationship between teaching and learning, what students do, how and why, matters in informing views of quality and in shaping the very nature of evidence sought to support such views and interpretations. Again, returning to Northfield's experience, despite his best efforts of teaching for enhanced student metacognition, he was continually confronted by apparent contradictions between that which he was attempting to pursue with his students and his students' "learned behaviours" in response. Therefore, simply implementing teaching procedures was not sufficient evidence of change to convince him that his efforts were positively impacting students' learning. He needed more. He needed to research his practice and to seek a diversity of evidence that change was meaningful – not only from his perspective, but also that of his students.

Northfield's research into his own practice revealed how aligning teaching actions with learning intents was synergistically aligned with the need to also explicitly link an articulation of a teacher's purpose with students' expectations; disparity required serious and ongoing attention – and was common. Just as teachers/teacher educators need compelling evidence of quality outcomes through practice, so too students require the same of the value to their learning. And that highlights crucial aspects of decision making, informed action and alignment of intent and outcomes that is so demanding for teachers and illustrates why it is such complex and sophisticated business.

The editors of this book have brought together a range of authors whose combined efforts begin to illustrate ways of better understanding the relationship of teaching and learning and how important that relationship is in the search for evidence that counts. Through better understanding pedagogy they make clear that is one way of better understanding the nature of evidence that informs views of quality in teaching and learning. That is something that is worthy of much more time and attention than is often the case when teaching and learning is viewed from the outside rather than the inside – the world of the classroom. This book offers a window into that work and invites others to do the same.

John Loughran
Sir John Monash Distinguished Professor
Executive Dean, Faculty of Education
Monash University

References

Berliner, D. C. (1986). In pursuit of the expert pedagogue. *Educational Researcher, 15*(7), 5–13.
Cochran-Smith, M. (2003). Teaching quality matters. *Journal of Teacher Education, 54*(2), 95–98.
Groundwater-Smith, S., & Mockler, N. (2009). *Teacher professional learning in an age of compliance: Mind the gap*. Dordrecht: Springer.
Hoban, G. F. (2004). Seeking quality in teacher education design: A four-dimensional approach. *Australian Journal of Education, 48*(2), 117–133.
Loughran, J. J. (2015). Thinking about teaching as sophisticated business. In D. Garbett & A. Ovens (Eds.), *Teaching for tomorrow today* (pp. 5–8). Auckland, NZ: Edify.
Loughran, J. J., & Northfield, J. R. (1996). *Opening the classroom door: Teacher, researcher, learner*. London: Falmer Press.
Mitchell, I. (2010). The relationship between teacher behaviours and student talk in promoting quality learning in science classrooms. *Research in Science Education, 40*(2), 171–186.

PREFACE

In the current education policy landscape, there is an increasing demand for concrete "evidence" demonstrating effective learning and teaching practices in Australian schools. However, the editors, who coordinate a large first-year education unit, felt that often this explicit link between evidence-based research/theory and learning and teaching processes was something that many pre-service and beginning teachers struggled to grapple with. Articulating the marriage of theory and practice in regards to how children/students learn and how teachers teach is something that not only needs to be at the forefront of teacher education, but that informs future research. It was the editors' discussions regarding how to best equip our future teachers that was the catalyst for this book. Not only did we feel that as teacher educators we needed to make these connections between theory and practice explicit to our pre-service and beginning teachers, but that we needed to highlight the "evidence" that already exists within our Australian classrooms so that it might inform our current learning and teaching practices while also informing our future research.

We would like to thank the many people involved in the production of this book. First, we would like to thank all of the authors who shared their expert knowledge and research in order to make explicit links between theory and practice and provide "evidence" of learning and teaching in Australian classrooms. We would also like to thank the external reviewers who acted as peer reviewers. The reviewers were extremely generous with their time and provided constructive feedback to ensure a book consisting of quality, evidence-based chapters. Our appreciation for this invaluable contribution goes to:

- Professor Mary Shephard Wong (Azusa Pacific University, USA)
- Professor Sharynne McLeod (Charles Sturt University)
- Professor Sue Grieshaber (La Trobe University)
- Associate Professor Rosemary Callingham (University of Tasmania)
- Associate Professor Shane Phillipson (Monash University)
- Dr Avis Ridgeway (Monash University)
- Dr Elke Emerald (Griffith University)
- Dr Erin Castellas (Swinburne University)
- Dr Ilana Finefter-Rosenbluh (Monash University)
- Dr Jennifer Rennie (Monash University)

- Dr Jill Abell (President of Australian College of Educators Tasmania and President of Network of Education Associations of Tasmania)
- Dr John Seelke (University of Maryland, USA)
- Dr Julie Choi (Melbourne Graduate School of Education)
- Dr Laura McFarland (Charles Sturt University)
- Dr Lenore Adie (Australian Catholic University)
- Dr Michelle Raquel (University of Hong Kong)
- Dr Sharryn Clarke (Monash University)
- Dr Tasha Bleistein (Azusa Pacific University, USA)
- Dr Tim Fish (Monash University)

Finally, we would like to thank Kathryn Garnier whose time, investment and care into this book could never be adequately measured. While Kathryn spent time organising and formatting the final draft of this book, it was the way in which she interacted and liaised with our peer reviewers to ensure that they were well-informed in regards to what they were to do and supported throughout the process which was more than commendable.

As you read this book, we hope that not only will you learn more about evidence-based learning and teaching practices in Australian classrooms but that you acknowledge the power of "evidence", research and theory in regards to their role to inform more effective learning and teaching practices.

Book development process

To ensure the integrity and quality of the research presented in this book, a double-blind review process was used for all chapters submitted for consideration to this book. Addressing the reviewers' feedback and the suggestions from the editors, the authors improved on their chapters and resubmitted their re-drafted work to the editors. As editors, we appreciate the collaborative and constructive nature of this review process. We are very thankful for the meaningful, constructive and detailed feedback from the reviewers and the time that the authors committed to ensure that their papers were of high quality.

CONTRIBUTORS

Megan Adams is a Lecturer in the Faculty of Education at Monash University. She has had extensive experience teaching from K-12 in Australian and international schools. Megan's research and teaching interests include pedagogy, STEM, collaborative practices and child development, with a special focus on transitions of families across countries using cultural-historical theory.

Sylvia Almeida is a Lecturer in environmental/sustainability and science education at Monash University. She has a strong teaching background with over 16 years' experience in a range of diverse settings as a teacher and teacher educator in India, Africa, the USA, the Middle East and Australia. Her research is mainly focused on environmental education, education for sustainability and teacher education. She is particularly keen on understanding ways in which environmental education for sustainability is implemented in various contexts, with a special focus on India.

Peter Joseph Anderson is from the Walpiri and Murinpatha First Nations in the Northern Territory. He is the Director of the Indigenous Research Engagement Unit at the Queensland University of Technology, he is also the Director of ARC Special Research Initiative National Indigenous Research and Knowledges Network (NIRAKN). His research theorises the understandings of the organisational value of academic freedom in Australian universities and also more broadly in the polar south. He researches in the areas of organisational leadership, Indigenous peoples' education and teacher and academic professional development.

Lauren Armstrong is a PhD Candidate and Teaching Associate at Monash University. She holds a Diploma in Children's Services, Bachelor of Early Childhood Studies, and Honours Degree of Bachelor of Education. Lauren has experience in long day care and crèche, and contributes to early childhood education through her research on educational and curriculum reform.

Melissa Barnes is a Lecturer in the Faculty of Education, Monash University. While her teaching career began in the USA, it is her teaching experiences in Germany, Vietnam, Australia and Brunei that have collectively shaped her understanding of language, literacy, assessment and teacher education in diverse educational contexts.

Nish Belford works in the Faculty of Education at Monash University as a Lecturer. Her current research targets to develop collaborative partnership with schools in implementing creative visual arts pedagogies to promote intercultural capability in young children.

Contributors xvii

Jill Cheeseman is a Lecturer of mathematics education in the Faculty of Education at Monash University. Before embarking on a career as an academic, Jill had extensive professional experience as a teacher of primary school and has worked as a teacher educator in a range of settings in Australia and overseas. Jill's research interests centre on how children learn mathematics and how teachers challenge children's mathematical thinking.

Renée Crawford is currently a Senior Lecturer in the Faculty of Education at Monash University and a Research and Evaluation Consultant. Her research interests are linked by discipline, a teacher-led belief about improving and strengthening educational outcomes and a commitment to innovative practice in teaching and learning. Renée's research focuses on teacher-led research practice in blended learning, team teaching in tertiary contexts, pedagogy and curriculum development and the utilisation of technology in education in an effective, contemporary and authentic way. This is informed by both current and historical perspectives.

Anna Fletcher is a Lecturer in the School of Education at Federation University, Gippsland Campus, where she teaches in the primary and secondary BEd and Masters programs. Anna is a formative assessment researcher with a particular interest in student voice, student agency and self-regulated learning. Her research tends to be framed by social cognitive theory, which combines students' intrapersonal factors, syllabus outcomes and the classroom context.

David Gilkes possesses a Bachelor of Education and a Master of Early Childhood Education (MECE). His Master's research (2013) explored parent perspectives on the importance of beauty and aesthetics in the early years of schooling. He has been an early childhood educator for 24 years and in 2014 was a recipient of a National Excellence in Teaching Award. He is currently a convener of the Tasmanian Reggio Emilia Network and has participated in five Study Tours for educators and leaders in Reggio Emilia, Italy. David also works part time as a consultant and has presented at a number of conferences and events.

Maria Gindidis is a Lecturer in the Faculty of Education, Monash University. Her teaching career began in Australian high schools. Her work as State coordinator of Bilingual Schools and leadership roles in the Department of Education influenced her current research in education leadership within culturally diverse and marginalised contexts.

Kitty Janssen is the Literacy and Numeracy Adviser as well as a PhD candidate of the Faculty of Education at Monash University. In her current role, her research interests concern preparing students for high stakes literacy and numeracy tests (LANTITE). Her PhD research interests are concerned with investigating the factors that influence adolescent sleep in order to better inform teaching practices around sleep. Kitty is an experienced secondary teacher in the fields of science, health and English as an Additional Language (EAL) with 17 years of secondary teaching experience in Australia and the UK.

Louise Jenkins is a Senior Lecturer in the Faculty of Education at Monash University. As a sociologist and performing arts practitioner, Louise's particular focus is on the development of music and drama as tools to support social inclusion for culturally diverse schools. Louise uses blended learning and team teaching to frame her approach to teaching and this is underpinned by pedagogy which reconsiders the role of the teacher and student in the classroom to facilitate student-centred learning.

Sarika Kewalramani is an early years science Lecturer at Monash University in the science curriculum, pedagogy and inquiry-based practices and has extended her experiences into cross-curriculum teaching and research. Research interests: Exploring parental involvement in students' science experiences in early years and beyond to the primary and secondary continuum and ways to meaningfully engage young children's learning of science, understanding pre-service teachers' professional experiences to enhance their knowledge and expertise around delivering science curriculum.

Damien Lyons is currently at Monash University as a Lecturer with responsibilities in teacher education and research in the area of literacy pedagogy. He is involved in a range of research projects focusing on online learning, teacher professional learning and literacy pedagogies to equip students with the skills and dispositions for 21st-century living, learning and working, using a range of methodologies including case study, narrative inquiry and phenomenology.

Jane McCormack is a speech-language pathologist and Adjunct Associate Professor in the School of Teacher Education at Charles Sturt University. Her PhD research focused on understanding the experiences of individuals with a history of childhood speech/language difficulties and the impact on their lives and their families. Her recent work with colleagues has explored ways of supporting children with speech, language and literacy needs, including the effectiveness of computer-based programs, and inter-professional practice.

Amber McLeod is the Director of Pathway Programs at Monash and teaches a range of units including digital technologies. Her research focus is on increasing digital competence in the community. This includes investigations into ways to increase pre-service teacher digital competence and the role of ICT in increasing access and equity.

Zane Ma Rhea is an Associate Professor at Monash University. Zane's research theorises cross-cultural understandings of the cultivation of wisdom and examines how higher education and schooling are harming or supporting the sustainable education of wise, global citizens.

Hilary Monk is a Lecturer in early childhood education at Monash University. Hilary's research interests include the ways in which young children's learning and development are shaped and reshaped by family and societal practices over time, professionalism and professionalisation of the early childhood workforce, child-centred/child-friendly methodologies and the use of visual data generation methods.

Deborah Moore is a Lecturer in education at Deakin University, working with Master of Teaching pre-service teachers. Deb's PhD research was an intergenerational narrative inquiry examining imaginative play places over time. Deb's research interests include researching with young children and, in particular, the methodologies that are most conducive to listening to young children, researching with children and their outdoor environments and environmental education for sustainability with children and with teachers.

Justen O'Connor is a Senior Lecturer in health and physical education at Monash University. His research interests include curriculum and pedagogy with a particular interest in diversity and inclusion; social, ecological and complex systems as drivers of physical activity and wellness for young people; and informal contexts for community sport and physical activity.

Sivanes Phillipson is a Professor of Education and Associate Dean International at the Faculty of Health, Arts and Design, Swinburne University of Technology. She is also the Routledge Series Editor for the Evolving Families Book Series. Her research interest and experience focus on family studies, in particular, parental involvement and expectations of culturally and linguistically diverse and disadvantaged young children and their educational outcomes.

Julie Rimes is an Adjunct Associate Professor at the University of Tasmania. Based in Tasmania, Julie works with schools in many parts of Australia. Her teaching career has seen her working with learners from early childhood through to post-graduate students in Australia, the South Pacific and the UK.

Corine Rivalland is a Lecturer in early childhood and equity and social justice education in the Faculty of Education, Monash University. Her research focus addresses alternative theories of child development, curriculum development, equity and social justice. Her work aims to contribute to the early childhood educational research with the view of implementing more equitable and socially just early childhood teaching and learning practices.

Peter Sellings is a Teacher Educator working in the Faculty of Education and Arts at the Mt Helen Campus of Federation University Australia. Peter has a long-standing interest in science and mathematics education and is committed to the development of teachers who can engage students by putting content in real-world contexts. He is currently researching how to build confidence and competence in mathematics pre-service teachers and how classroom-ready pre-service teachers feel at the completion of their course.

Michelle Smith-Tamaray is a Lecturer in the speech pathology program at Charles Sturt University. She has an interest in service delivery, access and equity of speech pathology services in non-metropolitan areas, ethics and working in teams. Michelle is particularly interested in how working collaboratively with others can improve outcomes for clients in many areas of speech pathology practice.

Lou Thorpe has been an early childhood educator for 20 years and she is currently the Educational Leader at New Horizons Preschool in Battery Point, Tasmania. Lou was a delegate on the 2011 Study Tour to Reggio Emilia and has been an active committee member of the Tasmanian Reggio Emilia Network Group. In 2016, Lou was a recipient of one of five REAIE Professional Development Scholarships. She has a number of published articles on early childhood education. Lou is passionate about the Reggio Emilia Educational Project, nature play and inquiry pedagogies.

Narelle Wood is a PhD candidate in the Faculty of Education at Monash University and teaches within pre-service teacher education courses. Her interests include creativity, teachers' beliefs and assessment strategies. With a background in both English and science, Narelle has worked on a number of interdisciplinary curriculum projects, especially in non-traditional education settings such as specialised gifted education programs.

1 Australian classrooms
Linking theory and practice

Melissa Barnes, Maria Gindidis and Sivanes Phillipson

Introduction

As Australia continues to enjoy economic growth and a high standard of living, the government prepares for Australia's future with an understanding that "a well-performing school system is fundamental to building Australia's 'human capital' and is integral to the nation's economic and social futures" (AGPC, 2012, p. iii). Teachers and schools, therefore, are an integral function of the economic and social future of a country. In other words, achieving a well performing school system has become a political, economic and social priority for Australia.

As part of this focus around a good school system, quality assurance for learning and teaching continues to be a central debate amongst policy-makers and the public, especially in light of Australia's standing in the international educational assessment platform. The benchmark for such international assessment is the Programme for International Student Assessment (PISA), an assessment taken by 15-year-olds in 72 countries around the world that measures reading, mathematics and science competencies (OECD, 2017). The Organisation for Economic Co-operation and Development (OECD), which aims to promote policies for the social and economic well-being of people around the world (OECD, 2017), administers PISA and argues that PISA has become "the world's premier yardstick for evaluating quality, equity and efficiency of school systems" (OECD, 2013, p. 11). This sentiment can be felt within Australia:

> Our performance both relative to other countries and in real terms has declined over time and there is a significant gap between our highest and lowest performing students. PISA results indicate there has also been a decline in the number of high performing students in mathematics and reading.
>
> (Australian Government, 2016, p. 1)

Therefore, the Australian Government's view of the quality and efficiency of the Australian school system is based heavily on measurable data from this international test. Due to the evidence of the decline in high performing students from PISA, it has provoked debates regarding the quality of Initial Teacher Education (ITE) programs and more specifically the quality of our teachers. Darling-Hammond (2015) argues, "The quality of teaching, most would agree, is signalled by how well students are learning" (p. 132). In a similar vein, the Australian Institute of Teachers and School Leaders (AITSL, 2011) argues that teachers "share a significant responsibility in preparing young people to lead successful and productive lives" and "build on national and international evidence that a teacher's effectiveness has a powerful impact on students" (p. 1). Not surprisingly, attention has shifted to teachers in how they facilitate learning and student test scores are increasingly being used as a measurement of teacher quality. In other words, to many, the decline in PISA scores signals a decline in teacher quality.

It is, hence, not surprising that Australian education policy is currently dominated by a discourse of data, evidence, quality and standards (Comber, 2013) affecting the way we (teachers, academics, parents, policy-makers, etc.) view education. In response to this trend, this book provides a snapshot of the *evidence and data* that are being collected in our classrooms within Australia. The chapters in this book seek to interrogate current views of learning and teaching, beyond what is measured in external assessments that capture only a limited view of student learning outcomes.

Outline of the book

This book features classroom-based research in an Australian context by exploring evidence-based learning and teaching practices. This book aims to marry theory and practice through authentic classroom research that addresses issues surrounding current learning and teaching practices. The chapters in this book explore a range of fundamental topics within education, including positive learning environment, student voice and assessment, which touch on the vital knowledge and skills needed for current and future teachers. In addition, these chapters make a clear link between teaching and learning processes and the theories that frame, shape and inform these learning and teaching processes. The studies presented in this book provide insights into learning and teaching in early years, primary, secondary and tertiary education. While most chapters are based on empirical, classroom research, there is a special chapter on Indigenous education, which discusses the historical and political influences which continue to shape Indigenous education, and provides practical steps for teachers, teacher educators and researchers in order to guide classroom-based practices that support a rights-based approach to Indigenous education.

This book is structured into three sections: *Understanding learning and learners*, *Encouraging learning through pedagogy*, and *Navigating structures and tools*.

Section I: Understanding learning and learners

The first section, *Understanding learning and learners*, showcases studies that focus on how students learn and makes connections between learning and learning theories (e.g., sociocultural theory, communities of practice, whole-brain teaching, inquiry-based learning). Additionally, this section highlights how aspects such as classroom environment, student voice and teacher and parent support enable the learning process.

- In Chapter 2, Jill Cheeseman, a mathematics educator, reflects on her observations of children in early primary classrooms and the role of the classroom in encouraging children to be curious learners of mathematics.
- Megan Adams, in Chapter 3, explores learning, teaching and assessment of mathematics with five-year-olds using Vygotsky's cultural-historical theory.

- In Chapter 4, Melissa Barnes presents findings of her action research study which experimented with the use of an educational social media tool, Edmodo, to encourage language development among Japanese students studying in a high school in Sydney.
- Maria Gindidis, in Chapter 5, applies a brain-based learning approach to explore how secondary teachers view language learning processes.
- Chapter 6 considers the influence of technologies on learning, identity formation and the rights of the child in the 21st century by using a sociocultural framework. Damien Lyons explores the meaningful use of technology in the classroom while keeping children safe.
- In Chapter 7, Deborah Moore gives "voice" to the young children in early childhood settings by exploring two case studies that highlight the value and important role of imaginative "hidden" play in children's lives.
- Chapter 8, the final chapter in this section, by Sarika Kewalramani, Sivanes Phillipson and Nish Belford, uses Vygotsky's sociocultural theory to investigate immigrant students' perspectives on the career counselling process in secondary school. This chapter argues for the important role of parent-school partnerships to help better support students' educational decisions and academic trajectories.

Section II: Encouraging learning through pedagogy

The second section, *Encouraging learning through pedagogy*, highlights classroom-based research that experiments with the use of a variety of teaching practices, approaches and strategies to encourage learning in the classroom.

- Chapter 9, by Julie Rimes, David Gilkes and Lou Thorpe, explores features of classroom experiences of young children in relation to the theory and practice of the Reggio Emilia Educational Project. This chapter argues that the role of active listening creates environments where children are active protagonists of their growth and development processes.
- In the following chapter, Peter Sellings explores how formative assessment can be used to determine whether or not students have made theory-practice connections. This study examines student-generated representations created by Year 10 science students and discusses how an assessment rubric can be used to determine students' level of understanding and inform future learning and teaching.
- Also emphasising the powerful role of assessment, Anna Fletcher, in Chapter 11, provides examples from her study in a Northern Territory primary school to describe and explore Assessment as Learning (AaL) and Self-Regulated Learning (SRL).
- In Chapter 12, Kitty Janssen, Justen O'Connor and Sivanes Phillipson discover how Year 7 students respond to group work. They reflect on the pedagogy of group work and the implications for student learning.
- In Chapter 13, Narelle Wood explores the concept of creativity and creative thinking by analysing a Year 9 English lesson. She interrogates the "creative moments" that occur in this narrative and that may have otherwise gone unrecognised if defined by common definitions of creativity.

- For the final chapter of this section, Chapter 14, Amber McLeod unpacks the use of digital technologies, and the theories underpinning them, to explore their pedagogical worth and how they promote student learning.

Section III: Navigating structures and tools

In the book's final section, *Navigating structures and tools*, structures such as policy and curriculum frameworks are drawn upon to explore their role in shaping learning and teaching in Australia. In addition, classroom-based studies that explore the use of inter-professional collaborations and teacher reflection as a tool to enhance learning and teaching practices are presented in this final section.

- Chapter 15, by Melissa Barnes, Deborah Moore and Sylvia Almeida, explores the implementation of a policy initiative aimed to prioritise Education for Sustainability (EfS) through the use of a smart meter program aimed to provide educational benefits and prioritise sustainability across content areas.
- In Chapter 16, Lauren Armstrong, Corine Rivalland and Hilary Monk present key curriculum changes within the Australian context, providing excerpts from the field, to explore the influence of curriculum reform. They write this chapter from an early years perspective.
- In Chapter 17, Peter Anderson and Zane Ma Rhea explore the current education policy landscape around Indigenous education and discuss how teachers, teacher educators and researchers can develop a rights-based approach to curriculum development and pedagogical practice in the First Nations education space.
- Jane McCormack and Michelle Smith-Tamaray, in Chapter 18, explore collaboration with a focus on supporting children's language and communication needs in the preschool and primary years. They argue that research into collaboration, and collaboration itself, can inform learning and teaching.
- Chapter 19, by Louise Jenkins and Renée Crawford, discusses the use of action research as a research method for reflective teacher practice and for an evidence base for effective learning and teaching.
- The final chapter in this section, by Nish Belford, also focuses on reflective practice but explores reflection on pedagogies of practice in art education. She draws from two art educators' reflections and explores how their experiences open up the possibilities for art educators to merge their personal interests and professional work to empower their own artistic practice.

The conclusion chapter of this book, Chapter 21, by Melissa Barnes, Sivanes Phillipson and Maria Gindidis, discusses the key themes and implications present in the studies discussed in the book.

Conclusion

This book is designed to highlight the power of classroom-based research as a tool for understanding learning and learners, encouraging learning through pedagogy and navigating educational structures and tools to enhance learning and teaching. In addition, the book seeks to acknowledge the work that is already being done within Australian classrooms to make stronger links between theory and practice, and provide insight into the types of evidence-based practices that do encourage learning and teaching. As the Australian Government continues to push for the need for concrete data and "evidence" of the health of our educational system, it is through these evidence-based studies presented in this book that the reader can begin to understand the power of research in the classroom. For pre-service teachers and teachers, the authors hope that this book provides explicit yet accessible links between the practical and theoretical components of learning and teaching. For teacher educators and researchers, we hope that these chapters provide current evidence but also act as a platform for future research in evidence-based learning and teaching within Australia.

References

AGPC (Australian Government Productivity Commission). (2012). *Schools workforce: Productivity Commission research report*. Retrieved on October 2, 2017 from: http://www.pc.gov.au/inquiries/completed/education-workforce-schools/report/schools-workforce.pdf

AITSL (Australian Institute of Teachers and School Leaders). (2011). *Australian Professional Standards for Teachers*. Retrieved on September 21, 2017 from: https://www.aitsl.edu.au/docs/default-source/apst-resources/australian_professional_standard_for_teachers_final.pdf

Australian Government (2016). *Quality schools, quality outcomes*. Retrieved on October 1, 2017 from: https://docs.education.gov.au/system/files/doc/other/quality_schools_acc.pdf

Comber, B. (2013). Teachers as researchers: A 'fair dinkum' learning legacy. *English in Australia*, 48(3), 54-61.

Darling-Hammond, L. (2015). Can value added add value to teacher education? *Educational Researcher*, 44(2), 132-137.

OECD (The Organisation of Economic Co-operation and Development). (2013). PISA as a yardstick of educational success. *Strong performers and successful reformers in education – Lessons from PISA 2012 for the United States*. Retrieved on October 2, 2017 from: http://www.oecd.org/pisa/keyfindings/PISA2012-US-CHAP1.pdf

OECD (The Organisation of Economic Co-operation and Development). (2017). *About the OECD*. Retrieved on October 2, 2017 from: http://www.oecd.org/about/

Section I
Understanding learning and learners

2 Creating a learning environment that encourages mathematical thinking

Jill Cheeseman

Introduction

As a mathematics educator, I am committed to classroom-based research. For me, the way that theory informs practice and practice informs theory is fascinating. While observing in early primary classrooms it struck me how important it is to create a classroom environment that encourages children to be curious learners of mathematics. This led me to analyse what the teachers were doing to create communities of investigative learners (Cheeseman & McDonough, 2016). In this chapter, stories of classrooms and the children in them will be shared to illustrate some of the practices of highly effective teachers of mathematics.

Background

The vignettes of classrooms will be drawn from a research project that was designed to closely examine the practices of "highly effective" teachers of mathematics with young children (Cheeseman, 2010). The teachers were first identified as highly effective based on the measurable improvements in children's mathematical learning over two consecutive years of the Early Numeracy Research Project (ENRP) (Clarke et al., 2002). During the final year of the project a case study was undertaken to identify the characteristics of effective teachers (McDonough & Clarke, 2003). A further study was undertaken by Cheeseman (2010) to describe in greater depth how effective teachers build communities of learners and encourage classroom interaction. In particular, how highly effective teachers:

- use a range of question types to probe and challenge children's thinking and reasoning;
- hold back from telling children everything;
- encourage children to explain their mathematical thinking/ideas;
- encourage children to listen and evaluate others' mathematical thinking/ideas; and help with methods and understanding (p. 265).

Teacher behaviours that promoted classroom interactions that stimulated mathematical thinking and reflection in the context of high teacher expectations were at the heart of the study. Each of the illustrative vignettes comes from the classroom of the highly effective mathematics teacher.

Theoretical underpinning

The theoretical basis of the study is one of social constructivism which holds that the construction of knowledge occurs within a social and cultural context where discourse is a vital component in establishing an effective learning context (Cobb, Wood, & Yackel, 1990; Cobb & Yackel, 1998; Sfard, Nescher, Streefland, Cobb, & Mason, 1998; Sriraman & English, 2010). It is a theory in which "learning is seen as a collaborative process in which adults and children search for meanings together" (Clark, 2004, p. 143). According to Vygotsky (1978, p. 57):

> Every function in a child's development appears twice: first on the social level, and later, on the individual level; first between people (interpsychological) and then inside the child (intrapsychological).

Vygotsky's zone of proximal development is probably his best-known concept. It argued that children can, with help from adults or children who are more advanced, master concepts and ideas that they cannot understand on their own. Social constructivism adopts a philosophical thesis that "mathematical knowledge grows through conjectures and refutations, utilizing a logic of mathematical discovery" (Ernest, 1991, p. 42).

Literature

Four elements of the research literature that underpins the study will be briefly described: the characteristics of effective teachers of mathematics, questioning, listening, and a perspective of young learners.

Effective teachers of mathematics

Groves, Mousley, and Forgasz (2006) produced a database of 185 projects and 726 publications relating to numeracy research and thereby mapped Australian research on primary school mathematics. The project report examined results under themes. Effective teachers of numeracy were found to:

- have high expectations of their students;
- focus on children's mathematical learning, rather than on providing pleasant classroom experiences;
- provide a challenging curriculum;
- use higher-order questioning;
- make connections both within mathematics and between mathematics in different contexts; and
- use highly interactive teaching involvement with students in class discussion (2006, p. 203).

These characteristics matched general patterns of characteristics of highly effective teachers of mathematics found in the ENRP as described by Clarke et al. (2002) that underpin the research described here.

Mathematical communication: Questioning and listening

The focus of the study was teacher-child interactions. The literature surrounding mathematical communication was particularly relevant to the study, especially mathematical *conversations*. Thornbury and Slade (2006) described the characteristics of conversation as: spoken, spontaneous, dialogic, synchronous, interpersonal (as opposed to transactional) and symmetrical in relationship. Classroom talk is different from conversation which:

> is a natural context for verbal scaffolding ... it has been argued that instructional talk that is modelled on conversation – that incorporates, for example, such features of conversation as reciprocal turn-taking, referential questions, elaborations, and continuing moves – is likely to be more effective than sequences of teacher-initiated display questioning.
>
> (p. 207)

For the purposes of this study, instructional talk modelled on conversation was a more precise descriptor than simply conversation. Certainly, questioning was a key to the study because it was a major part of effective communication by teachers (Gervasoni, Hunter, Bicknell, & Sexton, 2012; Roche & Ferguson, 2015). Teachers used questions that promote higher order thinking as a regular part of children's mathematical experience (Burns, 1985; Burton, 1984; Mason, Burton, & Stacey, 1982).

In addition to asking "good" questions (Sullivan & Clarke, 1991), careful listening to students has been shown to be an important aspect of teaching practice (Arcavi & Isoda, 2007; Carpenter & Fennema, 1992; Crespo, 2000). Davis (1997) described three different types of listening. These were: *evaluative listening* where the teacher was listening for something in particular rather than listening to the speaker; *interpretive listening* where the questions posed were information-seeking, required more elaborate answers and often some sort of demonstration or explanation; and *hermeneutic listening*. This description was "intended to reflect the negotiated and participatory nature of this manner of interacting with learners" (Davis, 1997, p. 369). In hermeneutic listening the teacher is a participant in the exploration of a piece of mathematics. Behaviours and understandings emerged that were unlikely to have arisen had the learners not been given the opportunity to interact. These behaviours were characterised by Davis as complex and dynamic interactions where learning is seen as a social process and the teacher's role is one of participating, interpreting, transforming and interrogating. This study found teachers who used hermeneutic listening as a regular part of their classroom practice.

Perspective of young learners

Another important aspect of this study was the view taken of young children where children were viewed as "experts in their own lives" (Langsted, 1994, p. 42). This study was designed to inquire into children's mathematical thinking and to gather their accounts of the classroom events. I view children as "beings not becomings" as voiced by Qvortrup, Bardy, Sgritta, and Wintersberger (1994, p. 4). In other words, I believe that children have important perspectives to contribute to making meaning of classroom interactions in the teaching and learning of mathematics. In the vignettes that follow the mathematical thinking of the children is important.

Methodology

In this study, teacher behaviours that challenge young children to consider their mathematical thinking were investigated. A *complementary accounts methodology* was used to study four "highly effective" teachers to capture some of the complexities of classroom settings and to collect rich data (Clarke, 1998, 2001). The methodology involved observing, videotaping and interviewing teachers and children to collect varying accounts of classroom events (Figure 2.1).

Four teachers who taught children aged five to seven years in the first three years of primary school participated in the research. Each teacher came from a different school and their schools represented a range of geographic and socioeconomic profiles in the Victorian school system. Three consecutive mathematics lessons taught by each teacher were observed and videotaped. Interviews were conducted with the teacher and several children after each observed lesson. These interviews were audiotaped for transcription and analysis. The various sets of data were used to construct a picture of the behaviours of each teacher.

Data were collected from "ordinary" mathematics lessons in the usual classroom setting at the usual time of day. Whole mathematics lessons were observed and videotaped. Interviews were conducted with the teachers and children soon after the lesson, to collect their perspectives. The multiple data sets were examined, analysed and compared in an iterative process to produce a creative nonfiction, or a story using facts and substantiated by quotes, which also went beyond the vignette to discover underlying meanings (Caulley, 2008). Each "case study story" was given to the teachers to make sure that what was written about them accurately represented them and their words. A cross-case analysis was then undertaken to search for common patterns of behaviour. The classroom stories in this chapter derive from these data.

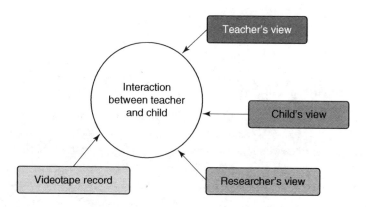

Figure 2.1 A diagram of complementary accounts methodology

Results and discussion

Two stories of the classroom will illustrate some of the ways in which teachers can effectively create learning environments that encourage mathematical curiosity.

Measuring Joey

Joey was legendary in the school as he had visited every year since he was a tiny puppy. Incoming Preps knew through the school grapevine that he would visit but they did not know when. This is a classroom story from the day he finally came to school.

Their topic for inquiry was *Pets*, so wherever sensible, mathematics lessons were integrated into this topic. The story *Mrs McTats and Her Houseful of Cats* (Capucilli, 2004) had been read to the children, then they made a pictograph of the cats that arrived each day at Mrs McTats' house. They also had made a graph of their pets and a frequency plot on the whiteboard with magnetic spots to vote for their favourite pets.

In preparation for Joey the children were asked to pose questions about him that could be answered by mathematics. The list was long and some of the ideas that the children suggested included: How long was his tail? How long was his fur? His ears? How tall was he? How big he was around the neck and the tummy (and various other linear measures). How many toenails did he have? Would his collar fit around their necks? How much did Joey eat? Each of the questions was recorded on the board with the initials of the child who posed the question.

On the day that he came to school the children were assigned to three groups and they had three activities to complete: playing in the classroom shop, playing a favourite dice game and measuring Joey. Each group had a turn with every activity by the end of the mathematics session.

The teacher, Mrs W, stayed with the group measuring her dog and expected the other children to be self-contained with their activities. At this point it must be said that Joey is a wonderfully calm and patient dog who obviously likes little children and is very used to being handled by them; very few dogs in my experience would match him.

Jessica and the dog

A group of children was working on the problem of how many dried food pellets Joey's bowl would hold when quite suddenly Jessica said: "Oh we could weigh him!" Mrs W found some bathroom scales and gave them to Jessica.

Mrs W: "What are you thinking?"
Jessica: "We could make him stand on the scales."

Mrs W called Joey and placed his front legs onto the scales but he moved away immediately.

Mrs W: "What could we do?"
Jessica: "We could try again."

The dog was placed onto the scales again but was even less keen the second time.

Mrs W: "What else could we do?"

14 Jill Cheeseman

There was a long pause.

Jessica: "We could weigh him times (sic) me."
Mrs W: "Do you mean with you?"
Jessica: "Yes. I can hold him."

With that, Mrs W weighed Jessica and wrote 19 kilograms on the board. Then she picked up the dog and gently handed him over to Jessica as she stood on the scales (Figure 2.2).

Other children who had become interested read the scales with Mrs W – they showed 28 kilos. The dog was released and 28 kilograms was written on the board. Jessica then worked with her friend using Unifix cubes to find the difference between 28 and 19. After some time she excitedly announced, "Joey weighs nine kilograms."

An examination of the conversational exchange shows that it is an example of hermeneutic listening where the teacher is a participant in the exploration of mathematics.

I was observing in the classroom but I was unsure whether the idea had really been Jessica's. In an interview after the lesson I used video-stimulated recall to prompt Jessica to talk. I paused the video just as Jessica made the suggestion to weigh Joey. The following exchange occurred:

Interviewer: "Can you tell me about your good idea for maths today please?"
Jessica: "I thought of holding Joey on the scales. I would know how much Joey weighed. So I hopped on the scales with him and I holded (sic) him. And then we took away 19 [from 28] because I was 19 and he was nine and so – that was nine kilograms and that's what he weighed."

The teacher's actions

From this exchange, it is clear that the teacher was facilitating the child's idea and encouraging her mathematical curiosity. The teacher took the question posed by the child as one

Figure 2.2 Sequence of actions of Jessica weighing the dog

that mathematics could answer. She encouraged the child to plan her data collection and to behave as a young mathematician (Fosnot & Dolk, 2001; Mannigel, 1992). She noted results in a natural way to keep track of numbers so that they could be used later and in doing so modelled how adults genuinely jot down numbers to work on later. She left the child to work out a solution using familiar countable materials. Finally, she encouraged Jessica to create a beautiful page in the book that the class was making about Joey to record all that she had done.

The "class on the stage" problem

Mrs B's Prep children were accustomed to solving problems in their mathematics lessons. The day that I observed them tackling The Class on the Stage problem was an interesting and memorable one for me. The lesson was introduced by having the children think and talk about when they had heard the word "half". Mrs B drew a poster of the ideas the children shared. She then asked individual children to divide a length of ribbon in half and a collection of counters in half. Having built the mathematical vocabulary and modelled halving of a continuous and a discrete quantity, she then set the problem of the day. The problem was:

> Miss G asked the class to go up on the stage for assembly.
> She asked half of the class to sit and half of the class to stand.
> How might that look?

The problem was read carefully and Mrs B made sure that the context was one the children could understand by connecting it to their everyday lives at school. There was a bit of chat as an aside, then the problem was read aloud again and this time Mrs B pointed to each word on the chart as she read it. Emphasis was then placed on half sitting and half standing to clarify and reiterate the problem.

The children were then told what was expected: they would draw something on a large piece of paper to show their solution to the problem. The children were told to get a sheet of paper and find a place to work. Mrs B called a group of four children to work with her on the floor. She told them that they were going to use materials to work it out. Mrs B had collected a container of two-coloured counters which she tipped onto the floor. Patrick and Jordan decided that they wanted something different so they were sent off to get the materials that they were going to use. Soon they returned with a container of plastic dinosaurs. Patrick demonstrated to Mrs B how the sitting down group would be tipped over onto its side while the standing would be upright dinosaurs. Mrs B then restated the problem and left them to get on with finding a solution.

Challenging mathematical thinking: The story of Jordan

Jordan was slow to get organised and Mrs B was quite insistent that he show her what he planned to do. Once he became engrossed with the task she devoted her attention to others in the group. From time to time she asked for an explanation or a justification of Jordan's thinking about what he was doing. He had placed two rows of dinosaurs on the paper, one row consisted of nine figures standing up and the other was of nine lying down. When he was asked what he had, he replied that he had half standing and half sitting. Mrs B pressed him for how he knew that. He said that they were equal. Mrs B said, "What is equal?" and got another dinosaur and put it at the end of the standing row. Jordan said that wouldn't be half because one was longer. It was clear what Mrs B was probing for. Was Jordan looking at the length of the two rows or the number of objects in each row? Could Jordan conserve number? Did Mrs B know something about Jordan's number understandings that made her keep questioning him? She still pressed for an explanation of why it was half. Then she was immediately satisfied when he explained that the numbers have to be the same in each half.

Jordan's focus was then swung by Mrs B to the number of objects in the whole "class". To find how many were in the class altogether Jordan counted to nine in twos and on from nine to 18 with support. He commented, "It's counting by nines". He added, "I could do it if I could count by nines". Mrs B asked him whether he could count on a calculator, then sent him to get one. As he was walking back to his workspace on the floor he had already keyed in the strokes to have his four-function calculator count by nines. (Mrs B later wrote this on his paper as 9 + = =). He sat on the floor calling out the sequence of numbers he was generating on the calculator display: 9, 18, 27, 36, 45, 54, 63, 72, 81, 90, 99, 108. He was rocking back and forth and smiling to himself. Mrs B was smiling too (Figure 2.3), then she said, "So if you could count by nines you could do it, or you could get the calculator to count by nines, couldn't you?"

Next Mrs B challenged Jordan to write down what he had done. Having worked with several other children Mrs B came back to Jordan. He had put out four rows of dinosaurs by that time and knew that there were 36 of them on the floor (Figure 2.4). Mrs B recapitulated what he had done and how many groups of nine he had begun with. She emphasised the groups of nine by recording what he told her as: 2 groups of 9, 18.

She then encouraged Jordan to think about his extension of the original problem, where he had two rows of people sitting and two rows standing: 4 groups of 9, 36.

Figure 2.3 Jordan enjoying his success at counting by nines

Encouraging mathematical thinking 17

Figure 2.4 Jordan had extended the problem beyond two groups of nine

Mrs B recorded Jordan's solution in symbols that made sense to him. There was a little comment by Jordan when Mrs B was drawing the stick figures sitting and standing. It had the familiarity of a child sitting beside his mother as she drew him a picture. Jordan sat close and smiled at Mrs B (Figure 2.5).

Jordan: "You're really good at that."
Mrs B: "I'm not really, I don't quite know what I'm doing with this leg. What will I do with that one? Anyway he's sitting isn't he?"
Jordan: "Mm."

Jordan proved to Mrs B that there were 18 in the whole class. He used the calculator to skip count by nines. Mrs B then issued another challenge: "If you would like to - have a go at counting by nines and see if you can see a pattern."

After the children had worked on solutions to the problem for about 40 minutes the class was given notice to finish and to pack up so that they could be ready to share what they had done. Three children, including Jordan, were asked to be ready to tell what they had done. The first child to share was Nicholas. By asking leading questions, Mrs B led him through a succinct description of his solution - six standing and six sitting was 12 altogether. She asked him to justify his solution in terms of the problem, then focused on the mental computation strategy that he used to find the total. She described how he was originally going to "count all" of the people he had drawn but she had challenged him to do something else. Nicholas then said that he remembered when they were using dice and he knew that six and six was 12. Mrs B then connected that to a previous time where they had found double letters and introduced "doubles" in numbers. She asked Jordan what you get when you double nine.

18 Jill Cheeseman

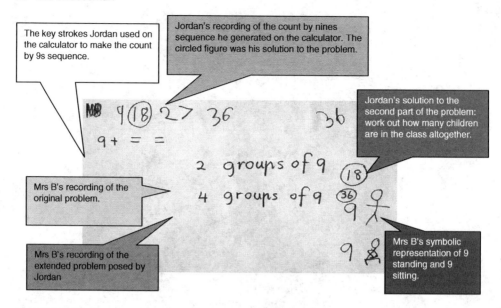

Figure 2.5 Jordan's work sample – front of the sheet of paper

He responded immediately with 18. Brianna was asked to talk about her work, especially to say how she changed her original solution and why. She originally had four children standing and five sitting. In asking Brianna to explain her thinking, Mrs B seemed to be emphasising the need for two halves to be equivalent in number. She was also praising the correction of flawed thinking.

Then Mrs B asked Jordan to report to the class. She set up the report by describing the fact that Jordan had dinosaurs and asked Jordan to describe what he did to start with. He talked about how he had nine sitting and nine standing and as he was doing so read his paper and he picked up his calculator and pressed the keystrokes to generate a count by nines pattern. Mrs B stopped him there to reiterate the process to get the solution.

Then using the thinking that Jordan did as an extension to the problem of the day Mrs B capitalised on the opportunity to have the class look at the sequence of numbers generated by counting by nines and to identify and predict some patterns. Children were then gathered around Mrs B to look at what Jordan found and to check what he had done. First Jordan generated the sequence of numbers he had produced by getting a calculator to skip count by nines. Then Mrs B challenged the children to explain why he had written the pattern as: 9, 8, 7, 6, 5, 4, 3, 2, 1. Lexie described them as "the numbers on the end" (Figures 2.6 and 2.7).

Mrs B then orchestrated a scenario where the children were able to predict the next number in the pattern and she even challenged them to search for a pattern in the tens column as well.

The children had been concentrating on mathematics for a long time and there were a few minutes until recess so Mrs B said that they could have a few quiet minutes to do what they wanted, to eat some "brain food" (fruit and vegetable snacks that they have close at hand) or to play with a calculator to do what Jordan did. It was very interesting to see that at least half of the class got a calculator to investigate numbers.

Encouraging mathematical thinking 19

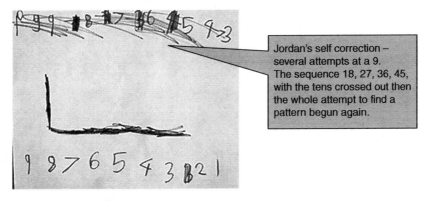

Figure 2.6 Jordan's work sample – back of the sheet of paper

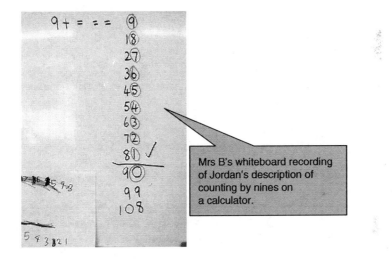

Figure 2.7 Jordan's work sample and Mrs B's use of the pattern he had found

A timeline of Mrs B's interactions with Jordan (Figure 2.8) reveals that Mrs B interacted with Jordan on ten separate occasions and on two of these occasions she spent an extended period of time engaged in conversation with him. The interactions with Jordan took a general form: raise a challenging question requiring thought and action, leave the child to do some mathematics, review and raise a new challenge, leave the child to do more mathematics, require a report of mathematical thinking. During the exchange with Jordan, Mrs B:

- Asked Jordan to demonstrate half of a continuous quantity;
- Required him to model the problem;
- Had him explain his solution;
- Expected that he justify that solution;
- Asked him to generalise the concept of half of a discrete quantity;
- Stimulated him to consider the "whole";
- Requested that he calculate the sum of two equal sets;

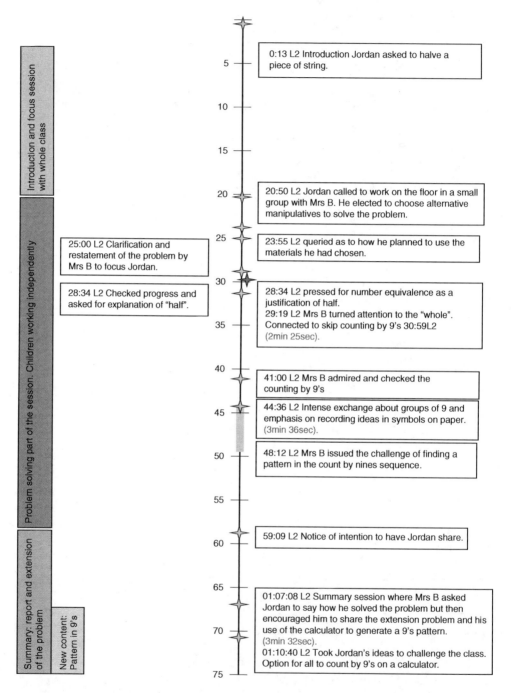

Figure 2.8 Timeline of Mrs B's interactions with Jordan

- Expected the transfer of his previous experience and knowledge of skip counting on a calculator to the current problem;
- Prompted him to link his skip counting by nine to "groups of nine", that is, connect repeated addition to emerging multiplicative thinking;
- Asked him to write and read two-digit numbers;
- Challenged him to search for pattern in number – the nines sequence;
- Expected him to describe what he did and what he found to other children.

Looking at this list of mathematical actions Mrs B required of Jordan makes plain the challenge she regularly expects her five- to six-year-olds to meet. This is the story of only one child in her classroom on one day and it might be assumed that Jordan is the only child who was given this attention and challenge.

In fact, Mrs B decided which four children she would give her intense focus and the rest of her class all received some attention during the mathematics lesson every day. With 21 children in her room she was able to have intensive conversational exchanges with every child about their mathematical thinking every week. During such exchanges, the children are called on to demonstrate, model, explain, calculate, justify, generalise, transfer, connect and describe their mathematical thinking. These are powerful mathematical behaviours that establish the habits of mind of young mathematicians. The story is an example of a teacher's practice that embodies all of the features of effective teachers of mathematics described by Groves, Mousley, and Forgasz (2006).

Conclusion

Highly effective teachers have a clear learning path in mind for the children in their classes, and for individuals within the class, and it is at the "cutting edge" of each child's understanding that the teachers are attempting to work. They question and evaluate each child's conceptual development, put that knowledge into the context of a broad knowledge of a mathematical framework, then make "on the run" judgements about how best to press for further understanding. Sometimes they offer linking ideas to connect the child to past experiences in mathematics, sometimes they offer a slight variation on the problem and sometimes they ask a question that requires the child to think generally about what has happened. They use a range of techniques to suit the event and to press the child's thinking in their zone of proximal development (Ernest, 1991). Perhaps the most striking quality is the flexibility and the speed with which they consider and respond to situations as they unfold.

Implications

Studying the practices of highly effective teachers of mathematics with young children helps us to identify some of the features of their approaches to teaching and learning. One finding in particular, that had not hitherto been documented in the literature, was the interlinked conversational exchanges between teacher and child in mathematics lessons in the early years of primary school. These "strings" of conversational interactions support, extend and challenge children's thinking. The one-to-one interactions between teacher and child that were the focus of the large study by Cheeseman (2010) proved to be a revelation.

The mathematical conversations that teachers had with children as a regular part of their classroom practice during their mathematics lessons challenged young children to probe their mathematical thinking. Leaps of thinking took place as teachers elicited children's mathematical knowledge and supported children's construction of new thinking. This is the epitome of a social-constructivist theory in action where meaning is made in the moment between people (Cobb et al., 1990) and a context in which adults and children search for meanings together (Clark, 2004).

Recommendations

Based on my experiences in the classrooms of highly effective teachers of mathematics I offer three recommendations.

Plan time for close mathematical conversations with children

The daily close mathematical conversations that the teachers in the study (Cheeseman, 2010) had with children took planning and forethought. It was not planning in the sense that the teachers needed to know exactly what they were going to say and do, but in the sense that when they considered the lesson content and structure, they chose tasks that allowed them to spend time with individuals and with groups of children, conversing about the children's mathematical reasoning and extending the children's thinking with challenging questions. The planning involved making time within each mathematics lesson to listen to children; it also involved keeping the pressures of everyday life in the classroom isolated from the conversations about mathematical thinking. Teachers needed time to reflect during conversations in order to think about the children's insights, and to consider how to frame the next challenge. Therefore, planning for close mathematical conversations to occur is essential if children are to be challenged to think mathematically.

Expect thinking of children, including conjecturing, reasoning, justifying

The findings indicated that the teachers in this study had high expectations of the children's abilities to conjecture, to reason and to justify their mathematical thinking. The teachers' expectations were often expressed as questions. Children were asked to explain their ideas and to justify their thinking; they were expected to use the skills of young mathematicians. The children's ideas were queried and challenged and children were expected to defend their thinking. The teachers' high expectations created a sense of demand and the children rose to the challenge. Higher order mathematical thinking of young children is an achievable challenge. Therefore, expecting rigorous thinking of young children, including conjecturing, reasoning and justifying, is a way to enhance children's mathematical development.

Consider tasks and their potential to engage and extend children's thinking

The potential of tasks to engage and extend children's thinking was paramount and teachers then used these tasks to their full potential. They took time to let the children explore, investigate and, to some extent, struggle with the mathematical content of the tasks. If there was no challenge for a child, each of the teachers increased the level of complexity or extended the task with an extra requirement, so as to take the children's thinking into new mathematical territory. The teachers were in no hurry for children to reach solutions and were prepared to wait for children to think through the mathematics. Consideration needs to be made of the potential of tasks to engage and extend children's mathematical thinking. Teachers also need to consider flexible and adaptable ways in which they can then interact with children in order to reach the full potential of the mathematical opportunities presented to the child.

References

Arcavi, A., & Isoda, M. (2007). Learning to listen: From historical sources to classroom practice. *Educational Studies in Mathematics, 66*(2), 111-129.

Burns, M. (1985). The role of questioning. *Arithmetic Teacher, 32*(6), 14-16.

Burton, L. (1984). Mathematical thinking: The struggle for meaning. *Journal for Research in Mathematics Education, 15*(1), 35-49.

Capucilli, A. S. (2004). *Mrs McTats and her houseful of cats*. New York: Alladin Paperbacks.

Carpenter, T., & Fennema, E. (1992). Cognitively guided instruction: Building on the knowledge of students and teachers. In W. Secada (Ed.), *Researching educational reform: The case of school mathematics in the United States* (pp. 457-470). (A Special Issue of *International Journal of Educational Research*.)

Caulley, D. (2008). Making qualitative research reports less boring. *Qualitative Enquiry, 14*(3), 424-449.

Cheeseman, J. (2010). *Challenging children to think: An investigation of the behaviours of highly effective teachers that stimulate children to examine their mathematical understandings*. (PhD), Monash University, Melbourne.

Cheeseman, J., & McDonough, A. (2016). Fostering mathematical curiosity. In A. Macdonald & S. Dockett (Eds.), *Early childhood mathematics education: The legacy of Bob Perry* (pp. 142-151). Albury, Australia: Charles Sturt University Press.

Clark, A. (2004). The mosaic approach and research with young children. In V. Lewis, M. Kellett, C. Robinson, S. Fraser, & S. Ding (Eds.), *The reality of research with children and young people* (pp. 142-162). London: Sage Publications.

Clarke, D. J. (1998). Studying the classroom negotiation of meaning: Complementary accounts methodology. *Journal for Research in Mathematics Education. Monograph, 9*, 98-111.

Clarke, D. J. (2001). Complementary accounts methodology. In D. J. Clarke (Ed.), *Perspective on practice and meaning in mathematics and science classrooms* (pp. 13-32). Dordrecht: Kluwer.

Clarke, D. M., Cheeseman, J., Gervasoni, A., Gronn, D., Horne, M., McDonough, A.,,... Rowley, G. (2002). *Early Numeracy Research Project: Final report*. Fitzroy, Victoria: Mathematics Teaching and Learning Centre, Australian Catholic University.

Cobb, P., Wood, T., & Yackel, E. (1990). Classrooms as learning environments. In D. Robert, M. Carolyn, & N. Nel (Eds.), *Constructivist views on the teaching and learning of mathematics* (Vol. 4, pp. 125-146). Reston, VA: NCTM.

Cobb, P., & Yackel, E. (1998). A constructivist perspective on the culture of the mathematics classroom. In F. Seeger, J. Viogt, & U. Waschescio (Eds.), *The culture of the mathematics classroom* (pp. 158-190). Cambridge: Cambridge University Press.

Crespo, S. (2000). Seeing more than right and wrong answers: Prospective teachers' interpretations of students' mathematical work. *Journal of Mathematics Teacher Education, 3*(2), 155-181. DOI:1573-1820.

Davis, B. (1997). Listening for differences: An evolving conception of mathematics teaching. *Journal for Research in Mathematics Education, 28*(3), 355-376.

Ernest, P. (1991). *The philosophy of mathematics education*. London: Falmer Press.

Fosnot, C., & Dolk, M. (2001). *Young mathematicians at work: Constructing number sense, addition, and subtraction*. Westport, CT: Heinemann.

Gervasoni, A., Hunter, R., Bicknell, B., & Sexton, M. (2012). Powerful pedagogical actions in mathematics education. In B. Perry, T. Lowrie, T. Logan, A. McDonald, & J. Greenlees (Eds.), *Research in mathematics education in Australasia 2008-2011* (pp. 193-218). Rotterdam: Sense Publishers.

Groves, S., Mousley, J., & Forgasz, H. (2006). *Primary numeracy: A mapping, review and analysis of Australian research in numeracy learning at the primary school level*. Canberra, ACT: Commonwealth of Australia.

Langsted, O. (1994). Looking at quality from the child's perspective. In P. Moss & A. Pence (Eds.), *Valuing quality in early childhood services: New approaches to defining quality* (pp. 28-42). London: Paul Chapman.

Mannigel, D. (1992). *Young children as mathematicians: Theory and practice for teaching mathematics.* Wentworth Falls, New South Wales: Social Science Press.

Mason, J., Burton, L., & Stacey, K. (1982). *Thinking mathematically.* London: Addison Wesley.

McDonough, A., & Clarke, D. (2003). Describing the practice of effective teachers of mathematics in the early years. In N. A. Pateman, B. J. Dougherty, & J. Zilliox (Eds.), *Proceedings of the 27th Conference of the International Group for the Psychology of Mathematics Education* (Vol. 3, pp. 261-268). Honolulu, HI: PME.

Qvortrup, J., Bardy, M., Sgritta, G., & Wintersberger, H. (1994). *Childhood matters.* Vienna: European Centre.

Roche, A., & Ferguson, S. (2015). What do you notice? Cultivating noticing and questioning in mathematics. *Prime Number, 30*(2), 5-7.

Sfard, A., Nescher, P., Streefland, L., Cobb, P., & Mason, J. (1998). Learning mathematics through conversation: Is it as good as they say? *For the Learning of Mathematics, 18*(1), 41-51.

Sriraman, B., & English, L. (2010). *Theories of mathematics education: Seeking new frontiers.* Berlin/Heidelberg: Springer.

Sullivan, P., & Clarke, D. (1991). *Communication in the classroom: The importance of good questioning.* Geelong: Deakin University.

Thornbury, S., & Slade, D. (2006). *Conversation: From description to pedagogy.* Cambridge: Cambridge University Press.

Vygotsky, L. (1978). *Mind and society: The development of higher psychological processes.* Cambridge, MA: Harvard University Press.

3 "Why do we have to do addition? I already know addition"

A cultural-historical perspective of collaborative learning, teaching and assessment in early years mathematics

Megan Adams

Introduction

The way learning informs teaching and teaching informs learning is the basic component of education. While researching the everyday life of children (Adams, 2014), the way young children work together to support each other's learning can be observed and explored. Often the support between children occurs beyond the gaze of an adult. In this chapter, the way the more capable other (Vygotsky, 1987) directs the process of mathematical learning is explored in relation to the possibility of collaborative learning, teaching and assessment. The documentation of children's conversations during play highlights the possibilities for learning, teaching and the assessment process.

Background

The conversations documented in this chapter originate from a research project that investigated the everyday life of children in home and school settings (Adams, 2014; Adams & Fleer, 2016). The current study has its focus on two five-year-old Australian children attending a classroom in an Australian international school setting. The classroom was set up to invite children to work together on mathematical problems. In contrast to most subject-specific assessments in older age groups, early childhood teachers generally seek to understand the whole child in their learning setting. The challenge for teachers is to capture the dynamic and complex nature of children's learning (Fleer & Quinones, 2013) and provide evidence that reliable and valid assessments have been undertaken (Arthur, Beecher, Death, Dockett, & Farmer, 2015). Therefore, suitable assessments that inform learning and teaching are required to be designed. In this chapter, learning about mathematics is explored, followed by introduction of the terms assessment for learning, assessment of learning and assessment as learning. A discussion regarding documentation of children's conversations, the analysis of the conversations and a discussion on the implications for learning, teaching and assessment follow.

Learning about mathematics

Mathematics forms part of a child's formal and informal education from a very young age. It is important for young children to establish an understanding of foundational concepts that form the basis of mathematical learning (Sarama & Clements, 2004). There are various ways children learn about mathematics in their everyday life. This may include learning from parents, from older siblings, through informal play situations and from commercially available software (Thomas, Tagg, & Ward, 2002). Cohrssen (2015) suggests that although teachers have conversations with children as they play, it is less common to direct conversation towards mathematical learning. According to Sarama and Clements (2009, p. 17), there are "hypothetical learning trajectories" which is a way of conceptualising and/or understanding the processes of thinking that children move through as they learn about mathematical concepts. The trajectory has three components: a goal (directed towards a mathematical concept), a developmental progression (the process of thinking involved in understanding the concept) and instruction which helps move the child along the path (Sarama & Clements, 2004). Therefore, the teacher plays an important role in the child's process of learning mathematics.

The teacher's understanding of and capacity to explain mathematical concepts determine the level of understanding a child forms during the process of learning. Sarama and Clements (2009, p. 17) argue that the teacher's own knowledge of learning and understanding concepts "is essential for high-quality teaching based on understanding both mathematics and children's thinking and learning". Thomas et al. (2002) found the greater understanding a teacher has of mathematics, the better the children's performance. Determining how to facilitate children's learning trajectories is an important consideration and where assessment plays an important role.

Assessment

The three main types of assessment described in Australian curriculum documents are *assessment for, as* and *of learning* (see for example, Australian Department of Education and Employment and Workplace Relations, 2009, for the Early Years Learning Framework). Assessment **for** learning has its origin in formative assessment. In formative assessment, information is gathered on children's behaviour and learning and is used to inform future teaching and learning. According to Black and Wiliam (1998), in assessment **for** learning, formative assessment is extended to encompass the process where children and teachers together interpret evidence from assessment. Arthur et al. (2015, p. 259) state this "results in a clear purpose for learning and intentional teaching", similar to learning trajectories (Sarama & Clements, 2004). Assessment **for** learning informs teaching which informs learning, ideally leading to a spiral of learning and development.

Assessment **as** learning differentiates the role of the teacher and the learner. The focus is on metacognition (learning to learn) and the process of learning that is made explicit to the children (Earl, 2003). The teacher and the children work together to understand how all children learn, moving away from only the product or outcome of learning. Part of this process is the individual and group documenting and reflecting on the process of learning. Assessment **of** learning is usually summative and is set for the end of a learning period to understand achievement of children on a specific task or unit.

"Why do we have to do addition?" 27

There are various ways teachers collect and analyse information to assess the standard children are working towards. This can include gathering children's work from various contexts and sources such as images, written work, digital audio recordings, documenting social interactions (with peers and teachers), the children's questions, theories and ideas. The main purpose of gathering information is to analyse children's experiences of learning and to support and direct future teaching and learning (Helm, Beneke, & Steinheimer, 2007). In the early years and primary schools, this collated information is referred to as pedagogical documentation (Edwards, Gandini, & Forman, 2012) and informs learning, teaching, assessment and reporting to parents and other stakeholders related to education.

Theoretical underpinning

Pedagogical documentation can be understood as a dynamic mode of assessment because it relies on the interactions between teacher and learner. This type of assessment is structured on the process of learning to support the teacher's understanding of the learners' potential. Fleer and Quinones (2013, p. 238) argue that dynamic collection modes "capture the embedded and fluid nature of assessment practices". The dynamic nature of assessment is linked to Vygotsky's (1987) zone of proximal development (ZPD). The ZPD is directed towards the child's development and possible future learning. The concept supports understanding the role and significance of the teacher or more capable other in the assessment process. The ZPD is explained as "the distance between the actual developmental level as determined by independent problem solving and the level of potential development as determined through problem solving under adult guidance or in collaboration with more capable peers" (Vygotsky, 1987, p. 86). Therefore, assessment **for**, **of** and **as** learning are required to capture the dynamic relation between the more capable other and the learner in the process of child development. The ZPD can be used to support future teaching which informs future learning.

Methodology

The main aim of the current study, presented in this chapter, was to explore the process of collaborative learning, teaching and assessment as children engaged with mathematics concepts.

Procedure

In the larger study, data were collected over the course of six months, including images, video observations and field notes of the everyday lives of five expatriate families with young children experiencing relocation into Malaysia. Video data of the children at home and school and semi-structured interviews with parents, teachers and principals totalled 90 hours.

Data analysis

The analysis was completed by looking at the whole data set, then producing themes which related to learning and development. An iterative approach was used in the analysis of data, or, in other words, the videos were grouped and further revised and sorted. The video data were converted into short clips, which related to the aims of the research and the research question. In this instance, it was the child's conceptual understanding of addition that occurred during play and assessment at school.

The focus on children's learning of mathematical concepts was targeted using Hedegaard's (2008) three-stage approach to data analysis. Initially a *common-sense interpretation* was used, where details were processed in written form on a word processor and the data were organised into folders. The data extracted revealed the collaborative social interaction between two focus children on different occasions over a three-week period. The data drawn upon here stem from two learning episodes; first the focus children set up a stall and sold lemonade. In the second learning episode, the focus children played a mathematics game on the computer. On a third occasion, social interaction between the focus children and the teacher while completing a mathematics assessment was analysed. Any form of explicit explanation of a concept by participants was targeted. The second level of analysis is termed *situated practice interpretation*, this is where instances were linked together (lemonade stall, computer game and formative assessment), and conceptual patterns were located across the research site. This level included the focus participants learning, or signs of beginning awareness or understanding through discussion or application of mathematics concepts. The final level of data analysis is termed *thematic interpretation*, where video and interview data were connected with the research aims. Further, Hedegaard (2008) suggests that theoretical concepts are used for extraction of social relations and patterns located within the data.

Research ethics was granted and research protocols were adhered to; for example, to protect the anonymity of participants, all names are pseudonyms. The study continued over a six-month period. Families and focus participants (children, parents, teachers and significant friends) were filmed for six hours at home and six hours at school. The data drawn for this chapter originate from Bill's and his friend Mary's experience at school while engaging in mathematics lessons over a four-week period. In the learning episodes that follow, examples of the varied mathematics number work and assessment by the teacher are discussed.

Findings and discussion

The findings discussed in this chapter analyse three learning episodes. The first episode consists of Bill and Mary setting up a lemonade stall and using money to buy and sell lemonade. In the second episode Mary and Bill work collaboratively on a computer game and challenge each other's understanding. The final episode focuses on a whole class assessment task and the learning outcomes from the task. In addition to analysing the learning that occurs in these episodes, the teacher's and researchers' pedagogical documentation is drawn upon to further analyse these learning episodes.

A lemonade stall in the classroom, week one

On the first day the researcher was in the classroom, Bill and Mary had free time and set up a stall "selling" lemonade. Bill made coins by tearing up paper. Mary suggested they make the coins "more real" by writing numbers on the paper. Mary instructed Bill to write numerical values on the paper (1, 2, 3, 4, 5 and 10 cent coins). The children proceeded to play the game buying and selling lemonade. Both children were able to add, subtract and provide "change" with the "coins".

When playing the game, Bill said, "Two cents for each lemonade, and you want three lemonades". Bill touched each plastic cup twice saying, "One, two", moved to the next cup and touched, "three, four", moved to the final cup and counted, "five, six". Mary handed Bill two coins, one with the number five and the other with the number two. Bill looked at the coins and said, "No, there are only two, you have to give me six". Mary explained that with money five add two is seven and Bill needed to give her one cent change. Bill said he knew that five and two was seven but was adamant that he required six coins. Mary provided him with seven one cent coins and Bill provided one cent change.

Bill's understanding of money. From this play scenario, Bill is competent with one to one correspondence (touching and counting sequential numbers), adding numbers to six with the help of manipulatives (touching each cup twice) and understanding that change is provided. In this instance, Bill showed that he understood that one cup of lemonade was worth two cents (touches the cup twice) and that one coin represented one cent.

Mary's understanding of money. Mary understood that numerical values are written on coins (Mary wrote 1, 2, 3, 4, 5 and 10). However, Mary represented the numerical values by applying her knowledge of sequential counting to the coins and the size of the paper rather than following the conventions of the denominational value of the coins (1 cent was smallest, 10 cents placed on the largest pieces of paper rather than 1, 2, 5, 10, 20 and 50 cents).

The teacher was roaming around the classroom documenting children's play. She entered into the play space towards the end of Bill and Mary's game. The teacher wrote the following (notes were made into full sentences by the researcher):

Bill and Mary's developing concepts. Bill and Mary set up a lemonade stall. Both need support to understand grouping of numbers in relation to the assigned value of the coin. This could be achieved through: (1) the introduction of real money in play and making sure the children's attention is directed to the numerical values on the coin; (2) children provided with opportunities to group numbers to ten with manipulatives and be directed by the use of open-ended questions, for example, "How many ways can you make five?" Then use real money.

The following section combines a discussion of the children's data while setting up and selling lemonade and the teacher's documentation regarding the children's mathematical understanding and future learning in relation to assessment *for* learning.

The anecdotal notes made by the teacher were to be placed in the children's individual portfolios; there was a missed opportunity to take assessment *for* learning to the next level where children and teachers together interpret evidence (Black & Wiliam, 1998). The teacher observed the children and determined where to go next without having a conversation with the children about their mathematical understanding. This substantiates Cohrssen's (2015) suggestion that teachers tend not to engage children in mathematical conversations during play. However, starting a conversation may have led to a deeper understanding of each child's concept of money. The teacher did not realise that Mary was the more capable other supporting Bill to write numerical values on the coins and was able to add the five and two cent coins and ask for one cent change. In group time the teacher could have provided the opportunity for Bill and Mary to explain what they were playing and why the numbers were on the paper, the reasoning behind the sequential numbers and the size of the paper in relation to the numbers on the paper "coins". The teacher could use this as a time to document children's learning and understanding as they explain what was being played and why. As Thornbury and Slade (2006) argue, conversations and making explicit mathematics concepts is important to gauge children's understanding of mathematics.

Children learn from each other through informal play situations (Thomas et al., 2002). In the shop scenario discussed above, Mary is the more capable other (Vygotsky, 1987) and is supporting Bill's beginning understanding of denominational money. Mary's explanation to Bill supported her own understanding. To fully gauge each child's understanding, conversations would enable the teacher to assess where to direct future learning with the concept of money.

A computer game in the classroom, week two

During the second week of data gathering, Bill and Mary were instructed to play a multiplayer addition game, working with numbers to ten on the computer. Mary and Bill completed addition to ten very quickly. Mary suggested they move to a higher level by increasing addition with numbers to 20. At the next level, Mary was quicker than Bill who showed displeasure and stated, "That's not fair, how do you do it so quick?"

Mary explained in an excited voice, "I'll tell you, I just did 12 and eight. So, I hold ten in my head and then just go two add eight, which is ten. Then get the ten in my head so ten and ten is 20!"

Bill stated, "I don't get it! Where do you hold the ten in your head? Anyway, where does the ten and the two come from?"

Mary explained, "Well you've got 12 so ten add two is 12. I hold that ten in my head and add that two and the eight, which is ten, so then add that ten and the ten in my head and get 20. Now you do it. The game is showing 13 and seven". Bill replied, "I see it now, so all you're doing is, is well making the numbers smaller, then bigger. So, it is seven and, and, then 13 is three and, and, and um, ten so that's seven and three (says ten in a whisper and touches his head) and ten is 20?" Mary said, "YES! Next, 16 and four?" After a few seconds, Bill touched his head and replied, "20 because four and, and, and six is umm, ten and the other ten (touching head) is 20! YAY! I am going to beat you now!" The game resumed, Bill's addition speed increased exponentially.

Bill's understanding of addition. Bill was able to complete mental addition to ten without manipulatives (such as fingers). Bill was developing a working knowledge of addition to 20. Initially he did not understand Mary's explanation of separating 12 into a ten and two units by keeping aside the ten and adding the units (the problem is 12 + 8 so 12 = 10 + 2; which is 2 + 8 = 10, then 10 + 10 = 20). In the second attempt, Bill spoke of making the numbers smaller, showing an understanding of subtraction ("breaking" the 12 = 10 + 2), then making the numbers (units) bigger by adding the units (2 + 8) and the base tens (10 + 10). Bill seemed to use verbal language to create a visual image, which he used as a tool to support addition. He used the touch of his head to remember the initial ten in the equation. Bill was able to verbalise the question to help direct Mary to answer to support his learning.

The teacher was not in the vicinity of the children when they were playing on the computer and making verbal computations, therefore the researcher made notes and analysed the children's conversation:

Bill and Mary's developing concepts. Bill initially required support with mental addition skills to 20. Future learning may include further patterns of addition and subtraction, grouping and adding numbers. Mary was able to verbalise the process of addition with numbers to 20. From Mary's explanation, she understood that ten units made base ten. Mary utilised this knowledge by keeping the tens separate from the units and adding the units together, then the tens. Being able to explain this twice in slightly different ways meant that Mary was working at a sophisticated level. From this example, there is not enough information to determine the level of Mary's developing addition skills. Therefore, to develop future learning for Mary, the teacher would ideally engage in conversations and observe how far she could progress with varying options on the computer program.

Although the teacher cannot be everywhere in the classroom at one time, there are certain ways that assessment **as** learning (Earl, 2003) or metacognition (learning to learn) can be structured. In this example, Mary develops an explicit opportunity to explain her understanding to support Bill's conceptual knowledge of addition. This type of experience is a powerful way to show that children can be explicit and explain their mathematical thinking. This could be utilised during group time to get Mary and Bill to explain how they add numbers together. The way Mary and Bill work together highlights the reciprocity between questions and answers and the way framing and answering questions contributes to learning and teaching. Hedegaard (2005) suggests that the ability of formulating a question is part of the developmental process within the ZPD. Roth and Radford (2010) extend this by stating the understanding developed between the person asking the question and the person answering the question is important as each participant is required to understand the other's position and level of comprehension. Therefore, conditions have been created for the process of learning (Chaiklin, 2003) by both participants. Bill was able to refine the questions asked so Mary could rephrase the explanation of how to complete mental addition.

Assessment in the classroom, week three: A whole class assessment task

Throughout the three weeks the teacher provided opportunities for children to work individually and together on counting, solving addition problems with and without manipulatives with numbers to five, ten and 20. This provided fluidity with the formation of groups and the way learning goals were met. The teacher roamed between groups and spent time with each child. The final data collection session was in week three where the teacher provided an assessment **of** learning at the end of a period of work.

Bill's teacher divided the class into four groups to complete an assessment of learning. Group one was invited to sit on the mat and work with the teacher, group two was provided with objects and a sheet with addition to ten, the third group was provided with a sheet of addition to ten and no objects, the final group including Mary and Bill was provided with a sheet showing addition to 20. The teacher instructed the whole class on what was expected and began working with the group of children on the mat.

Bill sat at a table next to Mary and stated loudly, "Why do we have to do addition? I already know addition!" Mary looked at Bill and nodded in affirmation.

The teacher suggested Bill start and complete the test quietly.
Bill retorted, "I already did, I'm on number 12!"
The teacher proceeded to work with a small group sitting in front of her.
Bill stated, "I've finished!" Mary stated, "Me too!"

The teacher marked Bill's work, he scored 20/20. The teacher commented on Bill's reversal of numbers and stated, "We need to work on that, Bill". Bill was directed to place the test sheet in his mathematics folder so his parents could see his work at the end of the semester.

Bill's understanding of the formative assessment task. Bill questioned why he was required to complete the test as he already knew how to add. Bill was able to understand the test and added the numbers quickly without any form of manipulatives.

Mary's understanding of the formative assessment task. Mary agreed with Bill and questioned why they were required to complete the test. Mary was quicker than Bill at completing the test.

Bill and Mary's teacher was aware that the two children had worked together on the majority of activities set out in the classroom over the previous three weeks. However, the teacher was not aware that the children had extended each other and were able to work competently with addition to 20. Bill and Mary were able to complete the assessment task quickly with a 100% success rate. The only area the teacher commented on was the correction of number reversal with which Bill needed support. Thompson, Rowe, Underwood, and Peck (2005) argue that adults are often surprised at children's mathematical ability and understanding. Sarama and Clements (2009) argue that teachers are usually aware when mathematical problems are too challenging for children, by contrast they tend to overlook tasks that are not challenging enough. The example of Mary and Bill's test highlights this point exactly.

The test does not highlight the ZPD. Instead it replicates scaffolding (Bruner, 1975) where instruction is provided and then taken away as the child is able to complete the task independently. In this example of assessment, the assessment was oriented towards "yesterday's development" (Vygotsky, 1987, p. 211), that is, what Mary and Bill can already achieve. This type of assessment captures a "snapshot" of what the children are capable of but not their potential. The assessment was a missed opportunity for the teacher to engage with the children and find out where to direct future learning. Therefore, it is important for teachers to have sound knowledge of the process of learning trajectories and understanding of mathematical concepts that become more complex over the course of time (Sarama and Clements, 2009). This provides opportunities for the children to be extended and extend themselves towards "tomorrow's development" (Vygotsky, 1987, p. 211). The example discussed here substantiates Thomas et al.'s (2002) research as the greater understanding a teacher has of mathematics, the better the children's performance. Therefore, determining how to facilitate children's future learning is an important consideration for teachers.

Implications

Based on this experience of the two children and their teacher, there are three implications provided that aim to support classroom teachers' understanding.

"Why do we have to do addition?" 33

Classroom practices that can be used to inform assessment for learning

Children can and do co-construct meaning of mathematics through their own conversations in play. These conversations can be used for summative assessment as a way to gauge each child's understanding of mathematical concepts. Quality classroom practice involves providing children with the opportunity to think, make their own theories (Vygotsky, 1987) and explain how they worked out an answer. Providing a routine for group discussion to share how children problem solved mathematical questions helps the child and the whole class with their mathematical understanding. There are two possibilities: first, children can record their own mathematical conversations, or second, teachers can spend time observing and listening to children's conversations and carefully document these through various means (written, images, digital recordings). Pedagogical documentation can be used as assessment **for** learning to support future learning and presented to parents to show each child's progress. There is a clear implication for teachers to provide routine spaces for children to talk about how they worked out a mathematical problem.

Classroom practices that can be used to inform assessment as learning

It is important for teachers to spend time with children to discuss assessment procedures. Part of this process is the individual and group documentation and reflection on the process of learning (Earl, 2003). There are implications for teachers when making explicit comments about learning to learn. This begins with teachers having confidence in their own mathematical abilities and allowing space and time for children to reflect and make explicit their own theories and understanding. Working within the ZPD informs this process.

Classroom practices that can be used to inform assessment of learning

It is important for teachers to find ways to gain an understanding of what the child knows and most importantly where to direct future learning. If the teacher is not aware of each child's understanding, there is scope for missed opportunities. The test that Mary and Bill completed did not add anything to what was known about the children's understanding of the mathematical concepts of addition, it was situated on yesterday's development (Vygotsky, 1987). Further, the children were frustrated when asked to complete the assessment as they "already know addition". This "snapshot" approach is contrary to Vygotsky's theory which positions the ZPD to "determine the domain of transitions that are accessible to the child" (p. 211). The child and more capable other extend the learning together through their ongoing collaboration, it is a continual and reciprocal process. Vygotsky's conception of the ZPD provides a way to capture dynamic movement in relation to a child's thinking processes, providing the assessment is placed in context and enables conceptual reciprocity between the participants. There is a clear implication for teachers to listen to children's talk during play and structure the assessment to an appropriate level; this does not always require testing. However, the most important implication is understanding that the ZPD and scaffolding are two separate and quite different concepts (Chaiklin, 2003). The ZPD is a dynamic, future-oriented concept related to children's learning and development, based on reciprocal understanding of both parties as they work together in context. By contrast, scaffolding is based on teaching techniques which include demonstrating how to solve a problem and offering support only when required and taking support away when no longer necessary.

References

Adams, M. (2014). Emotions of expatriate children and families transitioning into Malaysia: A cultural-historical perspective. *Asia Pacific Journal of Research in Early Childhood Education, 8*(2), 129-151.

Adams, M., & Fleer, M. (2016). The relations between a 'push-down' and 'push-up' curriculum: A cultural-historical study of home-play pedagogy in the context of structured learning in international schools in Malaysia. *Contemporary Issues in Early Childhood Education, 17*(3), 328-342. DOI:10.1177/1463949116660955

Arthur, L., Beecher, B., Death, E., Dockett, S., & Farmer, S. (2015). *Programming and planning in the early childhood settings.* Australia: Cengage Learning.

Australian Government Department of Education Employment and Workplace Relations (2009). *Belonging, being & becoming: The early years learning framework for Australia.* Canberra, Australia: Commonwealth of Australia.

Black, P., & Wiliam, D. (1998). *Inside the black box: Raising standards through classroom assessment.* London: School of Education, King's College.

Bruner, J. (1975). From communication to language. A psychological perspective. *Cognition, 3*(3), 255-289.

Chaiklin, S. (2003). The zone of proximal development in Vygotsky's analysis of learning and instruction. In A. Kozulin, B. Gindis, V. Ageyev, & S. Miller (Eds.), *Vygotsky's educational theory in cultural context* (pp. 39-64). EBook: Cambridge University Press.

Cohrssen, C. (2015). Assessing children's understanding during play-based maths activities. *Early Childhood Australia Blog.* Retrieved from: http://thespoke.earlychildhoodaustralia.org.au/assessing-childrens-understanding-during-play-based-maths-activities/

Earl, L. (2003). *Assessment as learning: Using classroom assessment to maximize student learning.* Thousand Oaks, CA: Corwin Press.

Edwards, C., Gandini, L., & Forman, G. (Eds.) (2012). *The hundred languages of children: The Reggio Emilia experience in transformation.* Santa Barbara, CA: Clio.

Fleer, M., & Quinones, G. (2013). An assessment perezhivanie: Building an assessment pedagogy for, with and of early childhood science learning. In D. Corrigan, R. Gunstone, & A. Jones (Eds.), *Valuing assessment in science education: Pedagogy and curriculum, policy* (pp. 231-247). Dordrecht: Springer Science+Business Media.

Hedegaard, M. (2005). The zone of proximal development as a basis for instruction. In H. Daniels (Ed.), *An introduction to Vygotsky* (pp. 227-252). New York: Routledge.

Hedegaard, M. (2008). Principles for interpreting research protocols. In M. Hedegaard, M. Fleer, Y. Bang, & P. Hviid (Eds.), *Studying children: A cultural-historical approach* (pp. 46-64). New York: Open University Press.

Helm, J., Beneke, S., & Steinheimer, K. (2007). *Windows on learning: Documenting young children's work.* New York: Teachers College Press.

Roth, M. W., & Radford, L. (2010). Re/thinking the zone of proximal development (symmetrically). *Mind Culture and Activity, 17,* 229-307.

Sarama, J., & Clements, D. (2004). Building blocks for early childhood mathematics. *Early Childhood Research Quarterly, 19,* 181-189.

Sarama, J., & Clements, D. (2009). *Early childhood mathematics education research: Learning trajectories for young children.* New York: Routledge.

Thomas, G., Tagg, A., & Ward, J. (2002). *Exploring issues in mathematics education: An evaluation of the Early Numeracy Project.* New Zealand: Dunedin College of Education Te Kura Akau Taitoka.

Thompson, S., Rowe, K., Underwood, C., & Peck, R. (2005). *Numeracy in the early years.* Melbourne: Australian Council for Educational Research.

Thornbury, S., & Slade, D. (2006). *Conversation: From description to pedagogy.* Cambridge: Cambridge University Press.

Vygotsky, L. S. (1987). Thinking and speech (N. Minick, Trans.). In R. W. Rieber, & A. S. Carton (Eds.), *The collected works of L. S. Vygotsky* (Vol. 1) (pp. 39-285). New York: Plenum Press.

4 Encouraging language development through an online community

Lessons learnt from an action research project

Melissa Barnes

This chapter provides an account of a classroom teacher's experience as she identifies a problem she has encountered in her classroom and then takes systematic steps to create a solution. Through this process of teacher inquiry, or action research as described later, she experiments using a social media tool to encourage English language interactions between her Japanese exchange students. The "evidence" of successful language learning reported in this study is minimal but the teacher's journey provides an honest account of how educators must continually approach new ways of learning and teaching, collect evidence of learning and then try new and more effective ways to address the problem again ... and again.

Communities of Practice

The learning theory "Communities of Practice" (CoP), as first introduced by Lave and Wenger (1991), is used to explore how learning occurs in an online learning community. To understand how this study was conceptualised, it is important to understand how learning is constructed, or viewed, in light of this theory. The concept of CoP has roots in the work of other social theorists such as Vygotsky (1978) and Bandura (1977) who argue that social and cultural dimensions play an important role in learning. Lave and Wenger (1991) argue that learning occurs as learners engage in CoP. A CoP is defined as "groups of people who share a concern, a set of problems, or a passion about a topic, and who deepen their knowledge and expertise in this area by interacting on an ongoing basis" (Wenger, McDermott, & Snyder, 2002, p. 4). Learning is viewed as a process in which a learner moves from legitimate peripheral participation to full membership (Lave & Wenger, 1991). In other words, beginners or novices involve themselves in the group or community but their skills and knowledge are limited and are continually developing as they engage in this community. The experts in the community help to develop and nurture not only the skills and knowledge of the beginners but their growing identity within the community. It is the motivation of the members, whether novice or expert, to learn the values and practices of the community in order to keep their identity as community members (Lave & Wenger, 1991; Woolfolk & Margetts, 2016).

Lave and Wenger (1991) conducted research on apprenticeships in a number of communities, such as midwives in an American Indian community and tailors in West Africa. Their findings suggest that learning, for the most part, did not occur through a one-way transmission of facts but was best facilitated through an equally beneficial mentorship relationship between apprentices and more experienced workers (see also Mercieca, 2017). Therefore, learning occurred through the regular social interactions within these communities, rather than through a traditional process of knowledge being handed down from "teacher" to "student". Therefore, at the heart of CoP is the notion that learning is socially constructed, or in other words, that learning occurs when people interact and negotiate meaning to create understanding. This, then, moves away from more cognitive views of learning which argue that learning and behaviours are determined by our individual thinking processes (Woolfolk & Margetts, 2016). CoP draws on human nature's desire to gather with one another, and in doing so, come together to solve problems and share concerns and ideas (Mercieca, 2017). Given that social networking and technology have provided new platforms for sharing, contributing and co-constructing meaning, CoP is situated as a useful lens to explore how learning occurs online.

Social media tools

The emergence and evolution of the World Wide Web, first as Web 1.0 and then as Web 2.0, has forever changed how societies access information and communicate. While Web 1.0 allowed website owners (not users) to create, edit and manipulate information or text displayed on the Internet, Web 2.0 opened the door for website users to do the same (Handsfield, Dean, & Cielocha, 2009). Therefore, the introduction of Web 2.0, or the "Social Web" as it is often referred to, has made it much easier for content to be generated and published by users (Kamel Boulos & Wheeler, 2007). These changes in technology have created opportunities for new approaches to teaching and learning, allowing for new ways to communicate and acquire information. Applications such as wikis, blogs and digital storytelling are increasingly being used in the classroom as learners can contribute, interrogate and edit resources on the web, rather than just consume them (Handsfield et al., 2009).

For the purpose of this chapter, social networking is defined as "the practice of expanding knowledge by making connections with individuals of similar interests" (Gunawardena et al., 2009, p. 4). Characteristics of social networking, such as interaction, sharing and contribution, seem to befit the goals of teaching and learning language as we attempt to encourage the co-construction of knowledge and the negotiation of meaning in learning. Comas-Quinn, Mardomingo, and Valentine (2009, p. 98) explain that "sharing is a key activity in the co-construction of knowledge advocated by social constructivism, but whilst it is clear that the proliferation of user-generated content, free sites and software seems to point to a previously untapped human desire for sharing, it has been observed that people are more interested in sharing their own experiences than in taking advantage of what others have to share". Therefore, students' personal interest in "sharing" can be harnessed to encourage the development of language by using the target language to negotiate meaning with their classmates while also building a sense of community.

There is a growing field of research focusing on the use of microblogging, or social media tools such as Twitter and Facebook. Many researchers argue that these tools can foster and build a sense of community within and outside the classroom (Gannon-Leary & Fontainha, 2007; Gunawardena et al., 2009; Lai, 2015; Lomika & Lord, 2012; Newgarden, 2009; Trust, 2015). However, Salmon, Ross, Pechenkina, and Chase (2015) contend that while community "belonging" is desirable in an online learning community, there is limited research to suggest that it is either aspired to or achieved in these learning environments. As argued by Newgarden (2009), the power of social networking is the ability to extend learning outside of the actual classroom. These online communities can provide a platform to share, collaborate and reflect (Barnes, 2016).

Edmodo as an online learning community

With the emergence of social networking tools, online learning communities allow language learners to share their common interest of improving their language skills by interacting with one another online. Through specifically designed educational social networking tools, such as Edmodo, language learners can not only negotiate meaning and engage in the target language through discussions but can share resources and information. Edmodo is a free social learning network for teachers, students and parents. It is a platform that tries to emulate Facebook, yet with more control. The teacher can moderate the content and students can be restricted in how they interact with each other. Students can contribute to the social media platform by responding to teachers' posts and links, posting on a public board, sending private messages to the teacher, uploading content and embedding video. Teachers can set assignments (which can be synced to the class calendar), create quizzes and set up a library. The library feature allows the teacher to upload documents and video. This tool can be used to store important course materials and allow for independent learning tasks.

Thibaut (2015) investigated how a Year 6 class in an independent school in Sydney used Edmodo as an educational tool. Drawing on social learning theory, which CoP is rooted within, data were collected through teacher and student posts on Edmodo over four months, in addition to in-depth interviews with participants. Thibaut argues that teachers play an important role in modelling the use of Edmodo by organising activities that make explicit links between students' "everyday activities in the classroom with online digital interactions" (Thibaut, 2015, p. 87). In other words, the teacher explicitly made links between face-to-face and online interactions to ensure that students understood that these online activities were beneficial for their overall literacy development. Overall, Thibaut (2015, p. 89) found that students were able to "share their ideas, knowledge and creations by engaging with an audience of 30 unique different voices". She also argued that Edmodo provided opportunities for engagement, for interaction and to "develop" one's voice within this online learning platform.

Trust (2015), on the other hand, examined teachers' actions in an Edmodo mathematics subject community with more than 300,000 members and found that they did not share many attributes of the traditional CoP framework. He argued that while they were a "community", shared a common "domain" (e.g., mathematics) and shared resources and knowledge related to their "practice", there was little evidence of mentoring, relationship building and becoming a full participant. Trust (2015) found that out of the 600 posts and 1,908 replies, only two members posted or replied on multiple occasions. In other words, different sets of people were replying on every new post. In addition, 74% of the posts received less than five replies which implied short-lived interactions rather than sustained communication.

Given this contradicting evidence between these two studies, the study discussed in this chapter explores how Edmodo is used and how 30 Japanese high school exchange students respond to Edmodo and whether it has the potential to move language students from peripheral participation (contributing but minimally) to full participation (taking a more active role) in an online community.

Methodology

While a CoP approach, with its roots in social learning theory, is used as a lens to explore the data in this study, this study uses an action research design as it was born from a classroom teacher's awareness of a "problem" and her desire to act on this problem to improve teaching and learning practices in her classroom.

Action research design

The impetus for this study was born from three InterCultural Education Today (ICET) teachers' discussions on how best to encourage English communication in a classroom of Japanese speakers. This then prompted an action research study that aimed to use social networking tools to encourage English language communication, with the hope that students would create their own online English learning community.

Action research was revived within educational circles in the 1970s through the work of British educators Lawrence Stenhouse, John Elliott and Clem Adelman as they introduced the concept of "teacher as researcher" (Burns, 1999, p. 28). This brought forth the idea of two worlds coming together, the researcher and the teacher, theory and practice. Action research has become a tool for educators to take an active yet systematic role in improving and changing current educational practices. In other words, teachers take active steps in improving educational practices but have few clear and documented plans to achieve this change. The first step in action research is identifying a problem or a problematic situation and then taking deliberate actions to bring about change or improve teaching and learning practices. Action research is often described as a series of cycles or phases, which involve planning, acting, observing and reflecting (Kemmis & McTaggart, 1988, as cited in Burns, 1999, p. 7).

Freeman's (1998) action research model, the "teacher-researcher cycle", consists of six elements: (1) inquiry, (2) question/puzzle, (3) data collection, (4) data analysis, (5) understanding and (6) making public. The action research employed follows Freeman's (1998) teacher-researcher cycle (see Figure 4.1) in order to *improve* what is already happening in the classroom through a cyclic process of identifying the problem, inquiring, collecting and analysing data and reflection. Therefore, this chapter documents the process of how a teacher-researcher identified, interrogated and acted on a problem, collected and analysed the "evidence" and then reflected on what she had learnt from the process before starting the process again, trying and experimenting with new approaches to the problem.

Encouraging language development 39

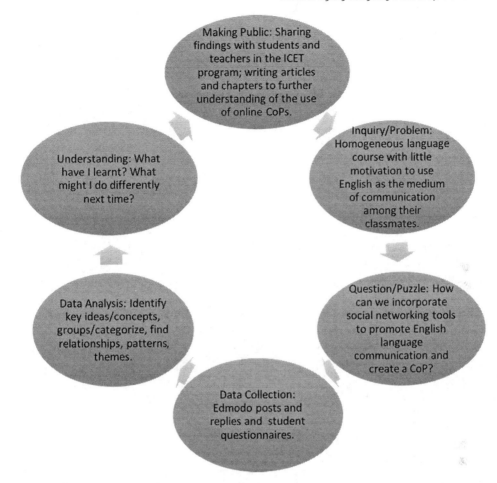

Figure 4.1 Action research plan

The context

The participants in this study consisted of 30 Japanese exchange students who studied in a high school in Sydney during the 2012 academic school year in a unique program called InterCultural Education Today (ICET). ICET was established in the early 1990s and placed Japanese high school students at different schools around Sydney with the vision that Japanese youth would be given the opportunity to expand their worldview and study and learn abroad. However, in time, it morphed into its current incarnation – a high school preparation program at one high school in Sydney. The 30 Japanese high school students in this study attended mainstream classes taking subjects such as mathematics, business, Japanese, health and physical education, while taking their English and history subjects with three ICET English as an Additional Language (EAL) teachers.

At the time of this study, ICET had two permanent classrooms at a high school in the Sydney metropolitan area and employed three teachers who were Teaching English to Speakers of Other Languages (TESOL) qualified and registered with the New South Wales

(NSW) Department of Education. Within the two ICET classrooms were ten desktop computers (20 in total) and a trolley with 15 laptops. Students had the opportunity to use these computing resources in the classroom and at designated times after school: three days a week for an hour and a half each day.

Before coming to Australia, the students were instructed not to bring a laptop of their own. The "no laptop policy" was implemented in 2009 after challenges with students who would isolate themselves in their bedrooms and not interact with their host family. While students could use their host families' home computer, they were also encouraged to use the desktops and laptops in the classroom. Many students would use the computers after school but primarily for personal communication purposes.

The problem

It became apparent early in the year to the teacher-researcher that it would take a great deal of effort, policing and creative thinking to encourage 30 Japanese high school students to speak to one another in English as their default was to communicate with one another in Japanese. While the teacher-researcher advocates the use of one's native tongue in language learning, as it's a powerful resource in language learning, she also acknowledges how difficult it can be for students to maximise engagement in the target language when they are situated in a classroom of students who speak their native language. In addition, students had access to laptops and computers both during class and after class but they were almost never used for educational purposes.

The plan

With the desire to encourage English language communication, the plan was to use web-based technologies to provide a platform for the students to communicate in English with one another. While two web-based technologies were explored, Edmodo and Glogster, for the purpose of this chapter only the use of Edmodo will be discussed. None of the three EAL teachers had any experience with Edmodo, providing a learning curve for both teachers and students. While there notably could have been a number of other "solutions" to encourage English language interactions among the students, at the time of this study the use of online learning tools was quite novel and something that was actively encouraged within the school.

Data collection and analysis (the "evidence")

Data were collected from 10 February to 19 November, 2012 (nine months) in the form of 183 posts and 164 replies on Edmodo and a student questionnaire distributed at the end of August. The student questionnaire was collected in August to present findings for a conference in September; however, Edmodo remained active until the students began exams in mid-November. The ICET program for the 2012 academic school year consisted of 30 Japanese students and three EAL teachers.

Edmodo posts or links were analysed in regard to the type and participation. In defining the type of task, the analysis identified the purpose of the post (e.g., a link to a resource, a presentation or discussion). The participation was analysed in two ways: Who was generating the post (e.g., teacher or student) and who was replying to these posts?

A student questionnaire was created by the teacher-researcher to primarily collect qualitative data on their attitudes and experiences regarding educational social media tools. The questionnaire was completed by 28 high school-age students, 17 females and 11 males, respectively. All questions were given in Japanese and English; however, responses were predominantly in Japanese. After responses from the questionnaires were translated, the data were then analysed by categorising and identifying key themes found among the responses, such as benefits, drawbacks, accessibility and engagement.

Results and discussion

Data were collected from Edmodo, in the form of posts and replies, and from student responses to a questionnaire. The following sections *analyse the data* from these two data collection instruments, demonstrating the fourth element in the teacher-researcher cycle process. In addition, the teacher-researcher's reflections and *understandings* (Element 5) are highlighted throughout this action research journey.

Edmodo posts and replies

In order to report on "what" occurred within the online learning community, the findings from the analysis of the Edmodo posts provide details on not only the purpose of the post (e.g., activity type) but "who" is generating the post and who is replying. The findings are discussed in relation to the lessons learnt by the teacher-researcher as she collected data, reflected on the results collected and considered more effective ways forward.

An early lesson: instruct and scaffold understanding of the online platform

The first post on Edmodo occurs on 10 February, 2012 by a student using an Edmodo post as a platform for answering a prompt given by the teacher in class (What will you do this weekend?), which is then followed by another 22 individual student posts. In class, the teacher asked the students to respond in English to this simple prompt on Edmodo as a way for them to begin navigating the online platform. It is to be noted that the teacher did not give an induction on using the platform or explicitly direct students to respond to each other's posts but had hoped that as the students "played around" with the platform they might discover the various ways they could use it to develop their language skills. Not surprisingly, of the total 23 posts on this first day, only two of the 47 replies to these posts are from peers with the remaining being an exchange between the teacher-researcher and the student who provided the original post.

This provides the first snapshot of the action research process. If it could be even referred to as a "community" at this point, this is a community that is controlled primarily by the teacher-researcher with little peer interaction. Instead of a community, it is an exchange between individual students and their teacher. The "evidence" from this first set of posts suggests that the teacher-researcher needed to provide more explicit instruction about this online platform, its capabilities and functions and ways in which they could use the platform to interact with one another in English. An important aspect of CoP is that community members maintain their own identity as they learn the values and practices of the community and whether they are novices or experts, they have something to contribute (Lave & Wenger, 1991; Woolfolk & Margetts, 2016). Therefore, if students had been better scaffolded in using and understanding the features of Edmodo, they may have taken more "ownership" and may have contributed more actively from the beginning.

Whose community? Allowing students to generate and control the content

Over the course of the nine months on Edmodo, there were 183 posts and 164 replies to posts. Of the 183 posts, 73% (n = 134) were tasks that were given by the teacher as an in-class activity or as homework and required a response in the form of a post, a presentation or a completed online poster (using the program Glogster). Of these 134 tasks, 40% (n = 53) were a student-generated response to a teacher prompt and the replies were primarily from the teacher but occasionally would elicit a response from one of five students who would occasionally comment on posts without being explicitly "instructed" to do so. This suggests that most students maintained "legitimate peripheral participation" as they contributed in minimal ways to the online community or as advised to do so, while five students began taking a more active role in the community by generating unprompted posts and replies.

As can be seen in Figure 4.2, 73% (n = 134) of the posts that were prompted by the teacher as an in-class activity or homework included the following activity types: Online posters using "Glogster", PowerPoint presentations, "Guess this place" activity (students described a place and their peers had to guess what place they had described) and letter writing. Of the remaining posts, 20% (n = 37) consisted of student-led discussions, 2% (n = 4) of teacher-generated polls and quizzes and 11% (n = 17) of teacher-generated links which primarily focused on grammar practice.

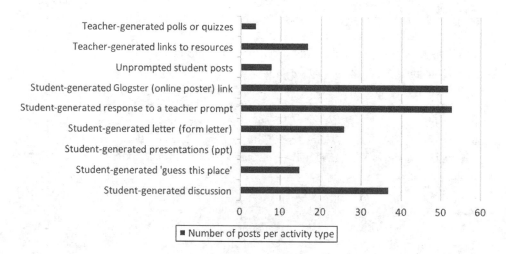

Figure 4.2 Number of posts per activity type

Encouraging language development 43

The action research cycle can be seen through the data collected from Edmodo as almost all of the posts (even though they were student-generated) were controlled by and dictated primarily by the teacher-researcher at the beginning of this study. In the process of reflecting on the types of activities and the lack of student replies, the teacher attempted to give more choice and control to the students. Until mid-July, most replies to a student-generated post consisted of a maximum of two student replies. The teacher-researcher then decided to experiment allowing students to create their own discussion questions and lead a conversation on Edmodo with their peers. Two students were to lead their own discussion on their topic of choice each week. While the teacher outlined some guidelines for the student-led discussion questions, such as ensuring they were appropriate for a classroom context, that the topic was something that every student could contribute to and that the question was open-ended and allowed students to provide different perspectives, most students created their discussion prompt with little scaffolding from the teacher. Ten of these student-led discussions had over 20 replies, with only six out of the 37 student-led discussions having under ten replies from peers.

As an example, on 24 August, 2012, a student-led discussion post, with 25 peer replies, provided this question prompt:

Why are you here (in Aus.) except to study English?

This post not only had students giving their responses but commenting on others with questions and encouragement. There was no teacher response.

Interestingly, only 4% (n = 8) of the total 183 posts over the academic year were completely unprompted. Of these unprompted student-generated posts, one was a student logging onto another student's Edmodo page and writing "I am smart" which then prompted 11 responses from peers. Four of these eight unprompted posts asked questions, such as:

What is the homework?

Why can Australian students use bad words in class and we can't?

The remaining three unprompted posts were reflective in nature, expressing and communicating two different students' unprompted thoughts and ideas. On 18 September, one student posted:

Although I finished listening in IELTS, I think my skill of listening has not been proving. Is my English skill weaker than before? Of course, I really need to study more and more. That is my wall that I need to break down. I have a no time to finish this year.

All but one of the unprompted responses were posted in the second half of the year, which may indicate that these students felt like they could reflect and discuss issues in English with their peers within this online community and that they were moving from legitimate peripheral participation to full participation.

In contrast, Trust (2015) argued that the move from peripheral participation to full participation of the 300,000 participants in his mathematics subject Edmodo group was not observed in the data due to different contributors and different groups of people being involved in different posts. This may be due to the large number of participants in his particular Edmodo group. However, in this study, most students knew each other from Japan so the problem was not engagement and/or sharing ideas and knowledge with one another but to do so with one another in English. Prior to trialling Edmodo, the students used English to interact with their teachers but would use Japanese to communicate with their Japanese peers when they communicated with one another face-to-face. Therefore, the data analysed from Edmodo show a shift from English use as a result of a teacher-prompted discussion and exchanges with the teacher to replies to the posts of their peers and unprompted social interactions using English (rather than Japanese) with their Japanese peers.

While students began taking more ownership of the content posted on Edmodo and engaged with it more readily, a look at the responses from the student questionnaire provides a different perspective and "voice" to the analysis of the Edmodo posts.

Student perceptions

The 28 students (out of 30) who completed the student questionnaire agreed that social media was popular in Japan, with half of the students using Facebook and Twitter every day. However, while social media played an integrative role in students' daily lives, the questionnaires revealed that only half of the students felt that Edmodo was beneficial in their English language classes. Those who felt that Edmodo was valuable argued that they could improve their writing skills, share their knowledge with others, discuss with friends, learn from others and improve their IT literacy.

On the other hand, nine students indicated that these social media tools were not beneficial, with three students arguing that it was not "fair" to use online tools if they were not allowed personal computers at home. One student commented, "It is not fair to be encouraged to use when there is not sufficient PC environment". An important element of an online learning community is that its participants can engage in collaborative and reflective practices (Salmon et al., 2015) outside or beyond the classroom (Newgarden, 2009). In the analysis of the Edmodo data, 73% (n = 134) of the posts were teacher-prompted and linked to classroom learning activities. While students did have access to computers, the times and the access were controlled by the teacher which does not promote a sustained learning community. It could be argued that an online learning community requires the freedom to interact without the constraints, such as time and location, that we usually place on classroom activities.

Another factor in the students' dislike of using Edmodo was the misunderstandings of the capabilities of these tools. For example, one student said that he/she could not make comments in Edmodo. This raises the issue that even though students are familiar with social media tools, they need to be explicitly instructed on the purpose and features of these web-based social media tools. In the questionnaires, several students commented that they would prefer to use Facebook rather than Edmodo, especially given that more than half of the students used Facebook as an educational tool in Japan. With the familiarity of using Facebook in their classes (e.g., teachers upload tasks, homework and videos), many students felt that Facebook was a better platform than Edmodo. This again raises the issue that students, and therefore teachers, need to understand the features of these tools. In addition, teachers need to explicitly teach students how to best utilise these platforms, incorporate them into lessons and then allow for flexibility in using them.

Implications for teaching and learning

In this action research project, the teacher-researcher explored how social media tools could be used to encourage communication and in turn create a CoP that would provide a space where students would share and interact with one another in English. As is common in action research cycles, there were several cycles that consisted of the teacher-researcher taking different approaches and using different activities to allow students a space where they learnt from one another and felt they had "voice" and membership within this online community. As action research provides evidence that is then reflected on to improve teaching and learning practices, this chapter does not claim to have "solved" the problem but places the teacher-researcher as a willing learner who aims to continually interrogate problems and learn in the process. There are several lessons learnt that can be drawn upon to inform teaching and learning within an online community space.

First of all, the restricted computer use was a recurring theme in the student questionnaires among the students and they felt they could not receive the full benefits of these social media tools due to not always having access to a home computer. As Wenger et al. (2002) argue, CoP require commitment and interaction on an ongoing basis. While the students enjoyed the social interaction that the social media tools afforded them, they needed to have more ease of access to these tools, particularly at home using their personal computers. Being a member of a community requires access to the tools needed to be part of that community. Equal access to the Internet, laptops and iPads is an important consideration when using online community platforms for teaching and learning purposes. Several studies have explored digital equity and disadvantaged students who may not have access to computers and/or the Internet (Chan, Hyung Park, Lau, Lau, & Yuen, 2016; Neal & Yelland, 2013).

Second, from the data that were collected, it became evident that students did not understand the purpose and the features of this web-based technology. In alignment with effective teaching practices, it becomes extremely important to be very explicit about the purpose of each activity. If students cannot see the value in these tasks, they will see the computer activities as fun and interesting but not educational. Thibaut (2015), in her study on the use of Edmodo with Year 6 students, argues that teachers must ensure that students are aware of the links between everyday face-to-face interactions and online interactions. As part of the action research journey, the teacher-researcher was prompted to reflect on this action research process, particularly how she might be able to better equip students to understand and fully interact with the features of Edmodo and then make cognitive links between how these online interactions develop their overall language ability. Additionally, it is important to introduce the various features of the technology and attempt to incorporate these in different activities and tasks as a scaffolding activity.

Implications for future research

Trust (2015, p. 79) argues that "the term 'online community of practice' is not a one-size-fits-all description of virtual spaces, platforms, and tools", and that further research is required to explore the different types of online communities and what features facilitate community building. While there is some evidence in this study that students took more ownership in generating and controlling the content in Edmodo, there was still a teacher presence aiding or distracting from students creating an English community of their own. The most telling "evidence" of the true nature of this CoP was that by the end of November when the students finished their academic year, there were no further posts but students continued to develop their sense of community with their Japanese peers on *Facebook* in *Japanese*. More research is needed to explore the role of the participants in regard to who facilitates the community building, how, and to what extent it is sustainable.

References

Bandura, A. (1977). *Social learning theory*. Englewood Cliffs, NJ: Prentice Hall.
Barnes, M. (2016). Encouraging communication through the use of educational social media tools. In D. Tafazoli & M. Romero (Eds.), *Multiculturalism and technology-enhanced language learning* (pp. 1-12). Pennsylvania: IGI Global.
Burns, A. (1999). *Collaborative action research for English language teachers*. New York: Cambridge University Press.
Chan, A., Hyung Park, J., Lau, G., Lau, W., & Yuen, A. (2016). Digital equity and students' home computing: A Hong Kong study. *The Asia-Pacific Education Researcher, 25*(4), 509-518. DOI:10.1007/s40299-016-0276-3
Comas-Quinn, A., Mardomingo, R., & Valentine, C. (2009). Mobile blogs in language learning: Making the most of informal and situated learning opportunities. *ReCall, 21* (1), 96-112.
Freeman, D. (1998). *Doing research: From inquiry to understanding*. New York: Heinle & Heinle.
Gannon-Leary, P., & Fontainha, E. (2007). Communities of practice and virtual learning communities: Benefits, barriers and success factors. *eLearning Papers, 5*. Retrieved on July 31, 2012 from: www.elearningeuropa.info/files/media/media13563.pdf
Gunawardena, C. N., Hermans, M. B., Sanchex, D., Richmond, C., Bohley, M., & Tuttle, R. (2009). A theoretical framework for building online communities of practice with social networking tools. *Educational Media International, 46*(1), 3-16.
Handsfield, L., Dean, T., & Cielocha, K. (2009). Becoming critical consumers and producers of text: Teaching literacy with Web 1.0 and Web 2.0. *The Reading Teacher, 63*(1), 40-50.
Kamel Boulos, M. N., & Wheeler, S. (2007). The emerging Web 2.0 social software: An enabling suite of sociable technologies in health and health care education. *Health Information and Libraries Journal, 24*(1), 2-23.
Lai, K. (2015). Knowledge construction in online learning communities: A case study of a doctoral course. *Studies in Higher Education, 40*(4), 561-579. DOI: http://dx.doi.org/10.1080/03075079.2013.831402
Lave, J., & Wenger, E. C. (1991). *Situated learning: Legitimate peripheral participation*. New York: Cambridge University Press.
Lomika, L., & Lord, G. (2012). A tale of tweets: Analyzing microblogging among language learners. *System, 40*(1), 48-63.
Mercieca, B. (2017). What is a community of practice? In J. McDonald & A. Cater-Steel (Eds.), *Communities of practice: Facilitation social learning in higher education* (pp. 3-26). Singapore: Springer.
Neal, G., & Yelland, N. (2013). Aligning digital and social inclusion: A study of disadvantaged students and computer access. *Education and Information Technology, 18*(2), 133-149. DOI:10.1007/s10639-012-9223-y
Newgarden, K. (2009). Annotated bibliography: Twitter, social networking and communities of practice. *TESOL E-Journal, 13*(2). Retrieved on May 5, 2016 from: http://www.tesl-ej.org/wordpress/issues/volume13/ej50/ej50m2/.
Salmon, G., Ross, B., Pechenkina, E., & Chase, A. (2015). The space for social media in structured online learning. *Research in Learning Technology, 23*, 1-14.
Thibaut, P. (2015). Social network sites with learning purposes: Exploring new spaces for literacy and learning in the primary classroom. *Australian Journal of Language and Literacy, 38*(2), 83-94.
Trust, T. (2015). Deconstructing an online community of practice: Teachers' actions in the Edmodo math subject community. *Journal of Digital Learning in Teacher Education, 31*(2), 73-81. DOI:10.1080/21532974.2015.1011293

Vygotsky, L. (1978). *Mind in society: Development of higher psychological processes*. Cambridge, MA: Harvard University Press.
Wenger, E., McDermott, R., & Snyder, W. M. (2002). *Cultivating communities of practice: A guide to managing knowledge*. Cambridge, MA: Harvard Business School Press.
Woolfolk, A., & Margetts, K. (2016). *Educational psychology*. (4th ed.). Melbourne, VIC: Pearson Australia.

5 Neuroscepticism
Investigating teachers' experiences using a Whole Brain Teaching method

Maria Gindidis

Introduction

The integration of neuroscience into teaching programs is developing and there is a trend towards including approaches claiming to be brain-based in classroom practice. This study investigates one such program, "Whole Brain Teaching" (WBT), a relatively new brain-based method of teaching that claims to enhance students' motivation and memory. The study was undertaken over the period of one school semester in a second languages program. It involved five primary school teachers and three secondary school teachers teaching Greek as a second language in an accredited after-hours community language program. Through systematic data collection of interviews and teacher journals, teachers reflected on WBT strategies introduced and used and how these contributed to both engagement with and recall of information, specifically set vocabulary in the second language. The study, a phenomenological, qualitative case study, explores the lived experiences of eight teachers who used WBT strategies, and who all advocated the positive impact of the WBT method without making links to learning theories or seeking evidence for research on the method.

Neuroscience and brain-based learning

Many attempts that integrate neuroscience into the classroom are referred to as brain-based (Jensen, 2008; Laster, 2008), brain-compatible (Ronis, 2007; Tate, 2003, 2004, 2005), brain-friendly (Biller, 2003; Perez, 2008) or brain-targeted instructional approaches (Hardiman, 2003). The field of neuroscience is complex and the accurate transfer of research findings to the classroom is often difficult (Ansari, Coch, & Scmedt, 2011; Devonshire & Dommett, 2010; Jolles et al., 2005). Misconceptions about the brain exist among professionals in education and claims loosely based on scientific facts have emerged in educational practice. Tate (2003) published an example of a brain-compatible approach in an article titled, 'Worksheets don't grow dendrites', suggesting that some educational practices "grow dendrites" and others do not.

There is no scientific evidence that worksheets or activities *grow dendrites*. Dendrites are structures found in the brain as part of a neuron that branch out from the soma or cell body of the neuron. These dendrites are responsible for retrieving information from other neurons and sending it to the soma, which then processes the information. Research has shown that dendrites will grow on their own even if they are isolated from other neurons. Recent findings suggest that neurons are genetically predisposed to grow even without environmental input; however, the environment around a neuron greatly influences its dendritic growth

(McAllister, 2000). Worksheets in the classroom have no connection to or impact on dendritic growth. Such gaps between neuroscience and education have enabled misconceptions about scientific findings to occur (Goswami, 2006). This lack of scientific evidence is where applications of neuroscience may have jumped beyond the data in today's classrooms.

Neuromyths, considered to be incorrect assertions or understandings about how the brain learns, include such ideas as "left and right brain learners", "critical periods for learning" and "types of food that influence brain functioning" (e.g., Geake, 2008; Purdy, 2008). These misunderstandings have served as a basis for popular educational programs, such as Brain Gym or the VAK approach (classifying students according to a Visual, an Auditory or a Kinaesthetic learning style). Whilst these programs claim to be "brain-based" or "brain-compatible", they, like worksheets that supposedly stunt dendritic growth, lack scientific validation (Krätzig & Arbuthnott, 2006; Lindell & Kidd, 2011; Stephenson, 2009; Waterhouse, 2006). Commercialisation, however, has led to a spread of brain-based classroom programs both in Australia and around the world. One such program is Whole Brain Teaching (WBT).

Whole Brain Teaching versus cognitive learning theory - the information-processing model

Over the past three decades due to technological advances with brain scanning and imaging, teachers have gained an increased understanding of how students think, reason and learn. Much of this gain, however, can also be attributed to the continuing development of a theoretical framework known as the information-processing model of human memory (Anderson, 1985; Atkinson & Shiffrin, 1968; Craik & Lockhart, 1972; Gagne, 1985). The model views human cognitive functioning as analogous to the operation of a computer. An understanding of the information-processing model clearly relates to programs such as WBT. WBT strategies used by teachers in this study can be linked to a number of known and researched concepts such as cognitive load theory (CLT), active learning, meaningfulness and automaticity.

WBT was first coined by Chris Biffle (2013, p. 4) who describes the origin of WBT as, "25 years of failure and then bingo ... the light goes on!" Biffle, a teacher in a community college teaching the students philosophy, began to experiment with new teaching strategies and came to the conclusion without any empirical evidence that he had discovered a classroom learning system linked to brain-based research. Biffle published his observations and new strategies making sweeping statements linking these to neuroscience breakthroughs or *neurofacts*. Such *neurofacts* included statements that students who engage in a physical learning activity employ the motor cortex, which is the most reliable memory storage area, located in a band across the top, centre of the brain. Biffle cites a number of similar *neurofacts* in his materials and publications, noting that WBT has the flexibility to allow teachers to put their own spin on techniques to meet each classroom's needs (Biffle, 2013, p. 60). Interestingly, all eight teachers in this study cited many *neurofacts* but were unable to describe the scientific structure and workings of the brain or whether this information supposedly from neuroscientific evidence was accurate.

What pre-service teachers and teachers often do not practice effectively is to examine the sources for statements made in programs such as WBT. Cognitive and neuroscience research explains that knowledge is based in activity. When animals and humans do things in their worlds, they shape their behaviour. Based on brain research, we know that likewise this shapes the anatomy and physiology of their brains (and bodies). When we actively control our experience, that experience sculpts the way our brains work, changing neurons and brain activity (Singer, 1995). Piaget's (1952) fundamental metaphor for knowledge was grasping ideas and facts with the mind and manipulating them physically and mentally. Mathematics illustrates this process directly in its fundamental operations, such as addition and multiplication, where objects are combined and grouped to produce numerical outcomes. Biffle's claims about learning and physical activity are not new or based on any new breakthroughs in the field.

Biffle (2013, p. 25) states that his primary goal in developing WBT was to devise a system that teachers would be able to willingly adopt to meet their particular students' needs. Each of the WBT strategies was cited as rigorously classroom tested, and several of these have, according to Biffle, now been researched for over ten years. The author of this chapter was unable to find any such empirical research or relevant peer-reviewed data findings. To make these claims for research and evidence, Biffle used teacher feedback received via email, from teacher conferences and from the WBT website from hundreds of teachers from locations all over the USA who used the techniques (Biffle, 2013, p. 25).

WBT also cites neuroscientific terms, one of which is *mirror neurons*; these, Biffle notes, are scattered throughout the brain and explain why people mirror others, or repeat what they are doing. In WBT classrooms, students mirror their teacher's actions and/or words and each other's behaviour (Biffle, 2013, p. 21). Again, this claim is not new, learning by observing and imitating others has long been recognised as a powerful learning strategy for humans. Recent findings from neuroscience, more specifically on the mirror neuron system, have offered further insight into the neural bases of learning by observation and imitation. Observational learning is considered both a basic and a powerful way in which people learn (Bandura, 1986). Science has noted that we may have evolved to observe and imitate each other (Sweller & Sweller, 2006). Cognitive load theory (CLT) argues that due to the way the brain architecture of humans is organised, learning by observing or imitating what others say or do is a more effective and efficient way of acquiring learning rather than trying to devise or construct it ourselves (Paas, Renkl, & Sweller, 2003). Mirror neurons are not new and whilst research grows in this field, their role in teaching and learning cannot be attributed to a "whole brain" system of teaching.

WBT also bases many teaching strategies on "understandings" of memory. Biffle cites two types of memory, short term and long term. Short-term memory is limited in capacity from three to seven items and is limited in duration; he states that some believe it to be only two seconds and others believe the memory to be lost in 15 to 18 seconds. Long-term memory, on the other hand, is unlimited in capacity because storing new information into long-term memory does not force other information out. WBT tells teachers that when information is repeated frequently enough, it will be stored forever (Biffle, 2013, p. 20). Hence, WBT uses much repetition consistently in strategies and techniques.

Studies of long-term memory and learning cite various types of information: declarative (semantic and episodic), procedural (how to do something) and imagery (mental images). As opposed to short-term memory, long-term memory has unlimited space. The crucial factor of long-term memory is how well organised the information is. This is affected by proper encoding (elaboration processes in transferring to long-term memory) and retrieval processes (scanning memory for the information and transferring into working memory so that it could be used). In general, we remember a lot less information than is actually stored there (Ericsson & Kintsch, 1995). WBT's claim that long-term memory stores information forever is in fact a *neuromyth*.

Lastly, according to Biffle (2013), habituation is one of the most important concepts in education. "Habituation occurs when an individual's response to a stimulus decreases after repeated stimulation" (Biffle, 2013, p. 22). Such an example can be likened to the fact that people will react to stimuli until they get used to it and don't even notice it anymore, like living on a busy street and hearing cars pass for the first few days, but not noticing it after that. With reference to the classroom setting, Biffle (2013) noted that an approach that works with students at the beginning of the year may not be successful a few months later.

The framework of "habituation" cited in WBT is not new brain research, it is informed by behaviourist and information-processing theories of learning. Whether for rote recall of facts as formulated in behaviourism (Skinner, 1953), or for skilful performance of algorithms or word problems as formulated through information-processing theories (Anderson, 1976, 1993), the basic premise of habituation is that repeated practice of routine problems leads to gradual adjustment to task constraints. Biffle's use of novelty in WBT to counteract this is not new in teaching. As this study was conducted in a second language learning context it is also worth noting that second language learning cognitive strategies such as imagery, elaboration, analysis, practice and inferencing explain how such strategies "operate directly on incoming information, manipulating it in ways that enhance learning" (O'Malley & Chamot, 1990, p. 44). Theories and methods of second language acquisition have a long history of research linking Total Physical Response (TPR) (Asher, 1969), gesture (McCafferty, 2002) and meaningful input of content (Krashen, 1980) to effective learning. WBT's claim that habituation is new cannot be evidenced.

There are seven teaching techniques that lay the foundation of a WBT classroom. With these techniques, eight areas of the brain, according to Biffle (2013), may be activated. When students are involved with a call and response, the prefrontal cortex is stimulated; students use their Broca's area when speaking, Wernicke's area whilst listening; and emotions awaken their limbic system. Memory formation uses the hippocampus and seeing registers the visual cortex. Anytime gestures are involved, the brain's motor cortex is triggered (Biffle, 2013). The above *neuro-talk* was offered and paraphrased by teachers in this study, both in interviews and in journal entries, as their reasoning for why WBT strategies were effective.

Methodology – phenomenology in classroom research

This study describes, interprets and presents the experiences and perceptions of eight teachers, using words to construct meanings, and is best framed as a qualitative study underpinned by phenomenology. This epistemology and choice for the research methodology can be best viewed using a graphic representation of the research process (Figure 5.1).

The research was primarily interested in the reality of what second language teachers experienced using WBT in classrooms. The study used phenomenology as a research design and Interpretative Phenomenological Analysis (IPA) as the tool by which various data sources were brought together or methods of data were corroborated to provide for accuracy in the evaluation of the data collected. The teachers are linked together by the second language they represent and all work in the same community language school. The choice of

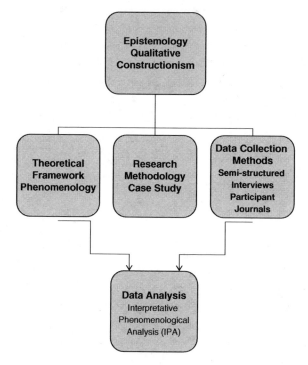

Figure 5.1 The research process

phenomenology as a research method provided a powerful basis for understanding subjective experience, gaining insights into people's motivations and actions and cutting through the clutter of taken-for-granted assumptions and conventional wisdom.

Phenomenology is a line of philosophy that emphasises the intentionality of human consciousness and the praxis of the so-called life-world, the world of lived experience. One of the characteristics of a phenomenological approach is that it's not interested in questions of existence, or a causal relationship of phenomena, but rather concentrates on searching for an understanding. The approach allows for the deconstruction of causal hierarchies and helps us see the world as an interactive weave (Heinämaa, 1996). The purpose of the phenomenological approach is to illuminate the specific, to identify phenomena through how they are perceived by the participants in a situation. This normally translates into gathering "deep" information and perceptions through inductive, qualitative methods such as interviews, discussions and participant observation, and representing it from the perspective of the research participant(s). Van Manen (1990, p. 10) notes that phenomenology used in research is an exploration of "the essence of lived experience".

The data collected and analysed were two semi-structured interviews with each teacher and a reflective journal each teacher submitted after each of the five WBT lessons they taught and reflected on. Given that experiences and perceptions of individual teachers are highly idiosyncratic and context-driven, the technique of "purposeful sampling" was employed to ensure a range of teacher perspectives from different contexts. Teachers in this study included experienced community languages teachers (minimum of ten years teaching background in a community language school) and less experienced (less than five years teaching background).

Each of the two semi-structured interviews was conducted over six months. In total, 16 interviews were conducted in 2015. Each of the interviews lasted for approximately 60 minutes. Each participant's reflective journal was collected over the last three months of the data collection period. The structure of the qualitative data collection, the passage of time over which the interviews were conducted, the internal consistency and external consistency of the transcription and noting or coding using IPA (Smith, Flowers, & Larkin, 2009, p. 83) were linked to Yardley's (2000) four broad principles for assessing the quality of qualitative research. These four principles – sensitivity to context, commitment and rigour, transparency and coherence and finally impact and importance – were implemented in this study.

A constructionist epistemology frames this research, within the constructivist "epistemology of practice" developed by Schön (1983) under the term "reflective practice" in which the researcher engages with interviews and interacts with the participant teachers in order to share their lived experiences, interpret those experiences and relate them to what is already known. The view of knowledge held by the researcher is that it is socially constructed (Crotty, 1998), with no true meaning but, rather, a multiplicity of meanings being "constructed by human beings as they engage with the world they are interpreting" (Crotty, 2003, p. 43). The researcher's belief in the value of many shared viewpoints, and opinions from a variety of perspectives, all of which are valid, underpins the relationship between the researcher, the research participants and the research purpose. This approach to the inquiry is aligned to the precepts of the social constructionist paradigm.

The constructionist researcher's task is not so much to discover realities by means of deductive analysis, rather the aim in constructionism is to construct meaning through engagement with world realities and the application of an inductive logic to the interpretation of those lived realities. This allows the researcher to generate theory and propose hypotheses. From the participants' diverse context-specific experiences, shared with the researcher in response to key questions formulated for the semi-structured interviews, theories are constructed. These theories show how concepts relate to each other (Neuman, 2007), given that interpretations and perspectives vary, for reality is subjective (Sarantakos, 1998). The collection and inductive analysis of multiple views of reality held by participants using a WBT teaching method allowed for new interpretations and more sophisticated constructions to emerge (Guba & Lincoln, 1985). The theoretical perspective taken in this study, that of phenomenology, is interpretivist by nature.

Table 5.1 serves as a snapshot and overview of all eight teachers.

Table 5.1 Overview of community teachers interviewed

Teacher	Language	Age	Years Teaching	Current Class	Student Number	Gender
Grace	Greek	51	26	Year 6	19	Female
Gloria	Greek	25	3	*Prep & Year 1	15	Female
Sophia	Greek	47	13	*Years 3 & 4	18	Female
Sonya	Greek	23	2	Year 7	17	Female
Anna	Greek	50	25	Year 1 & 6 & *HS	48	Female
Ari	Greek	59	34	Year 9	19	Male
Desi	Greek	22	1	*Prep & Year 1	15	Female
Diana	Greek	29	5	Year 8	27	Female

*Prep is Preparatory/Foundation, first year of schooling in Victoria. 5 Years old
*All names are pseudonyms
*Composite refers to mixed class of two or more ages
*HS refers to High School

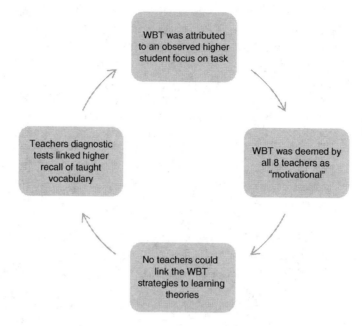

Figure 5.2 Overarching themes

Using a phenomenological theoretical framework together with IPA as the data analysis tool, the researcher has attempted to report on common themes that emerged across the data. On a methodological level, an IPA study involves a highly intensive and detailed analysis of experiences where patterns of meaning are developed and reported in a thematic form. These emergent themes are part of the overtly interpretative analysis, which position the descriptions as offered by participants in a wider, social, cultural and even theoretical context. This interpretative analysis affords the researcher an opportunity to deal with the data presented in a more speculative fashion; to think about what it means for the participants to have made these claims and have expressed their feeling and concerns about using WBT in their second language classrooms.

The graphic representation in Figure 5.2 presents the overarching themes that emerged from the analysis. Discussion of these themes presents the "collective voice" of all teachers.

Findings

Teachers in this study had all undertaken five, two-hour sessions of in-house school professional development. Their facilitator had attended a WBT conference in America and the sessions concentrated on WBT strategies. They used reflective journals to make observations about student focus on task and pre-test and post-test teacher-generated diagnostic vocabulary tests to collect data about recall. During the semi-structured interviews, no teacher was able to connect any of the WBT strategies to known learning theories and all made sweeping statements about learning.

When asked if she could link WBT to learning theories Sophia noted:

Neuroscepticism in a Languages classroom 55

Students have different learning styles.

- *50% are visual learners and prefer pictures, charts and written work.*
- *30% are kinaesthetic learners and need more hands-on activities.*
- *20% are auditory learners and they talk about what they are learning, is this what you mean? This is a learning theory linked to the brain's way of learning ... (pause) I think.*

When asked what they believed WBT contributed to their teaching Ari noted:

Children learn best when teachers teach new material first and review previously learned material. WBT and using the mirror strategy meant that I was reviewing and checking all the time and they (students) loved it. WBT creates a motivated class. It is a fantastic method.

Other participants commented that motivation was a definite observed positive in their WBT teaching:

Students are on high energy all the time, they are so motivated to learn. (Despina)

What was also interesting was that teachers often referred to time on task as *motivation*:

Students when using WBT were focused on the task, you could see how motivated they were. (Ari)

Also of importance were *brain facts* that were offered by teachers in interviews and documented in their journals. When asked where these were sourced from, all teachers cited the in-house WBT training in which they had participated. The following highlight such examples:

The brain performs better in a positive emotional state. Students must feel physically and emotionally safe before their brains are ready to learn. (Anna: journal entry)

The brain learns new information in chunks. Brain research states that children between the ages of 5 and 13 learn best when given chunks of 2 to 4 pieces of information. (Diana: journal entry)

Children ages 14 and older can learn up to 7 chunks at a time. Teachers should plan for these and teach Greek in small chunks. (Desi: journal entry)

The brain works on a time schedule. Children ages five to 13 learn best in five- to ten-minute sessions. (Grace: interview)

Students need a moment to rest their brain from a task. This increases their focus. (Sonya: interview)

WBT allows students to take time to stand up and stretch. The "teach - ok" strategy gives a 2-minute talk break, if you do this the brain will be more ready to stay on task and store information. (Gloria: journal entry)

In addition, one teacher spoke about the use of WBT gestures:

I really like the gestures because when I call on students and ask them a question, if it has no gesture, I can start to make the gesture, something clicks in their (student) brain – that's why it's called WBT – and they can remember and tell it. (Sophia: interview)

56 Maria Gindidis

Each of the teachers responded by saying that they definitely thought that WBT was much better compared to other teaching methods with which they were familiar. All the teachers noted in interviews that they planned on continuing to use WBT in their classrooms because it works and it is fun for both learners and teacher.

Lastly, teachers recommended that more teachers should use WBT strategies, but suggested taking it one step at a time. One teacher's advice was:

> You can make up your own (referring to gestures). It takes time, you need to be patient. The key with WBT is that you say a specific sentence or a phrase and then have the actions with it. All teachers should try it. (Gloria: interview)

When asked in interviews whether as teachers they recommend WBT one stated:

> Yes, definitely, because your 22 kids are engaged when you use WBT. They are seeing, hearing and repeating things and you are and they are having fun. (Ari: interview)

Although teachers in this study were resoundingly all positive about WBT, the information-processing theory of learning which provides a strong theoretical rationale supporting many of the WBT teaching techniques was not known to them. The study notes that an analysis of WBT is strongly connected to the information-processing model of learning and not to a newly created *brain-based model*; however, teachers in the study were unable to make such links both in their interviews and in their journals.

Implications of the study

Evidence from this study posits the view that there must be a greater and more meaningful dialogue between the educational and neuro-scientific communities. Whilst teachers in this study noted that WBT strategies used in their second language classroom created a more engaged classroom, motivating students and impacting on better recall of information, they also stated that they knew very little about how children learn. Teachers were unable to cite relevant evidence or link information-processing learning theories to the impact of the WBT strategies they used. They did, however, believe that WBT strategies were proven brain-based but were unable to give any scientific sources or cite research.

Research has demonstrated clearly that students learn best when they are actively involved in the learning process (Glover, Bruning, & Filbeck, 1983). The value that the information-processing model places upon a learner as an active rather than a passive participant in the learning process encourages participation by students, less teacher talk and more time spent using discussion, group activities and individual activities and exercises in the classroom setting. WBT, like many other programs that claim to be rooted in brain-based learning, Dubinsky (2010) warns, should be looked at with a watchful eye. She found that entrepreneurs have created a market with claims that brain-based programs are an effective instructional tool, yet had simply developed programs and products addressing classroom management strategies.

The limitations of this study included teachers' perceptions of measuring student engagement which is subjective and difficult to measure both qualitatively and quantitatively. The difficulty in defining levels of student on-task time includes how it looks in a classroom, the depth and breadth of engagement and if the engagement is aligned with the instructional objective. Students can appear to be on task through their compliance with completing classroom routines and tasks, yet the deeper and more complex levels of engagement that require more advanced cognitive skills such as synthesis and application create the complexities that surround measuring engagement.

WBT's mission statement is the creation of a learning environment that is based on high levels of student investment in learning with the goal of producing a deeper and more concrete experience. The use of WBT strategies such as mirroring claims to eliminate the option of being a passive learner. The goals of the WBT methods were cited by both Biffle (2013) and teachers in this study as fostering connectivity, empowerment, collaboration and team-building experiences for students. Attributing these goals solely to neurological findings of brain-based education perpetuates *neuromyths* in schools. The influence of these myths in the classroom is problematic, wasting money, time and effort, which could be better spent on the development of evidence-based practices (Pasquinelli, 2012; Sylvan & Christodoulou, 2010).

The implications of this study indicate that there is a need for more rigorous scrutiny of teaching methods which claim to be *whole brain-based*. This correlates with what Geake (2008, p. 12) refers to as a *critical filter* provided by those with enough specific knowledge to identify correctly the *neuromyths* in new programs destined for the classroom. This filter is predicated on a collaborative research alliance between classroom teachers and neuroscientists. Currently many teachers who follow the plethora of commercial brain-based learning methods are doing so with the belief they are improving student engagement or academic results when there is as yet no scientific justification for these activities. As 21st-century brain research further develops, additional findings with relevance for teaching and learning will continue to amass.

A critical filter and attention to evidence will assist both the profession and teachers to evaluate effective classroom teaching underpinned by known learning theories and be less likely to attribute such success solely to newly found *brain-based strategies*. Developing a critical filter in pre-service education courses and re-engaging with theories of learning such as the information-processing model in teacher professional development courses will deepen practitioner knowledge about how students learn.

Conclusion

We are in the infancy of brain research and its links to teaching and learning and there is much information and evidence that we still don't know. Dismissing it as a fad, premature or opportunistic could be seen as short-sighted and whilst *brain-based* methods and research seem conflicting, confusing and/or contradictory it is still a new frontier in education, one as teachers we need to stay curious and critical about.

Geake (2011, p. 12) concludes that "a cognitive neuroscience-education nexus should be a two-way street". Goswami (2006) similarly states that there is much that neuroscience can learn from classroom practitioners who need to be encouraged to collect data and offer feedback on important research questions. At the level of the classroom there is an acknowledged need for better two-way communication between the complex world of cognitive neuroscience and the equally complex world of education; the need, therefore, is strong for a *critical filter* to protect classroom teachers from *neuro-nonsense*. As this study collected data on WBT in the teaching of Greek as a second language it is apt to conclude with Aristotle's use of the term *phronesis*, a Greek word for a type of wisdom or intelligence specifically relevant to practical things. What teachers and theorists achieve in their classrooms and personal understandings of teaching cannot replace *episteme*, our collective theoretical accomplishment in developing a meta-discourse for teaching reform based on scientific knowledge (cf., Korthagen & Kessels, 1999).

References

Anderson, J. R. (1976). *Language, memory and thought*. Hillsdale, NJ: Lawrence Erlbaum Associates.
Anderson, J. R. (1985). *A series of books in psychology. Cognitive psychology and its implications* (2nd ed.). New York: W H Freeman/Times Books/Henry Holt & Co.
Anderson, J. R. (1993). *Rules of the mind*. Hillsdale, NJ: Lawrence Erlbaum Associates.
Ansari, D., Coch, D., & Scmedt, B. D. (2011). Connecting education and cognitive neuroscience: Where will the journey take us? *Educational Philosophical Theory, 43*, 37-42.
Asher, J. (1969). The total physical approach to second language learning. *The Modern Language Journal, 53(1)*, 3-17.
Atkinson, R., & Shiffrin, R. (1968). Human memory: A proposed system and its control processes. *Psychology of Learning and Motivation, 2*, 89-195.
Bandura, A. (1986). From thought to action: Mechanisms of personal agency. *New Zealand Journal of Psychology, 15*, 1-17.
Biffle, C. (2013). *Whole brain teaching for challenging kids (and the rest of your class, too!)*. Lexington, KY: Whole Brain Teaching LLC.
Biller, L. W. (2003). *Creating brain-friendly classrooms*. Lanham, MD: The Scarecrow Press.
Craik, F. I., & Lockhart, R. S. (1972). Levels of processing: A framework for memory research. *Journal of Verbal Learning and Verbal Behaviour, 11(6)*, 671-684.
Crotty, M. (1998). *The foundations of social research: Meaning and perspective in the research process*. London: Allen & Unwin.
Crotty, M. (2003). *The foundations of social research: Meaning and perspective in the research process*. London; Thousand Oaks, California: Sage Publications.
Devonshire, I. M., & Dommett, E. J. (2010). Neuroscience: Viable applications in education? *Neuroscientist, 16*, 349-356.
Dubinsky, J. M. (2010). Neuroscience education for prekindergarten-12 teachers. *Journal of Neuroscience, 30*, 8057-8060.
Ericsson, K. A., & Kintsch, W. (1995). Long-term working memory. *Psychological Review, 102(2)*, 211-245.
Gagné, R. M. (1985). *The conditions of learning and theory of instruction*. Fort Worth, TX: Holt, Rinehart and Winston.
Geake, J. (2008). Neuromythologies in education. *Educational Research, 50(2)*, 123-133. DOI:10.1080/00131880802082518
Geake, J. (2011). Position statement on motivations, methodologies, and practical implications of educational neuroscience research: FMRI studies of the neural correlates of creative intelligence. *Educational Philosophy and Theory, 43(1)*, 43-47.
Glover, J., Bruning, R., & Filbeck, R. (1983). *Educational psychology principles and applications*. Boston, MA: Little, Brown and Company.
Goswami, U. (2006). Neuroscience and education: From research to practice? *Nature Reviews: Neuroscience, 7*, 406-413.
Guba, E. G., & Lincoln, Y. S. (1985). Competing paradigms in qualitative research. In N. K. Denzin & Y. S. Lincoln (Eds.), *The landscape of qualitative research* (pp. 195-220). Thousand Oaks, CA: Sage.
Hardiman, M. M. (2003). *Connecting brain research with effective teaching: The Brain-Targeted Teaching Model*. Lanham, MD: Rowman & Littlefield Education.
Heinämaa, S. (1996). Feminism, science, and the philosophy of science. In L. H. Nelson & J. Nelson (Eds.), *Studies in epistemology, logic, methodology and philosophy of science* (pp. 289-308). London: Kluwer Academic Publishers.
Jensen, E. (2008). *Brain-based learning: The new paradigm of teaching* (2nd ed.). Thousand Oaks, CA: Corwin Press.
Jolles, J., Groot, R. H. M. D., Benthem, J. V., Dekkers, H., Glopper, C. D., & Uijlings, H. (2005). *Brain lessons*. Maastricht: Neuropsych Publishers.

Korthagen, F. A. J., & Kessels, J. P. A. M. (1999). Linking theory and practice: Changing the pedagogy of teacher education. *Educational Researcher, 28*(4), 4-17.

Krashen, S. (1980). The input hypothesis. In J. Alatis (Ed.), *Current issues in bilingual education* (pp. 144-158). Washington, DC: Georgetown University Press.

Krätzig, G. P., & Arbuthnott, K. D. (2006). Perceptual learning style and learning proficiency: A test of the hypothesis. *Journal of Educational Psychology, 98,* 238-246.

Laster, M. T. (2008). *Brain-based teaching for all subjects.* Lanham, MD: Rowman & Littlefield Education.

Lindell, A. K., & Kidd, E. (2011). Why right-brain teaching is half-witted: A critique of the misapplication of neuroscience to education. *Mind, Brain and Education, 5,* 121-127.

McAllister, K. (2000). Cellular and molecular mechanisms of dendrite growth. *Cerebral Cortex, 10*(10), 963-973.

McCafferty, S. G. (2002). Gesture and creating zones of proximal development for second language learning. *The Modern Language Journal, 86*(2), 192-203.

Neuman, W. L. (2007). *Basics of social research: Qualitative and quantitative approaches* (2nd ed.). Boston, MA: Pearson Education.

O'Malley, J. M., & Chamot, A. (1990). *Learning strategies in second language acquisition.* Cambridge: Cambridge University Press.

Paas, F., Renkl, A., & Sweller, J. (2003). Cognitive load theory and instructional design: Recent developments. *Educational Psychologist, 38,* 1-4.

Pasquinelli, E. (2012). Neuromyths: Why do they exist and persist? *Mind, Brain and Education, 6,* 89-96.

Perez, K. (2008). *More than 100 brain-friendly tools and strategies for literacy instruction.* Thousand Oaks, CA: Corwin Press.

Piaget, J. (1952). *The origins of intelligence in children.* New York: International Universities Press.

Purdy, N. (2008). Neuroscience and education: How best to filter out the neuro-nonsense from our classrooms? *Irish Educational Studies, 27*(3), 197-208.

Ronis, D. L. (2007). *Brain-compatible assessments.* Thousand Oaks, CA: Corwin Press.

Sarantakos, S. (1998). *Social research.* South Yarra: Macmillan Education Australia.

Schön, D. A. (1983). *The reflective practitioner: How professionals think in action.* New York: Basic Books.

Singer, W. (1995). Development and plasticity of cortical processing architectures. *Science, 270,* 758-764.

Skinner, B. F. (1953). *Science and human behaviour.* New York: Macmillan.

Smith, J. A., Flowers, P., & Larkin, M. (2009). *Interpretative phenomenological analysis: Theory, method and research.* London: Sage.

Stephenson, J. (2009). Best practice? Advice provided to teachers about the use of Brain Gym in Australian schools. *Australian Journal of Education, 53,* 109-124.

Sweller, J., & Sweller, S. (2006). Natural information processing systems. *Evolutionary Psychology, 4,* 434-458.

Sylvan, L. J., & Christodoulou, J. A. (2010). Understanding the role of neuroscience in brain based products: A guide for educators and consumers. *Mind, Brain and Education, 4,* 1-7.

Tate, M. L. (2003). *Worksheets don't grow dendrites: 20 instructional strategies that engage the adult brain.* Thousand Oaks, CA: Corwin Press.

Tate, M. L. (2004). *"Sit & get" won't grow dendrites: 20 professional learning strategies that engage the brain.* Thousand Oaks, CA: Corwin Press.

Tate, M. L. (2005). *Reading and language arts worksheets don't grow dendrites: 20 literacy strategies that engage the brain.* Thousand Oaks, CA: Corwin Press.

Van Manen, M. (1990). *Researching lived experience: Human science for an action sensitive pedagogy.* Albany, NY: State University of New York Press.

Waterhouse, L. (2006). Inadequate evidence for multiple intelligences, Mozart effect, and emotional intelligence theories. *Educational Psychology, 41,* 247-255.

Yardley, L. (2000). Dilemmas in qualitative research. *Psychology & Health, 15,* 215-228.

6 Literacy in and for the 21st century

Considering the pedagogical place of social media within 21st-century Australian literacy classrooms through the lens of childhood

Damien Lyons

Introduction

This chapter considers the place of social media within a 21st-century literacy discourse in Australian classrooms. Using a phenomenological narrative (Shacklock & Thorp, 2005) of three teachers in an Australian school we will reflect on an incident where Facebook was used by a group of eight Year 7 students inappropriately. Through reflecting on the incident, we will question, through a sociological lens, the place of social media teaching within a classroom literacy program, and wonder about the place this has when we consider what we mean by literacy in and for the 21st century. Within the digital world children can often be more skilled, risk oriented and willing to challenge power relationships (Gustafson, Hodgson, & Tickner, 2004). In Australia, children are more commonly being equipped with powerful technological tools for communication and learning. Laptops, tablets and smart phones are only tools, but the power they possess, and the influence they can create within social groups and communities, is vast. Therefore, considering the place of social media within a sociological landscape of childhood and 21st-century literacy pedagogy is the aim of this chapter.

Literature review

Defining literacy in the 21st century

At the heart of a rapidly changing world in the early part of the 21st century is a literacy discourse that is evolving to reflect the "new" ways we live, work and communicate, social media playing a significant part. While the illiterate of the 20th century were those who could not read or write, "the illiterate of the 21st century will be those who cannot critically interpret multiple sources of information" (Toffler, 1995, p. 22). This is not intended to be a binary opposition; rather, Toffler is suggesting that skills that were valuable in the 20th century are still necessary, but are not enough, for the 21st century. Literacy for the 21st century embraces and demands skills in multimodality, digital citizenship, information management and social media engagement, all within a context of fluidity and constant change (Crockett, Jukes, & Churches, 2011).

Definitions of literacy have arguably not changed for many years. For example, Bull and Anstey suggest that "literacy is represented as having the skills to successfully take part in everyday life, including economic and social contributions" (Bull & Anstey, 2005, p. 6). What has changed is the world in which children live and learn. It is this sociocultural context (Bonk & Cunningham, 1998) that arguably should be defining the thinking we do around literacy teaching and learning in and for the 21st century, in order to enable children with the skills and dispositions to be "literate" in time and place (Darling-Hammond, 2006).

However, a sociocultural view of literacy, which at its most simplistic level implies making meaning within a social context, has implications for the way we think about the teaching and learning of literacy in classrooms. In Australia, where high stakes standardised testing is being introduced and where, therefore, teachers are either directly or indirectly being encouraged to teach to the test to improve school data (Breivik, 2005), the notion of focusing on traditional literacies seems to endure, often at the expense of attention to the literacy practices in which young people are engaging outside of the classroom (Thomson, 2002). If literacy is a social discourse, and is constructed through discourse (Gee, Hull, & Lankshear, 1996), what is most striking are the power relations at play (Fullan, 2011). Children now have the ability to create and share meaning in ways that no longer can be controlled by schools or by the people who traditionally held power (Foo Seau, Ho, & Hedberg, 2005). This is often enacted through online social networks such as Facebook.

The world is changing, and changing rapidly. Industrial models of education that were once very successful, and that appear to be holding on within education systems (perhaps even being valued in some education systems), are today failing dismally beyond the classroom walls (Thomson, 2002). Employers are calling for skills that can be grouped under the heading of 21st-century skills, yet education systems are still struggling to place sufficiently high value on these skills (Crockett et al., 2011). In fact, there is some evidence in terms of high stakes standardised testing to suggest they may be edging towards the opposite (Robinson, 2011). The desire to embrace 21st-century literacy learning is apparent in many education curriculum documents, but in practice the value that is placed on this aspect of the curriculum seems at odds with the value that society places on these skills (Crockett et al., 2011). The world is radically changing almost everywhere, and at a pace that is faster than ever before, except in our schools (Prensky, 2010). Rather than focusing on policy or curriculum documents, it may be worth viewing this "wicked problem" through a different lens – the lens of childhood. By paying attention to how childhood is being constructed and enacted, we may find renewed energy to pay closer attention to the literacy practices children are enacting as part of their everyday life-worlds, and create renewed energy to build these literacy practices in as part of our literacy program.

Childhood and technology

Childhood conjures up many images, often influenced by our own childhood. David Buckingham's work on childhood constructions reminds us that while there are significant cries around the "loss of childhood", in actual fact, childhood has always been a social construction influenced by society in time and place (Buckingham, 2000). As we begin to think about how children are engaging with social media within a 21st-century literacy discourse, we need to question the popular commentators who promote social media as "evil" and a danger to childhood (Buckingham, 2007). Rather, we need to seek to understand how children are using social media to socially create their reality of childhood. In this spirit, we work to enable a safe and informed social construction of childhood reality (Silcock, Hocking, & Payne, 2013) for our children.

This small review of the literature has attempted to do two things. First, it has attempted to locate literacy within a 21st-century discourse – that is, suggesting we need to consider the social practices we use as a society in the 21st century to create meaning, and our classrooms need to reflect this better. Further, literature has been cited which suggests that classrooms are not reflecting this 21st-century discourse as well as they might for various reasons. Second, this literature review has offered an alternative view for justification around why we need to more closely consider the literature practices children are using to create meaning in their 21st-century world. This alternative view is around how we socially construct childhood. Specifically, drawing on the world of David Buckingham, who makes strong claims that childhood is a social construction in which children are active agents, ignoring the sociocultural influences of childhood in the 21st century is arguably a failure on the part of education systems around the world, including Australia.

Methodology

Introducing phenomenology

This chapter, which draws its data from a larger research project (Lyons, 2015), uses a phenomenological methodology to interpret a series of narratives from three teachers, to better understand an event involving the use of social media within a group of Year 7 students, which occurred in a school in Victoria, Australia, in 2015.

Phenomenology is the study of experiences, particularly as they are lived and structured through consciousness (Henriksson & Friesen, 2012). Phenomenology allows for the art and science of interpretation (Henriksson & Friesen, 2012), and thus also of the meaning. Phenomenology aims for understanding through description and explication of shared experiences, as well as the interpretation of stories that involve themes and patterns. Ultimately, a phenomenological analysis describes "the common meaning for several individuals of their lived experiences of a concept or a phenomenon" (Cresswell, 2013, p. 76). In the case of this chapter, phenomenology is being used to try and better understand the collective narrative of an event which is becoming more prevalent and problematic in our 21st-century world.

Research design and methods

The data for this chapter came out of a larger research project, which considered the pedagogical approaches to teaching literacy in and for the 21st century (Lyons, 2015). Data were collected using two methods. The first was an online diary, in which participants wrote a diary entry each week, for four weeks, reflecting on their literacy pedagogy. The second data collection activity was a one-hour semi-structured interview at the conclusion of the online diary activity. Ethics was obtained from the relevant school authority, and the University of London, where this study was conducted through. Data were collected in 2015.

Participants

This chapter draws on three teachers, who were located at the same school and were all directly involved in a literacy event which involved the inappropriate use of social media – specifically Facebook – by a group of Year 7 students. The participants have been given pseudonyms and their school has not been named.

Analysing the data

Data for this chapter were analysed in the following way:

(1) Developing narratives

Using the interview transcripts and online diaries, a narrative for each of the three participants was developed.

(2) Developing emergent themes

With narratives established, a reading was conducted to identify significant events, conversations, experiences and practices. These are considered "emergent themes" (Smith, Flowers, & Larkin, 2009).

> In looking for emergent themes, the task of managing the data changes as the researcher simultaneously attempts to reduce the volume of detail (the transcript and the initial notes) whilst maintaining complexity, in terms of mapping the interrelationships, connections and patterns between exploratory notes.
>
> (Smith et al., 2009, p. 91)

(3) Searching for connections across emergent themes

With the themes identified, the final stage was to produce a phenomenological narrative, which attempts to tell the shared story of the three participants. This is presented below.

Presenting the phenomenological narrative

In 2015, I was completing a research project, which was considering how teachers located in Victoria, Australia, were enacting literacy, with a particular focus on 21st-century literacy pedagogy (Lyons, 2015). Part way through the data collection phase of this research project an incident, which involved the inappropriate use of Facebook, occurred at one school, involving three teachers, which has formed the narrative for this chapter.

This narrative concerns itself with the misuse of Facebook by a group of 13-year-old students, who were in Year 7, at an independent school in Victoria, Australia. The narrative tells the story, through the experiences of the teachers, around what happened, the responses from various stakeholders and the reflections from the teachers concerned after the event.

Introducing the participants

The three teachers, who we will call Mary, Tony and Billy, had varying levels of experience and responsibilities within the school. At the time of the study, Mary was a teacher with 16 years' teaching experience and was the Head of Year 7 at the school. Tony was a graduate teacher with two years of teaching experience. Billy was an English teacher with nine years of teaching experience at various schools within Australia. The three teachers all had Year 7 teaching responsibilities in 2015.

Contextualising the narrative

The school within which this narrative is located is an independent P-12 school in Victoria, Australia. At the time this narrative was captured, the school had an enrolment of 453 students. The school had a principal and deputy principal, which formed the leadership team. There were 47 teachers and support staff in various permanent and part-time positions at the school.

The "incident"

In March of 2015 I received a phone call from Mary. She said to me:

> [Y]ou won't believe what is happening at the moment!

As Mary unfolded the story, it became clear that a group of eight Year 7 boys had created a private Facebook group, and subsequent page. The purpose of the group was to create a "hit list" of "uncool" kids – to take photos of them, post them to the Facebook page, and students who were part of the group could comment.

The school was unaware of this activity. Facebook, along with all other social media, was "banned" within the school, and at the time of this incident, no teaching around the use of social media was offered.

By the time I spoke to Mary, the principal of the school was aware of the Facebook page from a parent of a student who had been photographed semi-naked in the change rooms, and the photo had been posted to the Facebook page. The parent had obtained a copy of the photo and accompanying comments.

The school response

After a short investigation, the group of eight boys was identified. Both the students and their parents were interviewed to try and understand more fully the motives behind the actions.

The decision was made by the leadership team to suspend the eight boys for a period of one week. The principal addressed the school community via the newsletter and a school assembly. He pointed out that Facebook was banned at the school, and that he encouraged parents to "monitor" their children's social media activity. He remained committed to not adopting any teaching around the use of social media as part of the school's formal curriculum. An open invitation was made for counselling for any student who "wanted it".

The participants' responses

When I sat down with Mary, Tony and Billy two weeks after the incident had become public, it was clear they were collectively frustrated by a school directive, which they felt put children at greater risk, and violated their rights. As Mary stated:

> I can't believe they (the leadership team) have shut this down. We should be talking about it, helping students to understand what happened. And most importantly talking and showing students how to use Facebook safely.

Tony put it this way:

> [C]hildren have a right to learn to be literate ... don't they? Well, I hate to tell the "powers that be", but part of being literate in the 21st century is learning how to use Facebook and other social media platforms.

Billy was not as strong in her response. She offered the following insight:

> I just don't know what we do about it ... It's like we are opening a can of worms. Kids have been hurt, but I don't know if teaching kids how to use Facebook is the right decision.

It was also apparent from the participants' responses that the Year 7 children were talking about the incident, but they were more outraged than concerned. Mary offered the following insight:

> I have a significant number of my Year 7 students angry because we don't talk about things like Facebook ... the students all have Facebook accounts and use them all the time, yet we still make them write their homework in their paper diary ... I think students think we are from the "old days", and they are just doing what they like.

Billy was experiencing similar views from her students:

> [M]y Year 7 students are openly challenging me around what I'm teaching in my English class, asking me why we don't use "modern" things and constantly asking "why do we have to do this?" ... It's getting harder and harder to justify, although I'm not sure if I have the confidence to engage with all the technology they are using.

Tony offered a sobering and important reminder, saying:

> I think it's interesting, we are talking about it like it is something foreign ... and we are talking about devices, etc. ... our kids aren't talking about it in this way ... they see it as seamless ... you have a notebook to take notes ... you grab your phone to google something ... or to send a text to your mum to ask what time she is picking you up ... We are the ones creating the binaries ... kids have well and truly left us behind ... We should be learning from them ... rather than blocking and restricting.

Mary and Billy acknowledged Tony's point.

Based on the feedback from students and their own feelings, the three teachers in this study decided to talk with the leadership team about not only the incident, but trying to build a more seamless literacy pedagogy, which incorporated some of the 21st-century social discourses in which students were engaging.

The meeting happened, and Mary reflected on it in this way:

> I began by talking about this notion that we need to stop blocking things kids are using ... I understand why banning Facebook or any social media for that matter seems logical – they (the leadership team) are trying to protect the children. However, this isn't protecting them ... It's like saying you can't drive until you are 18 ... then you can have a car and you will be fine because you are 18! It just makes no sense. In the meeting, I tried to say that we need to start asking critical questions around how kids are living and learning and communicating, and start building that into our literacy pedagogy ... not just to be more relevant ... but to try and encourage our students to be more critical around how they use social media as an example.

The leadership team was not receptive to this, with Tony describing it this way:

> [W]ell, we were well and truly shut down! Like we didn't understand! The "boss" told us that he had to consider the reputation of the school and the safety of the children. I know we are a conservative school, but seriously are we that conservative that we can't teach or even talk about the stuff that's affecting kids' lives!

Billy was of a similar view:

> I came to this issue really unsure. But as I've thought about it, I know that we need to be teaching kids about the stuff that they are using in their lives ... This is about being literate! I mean that's what literacy is ... right? Making meaning in a social setting! Well, kids are using social media to "make meaning" ... they are just not doing it very well! They have a right to this learning ... don't they!

At the conclusion of the data collection phase of the project, Facebook, along with all other social media, was still banned, and no pedagogical consideration of social media was being considered within this school.

Discussing the phenomenological narrative

Inappropriate events, involving Facebook or other social media, similar to the one described, occur far too regularly in Australian classrooms, and are increasing in both sophistication and impact (Schifter, 2008). Further, it is still common for the explicit teaching of social media safety to be at best inconsistent, and at worst absent, within the teaching and learning program (Sandholtz, 2001).

This narrative demonstrates that even though there was an effort by people in authority to block the use of social media for children, it ultimately proved futile. A "battle" was being "fought" between children and adults over the way childhood was being socially constructed. On the one hand, there was a group of adults, who had overt power to take away social media because it "threatened childhood", while on the other hand there was a group of children who defied this and sought to create a different version of their childhood reality, one where social media was embedded. This was not a "battle" over whether technology could be used or not. This was a battle over identity, identity formation, power, power relations and the experience of childhood, within a 21st-century literacy discourse.

Within this narrative, it is apparent that the adults who had the power were intent on trying to isolate the children from a broader social world. As White and Wyn (2004b, p. 210) stated:

> Sociologists have found general agreement that immersion in digital communications is one of the defining features of the current generation, for whom traditional communication boundaries of time and space, of producer and consumer, have been crossed or blurred, as digital communications, released from limits of physical space, bring new ways of visualising and experiencing communities and offer new possibilities for constructing identities.

Children in this narrative did not see technology as "problematic". In fact, they had to struggle to see technology as a separate entity to their world. This would appear to support Gere's (2002, p. 198) comments suggesting that, "the ubiquity of digital technology, and its increasing invisibility make it appear almost natural to children". Therefore, the children in this narrative were not only "fighting" against their school culture, but attempting to make sense of why their school culture was attempting to disempower their socially constructed reality of childhood.

Children will make mistakes, in fact childhood should partly be about making mistakes in a safe and nurtured environment (Harwayne, 2001). What this narrative encourages us to pause and reflect on is the place communication tools and practices children are using in their out-of-school worlds have in the literacy curriculum, and what level of responsibility do we, or could we, have as teachers in equipping and enabling children to be critical and effective users. There is no way to know whether or not children in this narrative would still have made such a socially unacceptable choice around the use of Facebook, but there is some evidence to suggest that when practices are brought out of the shadows, made visible and public, and children are educated in effectiveness, the appropriate use improves (Auld, Snyder, & Henderson, 2012; Barnett, 2004).

Developing social relationships within an online and a physical world

This narrative highlights a point around the changing nature of communication in the 21st-century world of the child, which has implications for relationality; that is, how children live and communicate (Baran, Correia, & Thompson, 2011). This narrative was associated with an independent school, with a strong ethos around relationships. The hypocrisy within the narrative presented was the inability of the school leadership team to acknowledge the potential of social relationships within the online space, and the legitimacy children placed on this - to acknowledge that children can and do build and create meaningful relationships, which can and do harmoniously exist in the online and physical worlds. Of course, what this narrative identified is a harmful example of a social interaction and the breakdown of relationships. However, as the teachers in this study highlight so eloquently, when pedagogical expertise is put around teaching children how to build respectful relationships online, the positive outcomes increase (Brown & Slagter van Tryon, 2010). White and Wyn (2004b, p. 211) suggest "that digital technologies have had a profound impact on young people's lives and when schools embed meaningful teaching around how to build and maintain respectful relationships, they have the potential to create even further, far reaching changes to positive social relations". The power of social media is enormous in its ability to impact social relationships either positively or negatively. Children will continue to communicate in both online and physical spaces. I would suggest that blocking access is not effective. Blocking social media seems to put into conflict the way children see their world, and how they want to interact within their world.

Childhood identity construction in the 21st century

A key part of the challenge located within this narrative is differing views of how identity should be formed, nurtured and enacted.

Beck and Gernsheim (2002, p. 207) argue that a "social change over the past thirty years involves identity be constantly performed and enacted anew and that individuals are required to stage manage their own biographies". Beck and Gernsheim's comments have some relevance to this narrative. Children are social actors, and have identities that mould and change over time and circumstance. The ways that children enact their identity can be quite different to adults. For example, White and Wyn (2004a, p. 212) suggest that "digital technologies offer new opportunities for children to produce identities through the development and performance of identity in virtual spaces and this needs teaching and nurturing to help children understand". Beavis and Charles (2005, p. 357) have argued that "computers are a resource for children, enabling them to play with different identities and to challenge expectations". Indeed, children can create different identities in different realities. This is liberating, powerful and very dangerous if not understood by children. In this narrative, while the deliberate act of photographing in a private place and publishing the photos, and without permission, is alarmingly wrong, it does represent how children think about their identity, and when armed with powerful tools without the expertise or awareness to use them appropriately, how it can manifest itself in the creation of destructive behaviours that have lasting consequences. This, I would argue, is a key consideration of 21st-century literacy pedagogy. Children in the 21st century are enabled with powerful tools of communication and production (Wells & Lyons, 2015). Locating how to use these tools safely, responsibly and effectively for the appropriate and intended use seems a pedagogical goal worth pursuing, if only for the safety and security of children.

Conclusion

The 21st century is a world full of change, information, difficult choices and evolving expectations. In this context, understanding childhood, and how children are creating meaning in their social worlds, seems an important pedagogical goal to pursue. This is not to throw the baby out with the bathwater in terms of abandoning traditional literacy practices. Rather it is about considering a pedagogical architecture that seeks to understand the lived experiences of children, and to build skills and dispositions that allow them to engage meaningfully in their worlds using the tools and social practices that are reflective of their society in time and place. Allowing children a voice, and influence over their lives and their communities (including online), has the potential to add growth and nourishment to communities. In the 21st century, where much of the innovation is being driven by children, respecting their rights, nourishing their minds and facilitating their involvement has the potential to make lasting positive contributions. To my mind, this is partly literacy in and for the 21st century.

References

Auld, G., Snyder, I., & Henderson, M. (2012). Using mobile phones as a placed resource for literacy learning in remote Indigenous communities. *Language and Education, 24*(4), 279-296.
Baran, E., Correia, A.-P., & Thompson, A. (2011). Transforming online teaching practice: Critical analysis of the literature on the roles and competencies of online teachers. *Distance Education, 32*(3), 421-439.
Barnett, R. (2004). Learning for an unknown future. *Higher Education & Research, 23*(3), 247-260.
Beavis, C., & Charles, C. (2005). Challenging notions of gendered play. *Discourse, 26*(6), 355-367.
Beck, U., & Gernsheim, E. (2002). *Individualization*. London: Sage.
Bonk, C. J., & Cunningham, D. J. (1998). Searching for learner-centered, constructivist, and sociocultural components of collaborative educational learning tools. In C. J. Bonk & K. S. King (Eds.), *Electronic collaborators: Learner-centered technologies for literacy, apprenticeship, and discourse* (pp. 25-50). Mahwah, NJ: Lawrence Erlbaum.
Breivik, P. (2005). 21st century learning and information literacy. *Change: The Magazine of Higher Learning, 37*(2), 21-27.
Brown, A., & Slagter van Tryon, P. (2010). Twenty-first century literacy: A matter of scale from micro to mega. *The Clearing House: A Journal of Educational Strategies, Issues and Ideas, 83*(6), 235-238.
Buckingham, D. (2000). *After the death of childhood*. Cambridge: Polity Press.
Buckingham, D. (2007). Digital media literacies: Rethinking media education in the age of the Internet. *Research in Comparative and International Education, 2*(1), 43-55.
Bull, G., & Anstey, M. (2005). *The literacy landscape*. Frenchs Forest: Pearson Education Australia.
Cresswell, J. (2013). *Qualitative inquiry and research design: Choosing among five approaches*. London: Sage.
Crockett, L., Jukes, I., & Churches, A. (2011). *Literacy is not enough*. California: Corwin.
Darling-Hammond, L. (2006). Constructing 21st century teacher education. *Journal of Teacher Education, 57*(3), 300-314.
Foo Seau, Y., Ho, J., & Hedberg, J. (2005). Teacher understandings of technology affordances and their impact on the design of engaging learning experiences. *Educational Media Journal, 42*(4), 297-316.
Fullan, M. (2011). *Learning is the work*. Retrieved on February 5, 2018 from: http://www.coonabarabranhigh.com/c4e/documents/MichaelFullan.pdf
Gee, J. P., Hull, G., & Lankshear, C. (1996). *The new work order: Behind the language of new capitalism*. Sydney: Allen and Unwin.
Gere, C. (2002). *Digital cultures*. London: Reaktion Books.
Gustafson, J., Hodgson, V., & Tickner, S. (2004). Identity construction and dialogue genres – how notions of dialogue may influence social presence in networked learning environments. Proceedings of the Networked Learning Conference 2004, Lancaster, UK.
Harwayne, S. (2001). *Writing through childhood: Rethinking process and product*. Portsmouth, NH: Heinemann.
Henriksson, C., & Friesen, N. (2012). Introduction to hermeneutic phenomenology. In N. Friesen, C. Henriksson, & T. Saevi (Eds.), *Hermeneutic phenomenology in education* (pp. 1-14). Boston, MA: Sense Publishers.
Lyons, D. (2015). *Literacy in and for the 21st century*. (Doctor of Philosophy thesis), Deakin University.
Prensky, M. (2010). *Teaching digital natives*. Moorabbin: Hawker Brownlow Education.
Robinson, K. (2011). *Out of our minds. Learning to be creative*. West Sussex: Capstone Publishing Ltd.
Sandholtz, J. H. (2001). Learning to teach with technology: A comparison of teacher development programs. *Journal of Technology and Teacher Education, 9*(3), 349-374.
Schifter, C. (2008). *Infusing technology into the classroom: Continuous practice improvement*. Hershey, PA: IGI Global.
Shacklock, G., & Thorp, L. (2005). Life history and narrative approaches. In B. Somekh & C. Lewin (Eds.), *Research methods in the social sciences* (pp. 156-163). London: Sage.
Silcock, M., Hocking, C., & Payne, D. (2013). Childhood constructions of contemporary technology: Using discourse analysis to understand the creation of occupational possibilities. *Journal of Occupational Science, 21*(3), 1-14.

Smith, J., Flowers, P., & Larkin, M. (2009). *Interpretive phenomenological analysis*. London: Sage.

Thomson, P. (2002). *Schooling the Rustbelt Kids: Making the difference in changing times*. Crows Nest, NSW: Allen and Unwin.

Toffler, A. (1995). *Creating a new civilization: The politics of the third wave*. Atlanta, GA: Turner Publishing.

Wells, M., & Lyons, D. (2015). Navigating 21st century multimodal textual environments: A case study of digital literacy. In J. Keengwe, J. G. Mbae, & G. Onchwari (Eds.), *Handbook of research on global issues in next-generation teacher education* (pp. 43–61). Hershey, PA: IGI Global.

White, R., & Wyn, J. (2004a). *Youth and society: Exploring the social dynamics of youth experience*. Oxford: Oxford University Press.

White, R., & Wyn, J. (2004b). *Youth and society. Exploring the social dynamics of youth experience*. Melbourne: Oxford University Press.

7 Listening to the voices of young children in educational settings

Deborah Moore

Introduction

Listening to young children can be complex (Rinaldi, 2006). Rinaldi (2006, p. 65) cautioned that listening to the voices of young children should not be seen as a "simple natural act", rather it required a "deep awareness" by adults. On examination of the literature, there are two key assumptions commonly held by adults which add to the complexity of listening to the voices of young children. First, adults frequently assume they can instinctively listen to young children without the need for attentive effort (Clark, Kjørholt, & Moss, 2005). As a result of this lack of attention, adults do not fully listen to young children and therefore are commonly not aware of children's deeper thinking about what is important to them in their lives. Although Article 12 in the United Nations Convention on the Rights of the Child (1989) claims children have the right to discuss any matters that affect them, adults still do not always attentively listen to young children. The second assumption raised in the literature is that adults often consider young children are "not trustworthy" in the stories they tell about their lives (Clandinin, Huber, Menon, Murphy, & Swanson, 2016, p. 251) nor capable of telling valid stories for research purposes (Skelton, 2008). Research has also shown that as a result of this lack of trust in children's capacity for storytelling, young children's opinions, stories or conversations are often "excluded, marginalised, ignored or just seen as something cute or funny" (Dahlberg & Moss, 2005, p. 101).

This chapter examines two separate studies in which young children were involved as active participants within the research, illustrating both the challenges and the successes that are possible when listening to young children. In this chapter, two bodies of literature relating to the issue of listening to children are briefly discussed: first, how the phenomenon of listening to children has changed over time; and then, the way children's profound knowledge of place has not been listened to, or acknowledged, by adults. Next, the two separate studies are outlined where listening to the voices of young children was purposefully intended as a key objective of the research. Following this, the research design of these two studies is explained, one a comparative case study and, more recently, a narrative inquiry. The data generation methods and analysis processes are clarified; while the provision of empirical data from four young children allows for the examination of the way these methodological approaches and methods were conducted. Rather than dismissing the subjective stories of the young children participating in these studies, the data generated were valued and analysed to add to the body of literature around the importance of place to children.

Had these stories been considered simply "cute or funny", as Clark, Kjørholt and Moss (2005, p. 101) contend commonly occurs, the rich experiences of young children's construction of "hidden places" would not have been heard in these studies. Implications for future research with young children are discussed, and the chapter concludes with advocating for change in early childhood education through acknowledging what is important to young children.

The shifts in listening to the voices of children

Every era has its own version of what childhood means, the societal expectations of children and what children are considered capable of doing at that particular time in history (Cunningham, 2006). Looking back on earlier understandings of childhood, the notion of "childhood" has changed dramatically over time from a view of children as "miniature adults" in the 17th century (Pascoe, 2009, p. 216) to where, more recently, children are assumed to be "vulnerable and in need of constant protection" (Pascoe, 2009, p. 216). The image of vulnerable, needy children was originally fuelled by the dominant theory of developmental psychology from the 1960s through to more recent times. Developmental psychology dominated early childhood education and planning for many years and was based on Piagetian theories on the fixed stages of development (Arthur et al., 2015), reinforcing the assumption that children needed to be "filled with knowledge" from more "knowledgeable" adults (Dahlberg, Moss, & Pence, 1999, p. 44). However, more recently, many researchers have critiqued the dominance of developmental psychology and identified new ways of "understanding children's capabilities" (Arthur et al., 2015, p. 24). As a consequence of these new understandings of childhood, there has been a shift towards the sociology of childhood paradigm (James, Jenks, & Prout, 1998) in which young children were now seen as "social actors" capable of constructing their own knowledge (Corsaro, 2005; Dahlberg & Moss, 2005).

This is not to suggest, however, that the sociology of childhood approach to understanding children and childhood is not without its challenges. Shanahan (2007) explains there is an increasing dichotomy between the perception of contemporary childhood and what actually happens in reality. This is seen in Shanahan's (p. 415) claims that "children may have agency, but adults still monopolise the power; children may have voices, but it is the adults who control the conversation". What Shanahan is proposing here is that while it appears that children today seem to have more "freedom" than in the past, in reality, they are under more adult surveillance and subject to more "social regulation than ever before" (James, Jenks, & Prout, 1998, p. 7).

The complexity of listening to the voices of young children was suggested earlier in Rinaldi's (2006, p. 65) argument that adults should not assume it is unproblematic to "listen" to a child; and that, as adults, we need to welcome the "unknown". Silin (2005, p. 85) explained another dimension of this complex notion of listening to children, discussing how teachers need to listen carefully to children by "remaining silent at times" and not always "teaching through speaking". Insightfully, Silin (2005, p. 94) suggested, "when I speak, another doesn't ... in silence, we take up a position alongside of our students rather than in front of them". This body of work around the complexity of listening to children illustrates the need to take the role of listener more seriously than is commonly enacted by adults, more specifically, by teachers of young children. The following section details children's significant knowledge of place that is also commonly not listened to or taken seriously by adults.

Children's knowledge of place

In contrast to seeking children's "perspectives" or "flimsy opinions", Mayall (2008, p. 109) argued children should be acknowledged as capable of constructing and articulating their own knowledge. Relevant to this chapter, therefore, children should be seen as capable of constructing and articulating their own knowledge of places that are important to them. Interestingly, place-based researchers have proposed a strong link between children and place over many years of research (Hart, 1979; Moore, 1986; Rasmussen, 2004). These researchers found "spaces" with socially constructed meanings could be symbolically transformed by children into meaningful "places" for play. For example, children aged between four and 11 years in Hart's (1979, p. 205) classical study spoke in-depth of their experiences of place and the strong affiliation they had with particular trees and the importance of seclusion. These children also told of their search for trees, sticks and leaves to assist in "manipulating spaces to make places" to construct their hidden play places. Following Hart's lead, Moore's (1986, p. xiv) work on children's play places indicated their "hidden life" was still "not well understood, acknowledged or taken seriously" by adults. This apparent gap in adult understanding may have been due to an adult focus on their own agenda; or, children's reticence to talk about their "own made places" which Moore (1986, p. 46) considered to be children's "private knowledge". Despite this, however, he found there was a strong relationship between specific places and children's imaginative play practices "to create their own personal world" (Moore, 1986, p. 46).

Later, Rasmussen (2004), Clark (2007) and Lim and Barton's (2010) studies reinforced these findings in relation to children's relationship with place. In Rasmussen's (2004) and Clark's (2007) play place studies, children were asked to talk about the places they "preferred" to play. Both researchers found particular places triggered particular imaginative play practices. For instance, one child aged eight years old in Rasmussen's (2004, p. 157) study created his "own town" with houses, roads and fields on a "piece of land" with a "special meaning and name". Similarly, Clark (2007, p. 358) identified a number of different "spaces" where children chose to play when they were outside. For example, one child aged four years old created his own "imaginary space as a cave" in which, he said, he listened to "magic music from [his] magic radio". In Lim and Barton's (2010, p. 329) study, they concluded that place needs to be "interpreted and reconstructed by children". In all of these studies, children's knowledge of place was evident in the children's use of place and what these places meant to them.

Further to this research on places for children, a number of researchers have noted the importance of seclusion and the creation of "secret places" for children (Moser & Martinsen, 2010; Roe, 2007). For example, Roe (2007, p. 477) found children were able to find ways to feel "secrety" away from the adult gaze in "non-manicured" spaces; whilst Moser and Martinsen (2010) focused on the hidden "secret places" the majority of Norwegian early childhood educators provided for young children's play in early childhood settings.

The research mentioned in this section emphasises the importance of place to children; however, in reality, children's heightened sense of place is still not widely appreciated or listened to by policy-makers who regulate for clear, open spaces for "each child to be adequately supervised at all times" (ACECQA, 2013, p. 44). This information is important for teachers to consider in the pedagogical decisions they make for young children's environments and in the provision of materials, opportunities and spaces for play and learning.

Methodology: Listening to the voices of children in two studies

In this section I discuss the methodology and key findings from two studies I have conducted in which my intention was to listen to the voices of young children as a prime objective of the research. As an interpretative researcher, my understanding of reality and the way knowledge is constructed is seen through the social construction of multiple, shared meanings rather than one "universal and objective truth" (Dahlberg, Moss, & Pence, 1999, p. 5). This philosophical perspective informed the theoretical foundation of the two research studies on which this chapter is based. The first of these two studies was a comparative case study investigating young children's outdoor play preferences in two different preschool environments. One preschool had a large, bushy space with a wide variety of places for hidden play, whilst the other was sparsely vegetated, dominated by playground equipment, a large sandpit and a built cubby house (Moore, 2010). The second study was my doctoral research project that examined intergenerational imaginative play places using a narrative inquiry methodological approach inviting four families with three generations in each to tell stories of their childhood experiences (Moore, 2015). During both of these research projects children's knowledge and deep relationship with their own constructed places was heard through respecting, trusting and listening to the children's stories, and emerged as core dimensions of each study.

Comparative case study: Only children can make secret places

A case study methodology was used in the first study to collect a wide range of "more concrete, more contextual data" (Merriam, 1998, p. 31) to assist in an understanding of children's outdoor preferences in their play places. Yin (2009, p.11) confirms this strength of a case study, especially in the way it calls for the examination of "a full variety of evidence – documents, artefacts, interviews and observations". The "case" was to examine the phenomenon of children's preferences during outdoor play. Although two different sites were chosen, it is still classified as one case study with six preschool children aged four to five years old as participants. The analysis of data was conducted through a systematic framework of codes and categories to identify emerging patterns and themes amongst the rich, descriptive data collected (Creswell, 2007).

Drawing on Sumsion's (2003, p. 20) advice to researchers on the need to be "sensitive and humble" when researching with young children, I decided to use Clark and Moss' (2001) Mosaic Approach to generate data *with* the children. The underlying premise of the Mosaic Approach is that a wide variety of methods for data collection will encourage young children's participation in the research process, such as the use of drawing, mapping and walking tours of the centre. Clark (2007, p. 2) explained later that these data collection methods were closely aligned with Reggio Emilia's pedagogy of listening philosophy to assist researchers in the enactment of "visible listening" with children.

Listening to the voices of young children 75

The key finding from this case study was an understanding that young children need to construct their own meaningful "secret places" for play, and that adults are not able to construct these important places on children's behalf (Moore, 2010). To illustrate this key finding I provide brief extracts from empirical evidence involving two of the children from the study. The two children, John[1] and Alice, both attended the "bushy" kindergarten, but interestingly, the children in the "sparse" kindergarten also spoke of their wish to construct their own secret places in any way they could.

With great enthusiasm, I started the research asking the six children individually to explain to me what they liked to do when they were outside playing. Two months into the study, none of the children appeared to be particularly interested in talking with me or telling me anything other than monosyllabic responses to my carefully orchestrated questions. This pattern continued until one day when John declared he wanted to show me his "secret place", saying:

> I hide in a safe place. I hide down in the jungle. This is a secret place, but it looks like a jungle.

I realised at that moment that John had tried to show me these places previously but I had shut down the conversations by stating, "No, just stay here and tell me about it". By doing this I had slipped into dominating the conversation with John in a way I had tried hard to avoid as a kindergarten teacher and as a researcher. Nor did I listen to the child's voice telling me what was important to him. It was at that moment I also realised I needed to step back from the "interrogatory-framed questions" I had been using to demand answers from the children, and listen to their own knowledge, if and how they wanted to reveal it (Moore, 2014). When my approach to the way I listened to the children changed, the trajectory of the study changed dramatically. It was only then the children's stories of their deeply significant "secret places" were heard. From this point, I then respectfully asked each of the children if they had a "secret place" in the kindergarten playground, and if they would be happy to tell me stories about them.

One particularly rich example of these stories about secret place construction was from Alice, aged four years old, who explained that the reason why children make secret places is because they "invent things" when they are in there. She continued the explanation, saying:

> A secret place is very peace and quiet because it has a little hole in it so you can sneak in and no one can see you ... not a bit.

Earlier in the study, Alice had identified the climbing frames and the flying fox as places where she liked to play. In a palpable shift, Alice's stories were suddenly whispered in a shroud of secrecy as she continued her stories, saying, "Only children can make secret places ... lots of people come in here [around her secret place tree] but they don't know it's a secret place". Figure 7.1 is an illustration of Alice's "secret place" situated under and around a tea-tree in the kindergarten playground.

In Alice's drawing, her "secret place" can be seen to be attached to a particular tree; however, it was not hidden from view. In suggesting that others walked in and around her "secret place", Alice demonstrated her metacognitive understanding that a "secret place" could be symbolically hidden in plain view as well as physically hidden behind a scrubby bush or up a tree. This is important information for teachers in attempting to understand the

76 Deborah Moore

Figure 7.1 Alice's drawing of her "secret place tree" in her kindergarten playground

significance to children of making "secret places" and not to underestimate the meanings particular places hold for children. In listening to John and Alice's voices rather than asking irrelevant questions and demanding answers from an adult stance, these children's experience of secret place-making was clearly visible.

Intergenerational narrative inquiry: A place within a place

The second study highlighted in this chapter is an intergenerational narrative inquiry into the phenomenon of childhood imaginative play places, investigating if these places and practices had changed over time. Four families with three generations in each family were invited to tell stories about their lived experience of imaginative play places, with each family including a grandparent, a parent, an early primary and a preschool aged child (n = 16). A narrative inquiry methodology was deemed the "best fit" for this study as it allowed the deeper meanings of imaginative play places to be examined and questioned by both the researcher and the participants (Clandinin & Connelly, 2000). For the purpose of this chapter investigating listening to the voices of young children, only the research interactions with the young children in this intergenerational study will be highlighted. Given my previous research experience, and in line with this highly "relational research" approach (Clandinin, 2013, p. 81), I was aware of the need to trust and listen attentively to the children and follow their lead in our conversations.

Rather than looking at the linguistic patterns of children's narratives as is often the case in narrative research (Chase, 2011), a narrative inquiry allows for the researcher and participants to examine and question the multiple in-depth meanings of stories (Clandinin & Connelly, 2000). I was particularly aware that I did not want to offer "gimmicky tasks" (Albon & Rosen, 2014, p. 125) or a "pack of activities" (Waller & Bitou, 2011, p. 17) to manipulate the children's participation in the inquiry. Similar to the Mosaic Approach (Clark & Moss, 2001) implemented in the previous case study, I offered the children the voluntary engagement with a variety of multimodal methods. These methods included drawing, mapmaking, walking tours with photography and the collection of artefacts into memory boxes, but only if the children were interested in using these methods to assist in representing their knowledge of place and imaginative play.

The data generated were in the form of rich, subjective stories told by the children during four distinct conversational storytelling occasions. Conversational storytelling enables a more relaxed, informal and relational approach to interviewing participants than a formal question–answer arrangement often expected in research (Clandinin, 2013). Each of the children told their own unique stories about their experiences of imaginative play places in their homes, early childhood and/or primary school environments. The analysis of the data was conducted through a three-dimensional narrative inquiry model which assisted in the simultaneous examination of stories through "temporal, societal and place-based dimensions" (Connelly & Clandinin, 2006, p. 479). In this way, each child's individual context was seen to be influential on which stories the children chose to tell, and the way in which they told their stories.

Two children aged four years old who participated in this study, Frank[2] and Georgia, both had valuable stories to tell about the construction of their imaginative play places. Each of these young children told their stories on their own terms and in relation to their own agenda, so there were many times I needed to wait until it was convenient for each child to have a conversation with me. It was concerning to note that some of the teachers in the educational settings where these children attended suggested the children should just talk to me regardless of their interest in sharing their stories. This suggestion resonated with the slippage I had experienced in my previous research when I became interrogatory in my questioning rather than listening to the children attentively.

Similarly, both of the children approached the invitation to use the multimodal methods in their own unique and different ways. For example, while Frank was not at all interested in making maps of his imaginative play places, he was very interested in telling long, detailed stories about his places for pretend play while taking me on a walking tour of his kindergarten. However, this occurred only after everyone else had gone home. Without any reference from me about secret places, Frank announced that he constructed his "secret places" inside in his bedroom, outside in the garden at home as well as outside in his kindergarten playground. His heightened sense of agency to construct these places was evident in Frank's story extract below, seen here interspersed with the researcher's voice as the narrator, as follows:

> Frank's stories about his multiple secret places at kindergarten were quickly coming forth when he pointed out "that's my secret place ... and that's my secret place too ... I maked it up ... because I like to hide away". I was quite amazed that he even used the term "secret place" in the way that he did considering I had simply inquired as to where he played pretend at kinder. I was also amazed that he appeared to be so happy to tell

78 *Deborah Moore*

> me stories about these private and secret places, even the one he had made at home in a bush with his friend. I'm not sure if other children at kindergarten shared these secret places, but as Frank did not tell me about them until all the other children had left with their parents, I doubt the other children are supposed to know.
>
> (Frank, T&D, 31.5.13)

Frank's story extract confirmed the strong impulse for children to construct their own place for imaginative play that was evident throughout the inquiry. This narrative thread of purposefully constructing a "quiet, uninterrupted and private place" (Moore, 2015, p. 111) for imaginative play was consistently heard within all of the children's stories told in this study.

In Georgia's kindergarten experience, the whole group visited a local national park for once a week "bush" play. Interestingly, Georgia's imaginative play stories did not include any reference to the "built cubby" in her kindergarten playground; rather, the natural materials available to her in the "bush" enabled the construction of a "bush cubby" for pretend play. In contrast with Frank's disinterest in mapping, Georgia was especially engaged in creating a complex map with stick puppets that she invented to tell more stories about her play places, as seen in Figure 7.2.

In her mapmaking, Georgia drew her "bush cubby" and made two puppets representing a little girl and her Daddy using 3D materials, such as large sheets of paper, leaves, twigs, masking tape and drawing utensils. In Georgia's story, "the Daddy" was clearly not able to get into the cubby because of his larger size, symbolically representing Georgia's exclusion strategy of "others". The following story extract explains how Georgia used exclusion strategies to keep other children away from her "private play places":

> Georgia mentioned one way to keep other children away from her cubby was to "play very quietly", saying "I wanted to be quiet, to make them know … kind of not hear us, because we were too quiet … because we play our secret game and it's very hard to get into it".
>
> (Georgia, T&D, 20.6.13)

Figure 7.2 Georgia's mapmaking of her "bush cubby" using the 3D materials for mapping, illustrating her knowledge of place and exclusion strategies

In playing quietly, Georgia and her closest friend were passively excluding other peers from their cubby construction by not allowing other children to know the "secret game" rituals to gain entry into their imaginative play. This strategy also illustrates how Georgia was able to negotiate the adult-enforced discourse that "everyone must play together" so prevalent in early childhood playgrounds (Skanfors, Lofdahl, & Hagglund, 2009, p. 107). It is important for teachers to acknowledge this new way of understanding children's imaginative play rather than assuming it is necessary to enforce children's play with others as a matter of course. Once again, this important information would not have been heard if listening to young children's voices was not encouraged through this inquiry.

Conclusion

Pushing back against the assumptions adults often hold in listening to the voices of young children, this chapter has provided many examples of young children's competence and capacity in rich and trustworthy storytelling. Through listening attentively to the voices of the young children in both of these studies, the children's sense of place and knowledge of place-making were consistently illustrated. Had I continued to demand the answers to my adult-focused questions, John's tentative introduction to his "secret place in the jungle" would have been silenced by the sound of my own interrogatory questions. Similarly, Alice would have continued to talk only of climbing frames rather than whispering stories of her developing identity as an "inventor" at the base of her own "secret place" tree. If I had not listened attentively to Georgia's stories, I would have missed her comment that "Daddy was too big" to fit into the tree, which pre-empted her story about the need to exclude others from her "bush cubbies". And, finally, if I had not taken the time to wait and listen to Frank's voice at a time and place that he chose to tell me stories, his "secret place" stories would not have been available for this inquiry.

Implications for future research with young children

Recommendations for future research with young children are based on these two studies. A slower, less-adult driven research process in which the voices of young children have the time and the opportunity to be heard is suggested. Sumsion's (2003, p. 3) warning about "relinquishing [the] customary preoccupation with accumulating data" is of great significance here; instead, an appreciation of the importance of taking the children's lead is needed when researching *with* children. While adult-constructed multimodal methods were offered to the children in both of these studies, I was beginning to understand that children do not need adult assistance to formulate their own knowledge of place. It is the adults who need assistance from the multimodal communication platforms to understand what the children have always known about the need to make their own places for imaginative play.

Advocating for change in early childhood education

There are two key changes in early childhood education that can be derived from listening to the stories the children have told in these two studies. First, adults need to acknowledge the importance of private, hidden places for the development of children's highly creative, imaginative play. And second, ample time, materials and abundant opportunities need to be provided for young children to construct their own private play places in early childhood settings.

Both of these changes would have significant ramifications for Australian early childhood regulations mandating 100% supervision requirements at all times (ACECQA, 2013). However, it does need to be understood that this supervisory regulation is a matter of teacher interpretation of how these regulations are manifested in children's educational settings. For example, it is possible to enable young children to construct their own important places for "quiet, uninterrupted and private" play; to allow time to be alone without constant interruptions from adults or peers. It is possible for children to see out from bushy places without being seen behind a screen of bushy places in early childhood settings (Elliott & Davis, 2008); to allow a place, opportunity and time for children's highly creative play to be invented (Moore, 2015). These changes are possible if adults are prepared to reconsider an image of a child in need of constant protection; instead, to listen to what the voices of young children are actually saying is indeed important in their lives.

Notes

1 John and Alice are pseudonyms for the children in the case study, while the names "bushy" and "sparse" are descriptive names for the kindergarten centres to provide anonymity.
2 Pseudonyms used for these two young children in the narrative inquiry.

References

ACECQA (Australian Children's Education and Care Quality Authority) (2013). Guide to the National Quality Standards. Retrieved in August 2017 from: https://www.acecqa.gov.au/nqf/national-quality-standard

Albon, D., & Rosen, R. (2014). *Negotiating adult-child relationships in early childhood research*. London: Routledge Publishing.

Arthur, L., Beecher, B., Death, E., Dockett, S., & Farmer, S. (Eds.) (2015). *Programming and planning in early childhood settings* (6th ed.). South Melbourne, Australia: Cengage Learning Australia Pty. Ltd.

Chase, S. E. (2011). Narrative inquiry: Still a field in the making. In N. K. Denzin & Y. S. Lincoln (Eds.), *The SAGE handbook of qualitative research* (4th ed., pp. 421-434). California: SAGE Publications.

Clandinin, D. J. (2013). *Engaging in narrative inquiry*. Walnut Creek, CA: Left Coast Press.

Clandinin, D. J., & Connelly, F. M. (2000). *Narrative inquiry: Experience and story in qualitative research*. San Francisco, CA: Jossey-Bass Inc., Publishers.

Clandinin, D. J., Huber, J., Menon, J., Murphy, M. S., & Swanson, C. (2016). Narrative inquiry: Conducting research in early childhood. In A. Farrell, S. L. Kagan, & E. K. M. Tisdall (Eds.), *The SAGE handbook of early childhood research* (pp. 289-303). eBook Collection: EBSCO Publishing.

Clark, A. (2007). Views from inside the shed: Young children's perspective of the outdoor environment. *Education 3-13: International Journal of Primary, Elementary and Early Years Education*, 35(4), 349-363. DOI:10.1080/03004270701602483

Clark, A., Kjørholt, A.T., & Moss, P. (2005). (Eds.) *Beyond listening: Children's perspectives on early childhood services*. Bristol, UK: The Policy Press.

Clark, A., & Moss, P. (2001). *Listening to young children: the Mosaic approach*. London: National Bureau for the Joseph Rowntree Foundation.

Connelly, M. F., & Clandinin, J. D. (2006). Narrative inquiry. In J. L. Green, G. Camilli, & P. B. Elmore (Eds.), *Handbook of complementary methods in education research* (pp. 477-487). Mahwah, NJ: Lawrence Erlbaum Associates Inc.

Corsaro, W. (2005). *The sociology of childhood* (2nd ed.). California: Pine Forge Press.

Creswell, J. W. (2007). *Qualitative inquiry and research design: Choosing among five approaches* (2nd ed.). Thousand Oaks, California: SAGE Publications Inc.

Cunningham, H. (2006). *The invention of childhood*. London: BBC Books, BBC Worldwide Ltd.
Dahlberg, G., & Moss, P. (2005). *Ethics and politics in early childhood education*. London and New York: RoutledgeFalmer.
Dahlberg, G., Moss, P., & Pence, A. (1999). *Beyond quality in early childhood education and care: Postmodern perspectives*. London and New York: RoutledgeFalmer.
Elliott, S., & Davis, J. (2008). Introduction: Why natural outdoor playspaces? In S. Elliott (Ed.), *The outdoor playspace naturally for children birth to five years* (pp. 1-14). New South Wales: Pademelon Press.
Hart, R. (1979). *Children's experience of place*. New York: Irvington Publishers.
James, A., Jenks, C., & Prout, A. (1998). *Theorizing childhood*. Cambridge, UK: Polity Press.
Lim, M., & Barton, A. C. (2010). Exploring insideness in urban children's sense of place. *Journal of Environmental Psychology, 30*, 328-337.
Mayall, B. (2008). Conversations with children: Working with generational issues. In P. Christensen & A. James (Eds.), *Research with children: Perspectives and practices* (2nd ed., pp. 109-124). New York and London: Routledge.
Merriam, S. B. (1998). *Qualitative research: A guide to design and implementation*. San Francisco, CA: Jossey-Bass Publishers.
Moore, D. (2010). *'Only children can make secret places': Children's secret business of place*. (Master of Education [Early Childhood] thesis), Monash University, Melbourne, Australia.
Moore, D. (2014). Interrupting listening to children: Researching with children's secret places in early childhood settings. *Australasian Journal of Early Childhood, 39*(2), 4-11.
Moore, D. (2015). *A place within a place: Toward new understandings on the enactment of contemporary imaginative play practices and places*. (Doctor of Philosophy thesis), Australian Catholic University, Melbourne, Australia.
Moore, R. C. (1986). *Childhood's domain: Play and place in child development*. London: Croom Helm.
Moser, T., & Martinsen, M. T. (2010). The outdoor environment in Norweigan kindergartens as pedagogical space for toddlers' play, learning and development. *European Early Childhood Education Research Journal, 18*(4), 457-471. DOI:10.1080/1350293X.2010.525931
Pascoe, C. (2009). Be home by dark: Childhood freedoms and adult fears in 1950s Victoria. *Australian Historical Studies, 40*(2), 215-231. DOI:10.1080/10314610902865696
Rasmussen, K. (2004). Places for children - children's places. *Childhood, 11*(2), 155-173. DOI:10.1177/0907568204043053
Rinaldi, C. (2006). *In dialogue with Reggio Emilia*. London: Routledge.
Roe, M. (2007). Feeling 'secrety': children's views on involvement in landscape decisions. *Environmental Education Research, 13*(4), 467-485. DOI:10.1080/13504620701581562
Shanahan, S. (2007). Lost and found. The sociological ambivalence toward childhood. *The Annual Review of Sociology, 33*, 407-428. DOI:10.1146/annurev.soc.33.040406.131808
Silin, J. G. (2005). Who can speak? Silence, voice and pedagogy. In N. Yelland (Ed.), *Critical issues in early childhood education*. England: Open University Press.
Skanfors, L., Lofdahl, A., & Hagglund, S. (2009). Hidden spaces and places in preschool: Withdrawal strategies in preschool children's peer culture. *Journal of Early Childhood Research, 71*(1), 94-109.
Skelton, T. (2008). Research with children and young people: Exploring the tensions between ethics, competence and participation. *Children's Geographies, 6*(1), 21-36. DOI:10.1080/14733280701791876
Sumsion, J. (2003). Researching with children: Lessons in humility, reciprocity and community. *Australasian Journal of Early Childhood, 28*(1), 1-9.
United Nations Convention on the Rights of the Child (1989). Office of the United Nations High Commissioner for Human Rights. Geneva, Switzerland: United Nations, Committee on the Rights of the Child Publication.
Waller, T., & Bitou, A. (2011). Research with children: Three challenges for participatory research in early childhood. *European Early Childhood Education Research Journal, 19*(1), 5-20.
Yin, R. (2009). *Case study research: Design and methods* (4th ed.). Thousand Oaks, CA: SAGE Publications.

8 Student experiences of the career counselling process in secondary subject choices in Australia

A case for parent-school partnership

Sarika Kewalramani, Sivanes Phillipson and Nish Belford

Introduction

This chapter explores a unique topic of concern different from the other chapters in this book in emphasising parental role as mediators in children's future educational decisions. This study examines students' experiences and their thinking around their senior subject choices, as a result of schools' career counselling process involving students, their parents, the career counsellor and the subject teacher. Parents and teachers are known to be the mature partners in playing vital roles in the social context in which students learn, being key providers of guidance and support for student thinking around decision-making processes (Vygotsky, 1978). In particular, educators cannot overlook the significance of parental and other adults' role to develop high school students' (Years 10-12) thinking abilities around making career choices (Eccles, 1999). The Australian Department of Education Employment and Workplace Relations (DEEWR, 2011) has highlighted that significant career pathway advice and support occurs through less formal channels by parents and family members, as well as teachers. This is the case even though student subject selection and career pathway information and services are usually provided formally by career development professionals, such as the career counsellors in schools. As such, information services need to be tailored taking into account key players in career counselling, such as parents, teachers and career counsellors, to allow them to better support those making career decisions (NCDS, 2011). The Australian blueprint for career development emphasises the shared responsibility of schools and parents in supporting students to maximise their career development opportunities (MCEETYA, 2012). Although the quest of policy-makers in bringing together teachers and parents in the best educational interests of their children begins from the early years of education through to the primary years, this chapter especially brings to attention the significance of parent-school partnership in secondary schools as a continuum of children's learning.

Schools have the potential to work with parents to provide their children with the best possible educational and future career outcomes. Most educators and policy-makers in the early childhood and primary years seek to establish strong connections among parents, teachers and career counsellors in view of successful children's achievement outcomes (Holloway & Kunesh, 2015). Moreover, when there are expectations from teachers and parents to plan successful career counselling outcomes for children, schools have limited understanding and experience of how to implement this successfully (Lemon & Garvis, 2013). To date, few studies have explored the views from the "other side" (Holloway & Kunesh, 2015), namely students' perceptions of their experiences, which consequently during the career counselling process can exert an influence on intangible conceptions of student subject choices and career-making decisions. From an in-depth narrative analysis of three high school students' perspectives, this chapter discusses and examines their views to ascertain how parents and teachers can contribute in shaping their thinking about subject choices, which are considered as precursors to eventual career pathways. This chapter builds upon theoretical dimensions surrounding students' learning to reveal how students' perceptions of their parental beliefs and expectations alongside the teacher's and the career counsellor's role influence their subject choices.

Theoretical perspectives

The first theoretical premise guiding this research is rooted in Vygotsky's proposition that children's environment plays an essential role in the development of higher mental functioning (Vygotsky, 1978). This study considers the students' schooling environment to be comprised of "the significant other" persons such as their parents, teachers and the school career counsellor, who are more experienced in the students' learning environment. For instance, during parent–child interactions, parents act as the more knowledgeable other by transferring their knowledge and skills to their children, through the communication of their own educational experiences, cultural beliefs and resources (Vygotsky, 1978).

This study proposes that the students' interpretation and decision-making capacities in relation to their subject choices and career pathways, when taken together, are influenced by parent–child, student–counsellor and teacher–student interactions. Recognising the fact that students grow and learn at home, at school and in their communities, interactions with mature persons consisting of families, teachers and other school professionals, such as the career leaders and/or principals, may influence student thinking (Epstein & Jansorn, 2004). Hence, this study also draws upon Urie Bronfenbrenner's 1979 ecological approach to extend the concept of "the significant other" to give a holistic view of student interactions with key "significant others" impacting their subject choices. In this study's extended model (see Figure 8.1), students' environments are represented by the parents, teachers and career counsellors whose nested relationships and interactions are proposed to exert an influence on student subject choice thinking and career pathway decisions. Accordingly, the next sections in this chapter present the existing literature on the role of parents and school personnel, such as the career counsellors and teachers, to influence student subject choices.

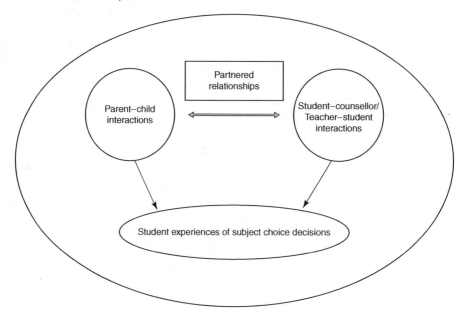

Figure 8.1 Ecological model showing nested relationships influencing student subject choice thinking

Student perceptions about parental role in their subject choice thinking

A number of studies have highlighted the significant effect of parental involvement on the educational careers of children (Eccles & Harold, 1996; Fan & Chen, 2001; Ule, Živoder, & du Bois-Reymond, 2015). For example, in Ule et al.'s (2015) study, there were accounts of parent-child interactions which demonstrated that parents and their children had a shared responsibility in terms of planning for future education. Additionally, by advocating for their children's subject choices, parents communicate their own aspirations and expectations, and the importance they place on their children's educational experience (Mayo & Siraj, 2015). However, what is important is that the nexus of parental expectations and aspirations for their children and the children's perceptions of the same can exert substantial influence on students' aspirations for their future careers.

With respect to seeking a holistic understanding of student perceptions of subject choice and career development, Morgan, Leenman, Todd, and Weeden (2013) articulated how the parental educational expectations predicted students' high school performance and college entry outcomes. Students in their study had internalised parental expectations as their own aspirations, and accordingly made decisions to determine their future educational trajectories. However, Morgan et al.'s (2013) findings were agnostic about the conditioned action of significant others that may determine student decisions of college entry, educational requirements and future job outcomes. Johnson's (2015) study in the USA revealed that economically disadvantaged students encountered many challenges in their educational experiences. These challenges included a deficiency in parental support and lack of communication of success and high expectations to their children. Coming from a minority background, the students perceived that their parents had limited background educational knowledge and experiences and the daily challenges (such as limited availability of technology resources) deterred parental involvement in children's academic decisions.

A Canadian study by Bloxom et al. (2008) provided unique insights into student perceptions of the effectiveness of high school career programs. A total of 888 Year 12 students completed a survey addressing their perceptions of involvement and effectiveness of career planning providers. Most of the students reported that they had a specific plan and had reached a stage of commitment and decision making, and only 12.5% reported having no career plans yet. When asked as to who students approach most for help, parents were ranked first followed by school counsellors. Moreover, the many facets of the career counselling services were strongly affirmed as being helpful in providing the right type of post-secondary education information based on student abilities and needs. This help included financial help resources for continuing education. Taking the findings of this study, it seems that though parental involvement is key to student subject choices, the parental role is confounded by the school career counselling process. The next section reviews further literature that focuses on career counselling as a process.

Student perceptions about the school career counselling process

Although there is an abundance of research establishing a link between parental involvement with school and adolescent academic performance (Johnson, 2015; Phillipson & Phillipson, 2007, 2012; Pomerantz, Moorman, & Litwack, 2007), less attention has been paid to what experiences students have and the implications they hold in the context of the career counselling and subject decision-making process. Moreover, perceptions relating to the school factors such as the teachers' and career counsellors' roles are rarely considered when attempting to investigate and eradicate the achievement gap (Johnson, 2015). The little research there is has found that young people from disadvantaged backgrounds do not necessarily lack aspirations, rather these students tend to lack a solid understanding of strategies needed to realise their career goals (Saha & Sikora, 2008). In line with this, Galliott and Graham (2014) have argued for the importance of Sen's concept of human capability (1992) and the role of teachers in the development of student career choice capability. They suggested a more appropriate approach is for teachers and school career leaders to examine students' current achievements, aspirations, career knowledge and educational experiences at home. Similarly, a recent study conducted by Durksen et al. (2017) urged the need to further investigate teacher-student interactions that encompass students' perceptions of subject choice, for example, student motivation and engagement in subjects such as mathematics and the confidence to pursue mathematics-based careers.

Shaunessy and McHatton (2009) asserted that students' experiences based on a wide range of teacher-student interactions can influence their viewpoints of subject selection and career aspirations. Their study recognised students' satisfaction with school experiences was linked with their sense of belonging and connection to school and the related achievement. Findings also reflected a wide range of student attitudes that included positive as well as negative feelings about teachers and the educational system, which seem to have some influence on student learning and academic achievement.

The literature review thus far has discussed the importance of student perceptions and relationships with not only their parents but also teachers and career counsellors in pursuing their educational career path. This current study, hence, is a crucial extension of the literature by examining student experiences of subject selection during the career counselling process. Student perceptions of parent-student and teacher-student interactions seem to empower or dominate students' thinking process while making career decisions. The next sections in this chapter, therefore, present the research design and data analysis and how the findings are interpreted through the lens of student perceptions, to further the literature in this area.

Research design

This study employed a qualitative case study approach. A total of ten students who attended low socio-economic status (SES) public secondary schools in the Western Metropolitan Region (WMR) of Melbourne, Victoria, took part in this study. Table 8.1 provides the profile and background of participating students. A brief analysis of the Australian MySchool (ACARA, 2014b) website was made to determine the choice of schools in the WMR. The contributing factor of the school's Index of Community Socio-Education Advantage (ICSEA) was taken into account when analysis of data was completed (ACARA, 2014a).

With respect to the school's career counselling process, the Career and Pathways Transition leaders' (CPTs) role was to liaise with the senior subject teachers to seek recommendations for their students' choice of subjects. In particular, the school had a formal recommendation process for mathematics-based subjects. During this process, the teachers informally recommended what subjects their students were capable of successfully completing and achieving a good Australian Tertiary Admissions Rank (ATAR) score. Most importantly, the CPTs played a critical role in organising career counselling of students, face to face interviews and sit-down meetings with parents regarding their children's subject choices.

Interviews

The recruitment of participants was completed in accordance with Monash University Human Ethics procedure. Data were collected using semi-structured interviews to gain insights of the

Table 8.1 Profile of student participants

Name	Ethnicity	Country migrated from	Parental occupation	Student (A-J) Year level
Student A	Italian	Italy	Accountant	Year 11
Student B	Spanish	Spain	Teacher assistant	Year 10
Student C	Polish	Yugoslavia	Teacher	Year 11
Student D	Serbian	Serbia	Homemaker	Year 11
Student E	Indian	India	Self-employed	Year 10
Student F	Indian	India	Factory worker	Year 11
Student G	Filipino	Philippines	Teacher assistant	Year 10
Student H	Indian	India	Home maker	Year 12
Student I	Bangladeshi	Bangladesh	Doctor	Year 12
Student J	Serbian	Serbia	Office worker	Year 12

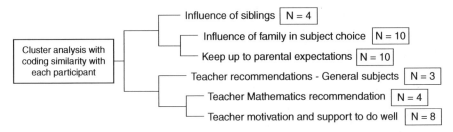

Figure 8.2 Cluster analysis with coding similarity with each student participant

student perceptions about the influence of their parents' beliefs and expectations regarding their subject choice and career pathway decisions. Students were also asked to comment on their school experiences involving the career counsellor and subject teachers during the subject selection process. Semi-structured interviews that lasted up to 60 minutes were conducted over a period of two school terms.

Data analysis

In the current context of this study, the potential of exploring student experiences to show the intersection of relationships between the parental influences and school personnel influences (CPTs and teachers) was best thought to be explicated through narratives. Taking Clandinin's (2007) narrative analysis approach, the aim was to provide insights into the experiences of the student participants' subject choice decision-making process. Following the protocols of narrative analysis, the sorting, comparing and clustering were completed as an inductive process taking into consideration the elements of student experiences of influencers of subject choice (Reissman, 1993). As seen in Figure 8.2, in this entire iterative process, recurring themes have been reported as frequency (N). In the next section, we report the student narratives that were organised as per the frequently occurring themes with the aim to accentuate the soundness of this study's theoretical concepts.

Findings

The findings in this study are presented as themes of narratives that have been captured using the ecological model that was presented in Figure 8.1. This model emphasised the important role of "the significant others" – parents, teachers and counsellors – in the ecological realm of students' thinking and decision-making environment. Due to the brevity of this chapter, the narratives of three student participants' experiences of their subject choices are presented and discussed.

Emma and her experiences of subject choices

Introducing Emma

Emma was in Year 11 and had chosen accelerated Year 12 business and Year 12 mathematics and her Year 11 subjects were English, psychology, health and human development and legal studies. She was born and brought up in Australia, and so were her parents. However, her grandparents were originally from Italy. At the time of the interviews, Emma's mother was an accountant at the same secondary school where she was studying. Her father was a manager at a telecommunication company.

Perceptions about parental role in influencing subject choice thinking

Emma perceived that her parents, particularly her mother, had an overbearing influence on her thinking around subject choice decisions. Although she believed that she was a self-motivated student and had chosen subjects that she enjoyed and in which she had an interest, she was still of the opinion that her family's beliefs and expectations, including her older brother's, had influenced her choice of mathematics-based subjects.

Role of parental beliefs and expectations

As Emma expressed the influence of parental beliefs and expectations:

> I think even mom and dad were brought up to value education as well because neither of their families were rich or anything. So they found it important that you learn and you do the best you could so that you could get the best out of life.

> I definitely feel like there is this expectation, especially because my brother was good at school and maths, I feel that there's definitely expectations of how I would do in each subject. I feel that the acceleration - doing both the Year 12 subjects - was influenced by family.

> I didn't want to do the maths methods because I knew it was going to be really hard and I feel like I'd rather do subjects that's a little bit easier that I knew I could do better in than do one that I'm going to struggle through. A bit of influence from brother given that he was in that kind of top student ... and then you feel like especially if it's in the family, you want to live it up to your parents.

As seen from Emma's utterances, parental beliefs seemed to have played a significant influential role in her choice of Year 12 accelerated subjects. She emphasised there was no room for her to be slack and she was expected to try hard and achieve her best in all her chosen subjects. That even meant to continue the family heritage of valuing going to university, and hence placing an expectation to choose subjects accordingly that would lead to a university-based course. This expectation can be seen in the way Emma talked about her perceptions of family obligation/expectations to choose the accelerated subjects just because her brother had experience in successfully completing them. She was not quite happy and professed that she might struggle with mathematics methods but on the whole agreed to pursue the subject as her brother had agreed to support her. Emma's narrative showed though that Emma's mother undoubtedly played a significant role in her subject choice thinking. It was clear that she had internalised her parental and familial expectations, wanting to live up to her mother's hopes and desires, and hence chose such subjects, as she further explains:

> Actually, mom was really keen on one of us becoming a lawyer, but - and she knows I'm not really interested in it, but she was still happy I chose legal studies but she doesn't

think anything to come out of it really. I don't really want to be a lawyer, but because I think that would make her happy if I was a lawyer.

As Emma exemplified even further, there seemed an apparent communication of her mother's own unattained career aspirations and desire of seeing her daughter become a lawyer. Emma perceived such career aspirations as communicated expectations that made her choose legal studies as one of her subjects, even though she did not really profess to know the future outcome of choosing legal studies. But the fact she wanted to make her mother happy was an indicator of internalised parental expectations.

Experiences during the school career counselling process

As a part of Emma's experiences of choosing her subjects during the career counselling process, her teachers were viewed as supporters and played an encouraging role in determining her choice of subjects. In contrast, Emma seemed to indicate that the career counsellors were not really influential, but rather a source of dissemination of university course information.

Teacher encouragement and support

Emma's English and mathematics teachers praised her and she valued this as an opportunity to do well and strive for better School Assessed Coursework (SAC) and ATAR scores. She gave her views as thus:

> I'm really good at English and like structuring answers and things like that for my SACs. All my teachers comment on my structure and encourage me to probably be more focused on speaking.

> In business, my teacher was helping me figure out how I'm going to get a good study score. And my math teacher, he's really helpful. He e-mails me all the time and he's always there if I ask for help.

> I guess teachers and what they've told you that you're good at, not in a strong way but it still makes you think about what subjects you want to do better in because it's what you want, only the best for your ATAR. It's what teachers say what they think you're capable of affects subject choices as well.

> I didn't really get much out of the career counselling session to be honest. I feel like I've got counselled by a teacher that I've never even had, doesn't know anything about me. I think it is a pointless thing that we do. If I really wanted to get counselled, I would talk to a teacher that knew me well, or something.

Emma perceived her teachers as actively involved and influential in her subject choice thinking. The teachers' support and advice on her capabilities, whether or not she was able to do well in her proposed choice of subject, acted as a contributor to her thinking and confidence in performing well. This was evident in her positive experiences of teacher-student interactions whereby her teachers were willing to invest time and effort to provide prior assistance and guidance for her prospective choices. She expressed such interactions to be helpful in predicting her subject choice judgements. On the other hand, career counsellors were seen to be only a gateway of formalising the subject choice process and were perceived to have no influence on her decisions.

Kul and her experiences of subject choices

Introducing Kul

Kul was in Year 11 and had chosen biology, chemistry, mathematics methods, politics and English. She was born and brought up in New Zealand and had moved to Australia when she was six years old. Her parents were born and schooled in India. Her mother completed only up to Year 10 whereas her father completed Year 12. At the time of the interview, Kul's mother was a housewife and her father was a truck driver.

Perceptions about parental role in influencing subject choice thinking

Role of parental beliefs and expectations

Kul's narrative indicated the powerful role of internalised parental beliefs and expectations. Her narrative unfolds her experiences while adapting to her familial values and mother's failed career aspirations.

> I was just in Grade 3. I remember my mom telling me that she wants me to be a doctor, but she didn't say you have to be a doctor. I was I think influenced by my mom more, because she had a dream of her daughter becoming a doctor and maybe somehow that is affecting me. She hasn't put it on me, but I just wanted to be a doctor and now it's like I want to be a surgeon. And yes they do value education, as an Indian thing. They're stricter education-wise. At the same time, my parents are more like do the best you can but aiming the full 100%.

As Kul narrated, her mother's own unrealised career aspirations and value for education seem to have been innately communicated to Kul. These communications appeared to have shaped her thinking of becoming a doctor. Although her mother expected Kul to try hard and achieve her best in test scores, there was an underlying cultural influence, which appeared to go hand in hand with their familial value of respecting education. So, in a way, Kul perceived her parents wanted her to get a better education and encouraged her to keep up with their expectations of achieving excellent study scores. Thus, it can be seen that Kul's mother's beliefs taken together with her expectations seemed to have mediated Kul's thinking around choosing science-based subjects, with a view to becoming a doctor.

Experiences during the school career counselling process

Teacher encouragement and support

Kul reflected on the importance of having a good teacher who can act as a motivator to develop a liking for a subject. In relation to career counsellors, Kul had a neutral standpoint where she perceived them to play no influential role in her subject choice decisions. She commented:

> It is because the teacher is really good and I actually now understand chemistry, and that kind of attitude like me liking chemistry as well. And if I talk to her about becoming a doctor, she encourages me how I can get that ATAR, I can get into that career.

> I've talked to my maths teachers as well. They've encouraged me in that way and have said you can do that maths methods subject.

The key element arising here is that Kul saw her chemistry and mathematics teachers to not only inspire her, but also to instigate her to develop a "liking" for the chosen subject. Through her positive interactions with her teachers, Kul perceived the teacher to be a role model in guiding her and giving her suggestions on how to achieve better ATAR scores in chemistry and mathematics and meet her career goal of becoming a doctor. Moreover, Kul considered the career counsellor to be of no further help in terms of encouraging and promoting motivation in her subject choice decisions.

Afraan and his experiences of subject choices

Introducing Afraan

Afraan was in Year 12 and had chosen biology, chemistry, mathematics methods, physics, human and health development and English. He was born and brought up in Bangladesh and had moved to Australia when he was seven years old. His parents were born and schooled in Bangladesh. At the time, Afraan's mother was working as an obstetrician whereas his father was a tradesperson.

Perceptions about parental role in influencing subject choice thinking
Role of parental beliefs and expectations

Afraan's narrative showed some strong views around his parents' high expectations of wanting him to study medicine. He seemed to take a considered view of his parents' wishes in trying to realise his own aspirations of becoming an engineer and future researcher.

> They expected that I would go to university and do something respectable and have a good prospect in the future. My goals align with their expectations but there was a point where their expectations went a bit too high and that pressurised me especially towards the end of schooling. Because that felt like she was just forcing me to do something that's going to take away from my high school life and confine me to studying 24/7. But in the end it didn't happen so. I didn't get into medicine. They can't force me to do medicine. I'm thinking of going into engineering or into a field of research with the subjects I'm doing.

Although Afraan's parental beliefs and desires of choosing a respectable career were clearly seen in his own repertoire of believing the same, his thinking about his future career did not completely align with his parents. His admittance of being rebellious was strongly present in his perceptions of high parental expectations; however, it was quite subtly narrated. There was an obvious internalised belief of choosing a respectable career as promoted by his parents, hence his reasoning for choosing subjects that will lead him to an engineering career.

Experiences during the career counselling process

Teacher encouragement and support

Afraan's perceptions of his teachers' role in his subject choice were quite positive. He was of the view that:

> My teachers cared a lot. They'd always give me feedback. They tell me if they're dissatisfied with my score or if they are satisfied with my score, they'd always tell me this is good and this is not. She had actually given me some advice on what's good for me and not to set my expectations too high to a point where I wouldn't make it into anything.

Here, Afraan highlighted the pivotal role of his teachers to be caring and understanding of his abilities and provide him advice accordingly. It appeared having such conversations with his teachers made Afraan think and realise his own capabilities of pursuing a realistic career goal and, hence, make viable subject decisions.

Lessons learnt from the student narratives

The literature to date has shown that there has been little focus on examining students' experiences of choosing their senior secondary subjects within the context of the career counselling process. The aim of this study was to fill this gap in understanding these perceptions in an Australian context. The ecological model (see Figure 8.1), drawn in conjunction with Vygotsky's sociocultural theory (1978), frames the role of parents, teachers and counsellors as partnered relationships; yet findings from this study (students' perspectives) reveal the roles of "the significant others" from distinct standpoints in influencing their subject choice. Partnered relationships among parents, teachers and counsellors were not signalled through students' responses, although communication or collaboration from these "significant others" can overall benefit or influence students' decisions. As described by the participants, there were aspects of their parental beliefs and expectations to affect or empower their subject choice thinking. Students' experiences also reflected how they were supported by their teachers in terms of providing support and inspiration while making informed career pathway decisions. In discussing these elements of subject choice thinking and decisions as depicted by the students, a couple of key lessons are derived from the three student narratives.

> *Lesson 1: The perspective of high parental aspirations and expectations of their children as influencers of student subject choice thinking.*

Lesson 1 emphasises how within parent-child interactions, parents communicate their beliefs, high expectations and own past unachieved career aspirations into children's thinking around subject choice decisions. Ule et al. (2015) provided evidence of how parental educational aspirations and plans for their children's future have substantial influence on students' academic trajectories. Because children in their study regarded parents as trustworthy and their primary advisers who will always consider their best interests, they reciprocated positively to parents' high expectations. While Ule et al. (2015) did not examine the influence of parental educational expectations on students' perceptions of secondary subject choice, their work demonstrated how students acknowledged the influential role of parental involvement in future educational decisions. As such, parental beliefs and high expectations are key influencers, which is congruent with years of research around this concept (Mayo & Siraj, 2015; Morgan et al., 2013; Phillipson & Phillipson, 2007, 2012). Yet, Lesson 1 signals an important message to the key influencers, that is, parents and the career counsellors/teachers, being the more knowledgeable others in understanding students' career pathway decisions. This study's enquiry into students' perspectives identifies what is critical in terms of Vygotsky's sociocultural theory (1978), how parents in their capacity as the more mature and experienced partner mediate students' thinking to envision or secure viable subject choices and realisable future educational outcomes (Galliott & Graham, 2014). With the students' recognition of parent-child positive interactions, it can be argued that parental beliefs, values, expectations and past educational experiences have a mediated action on subject choice thinking.

Lesson 2: The influential role of teacher-student interactions in student subject choice decisions.

In addition to their parents, the students also recognised the teachers' role to be the next "significant other". Students were heavily reliant on information from their teachers, particularly with respect to mathematics-based choices and the related pathways. These findings are consistent with Galliott and Graham (2014) who argued student-informed career choice capability is highly in need of the right kind of career pathways information, guidance and support as provided by teachers. Emma's, Kul's and Afraan's experiences are examples of how teachers can be a source of inspiration and guidance, which enables students to comprehend and empower their subject choice and career decisions (Shaunessy & McHatton, 2009). This study signifies teachers' roles as the more experienced partner in preparing students' competencies, whereby teacher-student interactions serve as an interactive loop along with parents' input for student reasoning of their subject choice decisions. Again here, Vygotsky's sociocultural theory provides evidence that career counsellors/teachers' interactions as the next significant other have the ability to establish positive mediated effects in shaping students' informed career choice options. These can be achieved by the right kind of career pathways information, subject choice recommendations, guidance and support as provided by teachers and career counsellors.

With respect to the career counsellor's impact on subject choice decisions, the students admitted that, compared to their teachers, the career counsellor's role was negligible in terms of the guidance and encouragement provided. Such findings are in contrast to Bloxom et al.'s (2008) study, in which students took a proactive stance and affirmed the effective role of career counsellors that was perceived to be helpful in making career choices. Thus, from Lesson 2, it can be argued that within the realm of parent-child interactions, although parents take the superior role as the significant other in transferring their beliefs and high expectations, albeit exerting a positive influence on their children's subject choice thinking, the role played by the teachers cannot escape scrutiny. In other words, when students feel supported by their teachers in encouraging them to build on their academic capabilities, and accordingly choose subjects, this may further enhance students' overall career choice success.

In sum, the current study's findings provide evidence for the ecological model (Figure 8.1) in reinforcing the significance of parent-school partnered relationships within the domain of secondary student subject choices. Taking the students' positive assertions on influences of both parent-child and teacher-student interactions, parent-school partnership can be the conjuncture to the subsets of such nested relationships. As such, students' future career decisions can be an outcome of parent-school partnered relationships, in which schools and parents work together to deliver opportunities, and viable and meaningful experiences to enhance student subject choice thinking (Sheridan & Kim, 2015).

Conclusion and implications

The lessons learnt highlight and equally provide evidence for Vygotsky's sociocultural theory (1978) in relation to how the inherent parental values, beliefs and educational expectations can be passed down to their children in their everyday interactions. This can mediate students' own future educational decisions. In addition, the study also offers novel contributions to qualitative research in understanding how students' interpretations and their decision-making capacities around their subject choices and career pathways are influenced by both parent-child and teacher-student interactions. Teachers, as supportive figures, play a pivotal role in the students' decision-making environments. Taken together, student subject choice is a three-way process involving significant interactions between the more knowledgeable others – teachers, parents and the students. This chapter reinforces the importance of Vygotsky's sociocultural theory and argues how parent-school partnership can be transformative in enabling students to make informed career choice decisions.

Although this discussion was specific to the secondary schooling context, the lessons learnt have the potential to aid teacher educators, throughout the continuum of early years through to secondary, in understanding their students' needs and educational interests. Teachers, through such an awareness, can then accordingly build students' capabilities for making educational decisions. Given the vast expansion of immigration, cultural diversity and the importance of parent-school involvement in a myriad of student programs, where children have to make informed choices, teachers can engage in parent-school collaboration practices to enhance students' educational outcomes (Theodorou, 2008). Future research agenda should investigate the role of families in facilitating such student experiences and develop policies to help parents and teachers support their children's academic trajectories (Henriksen, Dillon, & Ryder, 2014). In addition, taking a closer look at teacher-student relationships and interactions to have an influence on subject choice can provide policy-makers with information to address the ways in which building students' decision-making competencies can even begin in the primary schooling years.

References

ACARA (Australian Curriculum and Assessment Authority). (2014a). *Guide to understanding 2013 ICSEA values: Fact sheet*. Retrieved on May 11, 2015 from: http://www.acara.edu.au/verve/_resources/Guide_to_understanding_2013_ICSEA_values.pdf

ACARA (Australian Curriculum and Assessment Authority). (2014b, May). *MySchool*. Retrieved on May 12, 2015 from: http://www.myschool.edu.au/

Bloxom, J. M., Bernes, K. B., Magnusson, K. C., Gunn, T. T., Bardick, A. D., Orr, D. T., & McKnight, K. M. (2008). Grade 12 student career needs and perceptions of the effectiveness of career development services within high schools. *Canadian Journal of Counselling*, 42(2), 79-100.

Bronfenbrenner, U. (1979). *The ecology of human development: Experiments by nature and design*. Cambridge, MA: Harvard University Press.

Clandinin, D. J. (Ed.). (2007). *Handbook of narrative inquiry: Mapping a methodology*. Thousand Oaks, CA: SAGE Publications.

DEEWR (Department of Education Employment and Workplace Relations). (2011). *Rationale and options for a National Career Development Strategy*. Retrieved on May 14, 2015 from: https://docs.education.gov.au/system/files/doc/other/nous_group.docx

Durksen, T., Way, J., Bobis, J., Anderson, J., Skilling, K., & Martin, A. J. (2017). Motivation and engagement in mathematics: A qualitative framework for teacher-student interactions. *Mathematics Education Research Journal*, 29(2), 163-181. DOI:http://dx.doi.org/10.1007/s13394-017-0199-1.

Eccles, J. S. (1999). The development of children ages 6 to 14. *Future of Children*, 9(2), 30-44.

Eccles, J. S., & Harold, R. D. (1996). Family involvement in children's and adolescents' schooling. In A. Booth & J. F. Dunn (Eds.), *Family-school links: How do they affect educational outcomes?* (pp. 3-34). Mahwah, NJ: Erlbaum.

Epstein, J. L., & Jansorn, N. R. (2004). School, family and community partnerships link the plan. *The Education Digest*, 69(6), 19-23.

Fan, X., & Chen, M. (2001). Parental involvement and students' academic achievement: A meta-analysis. *Educational Psychology Review*, 13, 1-22.

Galliott, N. Y., & Graham, L. J. (2014). A question of agency: Applying Sen's theory of human capability to the concept of secondary school student career 'choice'. *International Journal of Research & Method in Education*, 37(3), 270-284. DOI:10.1080/1743727X.2014.885010

Henriksen, E. K., Dillon, J., & Ryder, J. (2014). *Understanding student participation and choice in science and technology education*. the Netherlands: Springer.

Holloway, S. D., & Kunesh, C. E. (2015). Cultural processes and the connections among home, school, and community. In S. M. Sheridan & E. M. Kim (Eds.), *Processes and pathways of family-school partnerships across development: Research on family-school partnerships* [E-reader version] (pp. 1-15). DOI:10.1007/978-3-319-16931-6_1

Johnson, M. M. (2015). Teacher perceptions and the impacts on the academic achievement of minority students from low-socioeconomic backgrounds (PhD thesis). Northcentral University, Prescott Valley, Arizona, USA.

Lemon, N., & Garvis, S. (2013). What is the role of the arts in a primary school?: An investigation of perceptions of pre-service teachers in Australia. *Australian Journal of Teacher Education*, 38(9). http://dx.doi.org/10.14221/ajte.2013v38n9.7

Mayo, A., & Siraj, I. (2015). Parenting practices and children's academic success in low-SES families. *Oxford Review of Education*, 41(1), 47-63. DOI:10.1080/03054985.2014.995160

MCEETYA (Ministerial Council for Employment, Education Training and Youth Affairs). (2012). *The Australian Blueprint for Career Development, Commonwealth of Australia, Canberra*. Retrieved on May 14, 2015 from: https://docs.education.gov.au/documents/australian-blueprint-career-development

Morgan, S. L., Leenman, T. S., Todd, J. J., & Weeden, K. A. (2013). Occupational plans, beliefs about educational requirements, and patterns of college entry. *Sociology of Education*, 86(3), 197-217. DOI:10.1177/0038040712456559

NCDS (National Career Development Strategy). (2011). *Research Project - Element 2: Synthesis Report*. Retrieved on September 15, 2015 from: https://docs.education.gov.au/node/20390

Phillipson, S., & Phillipson, S. N. (2007). Academic expectations, belief of ability, and involvement by parents as predictors of child achievement: A cross-cultural comparison. *Educational Psychology*, 27(3), 329-348.

Phillipson, S., & Phillipson, S. N. (2012). Children's cognitive ability and their academic achievement: The mediation effects of parental expectations. *Asia Pacific Education Review*, 13(3), 495-508. DOI:10.1007/s12564-011-9198-1

Pomerantz, E. M., Moorman, E. A., & Litwack, S. D. (2007). The how, whom, and why of parents' involvement in children's academic lives. *Review of Educational Research*, 77, 373-410.

Riessman, C. K. (1993). *Narrative analysis: Qualitative research methods series, No. 30*. Newbury Park, CA: SAGE Publications.

Saha, L. J., & J. Sikora. (2008). The career aspirations and expectations of school students: From individual to global effects. *Education and Society, 26*(2), 5–22.

Sen, A. (1992). *Inequality re-examined.* Cambridge, MA: Harvard University Press.

Shaunessy, E., & McHatton, P. A. (2009). Urban students' perceptions of teachers: Views of students in general, special, and honours education. *The Urban Review, 41*(5), 486–503. DOI:http://dx.doi.org/10.1007/s11256-008-0112-z

Sheridan, S.M., & Kim, E. M. (2015). *Processes and pathways of family-school partnerships across development* (Research on family-school partnerships; volume 2). London: Springerlink. DOI:978-3-319-16931-6

Theodorou, E. (2008). Just how involved is 'involved'? Rethinking parental involvement through exploring teachers' perceptions of immigrant families' school involvement in Cyprus, *Ethnography and Education, 3*(3), 253–269. DOI:10.1080/17457820802305493

Ule, M., Živoder, A., & du Bois-Reymond, M. (2015). 'Simply the best for my children': Patterns of parental involvement in education. *International Journal of Qualitative Studies in Education, 28*(3), 329–348. DOI:10.1080/09518398.2014.987852

Vygotsky, L. S. (1978). *Mind in society: The development of higher mental process.* Cambridge, MA: Harvard University Press.

Section II
Encouraging learning through pedagogy

9 Hundreds of messages on a leaf

Inspirations from Reggio Emilia

Julie Rimes, David Gilkes and Lou Thorpe

Introduction

This chapter explores classroom practice in the early childhood domain and situates that discussion in some of the values, philosophies and practices of the Reggio Emilia educational project. It is intended to serve as a tool for practitioners who seek to extend and enrich children's learning from birth to six years. Consistent with *Belonging, Being, & Becoming: The Early Years Learning Framework for Australia* (2009, p. 5), this chapter aims "to assist educators to provide young children with opportunities to maximise their potential and develop a foundation for future success in learning". The classroom experiences shared and the underpinning theory behind such experiences are intended to provide a provocation for teachers as they reflect upon practice in their own contexts.

A distinguishing aspiration of the educators who work within the infant-toddler centres (zero to three years) and preschools (three to six years) of Reggio Emilia, and those who are inspired by them, is their desire to keep abreast of the latest research in child development, pedagogy and education. These are educators who have a desire to continue to formulate new interpretations and new hypotheses about learning and teaching and possess an attitude of *teacher as researcher* (Edwards, Gandini, & Forman, 2012). Another key distinguishing feature of a Reggio-inspired educator is the process of focusing on daily observations of the practice of learning (Fraser & Gestwicki, 2001), as they learn alongside children.

This chapter is a study of the lived experience of human learning, including the professional practices of pedagogy. Using a hermeneutic phenomenological research methodology (van Manen, 2014), it identifies and explores the distinguishing features of the classroom experiences of young children in relation to the theory and practice of the Reggio Emilia educational project. Focusing on the core interwoven themes of listening, documentation and democratic classrooms, the chapter reveals how learning is a process of both individual and group construction. Using examples and documentation from one classroom setting, the researchers examine how, as Reggio-inspired educators, the pedagogy of active listening coupled with a strong image of the child as capable and competent creates a climate where children are active protagonists of their growth and development processes. The chapter explores how, once teachers have prepared an environment rich in materials and possibilities, they observe and listen to the children in order to know how to proceed with their work.

This chapter provides descriptions and reflections of practice in order that teachers can reflect on these ideas in their own context, keeping in focus always the relationships and learning that are in process locally and through this process consider possible ways to construct change.

Setting the context

In Northern Italy in the late 1960s, within the context of the emerging Italian feminist movement and of social protests advocating for better social services, child care and schools for young children, the city of Reggio Emilia developed an innovative and constantly evolving system for the education of young children. Right from the start in Reggio Emilia, there has been a desire for parents, community members, new immigrants, educators and children alike to be viewed equally as citizens and included as owners, collaborators and participants of the educational project. Teachers, moreover, collaborated with educator and school psychologist Loris Malaguzzi (Hall et al., 2010) in many ways, including developing some shared understandings around documentation, environments for learning, and articulating a strong image of the child. So the seeds of hope and possibility for the educational project in Reggio Emilia were planted in Italy at the end of WWII as the citizens of the city demonstrated their "collective responsibility and the desire to create a better society for their children" (Learning and Teaching Scotland, 2006, p. 2). From the beginning, there has been a commitment to progressive thinking and the development of a philosophy of education that centres on the child (Edwards, Gandini, & Forman, 1998). One of the primary tenets is the concept of the "child as citizen" (Rinaldi, 2013, p. 23). This concept has had huge implications for all levels of society and has led those concerned with education in Reggio Emilia to re-examine their very concept of "citizenship", to truly question and re-conceptualise the relationships between participation and democracy. Again, Rinaldi (2013, p. 21) is enlightening in this regard:

> To educate means building together identity and future. For this reason the early childhood centres and schools, in an educating community, play a primary role for the children that have to learn to become citizens of a community but also citizens of the world.

It is also important to note, as leading international educator and Reggio collaborator and writer Gandini (2003, pp. 25-27) explains:

> Educators in Reggio Emilia have no intention of suggesting that their program should be looked at as a model to be copied in other countries; rather, they consider their work as an educational experience that consists of reflection of theory, practice, and further careful reflection in a program that is continuously renewed and readjusted.

It is a mistake, therefore, to see Reggio Emilia as a recipe or a methodology; it is not a pre-defined curriculum ready for implementation in Australian educational settings. Rather, it is complex and multilayered and any attempt to do it justice in a few paragraphs does not give credit to the depth and history of the work of our colleagues in this Italian city. For the purpose of this chapter, however, it is important to summarise, albeit very briefly, what we believe to be some of the key *interconnected* principles (Reggio Children, 2010) of the Reggio Emilia educational project:

- All children have **rights** and are **active protagonists** in their learning and growth processes. They are innately curious and constantly seek engagement with others and their environment.
- Children possess **a hundred languages** – a multitude of ways to express and represent ideas and theories, to make connections and understand and encounter otherness.
- **Participation** is a value that is played out daily through relationships. Educators, children and families are considered stakeholders in the educational project. It is a reciprocal, democratic culture and attitude which recognises solidarity and belonging.
- A commitment to active **listening** exists between adults, children and the environment. It is considered a crucial element for dialogue, learning and change.
- **Children learn and make meaning through a process of co-construction** – in relationships with peers, adults and the environment. Through a supported attitude of research and in a kind of "dance" between joy and wonder, curiosity and uncertainty, challenge and risk, children build their understandings.
- Shared **research** between adults and children is recognised as a priority of everyday life and vital for making sense of the world. **Educational documentation** makes visible and explicit the learning processes of the adults and children. It involves "thinking about thinking" and "learning how to learn" – an ongoing process of reflection and professional learning – an attitude of "teacher as researcher".
- *Progettazione* is a term used in Reggio Emilia which can be described as an active process of designing the teaching and learning opportunities. It is a constant and evolving process of establishing hypotheses, conducting observations, interpreting documentation and re-launching thinking. It is the opposite to predefined curricula and programming.
- The **environment** is considered a fully participating element in learning. It is shaped by, connected to and influences significantly the projects and research of both the children and the adults.

These principles are central to deepening understandings of the discussion section of this chapter. For this chapter to be relevant, it is vital to make links between the principles of the Reggio Emilia educational project and how these can be *interpreted* in an Australian context; further, they are necessary in building connections between theory and practice.

We can see from the principles shared that an unwavering belief in children as curious, competent and capable citizens who actively engage in learning from the moment they are born is vital. These are children who seek out relationships with others in an attempt to understand themselves and the world around them; children who are respected for their own identity and recognised as protagonists in the construction of sense and meaning; children who are *not*, as many areas of society would lead us to believe, in need of direct instruction of meaningless "one-size-fits-all" curriculums or preparation for tomorrow's workforce. Neither are they incapable of offering to others complex and creative theories and understandings. As *The Early Years Learning Framework* (2009) notes: "Children actively construct their own understandings and contribute to others' learning. They recognise their agency, capacity to initiate and lead learning and their rights to participate in decisions that affect them, including their learning" (p. 9). It goes on to recognise the need for "viewing children as active participants and decision makers" (p. 9). Education is not about following recipes or measuring against set standards or predetermined outcomes, but potential and possibilities.

In this very brief summary, we see consistent reference to beliefs that all children are capable of learning; children learn best in environments that respect their individual development and personal interests; they learn best when the process of learning is dynamic and its outcomes are integrated into the lives of the young learners. Importantly, we observe the innate desire to learn can be heightened by caring, responsive and sensitive adults in the lives of the children.

Methodology

This research inquiry was underpinned by the philosophical writings of Heidegger (1977), Gadamer (1998) and Merleau-Ponty (1962) as influential representatives of the movement of hermeneutic phenomenology. There were two dominant understandings of this research. First, it is phenomenological, in the sense that the inquiry explores a particular phenomenon, the learning relationship in this early childhood setting; second, the inquiry is hermeneutic, which can be defined as the theory and methodology of interpretation. In this inquiry, the writers seek to render what is being said by the children in the classroom and then, through careful listening, interpret and disclose essential meanings of the phenomena. Phenomenology becomes hermeneutical when its method is taken to be interpretive, rather than purely descriptive.

A simple definition of phenomenology is offered by Grbich (2007) who states that phenomenology is an approach to understanding and interpreting both the hidden meanings and the essences of an experience together. Max van Manen (1990), who considers phenomenology as the most appropriate method to explore the phenomena of pedagogical significance, elaborates phenomenology as a response to how one orients to lived experience and questions the way one experiences the world.

Max van Manen (2014) suggests the practice and use of phenomenological methods in the contexts of everyday living and for those engaged in educational practice and reflection as it requires a very careful attention to what is being observed and the descriptive outcome is, of its nature, greater than the sum of its parts. The purpose of hermeneutic phenomenological research is to illuminate and reflect upon the lived meaning of basic experiences.

Data were collected from the one research site – a class of 18 four- and five-year-old children attending kindergarten in the southern suburbs of Tasmania's capital city, Hobart. In this classroom, there is one teacher (David) and one teacher assistant/co-educator (Christine). In the following Discussion section, the photographs taken and the conversations recorded were collected by these two people. Observations (which can take many forms, including photographs, extensive note taking, transcribed conversations, video, etc.) are central to the way Reggio-inspired teachers think about documenting the learning processes of both the children and the adults. The data collected in these observations are always analysed and interpreted to look for possibilities and deepening understandings and potentiality for taking the learning further. Consistent with this way of working, the practitioners used a hermeneutical phenomenological approach to analyse and explore their observations under the key terms of the themes of listening, documentation and democratic classrooms.

What follows in the Discussion section is a series of snapshots from classroom practice in a kindergarten class. Here one of the co-authors of this chapter, David, describes a series of learning experiences that took place in his classroom during 2017 at a point when the children's discussions were focused around the differences between machines and living things. When conversations between David and the children are included in the Discussion section, it is important to note that Christine, David's co-educator, is transcribing these, usually in the class "morning meeting" time, so that David can be fully involved in the interactions. As a teacher who has been inspired by the Reggio Emilia educational project for some time, David is committed to the power of active listening. As Rinaldi (2006, p. 125) expresses it, "if we believe that children possess their own theories, interpretations and questions, and that they are co-protagonists in their knowledge-building processes, then the most important verb in educational practice is no longer to talk, to explain, to transmit, but to listen". It is only through an attitude of active listening that we can truly hear the voice of the child and be open to the many pathways and possibilities that can present themselves.

Discussion

In this section, we will unpack how listening, documentation and democracy are evident in daily practice. To do this, we will place ourselves into the context of David's classroom of four- and five-year-old children. Before proceeding with the discussion, however, let's look back to the time when David and his co-educator, Christine, first encounter and come to know a group of children – that time at the beginning of a school year, when the children come to kindergarten with their minds full of enthusiasm, curiosity and a desire to engage with others. Right from the start of the year, David and Christine make it a priority to establish genuine and authentic relationships with each child and family, positioning themselves *alongside* the children and families as co-learners and co-constructors of knowledge. As Reggio-inspired educators, they challenge the notion of children as having needs and deficiencies, instead choosing to view them as competent, capable citizens who actively seek out new ways of making meaning. David and Christine continuously look for opportunities to actively listen and to create environments rich in democratic and respectful interactions, ensuring that all children feel that they belong and are part of a community of learners and researchers. It is important to understand some of the values that drive these educators to understand more fully the following snapshot of practice.

So, let's place ourselves in the context of David's kindergarten classroom. It is the middle of the school year. The children have been interested, for several weeks, in investigating the differences between machines and living things and engaging in various explorations around this area. A particular area that was captivating the children's interest at this time was the purpose of the brain and how it connects to everything, as the images of children's ideas and theories in Figure 9.1 show.

During one particular morning meeting time with the whole class (18 children), Christine (David's co-educator) recorded the following "brain conversation" as part of her regular practice of listening and documenting:

David (teacher): Natalie did a drawing of her brain last week that talked about how she uses it for her imagination and dreams. Lots of you told me about how you use your brains for ideas. How does your brain do this? How does it give you dreams, ideas and imagination?

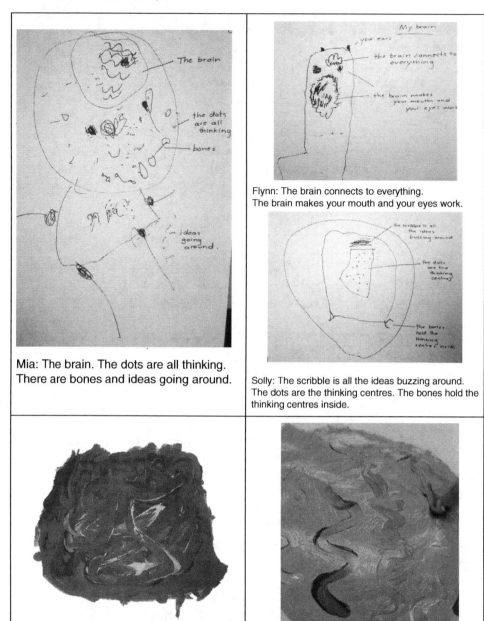

Figure 9.1 Thinking about the brain – children's ideas and theories

Inspirations from Reggio Emilia 105

Brax: I don't have any dreams. I do on the first bit of my pillow. The first bit of your pillow has dreams on it and animals on it. The last part of my pillow doesn't have any dreams. Ideas come here *(tapping his head with his hand)*. They go up to your brain. Your brain is your head. And your dreams are in there.

Holly: When I'm holding a shell, it feels like the messages are all spikey ... like the shell ... going to my brain.

Ruby: My hand is feeling a leaf. It feels soft. There are hundreds of messages on a leaf. When I feel all the lines, they are all different messages.

Solly: Do you know the other day, when I was walking on my carpet, I trod on one of my Lego ... a Lego snake. I wasn't wearing any shoes. It sent a message to my brain. It started on my foot and the message went all the way up my leg, up here and all the way to my brain.

David (teacher): Ah! So, there are OTHER places on your body that can send messages? Other places besides hands...

Felix: Yes! Knees! I tripped on many rocks. I got a scrape on my knees. My brain said I was hurt. Ouch! The message said ouch because I knew I was hurt.

The "morning meeting" is a regular practice in this classroom and a time when the group comes together to discuss what has occurred the day before, to reflect on prior learning experiences, to solve problems and/or to look at new possibilities and directions. Crucial to this process is an active attitude and openness to listening. Rinaldi (2012, p. 239) reminds us that we need to, "observe and listen to children because when they ask 'why?' they are not simply asking for the answers from you. They are requesting the courage to find a collection of possible answers". The role of the teacher is vital. The teacher, through their questioning, offering of provocations and the space and time for thinking, has the ability to extend and deepen children's ideas or to penalise and close off the possibilities. For example, asking "Can you tell me more about that?", "I wonder why that happens?" or "What's your idea?" are questions that are far more open ended and give greater avenues of possibilities than questions that merely elicit a recall of facts or a "yes/no" response. The morning meeting is always recorded. In David's classroom, Christine scribes the conversation word for word, capturing *everything* that occurs – the ideas, the pauses, the conflicts and differences of opinion and the teacher's questions. The documentation gives value to the children's theories, helps construct their sense of belonging to a group, positions us all as a community of researchers – active protagonists and co-constructors of meaning – and importantly helps to create a kind of flexible and fluid map of the many possible pathways the learning may take. In thinking about democracy, Rinaldi (2012, p. 237) reminds us that practice such as this is what is at the forefront of creating a democratic community:

> The task of those who educate is not only to allow the differences to be expressed but to make it possible for them to be negotiated and nurtured through exchanging and comparing ideas. In this way, not only does the individual child learn how to learn, but also the group becomes conscious of itself as a "teaching place".

It is within a climate of reciprocal and respectful relationships that a learning community is created. So, what pathways for learning did the morning meeting conversation about brains open up? As a teacher, it is important to not only record a conversation (or take a photograph or piece of video) but also reflect upon and *interpret* the data collected. David and Christine reflect on the "brain conversation" at the end of the day. They wonder what possibilities are offered to them as teachers, what opportunities can be found in this conversation for extending and building on children's theories and meaning making, what possibilities are there for the children to make connections between ideas and concepts and what contexts or environments need to be created to re-launch thinking so that deeper and more authentic learning occurs. They also think about how the children can represent their thinking in a multiplicity of ways (can their thinking be represented by another medium, such as clay, for example?). On top of this, they are reflecting on the many ways they can make this learning visible. Lastly, and importantly, they start to formulate what questions they have as teachers about *how* and *why* the children are working in a particular way and begin to establish their own research questions about the children's learning processes. In this instance, *how do the children use different mediums to express their theories about how the brain works?* Establishing a research question helps to give focus to the documentation.

In interpreting the "brain conversation", David and Christine thought that Holly's and Ruby's comments were interesting and worth taking back to the group to re-launch the children's thinking, address their own research question and promote further investigations. The girls had commented:

Holly: When I'm holding a shell, it feels like the messages are all spikey ... like the shell ... going to my brain.
Ruby: My hand is feeling a leaf. It feels soft. There are hundreds of messages on a leaf. When I feel all the lines, they are all different messages.

As teachers, we look for occasions or opportunities that can take the learning deeper. This requires us to make a choice. Holly's and Ruby's comments were chosen by the teachers to take back to the group at another morning meeting time because they generated ongoing interest in the children and appeared to hold pathways to many new possibilities. This is not to say that the other children's comments didn't possess possibilities as well, but one of our roles as a teacher is to make intentional choices. If we do not, we risk shallow, superficial investigations rather than richer, more meaningful inquiry. Often the children's ideas and comments will drive the direction taken and give clarity to what choice to make. This can be an exciting time for a teacher. Malaguzzi (1998, p. 91) reminds us:

> All through the project, adults should intervene as little as possible. Instead they should set up situations, and make many choices that facilitate the work of children. The adults have to continually revisit what has been happening, discuss the findings amongst themselves, and use what they learn to decide how and how much to enter into the action to keep the children's motivation high.

After revisiting and sharing Holly's and Ruby's ideas with the group, the children decided to represent their theories about how messages are conveyed from your hand to your brain through the medium of drawing (Figure 9.2).

Inspirations from Reggio Emilia 107

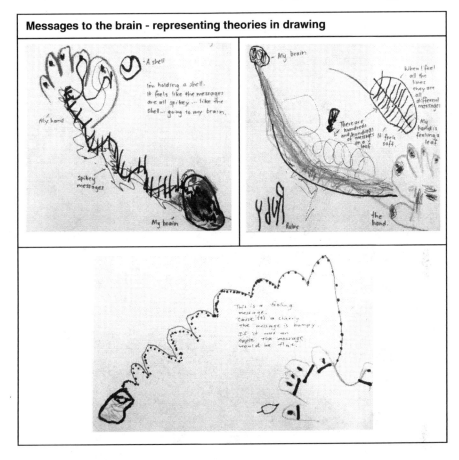

Figure 9.2 Messages to the brain – representing theories in drawing

These drawings were then shared with the entire group in the next morning meeting. This was an opportunity to have further discussions and articulate thinking and for David or the children to put forward proposals for further investigation. In this instance, Ruby's idea that there were "hundreds of messages on a leaf" was taken up as a provocation. David brought in a variety of different leaves – lettuce leaves, gum leaves, spiky banksia leaves and various herbs. The children explored the leaves with all of their senses and the following questions were put forward by both the children and teachers: What messages do we get from the leaf by looking at it with our eyes? By listening with our ears? By smelling with our nose? By touching with our hands? Could we taste any of the leaves? What messages were being sent to our brain (Figure 9.3)?

The next day the group explored the local bushland, feeling the trunks and leaves of different trees, taking Ruby's idea further (Figure 9.4).

The documentation of these sensory explorations, including transcribed conversations, photographs and anecdotal notes and so on, were looked at and interpreted by David and Christine, as well as offered back on many occasions to the children as a way of revisiting

Figure 9.3 Sensory explorations of a leaf

Figure 9.4 The bushland provides another context for learning

learning, deepening understandings and connections and fostering a climate of democracy. Millikan and Giamminuti (2014, p. 9) highlight that:

> Documentation is a democratic attitude; a way of being with children and honouring their voice. To us this means that documentation is not simply something you do (or must do to fulfil requirements for a regulatory body), rather it is something you are, or something you become.

Reflecting on the documentation redirected David and Christine back to the initial "brain conversation", where some children had been thinking about how messages can be sent from different parts of your body to your brain:

Solly: Do you know the other day, when I was walking on my carpet, I trod on one of my Lego ... a Lego snake. I wasn't wearing any shoes. It sent a message to my brain. It started on my foot and the message went all the way up my leg, up here and all the way to my brain.

It is our belief that children come to know ideas more richly when they are given both the time and contexts to really immerse themselves in them. They also need to be afforded the

Inspirations from Reggio Emilia 109

A message from a body part to our brain – representing our thinking in different media	
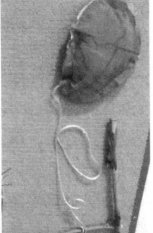	Holly made an eye with a CD, buttons and cut up straws. Holly: My eyes are looking at a shell. The message is curly because the shell is a little bit curly and straight.
	Solly made his foot out of sticks. His message had to travel a long way. Solly: I just stepped on my Lego snake. It sent a message to my brain … all the way up my legs!
	Natalie made a nose with sticks and gumnuts for nostrils taking a message to her brain. Natalie: It's smelling a pear. It smells beautiful. The message is bumpy because it's really hard to smell.

Figure 9.5 A message from a body part to our brain – representing our thinking in different media

opportunity to represent their thinking in other ways. Reggio Emilia educators continuously refer to the many different "languages" children possess (Edwards, Gandini, & Forman, 2012) and how they choose to communicate and express their ideas and theories. Millikan (2003, p. 36) says:

> Through their observations, the Reggio Emilia educators have become aware of children's desire to communicate and develop relationships with others, but also to communicate with others in their construction of skills and understanding. This has resulted in the educators exploring the possibilities inherent in children communicating through many different languages and the term "the hundred languages of children".

This metaphor is another important principle in the Reggio Emilia educational project. So, upholding this belief that children have "a hundred languages" for expressing themselves and making meaning, and remembering their previously stated research question of *How do the children use different mediums to express their theories about how the brain works?*, what other languages could David and Christine offer to the children at this point to take their learning deeper? In this instance, the children were keen to make three-dimensional representations of messages from different parts of their body to their brain. The images in Figure 9.5 show how three of the children chose to represent their thinking. All three children had made a brain from dyed calico that they had stuffed like a small cushion. Wire was agreed upon by the group as the best way to represent the "message", as it was pliable and equated well to their drawings of messages that were "curly", "bumpy" and so on. It was also a material that the children were familiar with and, as such, they were open to its many uses and potentialities. Each child had very different ideas for how to represent their body part, however, and, after some thinking, listening and planning together, the materials that the children thought they needed were sourced and collected; for example, Holly wanted an old CD and some buttons to make her eye.

Although these three-dimensional representations can be considered tangible products, it is the *process*, made visible through listening, documentation and democratic practice, that we consider to be the most important part of both the children's and the teachers' learning.

Conclusion

We're ending our discussions and unpacking of the "brain conversation" snapshot here but it is important to note that this was not the end. The children continued to explore their theories and understandings for many more weeks, each time taking their learning, both individually and as a group, to new and exciting places. This process of building theories together in a climate of joy, active listening, reciprocity and collaborative relationships is at the heart of co-constructed learning. Millikan and Giamminuti (2014, p. 11) point out that it is "through their *hundred languages*, children are also offered the possibility of being documenters themselves, making their ideas and theories visible, and through this process providing many different opportunities for adults to listen". Listening requires teachers who are open to experimentation, who are able to go with the unexpected and unpredictable nature of a student-led inquiry and who do not rely solely on any given schema or framework to inform their planning. We believe that our role as teachers is not to "teach" children but to give them the opportunities to express their understanding of the world in which they live. The "brain project" exemplifies respecting young students as legitimate, active citizens in our classroom and school; citizens who have a right to participate fully in their own learning.

As children participate in classroom, life they are also developing the skills to become active and participatory citizens, within their class, school and wider community and as citizens of the world. When children are given the opportunity to create something, to work together, to solve problems, to engage in a constructive dialogue, to share and to cooperate we begin to see the many, richly complex ways in which they co-construct knowledge. It opens up our eyes to the complexity in young children's learning, so that we too can learn from it. It shows us that a classroom can be a place of democratic practice, where children and teachers can work towards a common, shared goal. Listening and documentation can support the work of the children and teachers as both learners and researchers. Rinaldi (2013, p. 24) summarises our thoughts neatly by saying:

> The role of school can be defined as a fundamental place for the formation of the citizen ... This gives all of us, teachers first of all, a responsibility that is far more complex than the teaching of specific disciplines ... school is not a place only to transmit culture but to create it, to encourage critical thinking, creativity and relationship. No longer can schools simply be reproducers of knowledge. They are places where children and adults construct knowledge and their understanding of the world together.

This is our hope, that as teachers we are open to the many possibilities, to the many pathways, to the "hundreds of messages on a leaf".

References

Australian Government Department of Education Employment and Workplace Relations (2009). *Belonging, Being & Becoming: The Early Years Learning Framework for Australia*. Canberra, Australia: Commonwealth of Australia.

Edwards, C., Gandini, L., & Forman, G. (Eds.) (1998). *The hundred languages of children: The Reggio Emilia approach – advanced reflections* (2nd ed.). Westport, CT: Ablex Publishing Corporation.

Edwards, C., Gandini, L., & Forman, G. (Eds.) (2012). *The hundred languages of children: The Reggio Emilia experience in transformation* (3rd ed.). Westport, CT: ABC-CLIO.

Fraser, S., & Gestwicki, C., (2001). *Authentic childhood: Experiencing Reggio Emilia in the classroom* (1st ed). Belmont, CA: Wadsworth Publishing.

Gadamer, H. G. (1998). *The beginning of philosophy*. (Trans. R. Coltman). New York: Continuum.

Gandini, L. (2003). Values and principles of the Reggio Emilia approach. In L. Gandini, S. Etheridge, & L. Hill (Eds.), *Insights and inspirations from Reggio Emilia: Stories of teachers and children from North America* (pp. 25-27). Worcester, MA: Davis Publications.

Grbich, C. (2007). *Qualitative data analysis: An introduction*. London: SAGE Publications Inc.

Hall, K., Cunneen, M., Dunningham, D., Horgan, M., Murphy, R., & Ridgway, A., (2010). *Loris Malaguzzi and the Reggio Emilia experience*. New York: Bloomsbury Academic.

Heidegger, M. (1977). *The question concerning technology and other essays*. (Trans. W. Lovitt). New York: Harper.

Learning and Teaching Scotland (2006). *The Reggio Emilia approach to early childhood education*. Glasgow, Scotland: Learning and Teaching Scotland.

Malaguzzi, L. (1998). History, ideas, and philosophy. In C. Edwards, L. Gandini, & G. Forman (Eds.), *The hundred languages of children: The Reggio Emilia approach – advanced reflections* (pp. 49-97). Westport, CT: Greenwood Publishing Group.

Merleau-Ponty, M. (1962). *Phenomenology of perception.* London, UK: Routledge & Kegan Paul.
Millikan, J. (2003). *Reflections: Reggio Emilia principles within Australian contexts.* Castle Hill, Australia: Pademelon Press.
Millikan, J., & Giamminuti, S. (2014). *Documentation and the Early Years Learning Framework: Researching in Reggio Emilia and Australia.* Mt Victoria, Australia: Pademelon Press.
Reggio Children (2010). *Indications: Preschools and infant-toddler centres of the municipality of Reggio Emilia.* Reggio Emilia, Italy: Reggio Children.
Rinaldi, C. (2006). *In dialogue with Reggio Emilia: Listening, researching and learning.* Oxford, UK: Routledge.
Rinaldi, C. (2012). The pedagogy of listening. In C. Edwards, L. Gandini, & G. Forman (Eds.), *The hundred languages of children: The Reggio Emilia experience in transformation* (pp. 233–246). Santa Barbara, CA: Praeger.
Rinaldi, C. (2013). *Re-imagining childhood: The inspiration of Reggio Emilia education principles in South Australia.* Adelaide: Government of South Australia.
van Manen, M. (1990). *Researching lived experience.* Albany, NY: Suny Press.
van Manen, M. (2014). *Phenomenology of practice: Meaning-giving methods in phenomenological research and writing (developing qualitative inquiry).* Oxford, UK: Routledge.

10 Assessing student-generated representations to explore theory-practice connections

Peter Sellings

Introduction

Assessment is an integral part of the learning cycle and is necessary to determine where students are currently at, how to move them to the next level of understanding and to make judgements about whether or not learning has occurred. Assessment becomes formative assessment when the teacher uses it to modify the teaching or learning that occurs next. This study examines how student-generated representations can be used by teachers as a formative assessment tool to explore how well theory-practice connections have been made in science. It presents a specific example of where Year 10 students (n = 21) in an Australian school were asked to link what they saw in a flame test experiment to the theory that had been studied by the class previously. This linking of theory-practice was explored through students being asked to draw a representation of why the flame in a flame test experiment changed colour as an "exit slip" task. An "exit slip" is a tool that can be used by teachers to collect information about the lesson (Marzano, 2012), and this information can be used as valuable formative assessment data (Conderman & Hedin, 2012) to determine understanding and shape future learning. The "exit slip" representations were assessed using a purpose-designed rubric to determine the level of student understanding. Four very different student-generated representations are presented in this study, with each being used to determine the connections that students made between the theoretical discussion of how electrons can move between particular shells in atoms and the experience of completing flame tests in a laboratory situation.

This study highlights one way that formative assessment can be used in the classroom to shape the teaching that occurs later. It draws on work by Black and Wiliam (1998) who espouse the importance of formative assessment in the classroom, suggesting that it helps to raise overall student achievement. This need for formative assessment to determine where a child is currently at with their learning is one that fits well with the theories of Vygotsky (1896–1934) who suggests that the zone of proximal development (ZPD) of a particular child needs to be identified by educators before further teaching takes place (Vygotsky, 1935/2011).

Literature review

This literature review has distinct sections. First, it will present literature examining formative assessment and how this type of assessment can be used to shape the teaching and learning that take place in a class. Second, literature on student-generated representations, how they can be used in classrooms and how they can demonstrate representational competence will be explored.

Formative assessment

In very broad terms, assessment activities provide the teacher with information about the progress of students. Black and Wiliam (1998, p. 2) suggest that assessment is formative when "the evidence is actually used to adapt the teaching to meet student needs". This contrasts with summative assessment which is generally associated with high stakes testing, where students complete a test to evaluate their understanding of the learning outcomes studied, rather than the assessment being used to shape the future teaching and learning (Dixson & Worrell, 2016).

Formative assessment has been used in a range of settings with authors such as Trauth-Nare and Buck (2011) suggesting that formative assessment should be seen as a cycle that should be used regularly in classes. Formative assessment can be used in a number of different ways in the classroom. It can be used at the beginning of a topic to determine where students are at (Treagust, 2006) or as part of the teaching process, so that teachers are able to determine how well a particular concept is being understood and whether or not students have any misconceptions about the concept. Teachers can then make a decision to move forward or explore and correct misconceptions identified, thereby assisting the student to move forward with their learning (Black & Wiliam, 2009; Trauth-Nare & Buck, 2011; Treagust, 2006; Wiliam, 2011). Formative assessment can be implemented in classrooms in many different ways including "exit slips" (Conderman & Hedin, 2012; Marzano, 2012), self- and peer assessment (Black & Wiliam, 1998), and through the use of diagnostic testing (Treagust, 2006).

Conderman and Hedin (2012) suggest that "exit slips" can provide valuable formative assessment information for teachers. They describe an "exit slip" as a response from a student to a teacher-created prompt, which focuses on an aspect of the lesson that the students have just experienced. Students submit these responses before leaving the classroom (Conderman & Hedin, 2012), giving the teacher time to examine them before the next class. Moorehead and Grillo (2013) suggest that "exit slip" responses can be used to group students for future lessons based on their response to the prompt and suggest that some of these groups could be asked to work independently, while other groups would need to revisit aspects of the previous lesson.

Student-generated representations

A representation can be thought of as the act of capturing an idea, a concept, a relationship, an observation or phenomena in a form that can be interpreted (Greeno & Hall, 1997). The use of representations can lead to the development of cognitive skills, with different forms of representations developing different cognitive skills (Eisner, 1997).

In the teaching of science and mathematics, multiple representations are seen as important to assist teaching, learning and understanding of the key ideas (Ainsworth, 2006; Hubber, Tytler, & Haslam, 2010; Waldrip & Prain, 2006). The use of multiple representations that are different in form is known as multimodal representation (Tang & Moje, 2010; Waldrip,

Prain, & Carolan, 2010; Yore & Hand, 2010). There is growing recognition that student learning in science can be enhanced by using multimodal representations (Hand & Choi, 2010; Olson, 2008; Waldrip et al., 2010; Waldrip & Prain, 2006). Non-standard representations that are generated by students in response to an experience are known as student-generated representations (Waldrip et al., 2010; Waldrip & Prain, 2012a).

Representations can play a vital role in providing cues for students trying to recall important learning concepts and can be used by students to demonstrate understanding and reasoning. Representations are an excellent medium for thinking and can be a great starting point for learning discussions (de Bono, 1992). There is now growing evidence that getting students to generate their own representations as part of their learning allows students to demonstrate their thinking, construct a logical scientific argument and show the reasoning that they have used to arrive at a particular conclusion (Greeno & Hall, 1997; Hubber et al., 2010; Tytler, Haslam, Prain, & Hubber, 2009; Waldrip & Prain, 2012b). Student-generated representations need to be used in a way that allows students to refine existing knowledge to enable students to better understand key concepts (Hubber et al., 2010; Waldrip et al., 2010). There are many different ways that representations can be explored in a classroom setting and the pedagogies within a classroom must allow students to explore them in suitable ways (Tytler et al., 2009). Recent research into the use of student-generated representations in science and mathematics education shows considerable promise in terms of improving student outcomes (Ainsworth, Prain, & Tytler, 2011; Tytler et al., 2009; Waldrip, Prain, & Sellings, 2013; Waldrip & Prain, 2006). Outcomes such as depth of learning (Tytler et al., 2009; Waldrip & Prain, 2006), student engagement (Ainsworth et al., 2011; Hubber et al., 2010), reasoning skills (Tytler et al., 2009; Waldrip & Prain, 2012b) and concept development (Parnafes, 2012; Waldrip et al., 2013) are all suggested to have improved through the use of student-generated representations.

Demonstrating representational competence

When representations are created, it is important that they contain information that makes the message that the creator is trying to convey clear. This clarity of meaning of a particular representation is described as representational competence (diSessa, 2004). A study by diSessa (2004) investigated levels of representational competence in students by assessing Grade 6 student-generated representations against a set of seven competencies, finding that students can productively design new representations that can be as useful in learning as standard representations. DiSessa's (2004) study highlights that by allowing students to design representations, their understanding of a particular concept can be determined.

This notion of examining representational competence is one that has also been researched in other contexts by Kozma and Russell (2005) and Nitz and Tippett (2012). In a study involving university-level science students, levels of representational competence were examined in a slightly different way to that espoused by diSessa (2004). Kozma and Russell (2005) suggest that rather than the use of criteria, levels that describe general attributes of representations can be used to determine the competence level of a particular representation. This approach, described by Kozma and Russell (2005), examines the representation as more of a "whole entity" and what it demonstrates in terms of relationships to related concepts or phenomena rather than looking for specific features such as those described by diSessa (2004). Nitz and

116 *Peter Sellings*

Tippett (2012) assessed representational competence by using multiple representations and asking students to explain which representation best explained a particular situation, and why they believed their chosen representation provided the best explanation. Based on student responses, it is then possible to determine current skill levels of students and therefore areas for future study (Nitz & Tippett, 2012).

The criteria espoused by diSessa (2004) to determine representational competence of student-generated representations were developed after groups of students made critical judgements of representations. DiSessa (2004, p. 213) suggests that there are seven competencies any representation could show to demonstrate understanding of a particular concept. These competencies are:

- fidelity (how complete and accurate is the representation?);
- systematicity (is the representation consistent with both theory and observation?);
- univocality (does the representation have a unique interpretation?);
- simplicity (does the representation use unnecessary complications?);
- autonomy (can an untrained eye understand the representation?);
- conventionality (does it follow acceptable conventions?); and
- alignment (does the representation link information between different parts?).

This study draws on the work of diSessa (2004), Kozma and Russell (2005) and Nitz and Tippett (2012) to determine the representational competence student-generated representations demonstrate. This representational competence demonstrated by students will then be discussed in terms of students' understanding of links between theory and observed phenomena.

Methodology

This study was conducted in a Year 10 science class (n = 24) at a mid-sized regional secondary school that is considered to be slightly lower than average in terms of socio-economic status. Twenty-one students chose to participate in this study with their participation being optional. The teacher was an experienced teacher with 15 years' experience teaching senior chemistry and junior science. The teacher worked in her usual way with the class, presenting theory before organising the students to complete an experiment. As part of the write up of the experiment the students were asked to draw a response to a particular question (i.e., they were asked to produce a student-generated representation). The research question for this study was, "Can student-generated representations be used as a form of formative assessment to determine the links that students make between theory and observed phenomena?"

These student-generated representations were then analysed for levels of representational competence using a purpose-designed rubric (see Table 10.1) based on five of the seven competencies described by diSessa (2004). This purpose-designed rubric was developed by the researcher after discussion with the teacher involved. The two competencies suggested by diSessa (2004) that were not used to assess the student-generated representations were univocality and simplicity. Univocality and simplicity were omitted due to the teacher suggesting that since there was a distinct answer to the question that would be posed, the teacher believed that these two competencies were less appropriate for the set task than

Table 10.1 Assessment rubric (total = 15 points)

Criteria	High (three points)	Medium (two points)	Low (one point)	Not shown (zero points)
Fidelity	A complete representation that accurately depicted the situation.	A complete representation that demonstrated an understanding of some elements of the situation.	A representation that could have included more detail to demonstrate an understanding of all elements of the situation.	Little or no detail in the representation.
Systematicity	This representation used appropriate rules of correspondence.	This representation used some appropriate rules of correspondence but also contained other elements.	This representation used few appropriate rules of correspondence.	There was little or no use of appropriate rules of correspondence.
Autonomy	This representation was comprehensible and required no commentary from its creator.	A comprehensible representation that required some explanation from its creator.	A representation that could not be understood without extensive explanation from its creator.	The representation made little or no sense even after explanation from its creator.
Conventionality	All conventions were used correctly when depicting the situation being studied.	Most conventions were used correctly when this representation was developed.	Some conventions were used correctly in the development of this representation.	There was little or no evidence that conventions had been used to develop this representation.
Alignment	Links were correctly shown between different parts of the representation.	Some links were correctly shown between different parts of the representation.	The different parts of this representation were not linked properly to demonstrate an understanding of concepts.	There were no links shown between parts of this representation.

the other five competencies. The teacher was interviewed after the student-generated representations had been assessed to elicit her view on the usefulness of the student-generated representations as a determination of the theory-practice connection.

The topic that was explored through student-generated representations in this science classroom was electron excitation with theory being presented to students in a previous lesson about how electrons become excited and "jump" between electron shells, then return to their original (ground) state through the release of light energy of a particular wavelength (and therefore colour). The experiment carried out by students involved them using a flame test to examine five different compounds, one of which was an unknown compound which they were asked to identify by their results from the other four tests. At the conclusion of the flame test experiment, students were asked to draw a diagram in response to the question, "Why did the flame change colour?" All students were asked to respond to this question individually with little or no discussion about how they should respond to the question. These representations were used as an "exit pass" from class with the teacher explaining that she would look at the representations to determine how well each student understood the concept.

Results and discussion

The results are discussed as four specific cases, each of which was typical of a number of representations drawn.

The first student-generated representation was created by Abby and is shown in Figure 10.1. This representation was similar to three other representations in the class.

Abby's drawing showed little or no understanding of why the flame changed colour during this experiment. It was, in fact, a drawing of what was done during the experiment. When the representational rubric was applied to this drawing by the researcher, it scored two out of a possible 15, indicating that the student could not link what was observed in the experiment to the theory that had been previously taught. This representation was awarded marks in only one of the five areas assessed, this being autonomy, with the researcher believing that it was possible to determine what the student meant by the representation. When the teacher examined this representation and the three that were similar, she remarked that the students did not demonstrate any understanding of the links between the experiment and the theory and suggested that the student had not answered the question posed.

Bert's flame test diagram, shown in Figure 10.2, is quite different to Abby's diagram as it shows electrons rather than the experiment being carried out. There were five other similar representations drawn by the students in the Year 10 class.

Bert's diagram received a score of six out of 15, as assessed by the researcher, as it still does not convey an understanding of why the flame changed colour. Bert's representation of the flame test connected the electron theory to the flame test. He recalled the word "jumping", a word which is often used to explain the behaviour of electrons. The other elements in Bert's drawing indicate that he has limited understanding of why the flame changes colour.

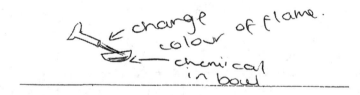

Figure 10.1 Abby's representation of the flame test

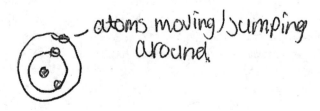

Figure 10.2 Bert's flame test representation

Bert's drawing is one that could not be used by an observer to properly understand the colour change that had been observed.

Carl's representation, shown in Figure 10.3, again has atoms depicted as the reason that the flame changed colour. There were five other representations drawn by members of the Year 10 class that demonstrated a similar level of understanding to that shown by Carl.

Carl's representation of the colour change in a flame test was clearly more accurate than Bert's and was scored as ten out of 15 by the researcher. His representation is interesting as it shows two "dots" (presumably electrons, given the narrative in between) in orbits in both of the diagrams; however, the "dots" are in different levels of orbits. This shows some understanding of what the electrons do, but it does not appear that Carl has understood that the colour change of the flame is produced when the electrons move back to their original orbital position. It was also interesting to note that Carl linked the heat (as energy) to the electron jumps, but did not show that the electron moved back to its original orbital position.

The final representation presented is Dana's, which contained the most detail of the four representations and was scored as 13 out of 15 by the researcher. This representation is shown in Figure 10.4 and is similar to four other representations drawn by the Year 10 students.

Dana's representation showed the highest level of understanding of any of the representations drawn because it showed electron movement due to the flame and then showed that these electrons move back to their original position. The writing contained in Dana's representation, however, did not correctly articulate why the flame changes colour, stating that "the electrons moved out by the flame, causing it to change colour", missing that the change of colour is due to the energy emitted by the electrons moving from their excited state back to their ground state. None of the representations drawn by the Year 10 students correctly

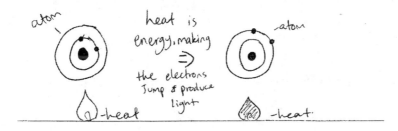

Figure 10.3 Carl's representation of the flame test experiment

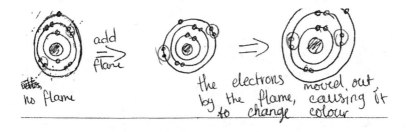

Figure 10.4 Dana's depiction of the flame test experiment

explained that the wavelength of the energy emitted when the electron moved back to its original shell caused the colour change phenomenon.

The representations of the four students showed the variability of student understanding of a particular concept and were used in subsequent lessons by the teacher to scaffold learning and move all students forward in their understanding. The teacher after viewing all of the representations at the end of the class expressed some surprise about how much the representations revealed about the level of understanding of each student, stating that they would need to revisit the theory to make sure the connections between the theory and the experiment were made. The teacher also expressed that they look at more explicitly discussing the links between the theory and the experiment both before and after the experiment.

The teacher, when interviewed about using the student-generated representational approach in a formative assessment way, made the following observation, "I thought it was excellent because it gave me an understanding of their level of understanding in a very simple form – draw what you think happened". This indicated that the teacher found it a useful exercise in terms of using the "exit slip" as a formative assessment task to modify the teaching based on the student responses. The teacher also remarked, "I found it really interesting because some really struggled with the higher concept of 'draw it'", highlighting that they were thinking carefully about the whole process used. The teacher later stated, "It's not something that I had thought of before ... whereas it is quite a creative way to get kids to show their understanding so it really helped me in my teaching", showing that the teacher had taken a lot away from this process.

These four examples of student-generated representations show one way that data collected as an "exit slip" can be analysed to determine the level of understanding of the students who drew them and how well they have connected theory to an observed phenomenon. The teacher's comments also highlight how the "exit slip" process can be used as formative assessment to shape the teaching and learning in future lessons, and the need to make explicit the links between lessons.

Implications and conclusions

This study has presented how student-generated representations can be used as formative assessment through an "exit slip" approach. This research indicates that a student-generated representational approach can be used to determine the level of understanding of students and the links that they have made between theory and observed phenomena. It is, however, important to note that this is one example only of the use of student-generated representations as a formative assessment tool and more research would need to be done to further test this conclusion.

This study linking student-generated representations to formative assessment supports the notion that student-generated representations can be used to improve student outcomes (Ainsworth et al., 2011; Tytler et al., 2009; Waldrip et al., 2013; Waldrip & Prain, 2006), highlighting that student-generated representations can be used to determine whether or not students have made links between theory and observed phenomena. The results of this study also suggest that formative assessment can be used to improve student understanding and then shape the teaching to move each student forward. This links well to Black and Wiliam's (1998) study that espouses that formative assessment can raise the standards of learning.

This research also gives an example of how a rubric can be used to assess student-generated representations using criteria previously described by diSessa (2004).

The research presented in this chapter also has a number of implications for teachers and pre-service teachers. It underscores the importance of:

- Using formative assessment to determine where students are at in their learning and then using this assessment to decide what needs to be taught next.
- Setting an "exit slip" task that is designed thoughtfully so that it generates useful data.
- Making explicit links between lessons and parts of lessons to enhance the understanding of the students.
- Recognising that what has been taught and what has been learnt can be very different.

The results presented also highlight the diversity of responses that students can give when "why" questions are asked rather than knowledge-based questions. Questions such as these allow the teacher to collect detailed knowledge on what students actually understand, thereby allowing them to determine future learning. The notion of getting students to create a representation in response to the "why" question shows promise as a method of formative assessment and could be used in a variety of subject areas.

Acknowledgement

The research described in this chapter was supported in part by an Australian Research Council Discovery Grant LP100200179 entitled *Improving regional secondary students' learning and well-being*.

References

Ainsworth, S. (2006). DeFT: A conceptual framework for considering learning with multiple representations. *Learning and Instruction, 16*, 183–198.
Ainsworth, S., Prain, V., & Tytler, R. (2011). Drawing to learn in science. *Science, 333*, 1096–1097.
Black, P., & Wiliam, D. (2009). Developing the theory of formative assessment. *Educational Assessment, Evaluation and Accountability, 21*, 5–31.
Conderman, G., & Hedin, L. (2012). Purposeful assessment practices for co-teachers. *Teaching Exceptional Children, 44*(4), 18–27.
de Bono, E. (1992). *Teach your child how to think*. London: Penguin.
diSessa, A. A. (2004). Metarepresentation: Native competence and targets for instruction. *Cognition and Instruction, 22*(3), 293–331.
Dixson, D., & Worrell, F. (2016). Formative and summative assessment in the classroom. *Theory into Practice, 55*(2), 153–159.
Eisner, E. W. (1997). Cognition and representation: A way to pursue the American dream? *Phi Delta Kappan, 78*(5), 348–352.
Greeno, J. G., & Hall, R. P. (1997). Practicing representation: Learning with and about representational forms. *Phi Delta Kappan, 78*(5), 361–367.
Hand, B., & Choi, A. (2010). Examining the impact of student use of multiple modal representations in constructing arguments in organic chemistry laboratory classes. *Research in Science Education, 40*(1), 29–44.
Hubber, P., Tytler, R., & Haslam, F. (2010). Teaching and learning about force with a representational focus: Pedagogy and teacher change. *Research in Science Education, 40*(1), 5–28.
Kozma, R., & Russell, J. (2005). Students becoming chemists: Developing representational competence. In J. Gilbert (Ed.), *Visualisation in science education* (pp. 121–146). London: Kluwer.

Marzano, R. J. (2012). Art and science of teaching: The many uses of exit slips. *Educational Leadership, 70*(2), 80-81.

Moorehead, T., & Grillo, K. (2013). Celebrating the reality of inclusive STEM education co-teaching in science and mathematics. *Teaching Exceptional Children, 45*(4), 50-57.

Nitz, S., & Tippett, C. (2012, August). *Measuring representational competence in science*. Proceedings of the 2012 EARLI Special Interest Group 2 Meeting, Université Pierre-Mendès-France, Grenoble, France.

Olson, J. K. (2008). The science representation continuum. *Science and Children, 46*(1), 52-55.

Parnefes, O. (2012). Developing explanations and developing understanding: Students explain the phases of the moon using visual representations. *Cognition and Instruction, 30*(4), 359-403.

Tang, K., & Moje, E. B. (2010). Relating multimodal representations to the literacies of science. *Research in Science Education, 40*(1), 1-5.

Trauth-Nare, A., & Buck, G. (2011). Assessment for learning. *The Science Teacher, 78*(1), 34-39.

Treagust, D. F. (2006, September). *Diagnostic assessment in science as a means for improving teaching, learning and retention*. Proceedings of the Assessment in Science Teaching and Learning Symposium, UniServe Science, University of Sydney.

Tytler, R., Haslam, F., Prain, V., & Hubber, P. (2009). An explicit representational focus for teaching and learning about animals in the environment. *Teaching Science, 55*(4), 21-27.

Vygotsky, L. S. (1935/2011). The dynamics of the schoolchild's mental development in relation to teaching and learning. *Journal of Cognitive Education and Psychology, 10*(2), 198-211.

Waldrip, B., Prain, V., & Carolan, J. (2010). Using multi-modal representations to improve learning in junior secondary science. *Research in Science Education, 40*, 65-80.

Waldrip, B., & Prain, V. (2012a). Learning from and through representations in science. In B. Fraser, K. Tobin, & C. McRobbie (Eds.), *International handbook of science education* (Volume 1, pp. 145-156). Dordrecht: Springer.

Waldrip, B., & Prain, V. (2012b). Reasoning through representing in school science. *Teaching Science, 58*(4), 14-18.

Waldrip, B., & Prain, V. (2006). Changing representations to learn primary science concepts. *Teaching Science, 52*(4), 17-21.

Waldrip, B., Prain, V., & Sellings, P. (2013). Explaining Newton's law of motion: Using student reasoning through representations to develop conceptual understanding. *Instructional Science, 41*(1), 165-189.

Wiliam, D. (2011). What is assessment for learning? *Studies in Educational Evaluation, 37*, 3-14.

Yore, L. D., & Hand, B. (2010). Epilogue: Plotting a research agenda for multiple representations, multiple modality, and multimodal representational competency. *Research in Science Education, 40*(1), 1-17.

11 Assessment to develop students' strategies and competence as learners

Anna Fletcher

Introduction

Assessment has been called "the bridge between teaching and learning" (Wiliam, 2011, p. 50), which reflects this chapter's exploration of how students' use of learning strategies can be developed when they engage in Assessment as Learning (AaL). The chapter's discussion of AaL as an evidence-based teaching and learning approach derives from a larger mixed-methods study (Fletcher, 2015), in which teachers and students from Years 2, 4 and 6 worked together on an AaL writing project. The term AaL refers to assessment that is designed to enable students to reflect on and monitor their own progress to inform their future learning goals.

Until recently, only a handful of studies had explored classroom assessment which enables the development of learner autonomy and students' engagement in self-regulated learning (SRL) processes. Encouragingly, this approach to incorporate formative assessment as part of learning and teaching is increasingly gaining an evidence base (see Andrade & Brookhart, 2016; Dinsmore & Wilson, 2016; Fletcher, 2016, 2017; Laveault & Allal, 2016). The literature includes various definitions of the concept and practice of formative assessment (e.g., Black, Harrison, Lee, Marshall, & Wiliam, 2003; Harlen & James, 1997; Perrenoud, 1998; Popham, 2008). However, here formative assessment is defined as assessment that is embedded as part of the learning process, and explicitly aimed at informing learners and teachers of the next steps needed to enhance a learner's understanding and skills. AaL is understood as an embodiment of formative assessment that positions learners as critically reflective connectors between task requirements and the learning process (Dann, 2002; Earl, 2013; Fletcher, 2016), as co-owners of their learning process. As Dann (2002, p. 67) points out, AaL is "most notably promoted through the process of self-assessment". Self-assessment refers to learning activities in which students reflect on what they have learnt so far, and identify strengths and weaknesses in their learning as they make plans to help them progress to meet their learning goals. As such, self-assessment is an SRL competence (Andrade & Brown, 2016; Harris & Brown, 2013) that requires the skills of reflection, task analysis, goal setting and monitoring one's learning progress. The term SRL denotes a learner's ability to control their thoughts, feelings and actions about a learning task by planning, monitoring and regulating the actions they take in pursuit of solving it (Zimmerman & Schunk, 2011). To conceptualise the skills and strategies needed for students to self-regulate learning, the study's theoretical framework combined situational influences such as task requirements; personal factors such as a learner's understanding and interpretation; and learning actions such as task analysis and goal setting.

Social cognitive theory

The study adopted social cognitive theory (Bandura, 1986; Zimmerman, 2011) to explore AaL as a classroom practice aimed at developing students' competence as learners, within the context of a writing project. Social cognitive theory works from the premise that human functioning is influenced by personal, environmental and behavioural factors, which mutually influence one another. As illustrated in Figure 11.1, from a social cognitive perspective, learning is shaped by the interplay among students' and teachers' *intrapersonal* influences (e.g., deductive reasoning, knowledge and skills, self-beliefs and emotional reactions, degree of motivation, interest); the *behaviour and learning actions* students and teachers engage in when working on the task at hand (e.g., clarifying and sharing learning intentions and success criteria, providing and seeking feedback); and the *situational* forces of the classroom context (curriculum demands, scaffolding and support from the teacher and peers, resources and exemplars). Learning and teaching are perceived to be influenced by the reciprocal relationship between these three domains of influences (Bandura, 2012; Fletcher, 2015). While these influences arguably shape all learning, this chapter limits its focus to writing as a process-driven learning activity.

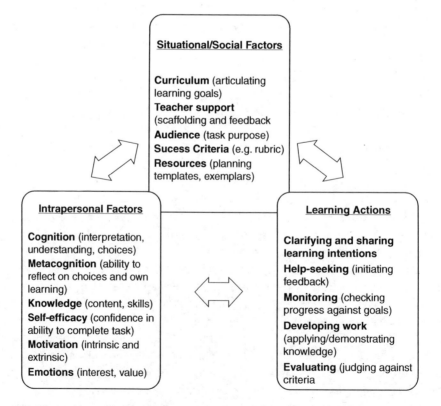

Figure 11.1 The reciprocal influences of learning. Adapted from *Student-Directed Assessment as a learning process for primary students* (Fletcher, 2015, p. 349)

Writing as a goal-directed process to develop students' SRL competence and strategies for learning

A set of distinctive thinking processes such as planning, monitoring, putting ideas into language and reviewing frame a writer's ability to compose text (Flower & Hayes, 1981). As such, writing is a goal-directed cognitive process that requires writers to identify high-level goals and supporting sub-goals. From a social cognitive perspective, the writing process illustrates the reciprocal relationship among the learner's interpretation of the task, existing knowledge and skills and ability to reflect on choices (intrapersonal factors); the task requirements and learning context (situational factors); and the learning actions students and teachers take. The present study used a three-phase AaL process – from here on referred to as the Student-Directed Assessment (SDA) process – to scaffold students' goal-setting steps, thus placing the student at the centre, as a director of the cognitive process. In this study, the AaL process consisted of three phases: *forethought, performance* and *self-reflection*. The forethought phase was constituted by task analysis, goal setting and identification of appropriate learning strategies. The performance phase involved students and teachers in monitoring and regulating students' learning. In the self-reflection phase, students and teachers evaluated the effectiveness of the strategies they had employed and identified the strengths and weaknesses of their approach. Scaffolded by their teacher and a planning template, the students drew on intrapersonal components, such as their knowledge and understanding, and applied these in the processes of writing.

Competence and self-efficacy

Competence refers to "a condition or quality of effectiveness, ability, sufficiency, or success" (Elliot & Dweck, 2005, p. 5), which provides a coherent basis to integrate findings from research into cognitive strategies and SRL (Elliot & Dweck, 2005). Competence depends on intrapersonal factors such as cognition and knowledge (Elliot & Dweck, 2005) and self-motivating beliefs (Zimmerman, 2011). Importantly, a student's perception of their own capability to learn or perform at designated levels – their *perceived self-efficacy* – helps determine what they do with the knowledge and skills they have, and the course of action they pursue (Bandura, 2012). Self-efficacy has been found to influence how much effort students will expend on an activity, and how long they will persevere when faced with obstacles in the task (Schunk, 1995; Schunk & Pajares, 2005). Yet, high amounts of self-efficacy will not produce a competent performance, if the requisite skills are lacking (Schunk, 1995). However, students' perception of control may impact on their competence beliefs (Connell & Wellborn, 1991, cited in Schunk & Pajares, 2005). In addition, students are more likely to sustain apt behaviour directed towards learning when they have a sense of controlling learning and performance (Schunk, 1995).

Methodology

The evidence base for this chapter's discussion of how SDA as a classroom practice supports learning and teaching derives from two research questions: (1) How do students in SDA groups use learning strategies and develop competence as learners? and (2) Do results in the writing project vary between SDA and Teacher-Directed Assessment (TDA) students?

The study adopted a mixed-methods approach by taking into account the perceptions and reflections of students and teachers as well as assessment results. In applying mixed-methods the researcher sought to *enhance* the understandings from the qualitative and quantitative evidence of learning and allow for *mutual corroboration* (Bryman, 2006) between the participants' qualitative accounts and quantitative data generated through students' planning templates and writing samples.

The school context

The study was conducted as a mixed-methods one-setting practitioner research study involving ten teachers and 256 students (121 boys and 135 girls) from classes in Years 2, 4 and 6 (students aged approximately seven, nine and eleven years), at an independent (non-government, non-religious) school in an urban area of the Northern Territory, in Australia. At the time of data collection, the school had an enrolment of approximately 700 students.

The position of the researcher has been described as being an "insider-outsider" (Dwyer & Buckle, 2009). As a long-standing member of staff at the school, thus well immersed in the setting, the researcher was predominately an insider. Yet, while the researcher was present when the writing projects were initiated in each class, the researcher was an outsider in the sense that she was not present in each class throughout the entire learning process. This relative distance helped avoid interview participants making the assumption that the researcher already was familiar with their experiences (Breen, 2007). Equally, not being in the classrooms throughout the learning process helped the researcher step outside the situation, which facilitated theorisation (Burton & Bartlett, 2005).

The study was approved by the relevant Human Research Ethics Committee. Informed written consent was gained from the school principal, parents/guardians of the participating students as well as the students and teachers themselves. To protect the anonymity of the participants, all names were replaced with pseudonyms before the data were coded and analysed. The participants were assured in writing that they were free to withdraw from the study at any time, without prejudice.

Design and instruments

The study was conducted as a writing project which ran over one school term (ten weeks). By employing a parallel sampling design (Leech, Onwuegbuzie, & Combs, 2011), the study provided a cross-sectional comparison between two groups, each representing Year 2, 4 and 6. Of the two groups, the SDA group used a planning template which was collaboratively developed by the researcher together with the teachers. The planning template for each of the three participating year levels targeted the relevant syllabus outcomes in the *Writing* strand of the Northern Territory Curriculum Framework for English (NTCF, 2009).

The other group, the TDA group, constituted the control group, which meant that they did not use a specific planning template to frame the AaL process, nor were the TDA students given a choice regarding the type of text they would write. However, students in the TDA group were provided explicit scaffolding by their teachers as they engaged in the writing project.

By contrast, students in the SDA group used their specific planning template, which had been designed to scaffold the forethought, performance and self-reflection phases of the

Table 11.1 Phases of the AaL process (Fletcher, 2017, adapted from Zimmerman, 2011)

Forethought phase	Performance phase	Self-reflection phase
Students:	Students:	Students:
• analyse relevant curriculum learning outcomes • split overall curriculum outcomes into partial, task-related goals • explore possible learning strategies to employ • create a checklist of strategies and partial goals to meet during the performance/drafting phase • determine timelines for partial goals	• monitor their understanding and seek help • check performance against partial goals to monitor progress • seek feedback	• identify strengths and areas to improve for next time • attribute reasons for success and challenges

learning cycle (Fletcher, 2015, 2017; Zimmerman, 2011). In the forethought phase, the teachers carefully supported the SDA students through the process of setting up the writing project (see Table 11.1). This required students to analyse the writing task, set partial goals for their writing project and identify appropriate learning strategies. The performance phase involved students monitoring and regulating their learning progress, with support – often in the form of conferencing – from their teachers. In the self-reflection phase, students and teachers evaluated the effectiveness of the strategies they had employed. In addition, both identified the strengths and weaknesses of their approach. Examples of how students and teachers used the template are provided in this chapter's results and discussion section.

In addition to the students' planning templates and their subsequent writing samples, the data collection included regular semi-structured email correspondence with the teachers throughout the writing project, with structured open-ended questions to prompt reflection. The study was also informed by two iterations of semi-structured interviews with teachers and students. The first iteration was conducted while the writing project was underway. The second iteration was conducted at the completion of the writing project. This gave the students, the teachers and the researcher time to reflect on the experience with the benefit of hindsight. All interviews were digitally recorded and transcribed by the researcher using voice-recognition software during the time of data collection.

Data analysis

The qualitative and quantitative data were collected at the same time, but analysed separately. An emerging approach was used to analyse the first round of interviews, which generated the initial set of emerging codes (Lankshear & Knobel, 2004). Further codes emerged during the re-reading of the interview transcripts, email correspondence with teachers and the planning templates, resulting in some 35 codes being identified from the data.

Repeated reading of transcripts generated identification of similar data, which were synthesised and interpreted though social cognitive theory (Bandura, 1986). Through this process of synthesis, the data were narrowed to eight thematic categories (Saldaña, 2013). Intrapersonal factors included: (1) *emotions*; (2) own *preferences* and *choices*; (3) *cognitive considerations* such as reflective learning, strategies and predictions; expressions of (4) *self-efficacy* and (5) *persistence*. Social and situational factors included: (6) *social considerations* such as references to peers, teachers and audience; (7) *value judgements* used to express a sense of authenticity and meaningfulness such as "real learning". The behavioural domain of social cognitive theory consisted of descriptive references to (8) *teaching and learning practices*.

To ascertain whether writing project results varied between SDA and TDA students, the NAPLAN marking rubric (MCEETYA, 2008) was used to mark all writing samples and provide the evidence base for the quantitative analysis. Students' NAPLAN scores from Year 3 and Year 5 were used as pre-tests in the study. Consequently, the study's writing samples from Year 2 students were omitted from the quantitative analysis as no NAPLAN pre-test scores were available for the group. Two markers, who had served on the NAPLAN marking panels in the Northern Territory, double blind-marked all the post-test writing samples. To explore the impact of SDA as a classroom practice, the statistical analysis measured the rate of growth from pre-test to post-test for each group by comparing means, standard deviations and effect sizes at pre- and post-test, post- and pre-test and any interactions.

Results and discussion

The planning template

The students' planning templates were each designed as a folded A3 sheet, consisting of three main sections to mirror the learning phases of forethought, performance and self-reflection. As illustrated in Figures 11.2, 11.3 and 11.4, the forethought phase was scaffolded in greater detail compared to the other two phases, to help develop students' autonomy as learners from the very beginning of the learning process. To contextualise how students used the planning template to develop strategies and competence as learners, examples follow of how Ruby and Leon, both Year 6 students, used the template.

The first forethought step (Figure 11.2) contained the relevant curriculum learning outcomes, which had been worded by the teachers in a manner that students would be able to understand and use as learning intentions and success criteria for the project. In relation to

1. What will I show that I can do?

Learning outcomes: <u>What</u> am I trying to do?

	Band 3	Extension
Text & audience	Write different types of texts using my own knowledge, experience, thoughts and feelings in my writing. Write for the purpose to inform, argue, persuade, move and entertain readers.	Write creative texts with a clear sequence, consistent plot and developed characters. Persuade the reader with convincing arguments and well-presented information in factual texts.
Structure	Write developed texts which are easy for the reader to understand. Use imagination, information and arguments in my writing.	Control the necessary spelling, grammar, punctuation and text structure to clearly communicate ideas and information in text.
Strategies	Use correct grammar and check that my writing is clear and effective.	Use a range of strategies to research, plan, compose, review and edit written texts to make sure that they are clear to the reader.

Figure 11.2 Forethought step 1: Engaging with the curriculum outcomes as learning intentions

Assessment to develop students' strategies 129

social cognitive theory, this section of the template represented a situational factor which framed the learning task.

On Ruby's and Leon's templates – like on most students' templates – no text was highlighted in this section. However, the teacher interviews indicated that the content had repeatedly been discussed in class: "Once they understood what was expected with the criteria – I went through that a couple of times – then they would just fly" (follow-up interview with Year 6 SDA teacher). This indicates that the template as a situational factor reciprocated with teaching actions. Yet, when students were interviewed, this section did not seem to have attracted their attention, as illustrated by the following segment with two Year 6 students:

Q: Can you tell me, why do you think you had to fill in this big planning template?
Jeremy: So that you can follow your storyline. So that you can plan it out and just write it ... and it will all be easier.
Frances: Uhm, it just helps us with our writing task.
Q: Okay, any other things on there that you think may have been put there deliberately?

(Both students looking at the planning sheet, long pause)

Q: So mainly to help you plan?
Both: Yes.

From a social cognitive perspective, Jeremy and Frances appear to describe intrapersonal and SRL considerations by acknowledging that the purpose of the template was to help them plan and monitor their writing. However, the curriculum section as a situational influence for goal setting is not spoken of, thus not demonstrating reciprocity with students' intrapersonal domain as an SRL factor.

The second step within the forethought process (Figure 11.3) provided students with a selection of strategies to refer to as they undertook the task of splitting the success criteria into partial goals to monitor progress against. This section of the planning template appeared more effective as a situational factor in prompting a reciprocal relationship with students' cognitive engagement as an intrapersonal factor. Many templates had particular sections or strategies underlined, indicating students' choices, which in turn suggest reciprocity with particular strategies for learning (learning behaviour) they intended to employ to self-regulate their learning.

In the forethought step 2 section, both Ruby and Leon had put ticks next to "How will my choice of words affect my reader?" Leon had also highlighted "Is it clear who is speaking in the text?" and Ruby had underlined sections in the "How should the text type be structured" dot-point. These choices were further elaborated on in section 4 of the planning template. Prior to section 4, students had to consider an additional forethought step by deciding on the type of text and audience they would target as they developed their writing sample (Figure 11.4). In this example, Leon chose to write a "play" for "children aged three to six", while Ruby had circled "Poetry" and "People in Darwin". Reconnecting with the reciprocal influences of learning, illustrated in Figure 11.1, Ruby's and Leon's templates indicated a reciprocal relationship among intrapersonal factors such as students' cognition, knowledge and emotions in the form of interest; situational factors such as audience and resources; and their future learning actions.

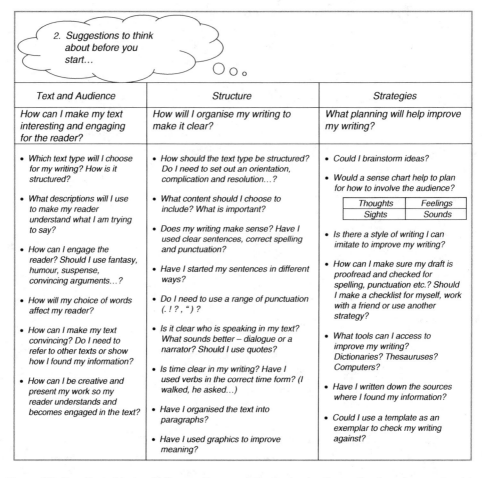

Figure 11.3 Forethought step 2: Suggestions and strategies for the writer to set as goals when planning and monitoring learning

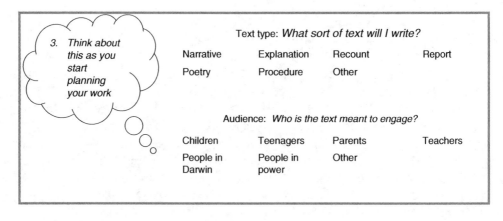

Figure 11.4 Forethought step 3: Determining text type and audience

Assessment to develop students' strategies 131

The middle segment of each template was designed as a transitional phase between the forethought and performance phases of the learning cycle. It consisted of a checklist section divided into three sub-headings: *text and audience*, *structure* and *strategies*. Each sub-heading had some space provided for students to scribe partial goals during the forethought phase, which then were used to prompt students' monitoring of their progress during the performance phase. Students commenced their writing projects during the performance phase by developing a draft and checking progress against the success criteria. As illustrated in Figures 11.5 and 11.6, Ruby's and Leon's planning templates reflected considerations they would keep in mind as they crafted their texts. Leon used key words and phrases in the

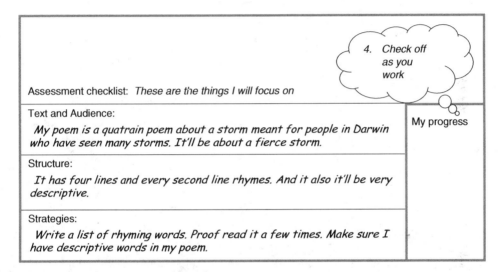

Figure 11.5 Transition between forethought and performance: Ruby's assessment checklist of things to focus on

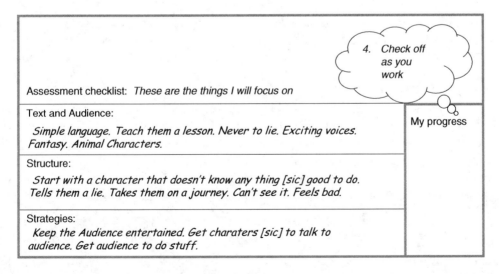

Figure 11.6 Transition between forethought and performance: Leon's assessment checklist of things to focus on

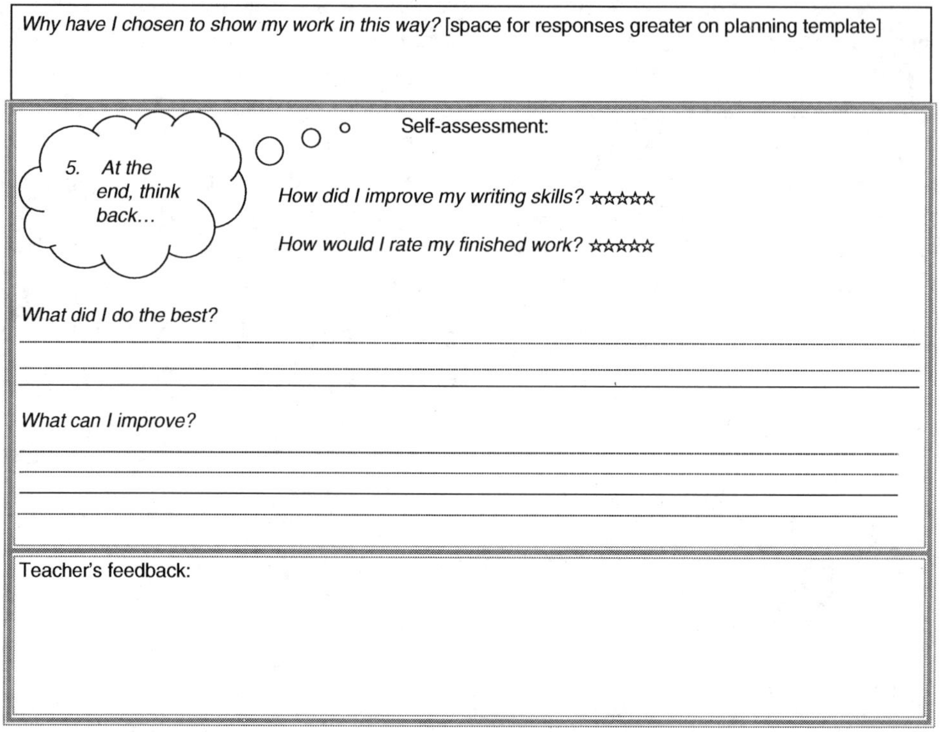

132   Anna Fletcher

```
Why have I chosen to show my work in this way? [space for responses greater on planning template]

                                    Self-assessment:
    5. At the
       end, think       How did I improve my writing skills? ☆☆☆☆☆
       back...
                        How would I rate my finished work? ☆☆☆☆☆

What did I do the best?
_____
_____

What can I improve?
_____
_____
_____

Teacher's feedback:


```

Figure 11.7 Self-evaluation phase

checklist as prompts to himself, suggesting that he used the checklist mainly for himself, to help plan and monitor his own learning. Ruby's checklist is written in a more mixed manner; the first point suggests that she is informing the reader of her plans to write a quatrain poem. The following two points appear more to be reminders for herself.

From a social cognitive perspective, Ruby's and Leon's checklists suggest an intrapersonal SRL focus in their function. However, the content of the checklists appears to emphasise the intended audience, which is a situational factor. In addition, Ruby's intended strategies illustrate that she had considered particular learning behaviours such as "write a list" and "proof read".

The final phase of the cycle entailed students evaluating how well their learning strategies worked and attributing reasons for their level of achievement in the task (Figure 11.7). In this section Ruby stated that she had chosen to write a poem because she likes reading them, thus again illustrating an intrapersonal dimension. Leon's template indicated that he had wanted to write a play for his younger sister, which again indicates a situational influence as well as intrapersonal factors such as motivation.

Students' demonstration of strategies and writing competence

To present evidence of AaL as a classroom practice that develops students' strategies and competence as learners, this chapter focuses on *Vocabulary*, which, as illustrated above, is an aspect of writing to which students such as Ruby and Leon gave much consideration. In the quantitative analysis (like NAPLAN), vocabulary competence was determined by the number of precise words in the writing. For example, one line of Ruby's poem reads "The leaves were dancing in the cold, cruel wind", in which "dancing" is a precise word, rather than the basic "blowing".

The planning templates provided a clear indication of students' awareness of the importance of precise word choices. For example, students identified intentions to use *descriptive words*, *rhyming words*, *adjectives* and *command verbs*. Of these, particularly the nomination of "rhyming words" and "command verbs" indicates metacognitive knowledge activation (Pintrich, 2004) and self-regulation with respect to task analysis and strategic planning (Weinstein & Hume, 1998; Zimmerman, 2008) because they explicitly connect with two specific types of text: poetry and procedures. The students' planning templates also indicated the intention as well as goals to *vary vocabulary*.

Comparison of vocabulary scores

The comparison of post-test scores showed a large effect size of greater competence among the Year 6 SDA students (see Table 11.2), compared with the TDA students in the same year level. This finding suggests that the Year 6 SDA group's writing samples displayed more "sustained and consistent use of precise words and phrases that enhance the meaning or mood" (MCEETYA, 2008, p. 10), compared with the Year 6 TDA samples. This greater level of competence among the Year 6 SDA group was further evidenced when the level of growth from the pre-test to the post-test was compared. In regard to level of growth, there was no difference between the SDA and the TDA groups at the Year 4 level. However, in Year 6, the SDA group demonstrated twice the level of growth compared with the TDA group (see Table 11.3).

Table 11.2 Difference between SDA and TDA students' pre-test and post-test scores in vocabulary

	CRITERIA	SDA Mean	SD	TDA Mean	SD	d
Yr. 4	Vocabulary (pre-test)	2.18	.38	2.21	.41	-.08
	Vocabulary (post-test)	2.89	.66	2.93	.59	-.06
Yr. 6	Vocabulary (pre-test)	2.66	.74	2.43	.34	.43
	Vocabulary (post-test)	3.41	.96	2.70	.89	.77

Table 11.3 Difference from pre-test to post-test in students' vocabulary scores

	CRITERIA	Post-test Mean	SD	Pre-test Mean	SD	d
Yr. 4	Vocabulary (SDA) (n = 40)	2.89	.66	2.18	.38	1.37
	Vocabulary (TDA) (n = 29)	2.93	.59	2.21	.41	1.44
Yr. 6	Vocabulary (SDA) (n = 76)	3.41	.96	2.66	.74	.88
	Vocabulary (TDA) (n = 84)	2.70	.89	2.93	.59	.44

Overall, as indicated by the planning templates, students demonstrated the ability to strategically plan by stating the intention to use precise vocabulary in their writing. In the case of the Year 6 SDA group, this intention resulted in substantially higher marks in the criteria of Vocabulary, compared with their peers in the TDA group. This finding points to the positive influence of goal setting as an SRL competence on learning (Flower & Hayes, 1981; Harris & Brown, 2013; Zimmerman & Schunk, 2011).

Teachers' situational influence on learning

The findings suggest that the AaL project prompted students to actively engage as learners and to seek help to inform their learning, at a time when they were receptive to feedback. Notably, the planning template may have served as a "challenges springboard" for both teacher practice as well as student learning, by requiring students to take on an active role in engaging in the detailed, explicit planning process. For the teachers, this meant giving more explicit instructions than they normally would, as part of the emphasised forethought stage of the learning process. For the students, the templates appear to have presented detailed planning considerations they needed to address as part of the forethought phase, prompting them to seek help.

Point-of-need teaching

Findings from the present study highlighted the teachers' practice in respect to providing students with individual feedback within the students' zone of proximal development (Vygotsky, 1978). The teachers' use of learning dialogues and targeted, small-group conferences to provide students with formative feedback emerged as a feature of the AaL process, as illustrated by Maria, a Year 2 teacher:

> I did small groups to start off with, to get an overview and then – yeah – a couple of sessions going through each part [of the planning template]. Some of them, I still – some of the kids still didn't quite understand, and more the fact that – it was just new to them. I'd go through each part again – especially with the bottom part, the strategy they used. Some of them found that bit hard to grasp. And did not realise that they are doing these things [applying strategies to solve a task] anyway ... I was conferencing with them, with their writing pieces, saying: Okay, so what did you do? Did you look through your work before you came to me? So, I had to talk them through it. But then we wrote down things they did.
> Follow-up interview with Maria

From a social cognitive perspective, Maria's description above illustrates how AaL is a process that facilitates point-of-need teaching as both a situational and a behavioural factor. The students' help seeking appears to have prompted Maria to have a dialogue with her students about learning strategies, clearly aimed at informing future learning. Her reference to the "couple of sessions going through each part" conveys how she guided students as they endeavoured to address the proximal learning goals and the overall learning outcome from the syllabus.

Time

From the interviews and email correspondence with teachers, three elements – time, confidence and experience – stood out, indicating important differences between how Year

4 SDA teachers and the Year 6 SDA teachers had approached the writing project. From a social cognitive perspective, this highlighted how teachers' intrapersonal influences, particularly their sense of self-efficacy, influenced both their teaching behaviour and the situational context in respect to how they conducted the writing project in their classrooms. While the SDA teachers in both Year 4 and Year 6 appeared to allow a similar amount of time in the forethought phase, clear differences emerged in the later phases. Monica, a Year 6 SDA teacher, noted:

> The project took longer than expected. We spent practically the whole term on the project. I do not think it could have been done any faster.

While all three Year 6 SDA teachers found that the writing project took longer than anticipated, none expressed concern about this. Instead, the Year 6 SDA teachers commented on how they could see that the students were engaging in deep and meaningful learning, which they reasoned benefitted the students. In an earlier email, when reflecting on how students had developed their drafts, Monica noted:

> Students really surprised me and worked well on their writing activity. [Jack] said that this was the first time he had written such a long story. Students like [Charlie], who are normally weak in writing skills, did well and never complained about having to write a recount. It really helped to have the assessment criteria (outcomes) that they had written themselves to refer back to.

Monica's quotes suggest that she extended the time originally allocated for the students to complete their writing task, because she felt confident in her judgement of indicators suggesting that the project benefitted students' learning. In particular, Monica's comments above resonate with earlier findings which suggest that students' perceived self-efficacy influences effort, persistence and motivation (Bandura, 2012; Schunk & Pajares, 2005). From a social cognitive perspective (Bandura, 1986), Monica's comments allude to how intrapersonal factors such as her own understanding, confidence and motivation reciprocated with learning actions and the classroom context.

Intrapersonal factors were also significant in respect to the Year 4 SDA teachers, who had less experience and who expressed concern in their interviews about having time to fit in the curriculum. Consequently, the Year 4 SDA teachers – in contrast to the Year 6 SDA teachers – allocated much shorter time for the writing project. This presents a reliability issue in respect to fidelity of implementation, and limits the statistical significance of this study's findings. Nevertheless, the evidence of learning generated in the study is informative. The aim from the outset of this mixed-methods study was to gain a nuanced understanding of how students' learning is shaped in a process that uses assessment as a meaningful learning process. However, future research is needed to explore this in more detail.

Conclusion

The study reported in this chapter originated from the researcher's practice-based belief, developed over years as a primary teacher, that AaL is a classroom practice that helps students become autonomous and competent as learners. Underpinned by social cognitive theory (Bandura, 1986), this chapter presents a detailed discussion of how SDA students engaged in their learning as part of a three-phase AaL process. The study emphasised the forethought phase of the learning process by presenting students with a writing task that scaffolded them to control and develop their thinking and understanding (cognition), their perceived ability to complete the task (self-efficacy) and what strategies they would use to plan and monitor their learning. The process was scaffolded by the teachers and framed by a planning template designed to emphasise the forethought phase of the learning cycle.

The findings paint a complex picture of AaL as a scaffolded and highly individualised form of goal-directed learning that is shaped by the reciprocal relationship among intrapersonal, situational and behavioural influences. Findings of the cross-sectional study suggest that the AaL process aided students' engagement in metacognitive processes such as monitoring, understanding, organising ideas and checking for consistency. This entailed students making strategic choices, with the support of the teachers, as the students planned and monitored their learning, thereby demonstrating SRL competence. As a consequence of students actively directing the AaL process (Dann, 2002; Earl, 2013; Fletcher, 2016), teaching became individualised and tailored around the students' learning needs. This in itself constitutes an auspicious pedagogical approach, which fuses SRL (Zimmerman, 2011), student choice, competence and motivation theories (Elliot & Dweck, 2005) into a structured format.

References

Andrade, H. L., & Brookhart, S. M. (2016). The role of classroom assessment in supporting self-regulated learning. In D. Laveault & L. Allal (Eds.), *Assessment for learning: Meeting the challenge of implementation* (pp. 293–309). London: Springer.

Andrade, H. L., & Brown, G. T. L. (2016). Student self-assessment in the classroom. In G. T. L. Brown & L. R. Harris (Eds.), *Handbook of human and social conditions in assessment* (pp. 319–334). New York: Routledge.

Bandura, A. (1986). Social foundations of thought and action: A social cognitive theory. Englewood Cliffs, NJ: Prentice-Hall.

Bandura, A. (2012). On the functional properties of perceived self-efficacy revisited. *Journal of Management*, 38(1), 9–44. DOI:10.1177/0149206311410606

Black, P., Harrison, C., Lee, C., Marshall, B., & Wiliam, D. (2003). *Assessment for learning: Putting it into practice*. Maidenhead, UK: Open University Press.

Breen, L. J. (2007). The researcher "in the middle": Negotiating the insider/outsider dichotomy. *The Australian Community Psychologist*, 19(1), 163–174.

Bryman, A. (2006). Integrating quantitative and qualitative research: How is it done? *Qualitative Research*, 6(1), 97–113. DOI:10.1177/1468794106058877

Burton, D., & Bartlett, S. (2005). *Practitioner research for teachers*. London: SAGE Publications, Ltd.

Dann, R. (2002). *Promoting Assessment as Learning*. London: RoutledgeFalmer.

Dinsmore, D. L., & Wilson, H. E. (2016). Student participation in assessment: Does it influence self-regulation? In G. T. L. Brown & L. R. Harris (Eds.), *Handbook of human and social factors in assessment*, (pp. 145–168). New York: Routledge.

Dwyer, S. C., & Buckle, J. L. (2009). The space between: On being an insider-outsider in qualitative research. *International Journal of Qualitative Methods*, 8(1), 54–63.

Earl, L. M. (2013). *Assessment as Learning: Using classroom assessment to maximize student learning* (2nd ed.). Thousand Oaks, CA; London; New Delhi: Corwin Press.

Elliot, A. J., & Dweck, C. S. (2005). Competence and motivation. In A. J. Elliot & C. S. Dweck (Eds.), *Handbook of competence and motivation* (pp. 3–15). New York: The Guilford Press.

Fletcher, A. K. (2015). Student-Directed Assessment as a learning process for primary students: A mixed-methods study. (Doctor of Philosophy thesis), Charles Darwin University, Australia. Retrieved from https://espace.cdu.edu.au/view/cdu:50323

Fletcher, A. K. (2016). Exceeding expectations: Scaffolding agentic engagement through Assessment as Learning. *Educational Research, 58*(4), 400-419. DOI:10.1080/00131881.2016.1235909

Fletcher, A. K. (2017). Help seeking: Agentic learners initiating feedback. *Educational Review*, [online] 1-20. DOI:10.1080/00131911.2017.1340871

Flower, L., & Hayes, J. R. (1981). A cognitive process theory of writing. *College Composition and Communication, 32*(4), 365-387.

Harlen, W., & James, M. (1997). Assessment and learning: Differences and relationships between formative and summative assessment. *Assessment in Education, 4*(3), 365-379.

Harris, L. R., & Brown, G. T. L. (2013). Opportunities and obstacles to consider when using peer- and self-assessment to improve student learning: Case studies into teachers' implementation. *Teaching and Teacher Education, 36* , 101-111. DOI:http://dx.doi.org/10.1016/j.tate.2013.07.008

Lankshear, C., & Knobel, M. (2004). *A handbook for teacher research: From design to implementation*. Maidenhead, UK: Open University Press.

Laveault, D., & Allal, L. (2016). Implementing assessment for learning: Theoretical and practical issues. In D. Laveault & L. Allal (Eds.), *Assessment for learning: Meeting the challenge of implementation* (pp. 1-18). London: Springer.

Leech, N. L., Onwuegbuzie, A. J., & Combs, J. P. (2011). Writing publishable mixed research articles: Guidelines for emerging scholars in the health sciences and beyond. *International Journal of Multiple Research Approaches, 5*(7), 7-24.

MCEETYA (Ministerial Council on Education, Employment, Training and Youth Affairs) (2008). *Writing-narrative marking guide*. Retrieved on December 13, 2010 from: http://www.naplan.edu.au/verve/_resources/napmarkguide08.pdf

NTCF (2009). *NT Curriculum Framework: English*. Darwin: Northern Territory Government. Retrieved on June 4, 2013 from: http://www.education.nt.gov.au/__data/assets/pdf_file/0014/2381/english_writing.pdf

Perrenoud, P. (1998). From formative evaluation to a controlled regulation of learning processes: Towards a wider conceptual field. *Assessment in Education: Principles, Policy & Practice, 5*(1), 85-104.

Pintrich, P. R. (2004). A conceptual framework for assessing motivation and self-regulated learning in college students. *Educational Psychology Review, 16*(4), 385-407.

Popham, J. (2008). *Transformative assessment*. Alexandria, VA: Association for Supervision and Curriculum Development (ASCD).

Saldaña, J. (2013). *The coding manual for qualitative researchers* (2nd ed.). London; Thousand Oaks, CA; New Delhi; Singapore: SAGE Publications.

Schunk, D. H. (1995). Self-efficacy and education and instruction. In J. E. Maddux (Ed.), *Self-efficacy, adaptation, and adjustment: Theory, research, and application* (pp. 281-303). New York: Plenum Press.

Schunk, D. H., & Pajares, F. (2005). Competence perceptions and academic functioning. In A. J. Elliot & C. S. Dweck (Eds.), *Handbook of competence and motivation* (pp. 85-105). New York: The Guilford Press.

Vygotsky, L. S. (1978). *Mind in society: The development of higher psychological processes*. London: Harvard University Press.

Weinstein, C. E., & Hume, L. M. (1998). Goal 2: Understanding the categories and characteristics of learning strategies. In C. E. Weinstein & L. M. Hume (Eds.), *Study strategies for lifelong learning: Psychology in the classroom* (pp. 23-41). Washington, DC: American Psychological Association.

Wiliam, D. (2011). *Embedded formative assessment*. Bloomington, IN: Solution Tree Press.

Zimmerman, B. J. (2008). Goal setting: A key proactive source of academic self-regulation. In D. H. Schunk & B. J. Zimmerman (Eds.), *Motivation and self-regulated learning: Theory, research, and applications* (2012 ed., pp. 267-296). New York: Routledge.

Zimmerman, B. J. (2011). Motivational sources and outcomes of self-regulated learning and performance. In B. J. Zimmerman & D. H. Schunk (Eds.), *Handbook of self-regulation of learning and performance* (pp. 49-64). New York; London: Routledge.

Zimmerman, B. J., & Schunk, D. H. (2011). Self-regulated learning and performance: An introduction and an overview. In B. J. Zimmerman & D. H. Schunk (Eds.), *Handbook of self-regulation of learning and performance* (pp. 1-12). New York: Routledge.

12 Groups in action
A closer look at how students respond to group work

Kitty Janssen, Justen O'Connor and Sivanes Phillipson

Introduction

Asking students to work in groups is relatively easy; ensuring that students have positive and productive learning outcomes from small-group learning is not. Although small-group learning has been used in classrooms for over four decades (Johnson & Johnson, 1974), how and when it should be implemented is still a subject of debate (see, for example, Hmelo-Silver, Duncan, & Chinn, 2007; Kirschner, Sweller, & Clark, 2006). This chapter explores how teachers may impact on the effectiveness of small groups for conceptual learning through task preparations, structuring of task and groups as well as the role played by the teacher.

Student-led small-group learning, also referred to as group work, cooperative learning and collaborative learning, is defined in this chapter as students working together in small groups to achieve a common goal on a subject of interest over an extended time without constant direct supervision of the teacher. It is considered that small-group learning has potential to lead students to authentic achievement and social equity through providing opportunities for active learning and substantive conversations (Cohen, 1994). Small-group learning may be an appropriate pedagogy for more complex tasks, as it allows for the cognitive load to be shared amongst the group (Kirschner, Paas, Kirschner, & Janssen, 2011). Yet Clark, Kirschner, and Sweller (2012) point out that small-group projects are most effective as a means of practicing recently learnt skills and content, not as an approach to making discoveries. The extent to which students will benefit from small-group learning will therefore depend largely on the aim of the learning and the task being presented (Kirschner, Paas, & Kirschner, 2009; Kirschner et al., 2011) as well as students' participation and the quality of students' discussion (Webb, 2009).

In this chapter, we explore how a teacher and three Year 7 classes responded to a sleep education unit using small-group learning. We discuss how task preparation, the structure of the task and groups and the teacher's role in the classroom impacted on the productivity of different groups in order to better understand small-group learning.

Small-group learning

Small-group learning can be implemented in different ways depending on the nature of the learning outcomes and task. Cohen (1994) suggests that ill-structured tasks are better suited to conceptual learning in small groups. An ill-structured task, as defined by Cohen, is a task

Table 12.1 Dimensions and elements of the Productive Pedagogies framework considered particularly relevant for conceptual learning in small groups

Dimension	Element	Associated research question
Intellectual quality	Higher order thinking	Are higher order thinking and critical analysis occurring?
	Deep understanding	Do the work and response of students provide evidence of depth of understanding of concepts or ideas?
	Knowledge as problematic	Are students critiquing and second-guessing texts, ideas and knowledge?
	Substantive conversation	Does classroom talk break out of the initiation/response/evaluation pattern and lead to sustained dialogue between students, and between teachers and students?
Supportive classroom environment	Social support	Is the classroom a socially supportive and positive environment?
	Engagement	Are students engaged in the task?
	Self-regulation	Is the direction of student behaviour implicit and self-regulatory or explicit?

that is not clear-cut and cannot be carried out by one individual. As such, ill-structured tasks require effective interactions which allow students to share ideas and hypotheses as well as exchange strategies and speculations. Cohen considers that productive outcomes may be considered in terms of higher order thinking and cannot be achieved without high-level conversation within small groups. More recently, Kirschner et al. (2009) concluded that social interaction within a team should allow for the formation of a collective knowledge structure. This interaction may be stimulated when members of the group are given a task that is interdependent: where all members depend on each other in order to complete the task (Kirschner et al., 2009).

The productive outcomes of higher order thinking through social interaction, as espoused by Cohen (1994) and Kirschner et al. (2009), align closely with the Productive Pedagogies framework (Hayes, Mills, Christie, & Lingard, 2006) – a framework which looks to improve academic and social outcomes by considering teaching practices. The Productive Pedagogies framework divides its 20 elements into four dimensions: intellectual quality, connectedness, supportive classroom environment and engagement with and valuing of difference. Although we consider that all four dimensions are important for a productive classroom, selected elements of the intellectual quality and supportive classroom environment dimensions (see Table 12.1) are considered particularly relevant to determining the productivity of small-group learning and conceptual learning.

Pedagogical processes used to promote the productivity of small-group learning

Implementing a pedagogy that yields intellectual quality, as well as a supportive classroom environment that allows for positive social interactions, can be a challenge for teachers (Hayes et al., 2006). This may be due to the different levels of teaching experience and student learning, as well as variation in students' content knowledge and communication skills. Webb (2009) explains that group members may show negative socio-emotional behaviour by insulting others or exhibiting off-task behaviour such as social loafing – where one or more members sit back and let others do the work. Webb, however, suggests that teachers can improve the likelihood of groups working productively by:

1   preparing students for the collaborative task;
2   structuring the task;
3   structuring the groups to promote positive student interactions;
4   taking on a facilitator role.

We will now consider each of these aspects in turn.

Preparing the students

Webb (2009) suggests that prior to undertaking extensive group work tasks, students should be prepared for the task. Preparations can range from a simple description of expected behaviours to extensive training in social skills. For example, she suggests that working with students on their social skills before or during the small-group learning can improve the functioning of the group. This approach, Webb suggests, reduces interpersonal conflict by helping members of the group to take responsibility for themselves and what is happening. Other studies suggest that teachers can prepare students by modelling appropriate ways of questioning, asking students to elaborate on their ideas and pressing students to explain their thinking in order to gain depth within student discussion in groups (Cohen, 1994; Murphy, Firetto, Wei, Li, & Croninger, 2016). They may also establish ground rules such as turn-taking mechanisms and setting group roles for discussion (Saleh, Lazonder, & de Jong, 2007).

Murphy et al. (2016, p. 28) suggest that students should be "primed" with new information on the topic so that they can make meaningful connections in a critical task. Similarly, Hmelo-Silver et al. (2007) suggest that mini-lectures or benchmark lessons can be used within inquiry learning to present key content information and ensure understanding and relevance. For highly functional groups, however, too much preparation and control may lead to micromanaging the process of thinking and talking (Webb 2009) and reduce the challenge of the task. The extent of the preparation of the students for the task must therefore be carefully considered so as to enhance, and not diminish, the productivity of small-group learning.

Structuring the task

There are many different ways in which a group task can be structured to make the groups more productive. Webb (2009) suggests that these can include explanation prompts, reciprocal questioning and structured controversy. When the teaching objective is conceptual learning, Cohen (1994, p. 20) suggests that tasks should aim to be less structured to allow for conceptual interactions which "foster maximum interaction, mutual exchange, and elaborated discussions". Yet, Cohen concedes that too little structure can lead to uncertainty in students, which may impede learning. Kirschner et al. (2009) reinforce this, noting the limitations of small-group learning when the task is too complex and when individuals within the group have difficulty sharing information. Kirschner et al. (2009) suggest groups are successful when they effectively share the cognitive load, fostered by creating interdependence. An interdependent task requires the distribution of different but crucial information amongst all the members so that they have to share information in order to achieve the task goal. Structuring groups can impact the effectiveness of this.

Structuring the groups

When structuring groups for productive learning, teachers may consider a number of factors such as students' friendships, common interests, ability or gender. Johnson (2009) points out that there are no magical formulas for creating effective groups – some work, others do not. Similarly, Webb (2009) and Murphy et al. (2016) indicate that there is no evidence for an optimal group composition.

Blatchford, Kutnick, Baines, and Galton (2003) argue that even when groups are decided upon by a characteristic, group composition will inevitably vary according to other factors such as the ability mix, the gender mix and friendships within the classroom. They recommend that students are involved in the formation of groups after being asked to consider the advantages and disadvantages of working alongside close friends. When considering how many students should be in each group, teachers must consider what is best for the productivity of the groups as well as what is manageable for themselves and their teaching. For example, they may consider that pairs will function better for a task but this number of groups may make it too demanding on the teacher to adequately support the groups. Larger groups, on the other hand, might be more manageable for the teacher but are likely to splinter into smaller sub-groups to complete the tasks (Blatchford et al., 2003).

Whatever the composition, Blatchford et al. (2003) suggest that groups must be given time and opportunity to develop trust, respect and strategies to overcome conflict. Whichever way the teacher decides to structure the groups will very much depend on the task, teacher, students and classroom context. The role played by the teacher in the classroom is also of great importance.

Teacher's (facilitator's) role during small-group learning

The teacher's role during small-group learning will vary depending on the task and learning outcomes. When setting up for conceptual learning, teachers need to refrain from providing direct instructions to allow students the freedom to interact independently within their groups (Blatchford et al., 2003; Cohen, 1994; Webb, 2009). Cohen (1994) argues that if the teacher, as an authority figure, takes too much responsibility for task engagement, student responsibility will diminish. Intervention is therefore only necessary when students are failing to progress or disagreeing in unproductive ways or to enable students to explore ideas more effectively (Cohen, 1994).

Researchers exploring inquiry-based learning approaches argue that teachers must be more than stand-off facilitators; providing explicit intentions for learning, just-in-time instruction, worked examples and clear formative feedback that is supportive rather than judgemental (Hmelo-Silver et al., 2007; Kirschner et al., 2006; Tomlinson, 2015). To get the maximum benefits from small-group work, Kirschner et al. (2009) suggest that teachers need to support learners to exchange resources through effective communication. Once groups are progressing, teachers should aim to progressively fade their control and authority to allow students to increasingly take responsibility to co-construct meaning (Murphy et al., 2016).

Having briefly explored the preparation, task structure, group composition and teacher's role within small-group learning, we now explore what happened when three Year 7 classes were asked to complete an ill-structured, student-led research project on adolescent sleep designed to stimulate conceptual learning through small-group learning.

The case study

In this case study, students were asked to work in small groups in order to explore the complex issue of adolescent sleep by completing an action research project. The aims of the project were to improve students' conceptual understandings of sleep, health literacy, the role of research in the development of health-promoting actions and the benefits of working in groups. The unit on sleep was implemented as part of a Year 7 well-being program at a relatively small Prep-12 independent school in Victoria, Australia. This unit and subsequent research responded to a concern raised by the school community about student sleep while developing their general capabilities, mainly their critical and creative thinking, personal, social, information and communication technology capabilities (ACARA, 2018). The unit was taught over a school term by an experienced teacher who had three Year 7 classes (a total of 86 students). The students were familiar with each other as most had been together in primary school. The teacher indicated that although students had some small-group learning experience from previous years, they had not conducted any meaningful small-group learning in his subject. The classroom was set up with two tables facing each other so that students sat in groups of four.

Method

After gaining ethical approval and permission from the parents and students, the lead researcher observed the three classes undertake the unit for 56 out of 69 lesson periods of 43 minutes. The observation also includes a one-period incursion and a four-period excursion (43 hours and 43 minutes of observation in total). During these lessons, the primary researcher acted as a moderate participant observer (Spradley, 1980), where, for the majority of the time, the observer sat at the edge of the room and wrote field notes of observations. On occasion, the observer took on a support role for the teacher, the role of expert for the students and the role of facilitator/organiser during the incursion and excursion. Before and after lessons, the researcher invited the teacher to discuss his reflections and address any questions or concerns. These conversations were audio-recorded where possible. Work samples were collected from student groups by the teacher and passed onto the observer, scanned and returned. The project was completed at the end of term two, 2015, after which semi-structured interviews of the teacher and 12 students (five individual interviews and two group interviews) were conducted. During the interviews, the teacher was asked about his perceptions of students' learning and the effectiveness of the unit. Students were asked about their understandings of disciplinary knowledge with regards to sleep, health promotion and the action research process in order to help determine their level of health literacy around sleep.

Analysis of the data was performed using a thematic analysis approach (Braun & Clarke, 2006) where observation notes, work samples and interviews were analysed for evidence of pedagogical process and group productivity. Pedagogical processes around small-group learning were analysed with reference to the frame by Webb (2009) discussed earlier: preparing students, structuring the task, structuring the group and the role of the teacher. Group productivity was analysed using the seven elements of the Productive Pedagogies framework (Hayes et al., 2006) in Table 12.1. The combinations of these seven elements were used as themes to establish three levels of productivity: productive, partially productive and unproductive, as described in Table 12.2.

Table 12.2 Descriptions of group productivity using the Productive Pedagogies (PP) framework (Hayes et al., 2006)

Elements of PP	Productive groups	Partially productive groups	Unproductive groups
Intellectual quality (higher order thinking, deep understanding, knowledge as problematic)	Some evidence that members achieved conceptual learning.	Evidence that some members achieved conceptual learning while others did not.	No evidence that members achieved any conceptual learning.
Substantive conversation (about the task)	Observed between all group members at least once every two lessons.	Observed between some group members at least once every two lessons. For most groups, one pair of students conversed well while the other(s) did not participate.	Rarely observed between group members.
Academic engagement in the task	Observed for all members for most of the time.	Observed for some (usually two) members while the other(s) sat quietly or were engaged in off-task behaviours.	Only observed for one or two members working individually, usually after heavy scaffolding by the teacher.
Self-regulation of behaviour	Observed for all members most of the time with little teacher intervention.	Observed for one or two members while the other(s) struggled to regulate their behaviour, attracting teacher intervention at least once every lesson.	Observed to vary greatly. Some members were disruptive and attracted teacher intervention at least once every lesson. Others were very passive and attracted little intervention.
Social support	Members were observed to support each other: answering questions, providing explanations and reminding each other of deadlines.	Engaged students were observed supporting each other. However, disengaged students were not supported unless prompted by the teacher.	Members rarely communicated with each other about the task and there was little to no evidence of social support.

Results

This section provides a brief commentary on how the different pedagogical processes outlined by Webb (2009) were applied in the case study. It will then provide a brief commentary on how these pedagogical processes impacted on the three types of groups. All participants are referred to with pseudonyms. Dates of interviews have not been provided as this could lead to identification of the participants.

Case study: Preparing the students

Prior to commencing their group investigation of sleep, students were provided with content knowledge around the topic of sleep and the research process so that they would be able to make meaningful connections with incoming information from their investigations (Clark et al., 2012; Hmelo-Silver et al., 2007; Murphy et al., 2016). In the first module of the unit, students were provided with activities that scaffolded current knowledge of the science of sleep and sleep hygiene practices, including an incursion from a sleep expert using direct teaching methods. The teacher then spent a lesson describing the process of research and its role in informing action using the RoadSafe health promotion campaign as worked examples. During this preparation phase, the teacher modelled the interactions expected of students during the task by encouraging critical discussions and asking open-ended questions (Cohen, 1994; Murphy et al., 2016). The preparation phase finished with an excursion to the university, which provided students with the opportunity to further understand health promotion campaigns and the research process in a lecture and subsequent workshop. The use of external experts during the preparation phase added to the authenticity of and connectedness to the task (Hayes et al., 2006). Interestingly, the teacher did not allocate any time to evaluate students' social skills for working effectively in groups nor did he prepare them for the social skills required to work in small groups, as suggested by Webb (2009).

Case study: Structuring the task

The task reflected an ill-structured group task comprising a series of sequential tasks too big for one person to complete, as recommended by Cohen (1994) and Kirschner et al. (2009). The groups' projects were deliberately open-ended in order to promote higher order thinking through interaction (Cohen, 1994). To further promote interaction, groups were given choice in terms of who they worked with, the aspect of sleep they wished to research, the research methodology (literature review, survey or interview) and the action they wished to take. Groups responded enthusiastically to this freedom and selected a range of aspects from the impact of technology, homework and extracurricular activities on sleep to the effectiveness of ear plugs in improving sleep quality. Actions varied from making movies around awareness to writing letters to the school principal. Group goals were explained to the students at the start of the project and on a daily basis: groups were asked to develop a research question, a research plan, a research instrument (e.g., survey or interview schedule) and a research report. Templates scaffolding each of these steps were provided. Finally, groups were asked to develop action plans from their findings. There were no specifications or support materials for this step, in order to allow groups freedom to develop their own ideas. The teacher informally assessed each task as groups completed them.

Although daily expected outcomes were set at the start of each lesson, groups did not have a reiteration of the overall goals until the rubric and checklist with deadlines of the summative assessment requirements were introduced in the third week (around lesson 9) of the project. The teacher had not released this information earlier as he felt that some groups would feel overwhelmed. He also wanted to see how groups progressed so that he could adjust the task and deadlines accordingly. Groups were not required to submit their final report for formal assessment until the final week of term. In terms of finding a balance between structure and uncertainty, there was significant scope for student input with uncertain outcomes. Overall, the task was considered authentic and in line with Productive Pedagogies as students could relate to the importance of adolescent sleep, familiar health promotion models, and were given choice to research an aspect of sleep they felt was worthy of a sleep-promoting action.

Case study: Structuring the groups

Students were given the freedom to choose their own groups of three or four at the end of the preparation phase. The teacher made this decision as he thought this would be most manageable for him and the students. Students had 15 minutes to form groups and were encouraged to move around to find students with similar interests during this time. Despite this approach, most groups were formed as friendship groups. In a few cases, students wanted to work alone or in pairs but the teacher insisted that students worked in groups of three or four, so these students and pairs were combined. By allowing students to choose their own groups based on interest and friendship, most groups, although not all, had existing relationships and group experience which might have improved group stability (Blatchford et al., 2003).

Case study: The role of the teacher

The teacher aimed to keep his interventions to a minimum aligning with Cohen's suggested approach (1994). Scaffolded templates and other supporting materials were provided in relation to the research process at the start of each lesson and on a just-in-time basis (Hmelo-Silver et al., 2007). This was designed to help groups manage any uncertainty around unfamiliar processes (Cohen, 1994). As suggested by Cohen, the teacher intervened more in groups who were struggling or not working productively. For example, he encouraged students who were not academically engaged to move seats so that it would be easier for them to participate. It was evident to the teacher that some members of some groups were socially loafing (Webb, 2009) and often off-task on their iPads. He responded by removing iPads that were in excess from the groups and increasing social pressure on students by asking those who were engaged to "start pulling people up if they are not doing something ... People will give you a number of excuses but there is no more time for excuses" (Field notes, 4 June, 2015).

Throughout the unit, the teacher checked groups' progress by asking them to explain what they had achieved at each stage of the research process. At the start, he asked them to show him their research questions, research plans and research instruments (e.g., survey or interview schedule). He then inquired as to their plan for collecting data. Once data were collected, he asked them how they were collating them. Once they were ready, he showed great interest in their findings and plans for action. Upon hearing about their work, he usually asked open-ended questions, listened and offered suggestions as appropriate. The teacher rewarded effort in the form of compliments, but did not provide groups with any formal feedback.

In the third week of the research project, the teacher identified that the majority of groups were not progressing sufficiently and decided to adjust expectations, provided groups with a rubric and checklist as well as clarified deadlines. He also cancelled the community exhibition, which had been planned for the end of the project, as he did not believe groups would be ready in time. He then increased the amount of intervention for the less productive groups and put in place consequences, such as staying in during break, for groups who did not complete their tasks by the deadline. Six groups were kept in during their break as a result. After one lesson, he reflected, "We got there in the end but it was a big push!" (Field notes, 11 May, 2015). During all the lessons, the teacher was extremely busy trying to ensure all students and groups were engaged and productive.

Pedagogical processes and productivity

We will now provide a brief commentary on how the pedagogical processes described for the case study impacted on the three types of groups – productive, partially productive and unproductive – as observed in the three Year 7 classes of the case study.

Groups as productive

Productive groups were students who worked well together based on respectful relationships and a mutual desire to do well. Productive groups appeared to have a good understanding of how to work effectively as a group: they would allocate roles, help each other out when needed and discuss their findings with each other in substantive conversations (Hayes et al., 2006). Productive groups appeared to benefit from existing relationships and prior group experiences to create group stability (Blatchford et al., 2003). One student, Allie, explained, "I like choosing my own groups because I usually go with the two girls I was with because we always work well together" (interview). These groups also benefited from the preparation tasks and were confident in conducting their research and relating their findings to the knowledge around sleep. The teacher extended these groups throughout their research projects by asking open-ended questions and filling in gaps of knowledge as needed. These interventions aided the groups and they progressed well.

Whole-class interventions by the teacher appeared to slow down these groups' progress, as described by Cohen (1994). One of the students interviewed, Jane, commented that she found it frustrating how the teacher kept interrupting them to give them instructions. It was concluded from the data that ten of the 22 groups worked productively. An example of the learning in a productive group is described in Case 1.

Case 1: Allie's group – an example of a productive group

Allie's group (Group 15) consisted of three students who researched the impact of homework on students' ability to sleep. This group hypothesised that students got too much homework and that they would send a letter to the principal to ask him to reduce the homework for students. The students decided upon the questions together and then allocated roles to each other: "We all had a job to do" (Allie, interview). Upon analysing interview data from students from four different year levels, the group concluded that the issue with homework was not the amount of homework people got, but that students were leaving it too late to do it. Therefore, they changed their action to an instructional video advising students to do their homework earlier. This group showed conceptual understanding of the research process and the impact of homework on sleep. They worked well together ensuring all students were engaged for most of the time. It is considered that part of this group's success was due to existing friendships, trust and respect arising from prior small-group learning experiences which enabled effective communication that allowed for the sharing of resources and a reduction in cognitive overload (Kirschner et al., 2009).

Groups as partially productive

Within partially productive groups, there was an observed disparity between the contributions of students. Some students appeared to have strengths that were optimally challenged by the task and consequently they appeared motivated and engaged. Others appeared to struggle with the task, perhaps due to a lack of meaningful connection with the task or not having a valued role to play within the group. These students may not collectively or individually have had the range of prerequisite skills and/or knowledge required to cope with the cognitive load of the ill-structured task (Kirschner et al., 2006). As a result, these students were less engaged in the substantive conversations which is an essential component of productive small-group work.

The division within these groups that impacted capacity for substantive conversations was often exacerbated by the seating arrangement around square tables where the more engaged pair sat next to each other and the less engaged person or pair sat across from them. This division within partially productive groups did not appear to shift from one lesson to the next as a result of the teacher's efforts to engage all students in a group. However, a shift was noted for some groups. For example, in Group 2-1, when two of the four members were away for a double lesson, leaving George and Scott in the group, George, who had shown little interest in the project to this point, became very engaged in helping Scott enter the survey data and even started analysing the results. For example, George was critical of the group's definition of family when he asked Scott, "Pets – I think pets are part of the family don't you think? [No response] I think pets are part of the family, so the total is ten" (Field notes, 20 May, 2015). When the other two students returned, George quickly disengaged and did not contribute to the project until the development of the action, despite the teacher's best efforts. In this case, it seemed that George did not feel he had a substantive role to play when the other students were there. This may have been because the focus of the more able and motivated student was on the production of their outcome (e.g., the report) and not the collective group learning or communication process. In this case, a shift to the importance of achieving the group goal through group learning, rather than the product, and scaffolding around roles in groups (Johnson, 2009; Saleh et al., 2007; Webb, 2009) or working in a smaller group (Blatchford et al., 2003) may have benefited George.

In partially productive groups, the more engaged students appeared quite tolerant of others who were not engaging. For example, one student, Leo, said of his group, "I reckon three of us worked really well. One of us did not work as well but he just got caught up playing games" (interview). This tolerance suggests an air of acceptance about roles and may have been the result of historic experiences of unchallenged group work practice, existing friendships and/ or the conciliatory contribution the student made during the development of their action. This observation suggests that increasing social pressure – as the teacher had done earlier by asking students to pull each other up – is an ineffective strategy for increasing engagement when groups are comprised of friends. It was concluded that eight of the 22 groups were partially productive. An example of a partially productive group is given in Case 2.

> **Case 2: John's group – an example of a partially productive group**
>
> John's group (Group 1-4) was a group of four who had not been allowed to work as two pairs. After the group decided upon their topic of sleep and technology, they effectively split their group in two pairs: one pair (John and Matt) would conduct a survey while the other pair (Andy and Jacob) interviewed fellow students. Both pairs collected their data separately, but when it came to collating the data, John and Matt agreed that they would each do a task. In the next lesson, however, it was evident that John had completed most of the task at home. This upset Matt but was readily accepted by the others.
>
> John: I've prepared the spreadsheet so I can enter the information.
> Matt: I've done it too.
> John: But I've got all six questions. Have you?
> Matt: The first two ... I was supposed to do it and I've done it. [Matt is looking upset]
> Andy: Just let John do it.
>
> (Andy walks off.) (Field notes, 9 June, 2015)
>
> This conversation continued between Matt and John for approximately ten minutes until the teacher came over to ask why Andy and Jacob were not doing any work. The ensuing conversation led to Andy and Jacob being allocated the role of developing the action. This satisfied the teacher but he did not realise that Andy and Jacob had little idea of the results and were therefore not in a position to complete the task. They simply sat and did nothing while the other two continued to work on the report. After a few minutes of silence, the researcher intervened and asked John and Matt to discuss their results with Andy and Jacob and decide upon an action as a group. By the end of the project, John typed up and printed the report at home and put it in a neat folder. The report was of a reasonable standard but it did not include the interview data. Jacob had drawn up a draft of the action at home but both he and Andy were absent from school

for the final week so it did not get finished. John and Matt included the draft action plan in the folder but did not care to improve upon it even though they submitted their projects with two lessons to spare. Whilst there was clearly interdependence of the sub-tasks allocated to the two pairs of this group (Kirschner et al., 2006), Matt and Jacob were comfortable only completing their individual goals and did not feel compelled to accomplish the overall team goal. These students' prior understanding of role allocation as part of small-group learning appears to have led students to be divided rather than united. It is considered that this group might have benefited from a greater focus on group progression within the assessments (Tomlinson, 2015) or preparation tasks around social skills (Webb, 2009). Alternatively, these students may have been more engaged if they'd been left to work as two pairs as initially requested – each with their own projects to complete.

Groups as unproductive

Students in unproductive groups were not observed to have had any substantial conversations or other aspects of intellectual quality past their initial conversation to decide on a topic. For the four groups identified as unproductive, the task preparations appeared to inadequately provide the prerequisite discipline knowledge on which to build understanding, the group skills they needed to work effectively together, a clear process outline with goals or the motivation to enable them to work effectively towards completing the task. For a number of students in these groups, the ill-structured nature of the task is thought to have led to cognitive overload (Kirschner et al., 2006). Subsequently, these groups relied heavily on the teacher to manage their behaviour and work. Even with substantive teacher intervention, students of three of the four unproductive groups were unable to complete the assigned tasks. For these three groups, this ill-structured task appeared to be balanced too far towards uncertainty, too unstructured in terms of criteria, deadlines and assessment.

For the fourth group, however, the teacher's scaffolding was sufficient to allow them to complete the multiple steps of the task albeit with little conceptual understanding and depth. This surprised the teacher and serves as an example of "teaching up" (Tomlinson, 2015) where additional support is provided to those students who are not able to complete a task. It is considered that all unproductive groups may have benefited from additional preparation around effective group functioning as well as a more structured task with increased scaffolding of content and process knowledge, worked examples, clearer deadlines and formative and summative assessment that rewarded effort. An example of an unproductive group is provided in Case 3.

Case 3: Jamie's group – an example of an unproductive group

The members of Jamie's group (Group 1-3) did little to no work for the first four weeks of the project. In this time, the group held substantive conversations but rarely around their topic. It appeared that all four students could be categorised as social loafers who expected that others would complete the work for them. The teacher tried to focus them on the work at least three times a lesson by asking them about their plans and offering suggestions (and then instructions) as to what they should do next.

They indicated that they would do it; however, as soon as he walked away from their table to help other students they would resume their off-task conversations. One student in particular, Jamie, was highly disruptive and appeared to be unable to regulate his behaviour. For example, when the Japanese teacher was the relief teacher for the class he yelled across the room to the teacher, "Do you know how to say photosynthesis [in Japanese]?" (Field notes, 19 June, 2015). The other students in the group were easily distracted by Jamie and appeared to enjoy his antics.

This group did not achieve much until they were threatened with lunchtime detention. At this point, the group did the minimal amount of work necessary to avoid the detention. This suggested that they were able to do the work; they were just not motivated to do it well or collectively. For example, when they had to write the report, each person wrote a paragraph without discussing an overall plan or direction for the report. When it became clear that the group was not going to do well, two members of the group worked together for a lesson in order to finalise the report and submitted it. In the meantime, Jamie and one of the other members made a video as part of their action; however, this was never submitted. This group demonstrated that they were capable of completing work when extrinsic consequences were in place. There was little evidence of any higher order thinking, deeper understanding or knowledge as problematic in completing the work. It is considered that the task may have held little meaning for these students and that the students' expectations of group work and their prerequisite cognitive and social skills to complete an inquiry positioned them as unproductive.

The teacher's reflections

During the final interview, the teacher concluded that he would be happy to repeat the project but that he would do it quite differently next time. He was disappointed at the work produced by the students and their ability to work effectively in groups. He thought this might be due to the length of the project as he felt some students' motivation waned as time went by. In hindsight, he realised that he had misjudged the students' capabilities as the task was:

> A bit hard for them. I genuinely think that I overestimated their capability because basically I based it on the capability of the upper end of the students [in the class] and I didn't really think enough how that was going to translate to the rest of the group.
>
> (Teacher, final interview)

The difficulty of the task meant that many groups needed continual help and scaffolding. Overall, he felt that questioning groups worked well though it was difficult to extend groups' thinking and manage classroom behaviour at the same time. He concluded that to gain greater control and enhance the quality of the student work he would make the task:

> A little more focused and possibly narrow the scope a little bit with it ... I'll be able to structure it a little bit more ... I can start collecting [reports] as examples and things like that will help.
>
> (Teacher, 15 June, 2015)

He explained that he intended to narrow the scope of the task by asking the class to decide on one topic on which everyone would work. He would then stipulate that all groups do a survey (with no option for interviews) as this would allow him to be more explicit in his instructions, worked examples, criteria and deadlines at the start of the unit. He also thought it would be better to do the unit later in the year so that he would have a better idea of the students' abilities and attitudes as well as the opportunity to work with students on knowledge and skills development for inquiry-based learning in small groups. In addition, he would exert more influence on the composition of the groups, ensuring some students wouldn't be in the same groups and allowing some students to work in pairs, presumably to ensure that there were fewer unproductive groups.

Discussion

In this case study, a teacher was observed as he implemented a critical inquiry unit on sleep using small-group learning with three Year 7 classes. The teacher is to be commended for his dedication, preparation, patience, reflexivity, openness, care and professionalism. The teacher's decision to repeat the unit with changes supports the idea that teaching is an iterative process from which lessons can be learnt, resources developed and processes refined. It also supports, in general terms, the notion that a critical inquiry using small-group learning can be a classroom feature that enhances classroom learning (Blatchford et al., 2003; Cohen, 1994; Webb, 2009). This case study demonstrates how the teaching and learning process could better support students' interactions through the pedagogical framework suggested by Webb (2009).

The preparation of the students for this unit of work concentrated on developing the student prerequisite discipline and process knowledge to support their inquiry learning. Whilst we feel this knowledge around sleep was well scaffolded, more could have been done to ascertain the extent to which learners comprehended this knowledge and were ready to apply it in more challenging ways through an open-ended group task. The preparation of the task lacked any meaningful development of the requisite social and communication skills for effectively working in groups. In hindsight, this was required for a number of the groups as students seemed to have developed group work practices from prior experiences. These prior experiences involved getting the job done (or not) rather than drawing upon collective strengths and the mutual exchange of ideas with all students participating. Therefore, preparation tasks that address what students may consider when choosing their groups as well as conceptual understandings of how to work effectively as a group are suggested for future projects. Blatchford et al.'s (2003) social pedagogy of group work offers a reasonable sequential approach to undertake this work.

The set task was ill-structured and open-ended in order to promote conceptual learning (Cohen, 1994) and social interaction. Yet we know even experts have trouble sticking to a broad, ill-structured task over a long period of time. In this case study, many groups struggled to progress through the tasks in a timely fashion and the lack of clarity around task expectations and lack of clearly structured milestones were likely to have made the task too complex for some students (Kirschner et al., 2009). Tomlinson (2015, p. 207) suggests a more structured approach where:

> The teacher develops meaningful practice for students at levels of difficulty slightly beyond their current points of development, designed to help them create conceptual schema for the content they are studying, and with support systems that enable them to accomplish the new level of challenge.

Tomlinson (2015) also suggests that tasks need to be differentiated by "teaching up" so that individuals can function at an optimal challenge point. He recommends that the teacher uses persistent formative assessment (pre-assessment and on-going assessment) in order to understand where each learner is in a learning trajectory at a given time. We believe that this process can also be used for small-group learning and will be of benefit to plan for each student's growth and monitoring of the group's progress. It is very much recognised that striking a good balance between structure and uncertainty for each student as well as each group is one of the many challenges of ensuring effective small-group learning. In line with the teacher's reflections, we therefore recommend providing or co-constructing clear group goals up-front that are scaffolded into meaningful steps which are linked to assessment (Tomlinson, 2015) in order to make the task more manageable for students.

We caution, however, of the risk in providing too much scaffolding which may limit the challenge and thinking (Webb, 2009). There is a need to strike a balance between fostering maximum interaction, mutual exchange and elaborated discussions while keeping the degree of uncertainty manageable (Cohen, 1994). There is a risk in lowering the teacher's expectations of students, as having high expectations of students is linked to achieving higher outcomes (Trouilloud, Sarrazin, Martinek, & Guillet, 2002). Our conclusion is, therefore, to argue that we should not try to find the one balance point for the whole class comprising different groups and individuals. We advocate for Tomlinson's (2015) teach up approach where expectations are high but scaffolding is provided for those groups who need it.

The implication is that, depending upon the learning intentions, teachers have to plan for differentiation. For productive groups, this may mean options for accessing resources that extend them or critically challenge their work. For less productive groups struggling with cognitive overload, it means providing access to additional resources with expert modelling, direct instruction, worked examples and templates. For unproductive groups, the scope of the project may be narrowed to one topic and one methodology for which there are additional resources. For less productive and motivated groups, such as Jamie's group, it means an increase in the structure that increases individual responsibility and puts a focus on meaning and relevance.

While differentiation is crucial to increase productivity, the teacher should also be prepared to consider adjusting group structure and size. A reduction in group size, at least initially, may be considered for students who struggle to gain a voice in larger groups whilst they are still developing communication skills and strategies. In this case study, it is thought that a number of students, such as George, Andy and Jacob, would have benefited from being in a smaller group. Alternatively, group roles may need to be further negotiated (Saleh et al., 2007) if regulation of behaviour continues to hinder learning. In this case study, an increase in accountability and access to meaningful roles may have helped focus some members of Jamie's group on the task.

The teacher's role in this pedagogy, therefore, is to continually work with students: listening, evaluating, questioning, offering suggestions and negotiating group dynamics. The teacher's skill is to be able to find the balance between structure and uncertainty so that there is time to extend groups' conceptual learning through scaffolding social interaction and skill development so as to facilitate the formation of a collective knowledge structure (Kirschner et al., 2009). Teachers may do this by exploring how the diverse strengths within a group may be put to better use when setting up the interdependent relationships of the task. The teacher's challenge is to try and get it right for all the groups. It is recognised that this is not easy and requires an iterative reflective process and the accumulation of resources. The main issue for the teacher in our case study was that the amount of support he had to provide to various groups was too high.

In order to keep the workload manageable for the teacher, we suggest dividing tasks and resources into focused chunks. Support resources should be developed that target different levels and groups supported to regulate their behaviour through identifying and utilising resources at a point of need (perhaps triggered at key milestones). Adequate preparation tasks, clearly defined goals and assessment criteria that reward group function, shared communication, effort and learning (and not just the final product) may also help motivate groups to progress. We recognise, once again, that the teacher's role to ensure productive small-group learning is far from easy.

Conclusion

This chapter explored the impact of one teacher on the productivity of the small-group learning in three Year 7 classes as he implemented a sleep education unit as part of a well-being program. From our observations, the teacher's reflections and work samples, we determined that of the 22 groups, ten were identified as productive, eight as partially productive and four as unproductive. The impact of the preparation activities, task and group structure and teacher's classroom role was different for each group type.

Our findings lead us to conclude that a small-group task for conceptual learning does not need to be a one-size-fits-all proposition and that consideration of group differentiation is needed. Differentiation may mean preparation tasks are varied, group size and composition altered, the focus on communication varied and tasks more or less scaffolded depending on group productivity. How a teacher may effectively implement such a differentiated task and find the right structure for each group is complicated and needs to be iterated with different groups. We consider that, despite teachers' best efforts, there will always be a mixture of group productivity (Johnson, 2009). Yet, there is merit in persisting as teachers and students will progress in their knowledge and understanding, allowing them to reap the benefits of more authentic learning experiences.

References

ACARA (Australian Curriculum, Assessment and Reporting Authority). (2018). *The Australian Curriculum*. Retrieved on February 1, 2018 from: https://www.australiancurriculum.edu.au/

Blatchford, P., Kutnick, P., Baines, E., & Galton, M. (2003). Toward a social pedagogy of classroom group work. *International Journal of Educational Research, 39*(1), 153–172.

Braun, V., & Clarke, V. (2006). Using thematic analysis in psychology. *Qualitative Research in Psychology, 3*(2), 77–101. DOI:10.1191/1478088706qp063oa

Clark, R. E., Kirschner, P. A., & Sweller, J. (2012). Putting students on the path to learning: The case for fully guided instruction. *American Educator, 36*(1), 6–11.

Cohen, E. G. (1994). Restructuring the classroom: Conditions for productive small groups. *Review of Educational Research, 64*(1), 1-35. DOI:10.3102/00346543064001001

Hayes, D., Mills, M., Christie, P., & Lingard, B. (2006). *Teachers and schooling making a difference: Productive pedagogies, assessment and performance.* Crows Nest, NSW: Allen & Unwin.

Hmelo-Silver, C. E., Duncan, R. G., & Chinn, C. A. (2007). Scaffolding and achievement in problem-based and inquiry learning: A response to Kirschner, Sweller, and Clark (2006). *Educational Psychologist, 42*(2), 99-107. DOI:10.1080/00461520701263368

Johnson, D. W. (2009). *Joining together: Group theory and group skills* (10th ed). Upper Saddle River, NJ: Pearson Education.

Johnson, D. W., & Johnson, R. T. (1974). Instructional goal structure: Cooperative, competitive, or individualistic. *Review of Educational Research, 44*(2), 213-240. DOI:10.3102/00346543044002213

Kirschner, F., Paas, F., & Kirschner, P. A. (2009). Individual and group-based learning from complex cognitive tasks: Effects on retention and transfer efficiency. (Report). *Computers in Human Behavior, 25*(2), 306. DOI:10.1016/j.chb.2008.12.008

Kirschner, F., Paas, F., Kirschner, P. A., & Janssen, J. (2011). Differential effects of problem-solving demands on individual and collaborative learning outcomes. *Learning and Instruction, 21*(4), 587-599. DOI:10.1016/j.learninstruc.2011.01.001

Kirschner, P. A., Sweller, J., & Clark, R. E. (2006). Why minimal guidance during instruction does not work: An analysis of the failure of constructivist, discovery, problem-based, experiential, and inquiry-based teaching. *Educational Psychologist, 41*(2), 75-86. DOI:10.1207/s15326985ep4102_1

Murphy, P. K., Firetto, C. M., Wei, L., Li, M., & Croninger, R. M. V. (2016). What REALLY works. *Policy Insights from the Behavioral and Brain Sciences, 3*(1), 27-35. DOI:10.1177/2372732215624215

Saleh, M., Lazonder, A. W., & de Jong, T. (2007). Structuring collaboration in mixed-ability groups to promote verbal interaction, learning and motivation of average-ability students. *Contemporary Educational Psychology, 32*, 314-331.

Spradley, J. P. (1980). *Participant observation.* New York: Holt.

Tomlinson, C. A. (2015). Teaching for excellence in academically diverse classrooms. *Society, 52*(3), 203-209. DOI:10.1007/s12115-015-9888-0

Trouilloud, D. O., Sarrazin, P. G., Martinek, T. J., & Guillet, E. (2002). The influence of teacher expectations on student achievement in physical education classes: Pygmalion revisited. *European Journal of Social Psychology, 32*(5), 591-607. DOI:10.1002/ejsp.109

Webb, N. M. (2009). The teacher's role in promoting collaborative dialogue in the classroom. *British Journal of Educational Psychology, 79*(1), 1-28. DOI:10.1348/000709908X380772

13 The Australian Curriculum, creativity and narrative accounts of the classroom

Narelle Wood

Creativity is a concept that everyone has an opinion about but is exceptionally hard to define. Colleagues have often remarked that I am a "creative teacher" and students have commented that they loved the "creative" work that we did in class. I have always enjoyed finding new ways to approach teaching or different concepts even amidst a changing educational landscape that is increasingly focused on standardisation and measurement to generate "meaningful" data (Ozga, 2009). While these changes in education have often challenged my practice, they have also prompted rich reflection on my part. At the forefront of these reflections are questions of teacher creative practice and creativity, such as: What does it mean to be a "creative" teacher? What place does creativity have in education? And how do teachers assess students' creativity? These questions seem especially crucial in a time when education policy and curriculum place a high importance on the concept of creativity and creative thinking, evident in documents such as the *Melbourne Declaration on Educational Goals for Young Australians* (MCEETYA, 2008), the Australian Curriculum (ACARA, n.d.a) and the Victorian iteration of this national curriculum (VCAA, n.d.a). These documents not only highlight the requirement for creativity to be embedded in the curriculum, they also in some instances stipulate that creativity and creative thinking are assessed.

Why is there an emphasis on creativity?

The priority of creativity in the curriculum stems partially from the *Melbourne Declaration* (MCEETYA, 2008). One of the aims outlined in the *Melbourne Declaration* document (MCEETYA, 2008, p. 8) is the development of "confident and creative individuals" who, as successful learners, "are creative, innovative and resourceful, and are able to solve problems". This idea of creativity as innovation or the ability to "approach problem-solving in new and creative ways" (MCEETYA, 2008, p. 5) is often seen as a solution to future local and global challenges of the 21st century (see Sawyer, 2014). The focus on creativity can therefore be considered a "fundamental attribute to enable adaptation and response in a fast-changing world" (Craft, 2003, p. 114). Continual renewal, revival and innovation, which might be clustered under the one heading "creativity", are seen as an integral part of a nation's economic success. Consequently, creativity is perceived as an employability skill able to address the fast-changing world of technology and job markets (see Gale, 2006; Harris, 2014; Pisanu & Menapace, 2014). The idea is that increasing students' creative capacity enhances the skills necessary to secure the economy of the future (see Gale, 2006; Harris, 2014).

The working paper by the Organisation for Economic Co-operation and Development (OECD) – *Progression in student creativity in school: First steps towards new forms of formative assessments* (Lucas, Claxton, & Spencer, 2013, p. 5) – highlights the typically fervent nature of the discourse surrounding creativity in schools, stating:

> Most people agree that schools need to develop creativity in students just as much as they need to produce literate and numerate learners. Yet across the educational world there is no widely used definition of what creativity is, no agreed framework for assessing its development in schools and few assessment tools specifically designed to track learners' progress … If creativity is to be taken more seriously by educators and educational policy-makers then we need to be clearer about what it is. We also need to develop an approach to assessing it which is both rigorous enough to ensure credibility and user-friendly enough to be used by busy teachers.

This excerpt also highlights the connection in contemporary educational practices between teaching students to think, including creative thinking, and improving educational outcomes (Maclure & Davies, 1991). In education, creativity has long been linked with knowledge, learning and problem solving and there have been a number of attempts to pin down a definition of creativity in ways that allow it to be teachable but also assessable. In order to find a viable definition of creativity, it is often assumed that the definition must offer a quantifiable framework that affords the assessment of the thinking process and the resultant, tangible, outcome. And yet despite the emphasis on creativity both globally (see OECD, 2014) and within Australia (see De Bortoli & Macaskill, 2014) there is little agreement on the nature of creativity in the significant body of literature exploring creativity, its meaning and application in education.

What counts as creativity in the Australian Curriculum?

The background documents of *General capabilities: critical and creative thinking* (ACARA, n.d.b) construct creativity as a skill that can be taught, with an emphasis on hypothesising and exploring possibilities in terms of solutions to problems. In the Australian Curriculum at present, creative thinking is categorised in the curriculum documents as one of seven general capabilities, grouping together critical and creative thinking. Underpinning the rationale for the *General capabilities: critical and creative thinking* are the concepts of productivity, innovation and problem solving. In fact, the Victorian Curriculum (VCAA, n.d.b, paragraph 7) makes the distinction between creativity and creative thinking, whereby "creative expression, creative endeavour and creative collaboration, are included in other learning areas and capabilities". Without making the distinction so explicit the Australian Curriculum capability descriptors similarly focus on creative thinking, stating that:

> By applying a sequence of thinking skills, students develop an increasingly sophisticated understanding of the processes they can employ whenever they encounter problems, unfamiliar information and new ideas.

(ACARA, n.d.b)

These definitions have been informed partially by some common frameworks used frequently throughout schools, namely de Bono's lateral thinking (2002) and Bloom's taxonomy (1956). It is interesting to note that while these frameworks are widely used in schools and are cited in the background documents for the *General capabilities: Critical and creative thinking* in the Australian Curriculum (ACARA, n.d.b), there are very few empirical studies that explore the effectiveness of such frameworks in teaching, enhancing and reliably assessing creativity. However, as they are both widely used and referenced in the Australian and Victorian curriculums, the definitions of creativity or creative thinking are worth consideration.

Creative thinking and de Bono's lateral thinking

de Bono (2002) argues that the purpose of the human brain "is to make stable patterns for dealing with a stable universe" (p. 2) by allowing "incoming information to organise itself into sequences or patterns" (p. 3) rather than considering "all possibilities at every point" (p. 6). Instead of this type of "what is" thinking, he proposes an alternative type of thinking, "what can be" thinking (p. 5). "What can be" thinking suggests moving from the well-worn thinking tracks and forging new patterns and "side tracks" that can result in an idea that is not immediately obvious but logical in retrospect. It is this combination of creative ideas and logic – divergent and convergent thinking respectively – that is the basis for de Bono's concept of lateral thinking. One way to engage in lateral thinking is the use of provocations. Provocations are distinct from brainstorming where "anything which is remotely logical … becomes a reality" (de Bono, 1986, p. 58). Provocations are a "deliberate and defined" (de Bono, 1986, p. 58) approach to exploring ideas, resulting in viable alternative possibilities. In order to accomplish what de Bono refers to as "what can be" thinking, he advocates a "think slow" approach, in other words, using extended periods of time to carefully consider all plausible ideas. This is another distinction from brainstorming and other models of creative thinking, which value a high fluency rate, that is, a large number of ideas in a short amount of time regardless of the plausibility of the ideas. In the think slow approach the thinker's attitudinal approach to thinking is changed to see thinking fast as a shortfall, avoiding jumping to conclusions, rather focusing on "extracting the maximum from one's own thinking and the thinking of others" (de Bono, 1986, p. 61). de Bono reasons that the slow thinker is more likely to reach the ideal solution to the problem, if more than a couple obvious solutions exists.

Creativity and Bloom's taxonomy

de Bono's concept of lateral thinking focuses on the creative thinking process in order to produce a viable and "unique" solution. Yet Bloom's (1956) taxonomy – a common framework applied in many schools to curriculum, task and assessment design – places emphasis on the product. The design of the original taxonomy was to help the broadening of educational goals, and develop a precision in specifying objectives that results in "easier to plan learning experiences and [preparation of] evaluation devices" (Bloom, 1956, p. 2). There is an emphasis on the preciseness of language in the assessment of the thinking process and as such the basis of the taxonomy is the "the *intended behaviour* of students – the ways in which individuals are to act, think, or feel as the result of participating in some unit of instruction" (Bloom, 1956, p. 12, author's emphasis). More recently, within a classroom context, the category of "create" (relabelled from Bloom's original category "synthesis" by Krathwohl, Anderson, & Bloom, 2001) emphasises that:

> Students should be able to synthesize material into a whole ... the student must draw upon elements from many sources and put them together into a novel structure or pattern relative to his or her own prior knowledge. *Create* results in a new product, that is, something that can be observed and that is more than the student's beginning materials.
>
> (Krathwohl et al., 2001, p. 85)

This definition of creativity clearly emphasises the result of creative thought processes similar to de Bono; the process of "synthesis" or "create" is incomplete until action is taken, the emphasis and therefore the evidence of creativity lies in the creative product, not just the creative thought process.

Exploring English teachers' perceptions of creativity

I mentioned in the introduction that the changing educational landscape and need for assessment and measurement had prompted rich reflection on my part. This resulted in asking questions such as: What does it mean to be a "creative" teacher? What place does creativity have in education? And how do you assess students' creativity? It became apparent in asking these questions that there may be a difference in how teachers understand and perceive creativity and the ways creativity is presented in the curriculum and policy documents. I was interested, for the most part, in the ways in which English teachers' beliefs and understandings of creativity were shaped by their teaching context – classroom and school culture as well as the educational policy and curriculum – and subsequently the way their understandings of creativity shaped their teaching practice – the types of work and assessment with which the students engaged.

Given the complex nature of creativity and teacher practice, and the influence of beliefs on practice, I decided to take a qualitative approach to the research, acknowledging that "worlds are multi-layered with many levels of interacting structures ongoing simultaneously" (Cupchik, 2001, p. 3). In order to explore these multi-layered worlds, I chose first to focus on English teachers, as an English teacher myself, and second to use narrative-based inquiry as it is "well suited to addressing the complexities and subtleties of the human experience in teaching and learning" (Webster & Mertova, 2007, p. 1).

Generating the data

Across the study there were 11 English teachers who participated in the research from a range of sectors, including government, independent and supplementary education (an educational context that is not bound by all of the typical institutional structures of formal schools; see Myers & Grosvenor, 2011). The narratives were generated from a combination of semi-structured interviews conducted before and after classroom observations.

The semi-structured interviews established an in-depth understanding of the complexities and nuances of the English teachers' understandings of creativity. The priority in the semi-structured interviews was "to keep the interview as close to a natural conversation as possible" (Csikszentmihalyi, 1996, p. 16). While the interviews were designed to take approximately 30 minutes, many participants chose to expand on their responses, sharing examples of their practice and discussing student work. These stories of classroom practices, taken from the transcripts of the interviews, along with the classroom observations, became the basis for the construction of cases.

The classroom observations provided an opportunity to observe teacher practice and the ways creativity is enacted in the classroom. The classroom observations were conducted in one lesson, as nominated by the participants. During the observations, I generated notes on the activities and discussion that occurred in the classroom, including the way the classroom was arranged and the classroom displays, or lack thereof. The observations often highlighted some of the complexities and tensions around creativity that the teachers had begun to acknowledge themselves throughout the first semi-structured interview. Subsequently, the discussions from the first interview and the classroom observations were used as part of a facilitated critical reflection in the second semi-structured interview. Using the data – the first semi-structured interview and classroom observations – participants were prompted to reflect on their understandings of creativity and their teaching practice. Once the data were generated, I set about constructing cases that consisted of details of the context of the educational settings and the classrooms, some background on the teachers themselves and a narrative that reconstructed parts of the classroom observation. Below is an example of one of the case studies generated through this research.

A reconstruction of the classroom

As I stated above, there were 11 participants in the study, but for the purposes of this discussion I would like to focus on Sarah. Sarah is the Head of English at a moderately high socio-economic status and academically focused school in the eastern suburbs of Melbourne. She has been at the school for over ten years and has been in the Head of English role for just over a term. Through her interviews she weaves in anecdotes of the school's work expectations – staff meetings frequently include audits of students' books examining the quantity of writing students have completed – and there is a whole-school focus on literacy, which several members of the English faculty are spearheading. The class she invites me to see is a Year 9 English class towards the middle of term two. Sarah refers to this class as her "lively little bugs", but she also laments the fact she is still getting to know them as her teaching situation is less than ideal. Sarah explains that she has, on a number of occasions, been taken out of her class to attend to her leading teacher role and therefore she does not feel she knows them as well as she should nor does she feel that the class is as prepared as they could be for their upcoming creative writing outcome. There is also the added issue that Sarah has taken on the "split" double – two lessons on a Tuesday, one in the morning and one in the afternoon – meaning that the lessons are even more disjointed than a "normal" timetable allocation.

Case 1 – Sarah's lively little bugs

It is midterm two, late Tuesday afternoon. Sarah is about to teach her lively little bugs, her Year 9's who, by her own admission, she is still getting to know. The faculty, in their planning at the end of the year, had decided to use a series of short stories in order to investigate setting, characterisation and narrative/character voice. Today's story was about character construction that will eventually lead to a creative response – a story from an alternative perspective, a descriptive piece or a newspaper feature article. I (Narelle) place myself somewhere towards the front of the room along the side of the U-shape; students casually come in, a few sit beside me and begin talking to Sarah.

Students: (Talking across each other) You're here Miss? Where were you this morning? Can you get someone good to cover next time? Will you be in class tomorrow?

Sarah: What did you do?

Students: (Only a couple of students respond) Not really that much. What were we supposed to do?

(Sarah spends some time explaining what the lesson should have been and how she will alter her lesson sequence to make sure students don't miss out on anything important. As a class they begin reading through 'Breakfast', a short story centred on a nameless female character whom is trying to feed her family breakfast in the aftermath of a nuclear holocaust. The lesson follows a familiar beat – read part of the story, ask questions, clarify information, read some more, repeat. Adorning the walls of the classroom are the literacy strategies Sarah is using, giving students and staff colourful reminders of what they "should" be doing, if perchance their eyes happened to glance in the direction of the posters and can make out what is written on them. The students continue to scribble annotations on their handouts.)

Travis: She's sick.
Sarah: Why do you think that is?
Travis: She's talking to dead people.
Sarah: What do you mean?
Travis: Sick as in psycho Miss. Well, sick as well, but psycho.
Violet: What do new-clear bombs do?
Brad: Explode!

(The class begins to snigger, not at the mispronunciation of "nuclear" but more Brad's blunt and honest response. Brad looks perplexed, he can't seem to figure out why the class thought his response was funny. He moves on, launching into a brief historical account of nuclear war. Sarah moves the class on to the next page.)

> Sarah: Remember to make annotations.
> Students: (Talking across each other) It's not very good. It's not really clear what's going on. Are they dead or alive?
> Brad: There are too many unanswered questions. I don't like these short stories. I'm left with too many questions.
> Narelle: (I momentarily step out of my role as observer) What is a good number of questions to be left with?
> Brad: A few questions are okay as long as they are not important ones.
>
> *(Brad begins to circle back to his discussion of nuclear war.)*
>
> Brad: Is this the 1950s and historically based or is it a futuristic nuclear war?
>
> Sarah: Why?
> Brad: That would change things.
> Sarah: How?
> Brad: I don't know, but it would.
>
> (Sarah directs the class to continue the discussion in their assigned literacy-circle groups. Brad's group gets straight to work. A couple of groups settle on talking about the weekend as they play with, and try to steal, the kinaesthetic toys that are flipping and flying around the classroom. A female student glances around the room, rolls her eyes and settles in to working independently, despite the presence of her group at her table. Three boys at the back of the room shuffle stationery backwards and forwards on their miniature toy skateboards until finally Travis, the owner of the travelling pencil case, looks up.)
>
> Travis: (Yelling) Hey Miss, was that chick alive or dead in the end?
> Sarah: What evidence can you find in the text?
>
> (Travis begins flipping through the story presumably looking for evidence. The group sitting by the back door slowly edge their chairs closer to the open door.)

Analysing the data through exploring what counts as creativity

The narrative above may not look like "typical" evidence in an empirical study and some may dismiss it as "subjective" and merely "anecdotal" (Doecke, 2013, p. 12). But as already discussed, narrative-based inquiry provides opportunities to surface some of the complexities in teaching that may not be evident in a quantitative approach. For instance, a possible way of approaching the analysis could be to identify to what degree de Bono's lateral thinking (2002) or Bloom's (1956) taxonomy is evident in the work in which the students are engaging. In terms of de Bono's lateral thinking there is arguably little evidence of "what can be" thinking. An argument could perhaps be made that Travis is engaging in "what can be" thinking in considering whether the "chick" was either dead or alive; he is slower to begin work and this may be interpreted as evidence of de Bono's "think slow" approach, and Travis may even be able to find evidence to support either or both interpretations of whether the female character was alive or dead in the end. But Travis, and Brad in his questioning of the date of the setting and the resolution of the story, is seeking absolutes. He wants to know the "right" answer. It is a clear example of "what is" thinking and this is perhaps not surprising given Sarah's comments in her first interview, stating that:

> The expectations on students in our subject [English] really limits their ability to go outside any box. You know, creative answers to questions aren't always necessarily rewarded as there's a certain response that's being looked for ... And we kind of taught them to be that way, and we're seeing that very much, even in just the simplest things.

Sarah articulates an interesting tension between the work she is doing within her classroom and the possibility for creative thinking within the subject. The analysis work that the students are engaged in is seen in terms of right or wrong, and yet this analysis work has been set to help inform the students' creative responses. However, even the extended creative responses themselves have been limited to particular types of genres and therefore further direct students to be creative in particular kinds of ways. If we examine the scene according to Bloom's taxonomy there is again very little evidence of the concept of how the taxonomy defines "create". There is clearly some synthesis of new ideas and previous experience – Violet's checking of the purpose of "new-clear" bombs and Brad's historical account of nuclear war – but this does not, at least in this class, result in a new or unique tangible product, which is an important aspect of Bloom's definition in both the original iteration and the updated iteration by Krathwohl et al. (2001). Brad, out of all the students, seems to be engaging in work that draws upon his previous experience and knowledge of other areas, but in his answering of questions on the handout, evidence of this prior knowledge is limited as he draws specifically from the text.

On the surface, there is little evidence of creativity through applying the OECD (2014) definition of creativity and creative problem solving. There are no obvious problems for the students to solve and Sarah does not explicitly state any of the activities in terms of problem solving, despite engaging in problem solving herself. She has walked into her class with an expectation to enact her plan for that class, but instead finds herself negotiating a new plan, one that addresses the needs of the curriculum as well as the needs of the students; the curriculum dictating she move on so that the unit is completed in a timely manner and yet the needs of the students demand more time be spent preparing for the assessment task. Sarah does not recognise this as a creative act, commenting in her second interview that it is "just what teachers do". There is also an implicit problem that students are working through, that being how to translate their analysis of the text 'Breakfast' and other short stories into their creative response. The handouts students fill out during the class capture the critical thinking work, but there is no work, at least explicitly, about how this analysis might be translated into the creative response.

Implications for teaching

When discussing the above scene and evidence of creativity with Sarah in the post-observation interview she does not recognise Brad's engagement with the material nor her problem solving as creative acts. Instead, she refers to Brad's comments as "pretty normal for him" and as stated above sees her own negotiation of classroom practice as also normal. As a consequence, for Sarah, creativity seems to be limited to particular types of creative acts, an issue she identifies in her first interview, stating that:

> I think from a teacher point of view, creativity and English can be a little bit stifled. I think a lot of the times we think we're being creative and in terms of our lessons or our teachings, or our approaches. And chances are we probably aren't being as creative as we think we could be. For students, I think it's the same.

This realisation that there may be a disjunction between how we view our teaching practice and the opportunities for creativity in the classroom has some interesting implications. It may, for instance, limit the opportunity for students to be creative in different ways, and/or for Sarah to teach creatively and assess creativity within this class. Furthermore, throughout Sarah's as well as all the other participants' interviews and observations, there is no reference to the types of creativity or creative thinking defined by Bloom (1956), de Bono (2002) or the OECD (2014). Therefore, not only is creativity and creative thinking viewed in particular albeit limited ways, the understandings of creative thinking are not ones that align with the operational definitions that have been afforded by the Australian Curriculum and organisations such as the OECD. The issue does not lie, however, with teacher understandings but with the way creativity and creative thinking have been constructed for particular curriculum outcomes and assessment. While the argument can be made, such as the view presented by Lucas et al. (2013), that focused definitions allow for easier identification and measurement of the concept in question, it also has the paradoxical effect of limiting the opportunities to teach, facilitate and encourage the development of creative skills. As a result, creativity or creative thinking potentially becomes a skill that is taught in distinct areas of the curriculum, or taught out of context devoid of any authentic purpose.

An alternative view of creativity

One possible way to expand the opportunities for teaching creativity and creativity thinking is to broaden the definition of the concept of creativity to encompass other perspectives – for instance, drawing on the view articulated in the literature that meaning making is a creative act (see Yandell, 2006, 2013). Similar in ways to Bloom's (1956) taxonomy construction of creativity, creativity as meaning making allows for students to draw on their previous knowledge and experiences and together with new knowledge and understandings, generate new interpretations and ideas. However, unlike Bloom's taxonomy, there is no need for a product in terms of something tangible or useful. Applying this definition to *Sarah's lively little bugs*, the possibility opens up of seeing this as a class where students and teachers are constantly engaged in creative acts. Take, for example, Brad's comment that "there are too many unanswered questions". In the above analysis drawing on de Bono's concept of lateral thinking, this appears as though Brad is seeking a definitive ending to 'Breakfast'. However, in applying a different framework for analysis, creativity as meaning making, it is possible for Brad's comment to be seen as creating an opportunity for discussion around the structure of short stories and how this might relate to reader interpretation and what constitutes a satisfactory ending. His comment is clearly drawing on his previous experience of and frustration with short stories and there is further potential to see how this critique manifests in his creative response. As another participant in this study states:

> I tend to approach [creativity] in the same way I approach teaching literature, that they [the students] are makers of meaning. And they're not apprenticeships of this subject but that they are contributing to knowledge.
>
> (Louisa, Year 12 literature teacher)

Consequently, classrooms are changed from places where students are assigned creative work under particular conditions to places where creativity – including creative thinking, creative expression, creative endeavour and creative collaboration – is common. This not only fulfils the *Melbourne Declaration*'s goal of developing "confident and creative individuals" (MCEETYA, 2008, p. 7) but also potentially broadens the scope for English teachers to develop their practice in creative ways.

Conclusion

There are many definitions and frameworks of creativity that can be used to analyse both teacher practice and student work. In doing so it is possible to surface and explore many "creative moments" that may otherwise go unrecognised. The broadening view of creativity to encompass creative thinking, problem solving, innovation, imagination, meaning making and other definitions afforded by the extensive body of literature may therefore provide "a brake on simply finding what we already knew/hoped/feared to be happening, and [give] us an opportunity to discover new phenomena or to re-see familiar events in a new light" (Freebody, 2003, p. 50).

References

ACARA (Australian Curriculum, Assessment and Reporting Authority). (n.d.a). *General capabilities: Critical and creative thinking*. Retrieved on October 4, 2017 from: www.australiancurriculum.edu.au/f-10-curriculum/general-capabilities/critical-and-creative-thinking/

ACARA (Australian Curriculum, Assessment and Reporting Authority). (n.d.b). *General capabilities: Critical and creative thinking*. Retrieved on September 22, 2014 from: v7-5.australiancurriculum.edu.au/generalcapabilities/critical-and-creative-thinking/introduction/background

Bloom, B. S. (1956). *Taxonomy of educational objectives: The classification of educational goals*. New York: D. McKay Co.

Craft, A. (2003). The limits to creativity in education: Dilemmas for the educator. *British Journal of Educational Studies*, 51(2), 113-137.

Csikszentmihalyi, M. (1996). *Creativity: Flow and the psychology of discovery and invention*. New York: Harper Collins.

Cupchik, G. (2001). Constructivist realism: An ontology that encompasses positivist and constructivist approaches to the social sciences. *Forum Qualitative Sozialforschung/Forum: Qualitative Social Research*, 2(1). DOI:http://dx.doi.org/10.17169/fqs-2.1.968

de Bono, E. (1986). Ideas about thinking: Excerpts from Edward de Bono's "Letter to Thinkers". *Journal of Product Innovation Management*, 3(1), 57-62.

de Bono, E. (2002). New thinking. *Think*, 1(1), 39-48.

De Bortoli, L, & Macaskill, G. (2014). *Thinking it through: Australian students' skills in creative problem solving*. Camberwell: Australian Council for Educational Research.

Doecke, B. (2013). Storytelling and professional learning. *English in Australia*, 48(2), 11-21.

Freebody, P. R. (2003). *Qualitative research in education*. Introducing Qualitative Methods series. London; Thousand Oaks, CA; New Delhi: SAGE Publications.

Gale, T. (2006). How did we ever arrive at the conclusion that teachers are the problem? A critical reading in the discourses of Australian schooling. In B. Doecke, M. Howie, & W. Sawyer (Eds.), *Only connect* (pp. 99-121). South Australia: Wakefield Press.

Harris, A. (2014). *The creative turn: Toward a new aesthetic imaginary*. Rotterdam, The Netherlands: Sense Publishers.

Krathwohl, D., Anderson, L., & Bloom, B. (2001). *A taxonomy for learning, teaching and assessing: A revision of Bloom's taxonomy of educational objectives* (Abridged ed.). New York: Longman.

Lucas, B., Claxton, G., & Spencer, E. (2013). *Progression in student creativity in school: First steps towards new forms of formative assessments*. OECD Education Working Papers, No. 86. OECD Publishing.

Maclure, S, & Davies, P. (1991). *Learning to think: Thinking to learn. The proceedings of the 1989 OECD conference*. Oxford: Pergamon Press.

Ministerial Council on Education, Employment, Training and Youth Affairs. (2008). *Melbourne Declaration on Educational Goals for Young Australians*. Retrieved on January 1, 2018 from: www.mceetya.edu.au/mceetya/melbourne_declaration

Myers, K., & Grosvenor, I. (2011). Exploring supplementary education: Margins, theories and methods. *History of Education: Journal of the History of Education Society, 40*(4), 501-520.

OECD (Organisation for Economic Co-operation and Development). (2014). *PISA 2012 results: Creative problem solving: Students' skills in tackling real-life problems* (Vol. V): OECD Publishing.

Ozga, J. (2009). Governing education through data in England: From regulation to self-evaluation. *Journal of Education Policy, 24*(2), 149-162.

Pisanu, F., & Menapace, P. (2014). Creativity and innovation: Four key issues from a literature review. *Creative Education, 5*(3), 145-154.

Sawyer, W. (2014). Polic(y)ing creativity. In B. Doecke, G. Parr, & W. Sawyer (Eds.), *Language and creativity in contemporary English classrooms* (pp. 17-33). Putney, Australia: Phoenix Education.

VCAA (Victorian Curriculum and Assessment Authority). (n.d.a). T*he Victorian curriculum: Critical and creative thinking*. Retrieved on October 4, 2017 from: victoriancurriculum.vcaa.vic.edu.au/critical-and-creative-thinking/introduction/rationale-and-aims

VCAA (Victorian Curriculum and Assessment Authority). (n.d.b). The Victorian Curriculum: Critical and creative thinking – Learning in critical and creative thinking. Retrieved on October 4, 2017 from: victoriancurriculum.vcaa.vic.edu.au/critical-and-creative-thinking/introduction/learning-in-critical-and-creative-thinking

Webster, L., & Mertova, P. (2007). *Using narrative inquiry as a research method: An introduction to using critical event narrative analysis in research on learning and teaching*. London: Routledge.

Yandell, J. (2006). Class readers: Exploring a different *View from the Bridge. Changing English, 13*(3), 319-334.

Yandell, J. (2013). The social construction of meaning: Reading *Animal Farm* in the classroom. *Literacy, 47*(1), 1-6.

14 Digital technology and learning

Amber McLeod

Introduction

To understand why information and communication technologies (ICT) could "transform education", the affordances of technology need to be explored. Technologies are tools that allow us to perform complex tasks more efficiently or effectively. For example, a telescope allows us to see further than we could with the naked eye and an electric mixer can whip cream faster than hand whisking. Technology also allows access to previously exclusive areas: in the past most people could not have attempted tasks such as making movies, but now film, edit and publish routinely using their smartphones. We also have unprecedented access to the most recent information: in the past a school project on Peru may have required students to spend hours in the library finding and reading dated books, but today, the Internet allows instant access to the most recent information including government websites, videos, online TV and radio stations, and even access to local Peruvians themselves on social media. The more advanced our technology becomes, the less time we spend gathering information and performing routine tasks, allowing us to spend the time on more advanced and imaginative pursuits. Learners are able to concentrate on developing higher order thinking skills (Alexander et al., 2013; Loveless, Burton, & Turvey, 2006).

Many of these skills that ICT apparently encourages are considered important for understanding of content and are also attractive to employers: thinking in critical and creative ways; being resourceful and showing initiative; and being able to solve problems that draw upon a range of learning areas and disciplines (MCEETYA, 2008). In this study, Kolb's (1984) experiential learning cycle (situated in constructionist thinking) was used to guide pre-service teachers (PSTs) in the creation of digital objects. Their reflections on the task were analysed to investigate their thoughts on the potential of ICT to develop deeper understanding of content knowledge and transferable skills in learners.

Literature review

Digital technologies are so pervasive that it is hard to imagine an education that does not include them. It has been argued that basic digital literacy, which has been described as a part of "multiliteracy" (The New London Group, 1996) or "new literacy" (Knobel & Lankshear, 2014), is, in fact, just literacy. More and more public (and private) services are increasing online accessibility and reducing face to face interaction and "digital interactions have now been mandated as the primary form of interaction for 80% of government services by 2017" (Australian Government Department of Health, 2013, p. 19). If school graduates are unable to access basic information can they truly be considered literate? The Australian Prime Minister, Malcolm Turnbull, answers this, declaring digital literacy to be as "fundamental as reading and writing" (Swan, 2015). It is often assumed that children who were born after digital technologies began appearing in homes and schools are naturally able to use technology. Prensky's (2001) term "digital native" gained currency when he suggested that young people had a common way of learning which was different to earlier generations. Despite many findings that this is a myth, the idea persists (Duncan-Howell, 2012; Margaryan, Littlejohn, & Vojt, 2011) and ICT is not always taught explicitly in schools. Indeed, the most recent National Assessment Program (NAP) ICT results indicate that only 52% of Year 10 students reached the proficiency level – a statistically significant drop from the previous results (NAP, 2015).

Transferrable skills (sometimes called 21st-century skills, applied skills or enterprise skills) are a list of skills currently deemed important for success in society and sought by employers and align closely with the higher order thinking skills desired for deep understanding of content knowledge. Knobel and Lankshear (2014, p. 101) suggest that developing "new literacies" (which includes digital literacy) will ready students "for a world in which there are few constants [as] the near future will involve artefacts, social relations, processes, routines … and practices barely imaginable now". After viewing 4.2 million Australian job advertisements, the Foundation for Young Australians (FYA) (FYA, 2015a) decided upon a list of such skills that includes problem solving, creativity, communications, teamwork, financial literacy, digital literacy, critical thinking and presentation skills. The increase in demand by employers over three years was highest for creativity (65%), critical thinking (158%) and digital literacy (212%) (FYA, 2015a). Results from another FYA (2015b) report indicated that the percentages of young Australians with low proficiency in problem solving (35%), digital literacy (27%) and financial literacy (29%), coupled with the NAP-ICT results discussed earlier, do not bode well for the future. FYA (2015b, p. 5) recommends schools develop transferrable skills in students "in ways that young people want to learn: through experience, immersion and with peers" and "engage students, schools, industry and parents in co-designing opportunities in and outside the classroom".

The question underpinning this research was: What is the best way to encourage teachers to consider the significance and potential of ICT in education?

Theoretical approach

To successfully integrate ICT in education, the relationship of the technology to the content of the lesson, the pedagogical approach desired and the context of the learning environment need to be considered. Mishra and Koehler (2006, p. 1018) recognised that "developing theory for educational technology is difficult because it requires a detailed understanding of complex relationships that are contextually bound". The TPACK model (Mishra & Koehler, 2006; Thompson & Mishra, 2007) is a conceptual framework which illustrates how the use

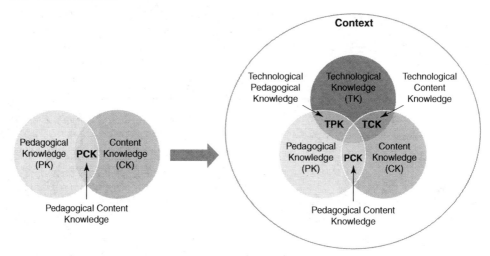

Figure 14.1 Adapted from Shulman (1986) and Mishra and Koehler's model (2006)

of technology adds to Shulman's (1986) model of pedagogical and content knowledge and helps us visualise where technology fits in our lessons. The evolution of Shulman's model into Mishra and Koehler's model is illustrated in Figure 14.1.

While technological knowledge has always been a part of teaching (e.g., a pencil or a microscope), it was not emphasised until digital technologies became prominent (Mishra & Koehler, 2006). Along with the Pedagogical Knowledge (PK), Content Knowledge (CK) and Pedagogical Content Knowledge (PCK) from the Shulman (1986) model, the TPACK model introduces Technological Knowledge (TK: knowing how to operate technology), Technological Content Knowledge (TCK: an understanding of how subject information and technology are related), Technological Pedagogical Knowledge (TPK: an understanding of how technology can be used in ways that emphasise different learning and educational theories) and Technological Pedagogical Content Knowledge (TPACK). TPACK is more than the sum of its parts and "represents a class of knowledge that is central to teachers' work with technology" (Mishra & Koehler, 2006, p. 1028).

While there are a wide range of learning theories that can be used with technology, consideration of the affordances of ICT need to be juxtaposed with the aim of the lesson. The same technology may be used for a number of different content areas and in varying contexts, and can be adapted for use with a variety of learning and education theories. For example, Behaviourism is reflected in an application that teaches times tables using online drills. Skinner (1958, p. 971) mentioned "teaching machines" as "devices which arrange optimal conditions for self-instruction". Drawing on constructivist ideas developed by Piaget (1952) and Vygotsky (1978), if the drills are in the form of a game – for example, a real-time mathematics race against online students from all over the world – it could be regarded as game-based learning (Jong, Shang, & Lee, 2010). Alternatively, rewarding students' efforts in online drills with game-like elements, such as virtual money for an online shop, is an example of gamification, where students are not playing a game, but game-design elements and principles are used (Wiggins, 2016; Gee & Hayes, 2013). Constructivism can also be seen in an online mathematics program that presents increasingly more difficult questions to determine the student's "zone of proximal development" and provides a "more knowledgeable other" in the form of animated online examples (Cicconi, 2014; Gee & Hayes, 2013).

Seymour Papert, a mathematian, educator and scientist, worked closely with Piaget and later developed a theory called constructionism, the theoretical basis of this study, which has close parallels with constructivism (Beisser & Gillespie, 2003). Similar to constructivism, learners actively build their own internal knowledge structures and view the world through these structures, which are tested and elaborated upon, using support and scaffolding from social contexts, until a satisfactory construct is formed (Thorsteinsson & Page, 2007). Unlike constructivism, in constructionism learners are encouraged to construct a product which then makes their knowledge structures public (Bruckman & Resnick, 1995; Papert & Harel, 1991). This allows learners to hear feedback on their knowledge structures and reflect and consider their constructs, perhaps reconstructing them. While this theory of learning can be applied more widely than with ICT, Papert had a strong interest in this area where students create, for example, their own computer games.

Examples of constructionism in action are student-centred approaches that allow students to use technology together in groups to create solutions for cross-discipline, real world problems and disseminate solutions to wide audiences who can react and comment, giving instant feedback (Knobel & Lankshear, 2014; Curwood, Magnifico, & Lammers, 2013). The students are motivated because their individual interests and skills are valued and they are doing something with visible impact in real time rather than a classroom simulation. A quick look at the media over the last few years reveals that students are already taking advantage of the affordances of technology when given the opportunity. One celebrated example was of 17-year-old Sydney Grammar School students, supported by chemists in an online research-sharing platform, producing the key ingredient in an expensive anti-malaria drug in their school science laboratory for $20 (Hunjan, 2016).

In this study, PSTs were asked to work in groups to create a personally meaningful product, a digital learning resource, which they would be able to use in their first year of teaching. It was hoped that PSTs would engage in a constructionist experience where they learnt from interaction with their peers, and co-constructed knowledge required. Kolb's (1984) experiential learning cycle (Figure 14.2), situated in constructionism, was chosen to guide the PSTs through a learner-centred experience ensuring that support and scaffolding from peers was available and reflection was highlighted.

Experiential learning theory places experience at the centre of learning and describes learning as "the process whereby knowledge is created through the transformation of experience" (Kolb, 1984, p. 38). Kolb and Fry (1975) argue that learners will enter the cycle at different points depending on their preferences, but the learning process involves a continuous cycle of a Concrete Experience (doing a task), Reflective Observation (reflecting on the task done and considering generalisation), Abstract Conceptualisation (making sense of what happened or devising a general principle), and Active Experimentation (putting what was learnt into practice, often in a new circumstance). Kolb (1984) emphasises the point that linking past experience with new concepts through reflection is needed for learning to occur.

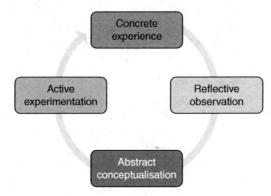

Figure 14.2 Experiential learning cycle (adapted from Kolb, 1984)

Methodology

While ICT is not always used well in education, the premise of this study is that when used in a considered way, it can help develop deeper understanding of content knowledge and transferrable skills. The background question that guided this study concerned how best we encourage teachers to consider the significance and potential of ICT in education. More specifically, this study investigated the following research question:

> When provided the opportunity to create their own digital learning objects, did PSTs see potential in digital technology to develop deeper understanding of content knowledge and transferable skills?

Participants, method and data collection and analysis

The cohort was 28 fourth and final year undergraduate PSTs and the task was from a pedagogy unit entitled "Practical learning". For their first assignment, PSTs wrote an academic essay on the benefits of practical learning. In the second assignment, groups of three or four were required to put their understanding of practical learning into practice and create and present a digital resource that could be used to teach their discipline to a Year 9 or Year 10 class and embodied the learning outcomes of the unit. Examples might include posters with QR codes that link to online quizzes or activities; computer games; webpages; videos; or blogs. Although some examples were given, there were no restrictions on the type of digital object that could be created.

The task was designed to incorporate transferrable skills, more specifically: creativity and ICT skills (required to make the digital object), communication and teamwork (PSTs were working in groups), presentation skills and critical thinking (PSTs were required to present their object and explain the connections to the unit content and to the Australian Professional Standards for Teachers (AITSL, 2014), and the Victorian Curriculum (VCAA, n.d.). A critical analysis of the digital object, using the SAMR model (Puentedura, 2010), was also required.

Finally, PSTs were asked to individually write a 500-word reflection on creating the resource. This formed the data for this study. Thematic analysis of the reflections was conducted. The task is outlined in terms of Kolb's experiential learning cycle in Table 14.1.

Table 14.1 Description of the task using Kolb's experiential learning cycle

Cycle stages	Description of task
Abstract conceptualisation	Grasping the theoretical content: Engaging with the theoretical content of the unit, in recognition that experience alone does not necessarily lead to learning or mean that learning will take place. PSTs attended class, participated in discussion and did readings. For their first assignment, PSTs wrote an essay explaining their understanding of the theory of the unit content.
Active experimentation	Coming up with the idea for a digital resource: PSTs were asked to work in groups to use ICT to begin putting their understanding of the theoretical content into practice. In this first step they had to explain their idea to the tutor and decide on which tools they would use to create the digital resource.
Concrete experience	Developing the resource: PSTs worked together to create the digital object.
Reflective observation	Trialling the resource: Each group trialled their object with peers and received feedback.
Abstract conceptualisation	Rethinking the resource: PSTs considered the feedback from the trial and discussed whether they thought changes should be made.
Active experimentation	Modifying the resource: PSTs redesigned their object to meet their new ideas of what the object should be.
Concrete experience	Presenting the resource: PSTs gave a demonstration of the finished product to peers.
Reflective observation	Reflecting upon their understanding: PSTs reflected upon "whether making something has helped you (a) engage more deeply with the content of this unit and (b) gain an understanding of AITSL standards".

Results and discussion

The results and a discussion of the findings are presented together in this section. A description of the themes which emerged from an analysis of the reflections is presented in three parts. First, findings from the PSTs' reflections on whether making digital objects help learners engage more deeply with the content of this unit (including an understanding of the Australian Institute for Teaching and School Leadership [AITSL] standards) are presented. This is followed by an analysis of the reflections in terms of the potential for learners to develop transferrable skills when using ICT. Finally, general comments from the PSTs about digital technology in education are presented.

Deeper understanding of the content of the unit

The PSTs' reflections showed strong agreement that creating and presenting the digital object had helped them engage more deeply with the content of the unit. While all PSTs inferred that they gained a deeper understanding of the unit content, 25 explicitly stated this. For example:

> When coding a program, students will have a better understanding of a topic or concept as it makes them critically think and evaluate their progress (as it did for me).

> By actually going through the process of making a digital resource I have definitely engaged more deeply with the content of this unit.

While all AITSL standards were mentioned, predictably, most PSTs (20) mentioned that engaging in the task had allowed them a better understanding of Standard 2 (know the content and how to teach it), specifically 2.6 (implement teaching strategies for using ICT to expand curriculum learning opportunities for students), as typified by this comment:

> Prior to beginning this task, I had not realised how frequently ICT was included in the AITSL standards. This emphasis on ICT serves to remind me of the significance of using such technology in the classroom, as well as how it may be used – as a resource to teach content knowledge or discipline-specific skills, or to teach the importance of safe ICT use – an important skill that students will need for their lives beyond the classroom.

While only 11 PSTs explicitly mentioned AITSL Standard 1 (know students and how they learn), or more specifically 1.2 (understand how students learn), it emerged as a strong theme as PSTs described a better understanding of what the learner might be experiencing, which influenced the digital object they ultimately created. Typical comments included:

> One of the key reasons I felt more equipped to answer this standard was because by creating the digital resource I was compelled to put myself in the seat of the learner.

> Although I have been a student for the last four years, this felt like the first time I compared my own feelings to what student thoughts might be if I had them embark on such an intensive creative task.

Three PSTs provided evidence of the development of deeper understanding of specific discipline knowledge through the process of creating the digital object. For example:

> I learnt an incredible amount about this period in history. This is in spite of the fact that I am a self-confessed history buff, and prior to beginning our timeline considered myself to be quite well read on the topic.

A final theme to emerge was the recognition that using ICT was motivating for many PSTs and higher engagement with the task had led to deeper understanding of the content. PSTs could also see the potential for using ICT to engage their own students in the future, for example:

> I believe the experience I have had ... has significantly developed my ability to see the potential of simple, previously bland lessons to become a much more interactive, engaging and motivating task with the help of ICT.

> This has allowed me to understand that by giving students access to coding programs, students will be far more engaged and motivated to learn as they will have the control over how the information is presented, as I experienced when I stepped into the role of a learner.

> Previously I had not realised how ICT may assist in encouraging students to a deeper level of thinking, I had seen it purely as a superficial engagement tool.

These findings suggest that PSTs had indeed considered the potential for digital technologies in education to develop deeper understanding of content knowledge.

The development of transferrable skills

There was recognition by PSTs that the task required the use of transferrable skills. Given the structure of the task, it was unsurprising that ICT, teamwork, collaboration and communication skills were the most often discussed. Problem solving, presentation and leadership skills were also mentioned. The development of critical thinking was mentioned in terms of the critical analysis required. Surprisingly, although three PSTs used the term "creative" when describing the task, none mentioned the development of creativity. Loveless et al. (2006, p. 4) suggest that creativity is often "perceived as 'having good ideas' or 'making pretty things', rather than the challenging, and often painful or frustrating experience that characterizes the practices of creative people – the 'hard fun' and the 'flow'". It is therefore possible that PSTs did not recognise the development of their creative skills as they were not aware they were being developed. While many PSTs indicated that their transferrable skills had been enhanced by the experience, others realised they had overestimated their ICT competence. A common comment was that working in groups allowed PSTs to learn from and support one another in terms of transferrable skills. Typical comments included:

> I do think my ICT skills were a limitation at times. However, I learnt a great deal from my group members about ICT platforms and skills.
>
> Before being set this assignment, I had never had any experience with coding or knowledge of what it involves. As we progressed through the weeks, my group found that coding is far more difficult and time consuming than we had initially intended.

A few PSTs reflected on how they anticipated that setting a similar task for their own students would develop transferrable skills, for example:

> I would be confident that they would be engaged in the task and effectively learning not only content knowledge, but practical history skills (such as research methodology, critical thinking and analysis) and ICT skills (such as responsible use of ICT, resource-checking and understanding how to embed files in a document or presentation).

This was accompanied by a recognition of the importance of transferrable skills for themselves as graduate teachers, but also for their own students' lives beyond the classroom. Typical comments included:

> More than ever, I believe the skills of critical analysis, evaluation and creation are important for teachers to possess because these skills enable teachers to measure the usefulness of resources in helping students to achieve challenging learning goals.
>
> Creating this resource also required a lot of thought and negotiation within our groups. This allowed me to interact with colleagues and negotiate our roles. This helped me a lot as in many cases, teachers are involved in team-teaching where they need to be able to communicate and negotiate effectively with others involved.

These findings suggest that through participation in this task, PSTs saw the potential for digital technologies in terms of developing transferrable skills and an increased understanding of why that was relevant to education.

General comments

Some PSTs included reflections that indicated a consideration of the significance of ICT in education. This was often framed as a growing confidence to incorporate ICT in their own classes, particularly as they had been required to use critical analysis to consider the pedagogical worth of the objects they created. The overall impression from the reflections was that PSTs were pleasantly surprised that they were able to complete the task to a level with which they were satisfied. They felt the effort was rewarded. Here is a sample of typical comments:

> While I am confident in using ICT, I don't automatically include it in my lessons – in fact in the past I have struggled to find interesting and relevant ways in which to do so. I have been reluctant to use ICT just for "the sake of it". Being exposed to the SAMR model and having an opportunity to put it into practice has helped me significantly in understanding how ICT may be used effectively in the classroom, as an improvement on some "non-digital" resources.

> It has presented a variety of challenges, such as learning a new online system, linking theory to practice and being intentional about how I am incorporating technology into a lesson.

Finally, on a pedagogical note, one PST illustrated perfectly the intention of the exercise, situated in constructionism, with this comment (emphasis added):

> I feel that I have created something that will be relevant and practical for students *and I am able to see what I have learnt*.

Conclusion

This study employed Kolb's experiential learning cycle to encourage PSTs, through the creation of digital learning objects, to consider the potential of ICT to develop deeper understanding of content knowledge and transferable skills. Following a constructionist approach, this research made learning visible to the PSTs, pointing them to where their understanding was incomplete. Working in social group settings PSTs scaffolded each other's learning, resulting in the development of considered digital learning objects and thoughtful reflections.

As a result, PSTs overwhelmingly suggested that they recognised the potential of ICT to develop deeper understanding of the unit content. They suggested that their own theoretical understanding of the unit had been enhanced when applied to a practical task and they could see clear connections to the AITSL standards, in particular 2.6 (ICT) and 1.2 (understand how students learn). PSTs also saw the potential of ICT to enable their own students to gain deeper knowledge of discipline content by constructing their own digital objects. There was a general consensus, based on PSTs' own experiences, that using ICT increased student motivation and that engagement would lead to better understanding of the discipline content.

In terms of developing transferrable skills, PSTs specifically mentioned the development of their own ICT, teamwork, collaboration, communication, problem solving, critical thinking, presentation and leadership skills. Surprisingly, no PSTs mentioned the development of creativity despite recognising the creative nature of the task. While some PSTs suggested their skills had been improved through participation in the task, others came away with a recognition of where their skills needed improvement (notably, teamwork, collaboration and communication skills). While many PSTs were pleasantly surprised that they were able to develop their ICT skills to a level that allowed the creation of complex digital objects, often with the support of group members, others had not realised the amount of effort required. Finally, PSTs indicated that they felt more confident in using ICT in the classroom, often overcoming a reluctance to use ICT for "the sake of it".

The implications of this research in terms of the broader question, how best we can encourage teachers to consider the significance and potential of ICT in education, are that engaging PSTs in the creation of their own digital learning objects, consistent with a constructionist approach, gives them an experience to reflect upon. Importantly, PSTs should be given more opportunities to develop their ICT and critical analysis skills so that they can recognise appropriate incorporation of ICT in education.

References

Alexander, S., Barnett, D., Mann, S., Mackey, A., Selinger, M., Whitby, G., ... & Griffin, P. (2013). *Beyond the classroom: A new digital education for young Australians in the 21st century*. Digital Education Advisory Group [DEAG], Commonwealth of Australia. Retrieved on February 2, 2018 from: https://docs.education.gov.au/system/files/doc/other/deag_final_report.pdf

Australian Government Department of Health. (2013). *Review of the personally controlled electronic health record*. Retrieved on February 2, 2018 from: https://web.archive.org/web/20170215230128/https://health.gov.au/internet/main/publishing.nsf/Content/17BF043A41D470A9CA257E13000C9322/$File/FINAL-Review-of-PCEHR-December-2013.pdf

AITSL (Australian Institute for Teaching and School Leadership). (2014). *National professional standards for teachers: ICT statements for graduate standards*. Retrieved on February 2, 2018 from: https://www.aitsl.edu.au/teach/standards

Beisser, S., & Gillespie, C. (2003). Kindergarteners can do it – so can you: A case study of a constructionist technology-rich first year seminar for undergraduate college students. *Information Technology in Childhood Education Annual*, 243-260. Retrieved on February 2, 2018 from: https://www.learntechlib.org/f/17766/

Bruckman, A., & Resnick, M. (1995). The MediaMOO project: Constructionism and professional community. *Convergence*, 1(1), 94-109. Retrieved on February 2, 2018 from: https://llk.media.mit.edu/papers/convergence.html

Cicconi, M. (2014). Vygotsky meets technology: A reinvention of collaboration in the early childhood mathematics classroom. *Early Childhood Education Journal*, 42(1), 57-65. DOI:10.1007/s10643-013-0582-9

Curwood, J., Magnifico, A., & Lammers, J. (2013). Writing in the wild: Writers' motivation in fan-based affinity spaces. *Journal of Adolescent & Adult Literacy*, 56(8), 677-685. DOI:10.1002/JAAL.192

Duncan-Howell, J. (2012). Digital mismatch: Expectations and realities of digital competency amongst pre-service education students. *Australasian Journal of Educational Technology*, 28(5), 827-840. DOI:10.14742/ajet.819

Foundation for Young Australians. (2015a). *The new basics. Australia: FYA*. Retrieved on February 2, 2018 from: http://www.fya.org.au/wp-content/uploads/2016/04/The-New-Basics_Web_Final.pdf

FYA (Foundation for Young Australians). (2015b). *The future of work. Australia: FYA*. Retrieved on February 2, 2018 from: http://www.fya.org.au/wp-content/uploads/2015/08/fya-future-of-work-report-final-lr.pdf

Gee, J., & Hayes, E. (2013). Nurturing affinity spaces and game-based learning. In J. Gee, *Good video games + good learning* (2nd ed.) (pp. 103-124). New York: Peter Lang.

Hunjan, R. (2016, Nov 30). Daraprim drug's key ingredient recreated by high school students in Sydney for just $20. ABC news. Retrieved on February 2, 2018 from: http://www.abc.net.au/news/2016-11-30/daraprim-nsw-students-create-drug-martin-shkreli-sold/8078892

Jong, M. S., Shang, J., & Lee, F. (2010). Constructivist learning through computer gaming. In M. Syed (Ed.), *Technologies shaping instruction and distance education: New studies and utilizations* (pp. 207-222). Hershey, PA: IGI Global.

Knobel, M., & Lankshear, C. (2014). Studying new literacies. *Journal of Adolescent & Adult Literacy*, 58(2), 97-101. DOI:10.1002/jaal.314

Kolb, D. A. (1984) *Experiential learning: Experience as the source of learning and development*. Englewood Cliffs, NJ: Prentice Hall.

Kolb, D. A., & Fry, R. (1975). Towards an applied theory of experiential learning. In C. Cooper (Ed.), *Theories of group processes* (pp. 33–57). London: John Wiley and Sons.

Loveless, A., Burton, J., & Turvey, K. (2006). Developing conceptual frameworks for creativity, ICT and teacher education. *Thinking Skills and Creativity*, 1(1), 3–13.

Margaryan, A., Littlejohn, A., & Vojt, G. (2011). Are digital natives a myth or reality? University students' use of digital technologies. *Computers & Education*, 56(2), 429–440. DOI:10.1016/j.compedu.2010.09.004

MCEETYA (Ministerial Council on Education, Employment, Training and Youth Affairs). (2008). *Melbourne declaration on educational goals for young Australians*. Canberra: MCEETYA. Retrieved on February 2, 2018 from: http://www.curriculum.edu.au/verve/_resources/National_Declaration_on_the_Educational_Goals_for_Young_Australians.pdf

Mishra, P., & Koehler, M. (2006). Technological pedagogical content knowledge: A framework for teacher knowledge. *Teachers College Record*, 108(6), 1017–1054. DOI:10.1111/j.1467-9620.2006.00684.x

NAP (National Assessment Program) (2015). *National Assessment Program – ICT Literacy – Years 6 & 10: Report 2014*. Retrieved on February 2, 2018 from: https://www.nap.edu.au/_resources/D15_8761__NAP-ICT_2014_Public_Report_Final.pdf

Papert, S., & Harel, I. (1991). *Constructionism*. New York: Ablex Publishing Corporation.

Piaget, J. (1952) *The origins of intelligence in children*. New York: International Universities Press.

Prensky, M. (2001). Digital natives, digital immigrants. *On the Horizon*, 9(5), 1–6. DOI:10.1108/10748120110424816

Puentedura, R. (2010) *Ruben R. Puentedura's Weblog: Ongoing thoughts on education and technology*. Retrieved on February 2, 2018 from: http://www.hippasus.com/rrpweblog/

Shulman, L. S. (1986). Those who understand: Knowledge growth in teaching. *Educational Researcher*, 15(2), 4–14. DOI:10.3102/0013189X015002004

Skinner, B. F. (1958). Teaching machines. *Science*, 128(3330), 969–977. Retrieved on February 2, 2018 from: http://www.jstor.org/stable/1755240

Swan, D. (2015, June 17). Turnbull says digital literacy 'as important as reading and writing'. *The Australian*. Retrieved on February 2, 2018 from: http://www.theaustralian.com.au/business/technology/turnbull-says-digital-literacy-as-important-as-reading-and-writing/news-story/4edd20335a2341cbe52879b4aef759d1

The New London Group. (1996). A pedagogy of multiliteracies: Designing social futures. *Harvard Educational Review*, 66(1), 60–93. DOI:10.17763/haer.66.1.17370n67v22j160u

Thompson, A., & Mishra, P. (2007). Breaking news: TPCK becomes TPACK! *Journal of Computing in Teacher Education*, 24(2), 38–64.

Thorsteinsson, G., & Page, T. (2007). Creativity in technology education facilitated through virtual reality learning environments: A case study. *i-Manager's Journal of Educational Technology*, 3(4), 74–86. Retrieved on February 2, 2018 from: http://files.eric.ed.gov/fulltext/EJ1069165.pdf

VCAA (Victorian Curriculum and Assessment Authority). (n.d.) *The Victorian Curriculum F-10*. Retrieved on February 2, 2018 from: http://victoriancurriculum.vcaa.vic.edu.au/

Vygotsky, L. S. (1978). *Mind in society: The development of higher psychological processes*. Cambridge, MA: Harvard University Press.

Wiggins, B. E. (2016). An overview and study on the use of games, simulations, and gamification in higher education. *International Journal of Game-Based Learning*, 6(1), 18–29. DOI:10.4018/IJGBL.2016010102

Section III
Navigating structures and tools

15 Education for Sustainability

A priority or an "add on"?

Melissa Barnes, Deborah Moore and Sylvia Almeida

Education for Sustainability in the Australian Curriculum

The term "sustainability" has no "universally accepted" definition (Davis, 2010, p. 2). However, there has been a more recent shift in the use of terminology from purely "Environmental Education" to "Education for Sustainability" to explain the role education plays in encouraging and understanding "sustainable living" as an interdependence between humans, other species and the environment (Davis, 2010, p. 2). In Australia, Education for Sustainability (EfS) has been part of the national agenda for over 30 years (Department of the Environment, Water, Heritage and the Arts, 2009). One of the first major moves towards joining the global trends was in 1984 with the National Conservation Strategy for Australia that focused on educating communities towards sustainable development and conservation (Gough, 2011). The Australian Government set up the national advisory council, network and research program in 2000 in recognition of the need for EfS and to develop policies that are based on sound research based on practice. The *Melbourne Declaration on Educational Goals for Young Australians* (MCEETYA, 2008, p. 4) acknowledged that:

> Complex environmental, social and economic pressures such as climate change that extend beyond national borders pose unprecedented challenges, requiring countries to work together in new ways. To meet these challenges, Australians must be able to engage with scientific concepts and principles, and approach problem-solving in new and creative ways.

The *Melbourne Declaration* set the background for the Australian National Curriculum (ACARA, 2016a, para. 16) which is underpinned by the belief that prioritising sustainability in the curriculum provides students with opportunities to develop an appreciation for "acting for a more sustainable future". Kuzich, Taylor, and Taylor (2015, p. 185) argue, however, that the curriculum reveals "a concerted lack of emphasis on a requirement for teachers to teach 'about' or 'for' sustainability". They argue that this is due to a lack of explicitness of what they are to teach and how they are to teach EfS within the curriculum documents, and suggest therefore that some teachers simply "ignore" EfS, as evident in the following quote:

> Although the Australian Curriculum provides an affordance for EfS, paradoxically it also provides a matching counter-affordance: if teachers are unfamiliar with the intent and purpose of EfS and find it too difficult to identify EfS elements in the curriculum

documents, there is a risk that teachers may choose to ignore EfS, especially if other mandated and assessed priorities compete with EfS. Consequently, the lofty intent of the new Australian Curriculum cross-curricular priority of sustainability may remain largely unrealized.

(Kuzich et al., 2015, p. 186)

Similarly, Kennelly, Taylor, and Serow (2011) suggest that the Australian Curriculum *assumes* all teachers have content knowledge within the field of sustainability, and are therefore able to understand and negotiate how to use the "sustainability icon tags" provided in the Australian Curriculum and link them to the topics they are teaching. It is important to note that these "icon tags" do not elicit reference to specific sustainability themes to focus on or how to teach related concepts and ideas.

To further their understanding of the attitudes, beliefs and experiences of teachers, Kennelly et al. (2011) conducted a case study with five teachers who had full-time teaching positions in New South Wales primary schools and had been teaching for between two and four school terms. In addition to in-depth interviews with the five teachers, interviews were conducted with school principals, other teachers, students and parents. Not surprisingly, prioritising EfS was often overshadowed by a focus on numeracy and literacy, which is a focus of the national assessment program in Australia. NAPLAN (National Assessment Program - Literacy and Numeracy) is an annual assessment taken by students in Years 3, 5, 7 and 9 (ACARA, 2016b). One of the principals interviewed argued that EfS was viewed as an "add-on event" (Kennelly et al., 2011, p. 216), suggesting sustainability is not a priority but rather an option. Another principal experienced pressure for improving numeracy and literacy within the school because this was what he was judged on. In contrast, he felt no pressure to encourage sustainability programs (Kennelly et al., 2011, p. 214).

One senior teacher commented in Kennelly et al.'s (2011, p. 213) study that, "Literacy and maths are our big focus because our NAPLAN results are not as good as they could be and the NAPLAN push is what you hear about and environmental education, I suspect, is at the bottom of the pile". Similarly, Kuzich et al. (2015) explored teacher and school leader perspectives in a school that was purposely designed to be a "sustainability community". However, their study revealed that even in a school with a strong EfS ethos, teachers found it difficult to engage with sustainability in their classrooms due to the pressures relating to NAPLAN testing. A teacher from the school explains:

> Unless you can justify sustainability [as] teaching literacy and numeracy [teachers] don't want a bar of it because they know they are getting assessed on the quality of their job based on their NAPLAN results! Whilst there is a great deal of goodwill within the school towards incorporating sustainability into the curriculum, a number of teachers talked about the priority need for 'results' in literacy and numeracy. Christine felt that the main driver in the school was literacy - not sustainability.

(Kuzich et al., 2015, p. 187)

This suggests that it is testing that often shapes, directs and determines what should be, and in reality what is, taught in the classroom. The current literature on the challenges of prioritising EfS in Australian schools (e.g., Kennelly et al., 2011; Kuzich et al., 2015) proposes that the complexities surrounding curriculum and assessment, as discussed above, play a role in

Education for Sustainability (EfS) 181

how EfS is positioned in Australia. Therefore, teachers' and school leaders' engagement with and promotion of EfS need to be understood as a part of a more complex system, in which there is a network of interrelated parts. In other words, we cannot fully understand the constraints and affordances relating to EfS until we recognise the various systems at play.

Systems thinking

Given the increasingly complex nature of the environment, the economy, politics and society, a new way of understanding our world is required. Systems thinking advocates analysing situations, events and issues as a whole rather than in isolation, which emphasises the interrelationships between parts (Shaked & Schechter, 2017). The United Nations Educational, Scientific and Cultural Organization (UNESCO) (2010) suggests that sustainability encompasses four major dimensions, namely the natural, economic, social and political, as represented in Figure 15.1. While this is a starting point in conceptualising sustainability from a systems thinking perspective, it is important to acknowledge other dimensions, such as culture and tradition, play an equally important role in understanding sustainability as a whole.

While the UN Decade of Education for Sustainable Development (2005-2014) may have prompted awareness about the urgent need for sustainable living (Davis, 2010), in reality, the world's resources and ecosystems are still in rapid decline (Goekler, 2003; Lapp & Caldwell, 2012). As researchers, we consider the use of systems thinking as a valuable theoretical framework in which to position this project because it provides the opportunity to be "bigpicture thinkers, able to consider the multidimensional and complex nature of the world and its problems" (Lapp & Caldwell, 2012, p. 492). Dominici (2015) takes this notion further by suggesting that systems thinking is a relevant way to think about contemporary environmental

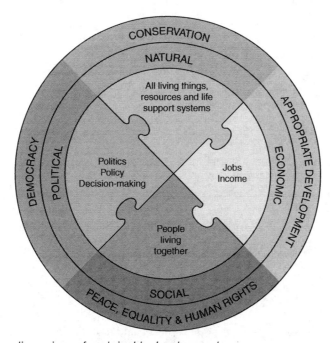

Figure 15.1 Four dimensions of sustainable development

problems as it demonstrates the interconnectedness of societal issues. He contends the need to consider a broader world view of multiple perspectives, rather than a "one size fits all" solution (Dominici, 2015, p. 1). Similarly, Goekler (2003, p. 13) argues that systems thinking allows for a "new vision" in which to seek solutions around sustainability, and states further:

> Systems thinking is simply a perspective, a language and a set of tools for describing and understanding the forces and interrelationships that shape the behaviour of systems. A system is defined as a collection of parts that interact to function as a whole and continually affect each other over time. Systems are not only interconnected, but they are coherently organised around some purpose.

Goekler's (2003) understanding of systems thinking is a useful starting point for this study, particularly in the way he highlights the interdependency between the elements embedded in a system (p. 11). For this study, systems thinking represents our understanding that individuals do not work in isolation; instead, teachers/school leaders/school communities operate within a range of "systems" that may encourage, enable, distract or constrain them in understanding, determining, negotiating and implementing EfS in practice. The systems at play in this study include the policies and curriculum that shape "what" is intended to be taught in classrooms alongside the schools with both school leaders (e.g., principals, business managers and lead teachers) and classroom teachers who are negotiating these policies and curriculum to coincide with their own professional identities.

Background of the study: The National Solar Schools Program

In line with its support for EfS, in 2008, the Australian Government launched the National Solar Schools Program (NSSP) which offered eligible primary and secondary schools the opportunity to compete for grants to install solar and other renewable systems. As a stipulation of the generous funding, schools were then required to provide their school communities with a Data Collection, Storage and Visualisation System (DCSVS) (DRET, 2013). As a consequence, the DCSVS would allow the school to communicate consumption and conservation of the school's resources to the wider school community, given that one of the five objectives of NSSP was to "allow schools to provide educational benefits for school students and their communities" (DRET, 2013, p. 85).

The Australian state/territory where this study was situated chose a smart meter website as their preferred DCSVS. The website itself was designed to provide live data that are collected from installed smart meters at each of the 86 participating schools, which gauged the consumption of electricity, solar, water and gas. On its home page, users are able to select a school from the dropdown menu or click on a map of the region with designated landmark points for each school. There is also a section on the left-hand side that offers information on current weather and temperature. Once the user chooses a school either from the dropdown menu or the map, there is some general information about the school and some of its key sustainability initiatives. There are options to check usage for electricity, solar, water and gas. The website also offers opportunities to compare the selected school's practice with another early childhood, primary or secondary school in the region. However, while the website provides this information, it lacks explicit pedagogical and/or curriculum links that would allow for clear educational benefits although this was a clearly stated aim of NSSP.

Five years after the start of NSSP, a report by the Department of Resources, Energy and Tourism (DRET) (2013, p. 88) stated that even with the implementation of NSSP and the Australian Curriculum's prioritisation of sustainability across content areas, less than 50% of surveyed schools nationwide incorporated the subject of energy efficiency in their learning materials. It was therefore timely, three years after this national report and eight years after the start of NSSP, that the DCSVS solution in one of the Australian states/territories was evaluated in regard to its promotion and implementation of EfS in schools.

Methodology

The aim of the study was to evaluate the smart meter website, or DCSVS, used by one Australian state/territory while also capturing the perspectives of teachers and school leaders on this particular tool and how it was used to promote student learning in EfS. For the purpose of this chapter, we focus on two main research questions:

1 How is the DCSVS used in the classroom?
2 What are the attitudes towards the DCSVS and how could it be improved to further EfS educational outcomes?

A mixed-mode design was utilised in this study, drawing on both qualitative and quantitative approaches "to answer different questions within the research topic" (Kervin, Vialle, Howard, Herrington, & Okely, 2016, p. 35). Data were collected through the anonymous online survey program Qualtrics. The surveys, one designed for teachers and the other for school leaders, were distributed to 86 local primary (some with an early learning centre) and secondary schools in July 2016. Teachers and school leaders (e.g., principals, sustainability leaders and business managers) were invited to participate. Given that the anonymous online survey was used to collect data from a potentially large data set, the researchers chose to approach some of the data quantitatively in order to collect and generalise information from a larger number of respondents, including the frequency of DCSVS use, purpose of use and attitudes. However, the survey also incorporated open-ended, qualitative questions allowing for deeper meanings and understanding of teachers' EfS practices and worldview of sustainability, which may not have been captured through the quantitative data. The survey also gauged educators' and school leaders' access to the resources and the opportunities afforded to them for better determining, understanding, negotiating and implementing sustainability into their educational practices. Therefore, a mixed-mode design was vital to answering the research questions of this study which was able to categorise frequency of use, purposes of use and attitudes but also give "voice" to the participants' perspectives.

The qualitative responses were thematically coded and emerging themes were identified. For example, some qualitative questions were categorised by discussing the website within a particular discipline (e.g., the website was useful for science) and according to teachers' current engagement with the website (actively uses the website, intends to use the website and has no interest in using the website). Before commencing this study, ethics approval was

184 Barnes, Moore and Almeida

gained by both the participating Australian state/territory Education Directorate and the authors' University Ethics Committee.

The survey captured the perspectives of 116 respondents – 66 teachers and 50 school leaders. Of the teacher participants, 49% were secondary teachers teaching Years 7-10 (n = 31), 35% were primary school teachers teaching F-6 (n = 23) and 5% early years teachers (n = 3). The remaining 11% reflected one teacher teaching College Years 11-12 and a mixture of K-6 teachers (n = 4), specialist science and sustainability teachers (n = 2), Years 6-8 teachers (n = 1) and support teaching staff (n = 1), as can be seen in Figure 15.2.

Of the 50 school leader participants, 46% were principals (n = 23), 34% were business managers (n = 17), 10% were deputy principals (n = 5) and the remaining 10% (n = 5) were a mixture of administrative staff (n = 2), sustainability coordinator (n = 1), business service officer (n = 1) and one unspecified (see Figure 15.3).

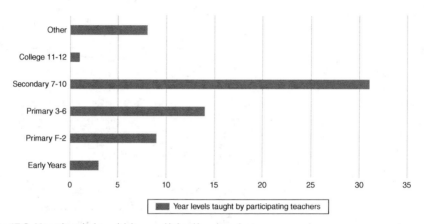

Figure 15.2 Year levels taught by participating teachers

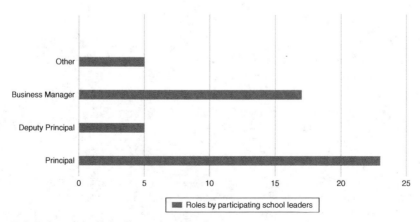

Figure 15.3 Roles of participating school leaders

Results and discussion

While this study revealed a number of themes, for the purpose of this chapter, the results and discussion will focus on how EfS is positioned in the participating Australian schools and how various "systems" such as mandated curriculum and policy, whole school approaches and individual teacher beliefs and attitudes toward EfS contribute to understanding how EfS is negotiated and implemented in schools.

Teachers' access and use of the smart meter website

An important finding from this study was that 82% (n = 54) of the teacher participants were not aware of the website, with 9% (n = 6) knowing about the website but not currently using it and only 9% (n = 6) using the website and finding it useful. This suggests that there has been a break-down in communicating policy from the policy writers to the school leaders to the teachers implementing it into the classroom. The Education Directorate had promoted the website to principals and business managers; therefore, how the school was to "trickle down" the information to teachers was up to each individual school leader. In addition, this points to the disproportionate efforts made in creating resources (especially digital) with little energy and effort spent in promoting this to end-users. There appeared to be limited effort to develop teachers' skills, confidence and knowledge about the resource itself, nor any reasons advocated as to why teachers should use this.

Also, schools, like many organisations, aim to position themselves in a way that makes them distinct and different from other organisations (Bartlett, McDonald, & Pini, 2015). These organisations often relate and position themselves in relation to their stakeholders (Bartlett et al, 2015; Brickson, 2007). Therefore, while some schools may position themselves as leaders in EfS, other schools may position themselves as leaders in literacy and numeracy, sport or music. This highlights that a school's identity and its relationship with relevant stakeholders (parents, students, policy-makers, etc.) may influence whether it makes a particular EfS initiative, such as the smart meter website, a priority in the school. Furthermore, systems thinking recognises that a school's identity and relationship with stakeholders are *part* of the complex system which influences the constraints and affordances of EfS in Australian schools.

The small number of teachers who used the website explained that they used it for purposes such as linking to STEM (science, technology, engineering and mathematics) curricula, motivating changes in behaviour among students and staff (e.g., turning off lights) and working with data that represent the "real use" of energy and water in their school. Surprisingly, only 6% (n = 4) of the teachers surveyed said they used the website to participate in sustainability challenges, such as Parliament of Youth and Earth Day.

While many teachers were unaware of the website, there seemed to be genuine interest from those initially unaware of the website with regards to how it could be used as a tool to promote sustainability across learning areas/subjects:

> I will now investigate the website to see what it can offer and then plan appropriately from there. Our sustainability committee may also use the data in their planning.

> I am a new teacher, but now that I know about the site I can use it in maths for calculations, kW per hour and per square metre, compare it to houses and other buildings.

Now I know about the website, I can use it as a resource in promoting sustainability.

A website such as this would link in very well with curriculum goals (Technologies). Has a link been provided on the - website? Who is responsible for informing teachers about this site? If I could receive their contact information I would happily email them to inquire about this website.

Now that I am aware of its existence, I will consider integrating use and data into health and civics.

I will now consult the website out of curiosity.

Given the interest from many of the teachers to utilise this website and link EfS into their teaching, there is a need to ensure that available EfS tools and resources are appropriately introduced to staff. Like a school's identity, teachers' professional identities are another *part* of this complex system, which in the case of EfS needs time to develop (Loughran, 2011) in conjunction with access to tools, resources and professional development.

EfS: a priority for school leaders?

In contrast to the majority of the teachers who were not aware of the website, the majority of school leaders were aware of the website; however, they used it only for purposes relating to resource management. When asked to tick purposes that were applicable to their school, 66% (n = 33) of school leaders said they used the website to identify problems (e.g., water leaks) and 32% (n = 16) to improve energy efficiency and reduce energy consumption. On the other hand, 22% (n = 11) stated that they did not know the website existed and 18% (n = 9) claimed that they did not use the website for any particular purpose.

Given that the majority of school leaders used the website to identify water leaks, improve energy efficiency and reduce energy consumption, it would suggest that schools as a whole in this particular state/territory view the smart meter website as a tool for resource management, not an educational tool. These beliefs and attitudes towards sustainability might also suggest why the website was not better promoted to teachers as an educational tool as there is a clear line drawn between a tangible resource (e.g., solar panels and gas heating which conserve energy and save money) and an educational one. Another *part* of the system influencing the constraints and affordances of EfS in schools is the financial gains that the overarching initiative, NSSP, provides. NSSP equipped schools with tangible resources, such as solar panels and gas heating, to help them save money. For many schools, this may have been the most attractive aspect of the initiative and therefore the website was always viewed as secondary for educational purposes.

School leaders have been known to be vital in providing support in a variety of ways, especially for whole school sustainability approaches (Kensler & Uline, 2016). Whole school approaches have been consistently shown to support better EfS implementation (Lewis, Baudains, & Mansfield, 2009; Shallcross & Robinson, 2008). Active support from their principals has been shown to "push" teachers to enable them to overcome some of the initial hesitancies in implementing EfS (Evans, Whitehouse, & Gooch, 2012). Therefore, this study suggests that if school leaders do not view EfS as important, it follows that their approach to sustainability will *impede* on the promotion of EfS in the classroom. With this said, it is important to recognise the school's identity, its relationships with stakeholders and the financial gains that this initiative provides schools as parts contributing to the broader issue in promoting EfS in schools.

When school leaders were asked how their school supported understanding and use of this website within their schools, they responded with:

> In all honesty, professional learning for staff has been mainly around literacy, numeracy and special needs education specifically. Whilst the website clearly links to maths and science concepts, teachers are not aware of the site and what it has to offer learning.

> We focus on literacy and numeracy along with student welfare and engaging parents. I'm not saying there is anything wrong with the website but it is a low priority ... No offence but this website is not core business so I'll avoid it as long as I can.

The above comments highlight the amount of pressure that schools are under to ensure that their students' literacy and numeracy skills are being adequately developed and improving at a competitive rate to other schools. This also highlights the role that literacy and numeracy (and the national tests which assess competency in these skills) play within this complex system. With a growing concern for accountability and test score data to compare, categorise and statistically depict the current state of Australian schooling, NAPLAN scores will continue to shape how and what students learn and how and what teachers teach in Australian schools. While future intentions are admirable, it is problematic that sustainability and EfS lack the accountability and support needed to ensure that teachers are guided and supported in its implementation. Even though the Australian Curriculum provides icons across curricula to signal to teachers that a particular topic can link to sustainability, the lack of explicit guidance and accountability (see Kennelly et al., 2011; Kuzich et al., 2015) results in sustainability falling between the cracks. Until schools, state and territory governments and teacher accreditation boards begin supporting and holding teachers accountable by providing authentic and relevant professional development and accessible and well-promoted sustainability tools, sustainability will continue to be deprioritised and demarcated from the rest of the curriculum. It cannot be assumed that all teachers have the knowledge, skills or desire to promote sustainability in their classrooms and therefore they need to be given explicit tools, resources and support to do so.

Overall, the findings from this study suggest that the smart meter website is not being prioritised by many of the participating schools in a way that positively influences educational outcomes and, more specifically, curricula outcomes. Similar to other states and territories in Australia, the state/territory government discussed in this study received a great deal of federal funding to provide sustainable resources (e.g., solar panels); however, these resources have been seen and utilised as tangible resources rather than educational. The smart meter website has allowed schools to measure and possibly modify their energy, gas and water consumption; however, an influence on educational outcomes is less evident. While there has been a great opportunity to prioritise sustainability by utilising tools, such as the smart meter website, to encourage EfS practices across the primary and secondary curricula, this has been left wanting. Now five years after DRET (2013, p. 88) reported less than 50% of surveyed schools nationwide incorporated the subject of energy efficiency in their learning materials, it does not appear that much has progressed in terms of prioritising sustainability across content areas and across educational sectors. With this said, however, this study evaluated *one* EfS initiative and school leaders' and teachers' non-engagement with this initiative cannot be seen as a direct correlation between all engagement with EfS resources and initiatives.

Buchanan (2012, p. 112) has argued that the need for education as an agent of change remains undisputed; however, this rhetoric of "societal change" reflected through education is not "enacted through practice at [a] personal level". Understanding the attitudes, beliefs and practices of teachers, school leaders, policy-makers and other stakeholders involved in promoting EfS in schools is invaluable in understanding the current status of EfS in schools and future steps in promoting skills, understanding and knowledge.

Implications for teaching and learning

Overall, the results of the study, and the evident lack of awareness and support of this particular sustainability initiative, suggest that for many sustainability is not a priority, nor is it cross-curricular. The first key implication for teaching and learning highlights the need for a more multifaceted, multimodal approach to the teaching and learning of EfS in Australian classrooms. First of all, a resource, like the smart meter website we have discussed in this study, in isolation may not cater for the variety of interests and needs of teachers, students and schools more broadly. Therefore, there needs to be a collection of resources that satisfy a variety of both teachers' and students' interests and learning and teaching styles. In addition, sustainability resources need to be coupled with explicit, targeted and practical support for ease and meaningful implementation. The second key implication is that there is a need for reflection on what sustainability is and how we can make practical and meaningful links to our everyday teaching and learning practices. This includes building awareness of how sustainability is situated within a broader system, which consists of economic, political and social dimensions (UNESCO, 2010). In addition, it is recognising that teachers and students require time to reflect on what sustainability means to them as engagement in EfS needs to be viewed as part of a continuum that acknowledges the different interest and knowledge levels. Teachers and students need to be offered time to internalise the meaning and practices associated with sustainability so that they continue to develop and explore EfS within the realm of their own interest and understanding.

Implications for further research

While this study examined both teacher and school leader perspectives, it was a small, baseline study to not only evaluate the use of the smart meter website in the participating state/territory Education Directorate, but to get a glimpse of EfS perspectives in schools. Further qualitative research is required to look at what is happening in classrooms and how teachers and students are negotiating and interpreting the EfS curriculum within schools and their communities.

References

ACARA (2016a). Cross-curriculum priorities. Retrieved on November 14, 2016 from: http://www.australian-curriculum.edu.au/crosscurriculumpriorities/overview/introduction

ACARA (2016b). *National Assessment Program*. Retrieved on November 10, 2016 from: http://www.nap.edu.au/about

Bartlett, J., McDonald, J., & Pini, B. (2015). Identity orientation and stakeholder engagement – The corporatisation of elite schools. *Journal of Public Affairs*, 15(2), 201-209.

Brickson, S. (2007). Organizational identity orientation: The genesis of the role of the firm and distinct forms of social value. *The Academy of Management Review*, 32(3), 864-888.

Buchanan, J. (2012). Sustainability education and teacher education: Finding a natural habitat? *Australian Journal of Environmental Education*, 28(2), 108-124.

Davis, J. (2010). Introduction. In J. Davis (Ed.), *Young children and the environment: Early education for sustainability* (pp. 1-17). Port Melbourne, Australia: Cambridge University Press.

Department of the Environment, Water, Heritage and the Arts. (2009). *Living sustainably: The Australian government's national action plan for education for sustainability*. Retrieved on November 1, 2016 from: http://www.iau-hesd.net/sites/default/files/documents/national-action-plan.pdf

Dominici, G. (2015). Systems thinking and sustainability in organisations. *Journal of Organisational Transformation and Social Change*, 12(1), 1-3.

DRET (Department of Resources, Energy and Tourism). (2013). *National Solar Schools Program Evaluation Report*. Retrieved on November 14, 2016 from: http://www.industry.gov.au/Energy/EnergyEfficiency/Documents/NSSP-Evaluation- Report-Final.pdf

Evans, N., Whitehouse, H., & Gooch, M. (2012). Barriers, successes and enabling practices of education for sustainability in Far North Queensland schools: A case study. *Journal of Environmental Education*, 43(2), 121-138.

Goekler, J. (2003). Teaching for the future: Systems thinking and sustainability. *Green Teacher*, 70, 8-14.

Gough, A. (2011). The Australian-ness of curriculum jigsaws: Where does environmental education fit? *Australian Journal of Education*, 27(1), 9-23.

Kennelly, J., Taylor, N., & Serow, P. (2011). Education for sustainability and the Australian curriculum. *Australian Journal of Environmental Education*, 27(2), 209-218.

Kensler, L., & Uline, C. (2016). *Leadership for green schools: Sustainability for our children, our communities and our planet*. New York: Routledge.

Kervin, L., Vialle, W., Howard, S., Herrington, J., & Okely, T. (2016). *Research for educators* (2nd ed.). South Melbourne, Australia: Cengage Learning Australia.

Kuzich, S., Taylor, E., & Taylor, P. C. (2015). When policy and infrastructure provisions are exemplary but still insufficient. *Journal of Education for Sustainable Development*, 9(2), 179-195.

Lapp, J., & Caldwell, K. A. (2012). Using food ethnographies to promote systems thinking and intergenerational engagement among college undergraduates. *Food, Culture & Society*, 15(3), 491-509.

Lewis, E., Baudains, C., & Mansfield, C. (2009). The impact of AuSSI-WA at a primary school. *Australian Journal of Environmental Education*, 25, 45-57.

Loughran, J. (2011). On becoming a teacher educator. *Journal of Education for Teaching*, 37(3), 279-291.

MCEETYA (Ministerial Council on Education, Employment, Training and Youth Affairs). (2008). *Melbourne declaration on educational goals for young Australians*. Retrieved on November 16, 2016 from: http://www.curriculum.edu.au/verve/_resources/National_Declaration_on_the_Educational_Goals_for_Young_Australians.pdf

Shaked, H., & Schechter, C. (2017). Systems thinking among school middle leaders. *Educational Mangagement Administration and Leadership*, 45(4), 699-718.

Shallcross T., & Robinson J. (2008). Sustainability education, whole school approaches, and communities of action. In A. Reid, B. B. Jensen, J. Nikel, & V. Simovska (Eds.), *Participation and learning: Perspectives on education and the environment, health and sustainability* (pp. 299-320). London: Springer.

United Nations Educational, Scientific and Cultural Organization. (2010). *Four dimensions of sustainable development*. Retrieved on November 10, 2017 from: http://www.unesco.org/education/tlsf/mods/theme_a/mod02.html?panel=2#top

16 The changing landscape of early childhood curriculum

Empowering pre-service educators to engage in curriculum reform

Lauren Armstrong, Corine Rivalland and Hilary Monk

This chapter focuses on the changes that have occurred in early childhood education (ECE) in Victoria, Australia. This is because unlike most other states in Australia, early childhood (EC) teachers in Victoria had no experience prior to 2009 in implementing a set curriculum framework. These teachers experienced the introduction of the *Victorian Early Years Learning and Development Framework* (VEYLDF), (DEECD & VCAA, 2009) and the national curriculum document, the *Early Years Learning Framework: Being, Belonging, Becoming* (EYLF) (DEEWR, 2009) simultaneously. The VEYLDF has since been updated (DET, 2016). The simultaneous introduction of the state and national curriculum frameworks may have led to greater confusion within the Victorian EC context, as educators and services attempted to understand these documents and translate them into their practice (Garvis et al., 2013). Although the content of the two documents are similar, the VEYLDF utilises language that is reflective of the Australian Curriculum (ACARA, 2016). In addition, the EYLF focuses on children from birth to five years of age, whereas the VEYLDF focuses on children from birth to eight years of age. As such, the VEYLDF is often used in the early years of the primary sector. Although this chapter refers to the Victorian EC context, it provides relevant information for all pre-service educators, as changes are visible throughout the country and across the EC, primary and secondary sectors. In addition, children enter ECE prior to attending primary and secondary school and it is therefore important for educators across all sectors to have some understanding of the sectors in which they are not teaching.

To demonstrate the significance of change in ECE, educational change theories are used throughout this chapter to explore ways of engaging effectively in meaningful change (Fullan, 2007; Pendergast, 2006; Wedell, 2009). Data from a study of long day care educators are included to offer insight into how educators have been experiencing change in the field. A poststructural lens (Hughes, 2010) and Foucauldian discourse analysis (Willig, 2013) were used to examine these data, with particular focus upon aspects of discourse, knowledge and power (Foucault, 1972, 1980). The study also acknowledged the subjective positioning (Willig, 2013) of educators in relation to curriculum change, and the presence of power in developing and implementing educational change (Fullan, 2007). Based upon these theories and findings, some useful strategies are offered to empower pre-service and in-service educators as they navigate their way through the uncertainty of change. This chapter begins by explaining the changing discourses within Australian ECE.

Changing discourses and evolving influences of society, politics and research

Change has played a prominent role in ECE – both historically and presently (Logan, Press, & Sumsion, 2016; May, 1997; Prochner, 2009). Due to the continual evolution of the EC sector, the presence of change and its related emotive responses (such as resistance) were visible as early as the 19th century (Prochner, 2009). The interrelationship between society, politics and the economic needs of the nation influences such changes. This ultimately impacts on fluctuating theoretical directions (OECD, 1998; Wilks, Berenice, Chancellor, & Elliott, 2008). In ECE, this has been visible through the evolution of global understandings of children's learning and development (Arthur, Beecher, Death, Dockett, & Farmer, 2015, p. 17; Copple & Bredekamp, 2009; Edwards, 2009). Recent research also indicates that educators face a range of issues and challenges regarding ongoing policy reforms and the prospect of further change in the field of ECE (Li, Fox, & Grieshaber, 2017).

Looking at the global and domestic development of ECE, a strong link can be made between the development of theory and policy which have been based on social, economic and political factors over time (OECD, 1998; Wilks et al., 2008). For instance, the *Convention on the Rights of the Child* (UNICEF, 1989) and its international standards concerning the care, protection and treatment of all children under the age of 18 years have been adopted in various forms by many nations around the world, and ultimately influenced the implementation of EC curriculum frameworks. Embedded within these frameworks was a range of valued learning outcomes and theories of child development and learning (DEEWR, 2009; Wilks et al., 2008).

Neuro-scientific research has also influenced ECE in recent years. This relates to the newly discovered significance of early brain development throughout the first seven years of life, particularly between the ages of birth and three years (Shonkoff, 2010), and more recent research into its connection with EC learning and development (Lally & Mangione, 2017; Nagel, 2012; Westell, 2016). This research is essential for pre-service and new educators to consider in terms of their own teaching and learning practices (Diamond & Whitington, 2015). Such research has impacted the value of ECE at societal, political and economic levels, as more investment in the development of quality EC programs is being made nationally and internationally (OECD, 1998; Wilks et al., 2008). At the same time, the connection between ECE and the enhancement of "human capital" is gaining value and momentum. This means that governments now perceive that investment in ECE can increase the economic productivity of the nation (Arthur et al., 2015, p. 17).

On a more local level, these influences can be seen through the landscape of ECE in Australia, as illustrated in Figure 16.1. Prior to reforms beginning in 2009, Australian ECE was strongly influenced by traditional developmental theories such as developmentally appropriate practice (DAP), Piaget's cognitive development theory and developmental milestones (Bredekamp, 1987; Copple & Bredekamp, 2009). Thus, the practices of educators were largely based on this approach for over two decades. Then in 2009, the EYLF was introduced as the national curriculum framework (DEEWR, 2009).

In Victoria, the VEYLDF was introduced simultaneously as a state curriculum framework (DEECD & VCAA, 2009). Both the national and state curriculum frameworks moved away

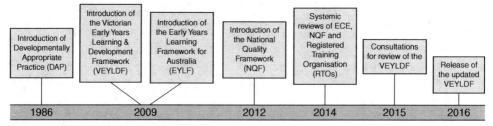

Figure 16.1 Timeline illustrating some key EC reforms in Australia (correlating with their date of introduction)

from focusing solely on traditional developmental theory to encompass much broader and holistic perspectives including contemporary approaches and terminology, based on sociocultural, critical, poststructural and postmodern theories. This means that educators were required to engage in the complexities of understanding these theories and translating them into practice. Moreover, the importance of economic productivity and human capital was central to these documents, with an emphasis on all young Australians becoming "active and informed citizens" (DEEWR, 2009, p. 5).

Adding to these complexities, the new *National Quality Framework* (NQF) emerged in 2012 to monitor and assess the quality of EC programs. The NQF included a set of quality standards known as the National Quality Standards and a new Assessment and Rating process (ACECQA, 2012). This was later followed by a systemic review into the "regulatory burden" of NQF, as it was viewed as adding to the time and workload of educators and services (ACECQA, 2013). The political influences continued in 2014, with a review of the Australian EC sector as a whole. This was conducted in an attempt to increase workforce participation by examining "the accessibility, affordability and flexibility of early childhood programs" (Australian Government Productivity Commission, 2014, p. 11). Since this time, a number of studies have been conducted to examine how educators in the Australian EC field have been understanding and implementing these reforms (Irvine & Price, 2014; Kilderry, Nolan, & Scott, 2017), and the workload and fatigue associated with these changes (Grant, Danby, Thorpe, & Theobald, 2016; Tayler, 2016).

The changing rules related to qualifications have been an additional political influence. Over time, these qualifications have evolved into a three-tiered system of certificates, diplomas and degrees. However, as these qualification requirements are relatively new, many educators remain unqualified. The vocational education and training and higher education sectors are predominantly the key training providers for these qualifications – although, more recently, the increasing demand for qualified educators has led to the roll-out of shorter courses offered by registered training organisations. As a result, inconsistencies in quality, content, duration and delivery of these courses have been identified, which ultimately led to a review in 2014-2015 (ASQA, 2015). These inconsistencies have added to the fragmented state of ECE and the diverse subject positions of educators in the field.

The presence of these changes and the diversity of teacher/educator courses available add yet another complex layer of change within the sector. This is important for pre-service educators, as it reflects the diverse levels of training and experience held by educators in the field. It also raises questions regarding how up-to-date these courses are in providing

Shifting theories of early childhood education

The direction of ECE has been influenced by numerous theories over time. These theories have essentially involved behaviourist, developmental, sociocultural, critical, poststructuralist and postmodern views towards teaching practices and children's learning and development (Arthur et al., 2015, p. 17; Copple & Bredekamp, 2009; Edwards, 2009). The historical influence of such a wide range of views suggests that theory has always been at the forefront of the sector. In particular, this can be seen through shifting perspectives (see Figure 16.2) regarding EC development, the image of the child, the amalgamation of education and care, the provision of quality, the significance of play and teaching and learning approaches. Figure 16.2 maps the introduction of a range of theories and approaches to learning and teaching.

Throughout their development and implementation, these theories and approaches have been progressively embraced by numerous countries around the world (Wilks et al., 2008). However, educators must acknowledge that these theories and approaches are continuing to evolve, as new knowledge and interpretations are established, disseminated and adopted (Hargreaves, 2003). In turn, new theories and approaches gradually filter into the sector over time. This has been particularly visible through the new focus on more contemporary theories and practices that are embedded within curriculum frameworks.

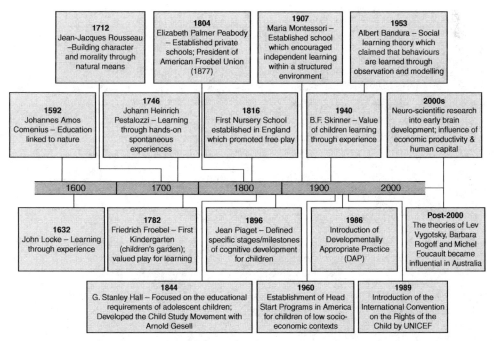

Figure 16.2 An illustrative timeline that shows some of the key theories and approaches which have influenced the progression of ECE in Australia over time

Times of change and uncertainty

In times of change and uncertainty, there is an urgent need to examine whether people are being supported effectively. According to Darling-Hammond (2000), teacher dispositions, their knowledge and skills and sufficient preparation and pre-service training are crucial for the successful implementation of educational reform.

There are numerous ways to define and interpret the concept of change; however, this chapter focuses on *educational change* which involves the progressive and systemic restructure of an educational context that is often essential during educational reform (Fullan, 2007; Wedell, 2009). According to Fullan (2007), successful engagement in effective and meaningful change requires both individual and collective understandings. As such, the way in which change is implemented may be affected by the comprehension of individuals and groups.

It has been explained that "organisations, including early childhood settings, are dynamic in that their people, hierarchies, structures and systems are continually evolving" (Rodd, 2006, p. 184). As such, this can lead to the occurrence of different types of change. As defined by Rodd (2006), these include:

- Incremental change (minor, cautious and gradual changes);
- Induced change (predetermined and systemic initiatives);
- Routine change (adjustments based on daily challenges);
- Crisis change (swift decisions based on urgency);
- Innovative change (imaginative resolutions that engage numerous participants);
- Transformational change (extreme organisational change).

It would be ideal to propose that ECE is in the midst of transformational change; however, it may be more accurately perceived as induced change. According to Rodd (2006, p. 185), "induced change results from a conscious decision to implement a change in people, processes, programs, structures and systems". This leads to the question of whose decision are the changes based on. In the case of Australian EC reform, these changes have been decided by government bodies, but the changes need to be implemented by individual educators and services. As such, this type of change can be problematic, as it can have a major impact on the individual and institutional contexts involved. Furthermore, it is understood that "complex change can only be successful if every member of the early years workforce learns to question the status quo, and rises to the challenge of reconceptualizing, approaching and performing professional roles, functions and responsibilities in different ways" (Rodd, 2015, p. 17).

Educators need to have an understanding of the change required in order to implement it effectively, but this requires time. According to the change literature, educational change comprises an eight- to 17-year cycle (Pendergast, 2006). However, Australian EC educators were given only one year to fully understand and implement the recent reforms (Garvis et al., 2013). This is visible in the rapid timeline of changes in Figure 16.1. It is clear that educators were required to deal with several reforms in succession. As such, educators may not have been provided enough time to understand and implement each of these changes effectively. Moreover, such changes require an understanding of the influences involved in their development.

The influences on educational change

So far, we have determined that educational change is influenced by national and global trends, and political and ideological perceptions which change over time (Wedell, 2009). When examining such changes, it is important to identify the *who*, the *how* and the *why* (Gorrell & Hoover, 2009). This relates to who initiates change, the scale of change and why the change is deemed necessary (Wedell, 2009). At a national level, change is often prompted by government departments and policy-makers. This is true for ECE, as state and federal government bodies generally initiate these reforms with support from policy-makers and leading EC institutions.

When attempting to implement change, it is essential that the contexts of all stakeholders are considered. In relation to educators, this can involve their beliefs, dispositions, strengths and weaknesses; their level of training, support, resources and workload; and their understanding of change and their preparedness to do so. Thus, educators need to acknowledge and be sensitive to the diverse contexts of their colleagues. This is particularly true in the Victorian context, as EC educators have been grappling with their understanding of two curriculum frameworks, the quality framework and tensions between qualifications, knowledge and experience. Based on this understanding, interview data from a recent study of Victorian long day care professionals are analysed and presented in the following section.

Methodology

Aim

The aim of the study was to examine how Victorian long day care educators were engaging with educational reforms and curriculum change. More explicitly, it sought to determine what strategies (supports and stressors) were being used by educators to understand, cope with and engage in curriculum change.

Sample

Eleven participants from a range of long day care settings in the south-east region of Victoria agreed to participate in this study. Participants consisted of educators, educational leaders (EL), directors and nominated supervisors (NS). The roles of EL and NS are considerably new, as they were established following amendments to the Education and Care Services National Regulations in 2011 (MCEECDYA, 2011). The decision to include these subgroups reflects stratified case sampling, which can involve the "sampling of usually typical cases or individuals within subgroups of interest" (Bryman, 2012, p. 419). This sample provided a rich data set, as participants held diverse levels of training, qualifications and experience.

Theoretical framework

The theoretical lens that framed this study draws upon poststructuralism, and Michel Foucault's concepts of discourse, power and knowledge (1972, 1980), while also using Willig's (2013) version of Foucauldian discourse analysis (FDA). To clarify, a poststructuralist perspective "seeks to understand the dynamics of relationships between knowledge/meaning, power and identity" (Hughes, 2010, p. 51). The concepts of knowledge, power and discourse provide a valuable lens to explore how educators engage with educational reform, and highlight that "everything and everyone can – and does – shift and change all the time" (Hughes, 2010, p. 50). These concepts are reflected by the shifting discourses and knowledge base of ECE, the power involved in the implementation of educational reforms and the subjective positions of educators and policy-makers regarding these reforms (Wedell, 2009).

In the Australian EC sector, Foucault's concepts of discourse, knowledge and power are evident through the dominant discourse of newly initiated reforms, the shifting knowledge and power embedded within those reforms and the privileged knowledge held by specific institutions. As such, these concepts have been relevant in deconstructing the meaning of change and reform for the purpose of this study.

Research method and design

A qualitative approach which supports a focus upon "the socially constructed nature of reality, the intimate relationship between the researcher and what is studied, and the situational constraints that shape inquiry" (Denzin & Lincoln, 2003, p. 13) was used. Qualitative research often uses a poststructuralist lens, as a way to frame the world and the interactions between people within it, while acknowledging the subjective position of the researcher (Hughes, 2010). As such, this study attempts to emphasise the "constant instability without attempting to *capture* or stabilise it" (Hughes, 2010, p. 50, original emphasis). Moreover, FDA has been utilised to explore the way in which specific processes, experiences and events are constructed by participants. All of these elements have been influenced by the research questions involved in this study.

Data generation

Data were generated through 30- to 60-minute, semi-structured interviews. To foster flexibility for participants, these interviews utilised face-to-face, telephone and group interview methods. Using knowledge gained through the literature and an understanding of the field, a set of base questions was constructed to prompt the direction of the interviews. These questions aimed to identify the discourses framing how participants engaged with the new reforms, and to ascertain significance of any differences and similarities between qualification levels, training and experience. The interviews were recorded and transcribed following ethical guidelines.

Analysis

The analysis process for this study involved thematic analysis, followed by Willig's (2013) version of FDA to examine the data, address the research questions and identify evidence of Foucault's concepts of discourse, power and knowledge (1972, 1980). Based on the works of Foucault, FDA was introduced in the 1970s within the field of Anglo-American psychology. It aims to explore the connections between discourse and social and institutional practices as well as the ways that subjects and objects are constructed by discourse.

Early childhood curriculum 197

Foucauldian Discourse Analysis
1. Discursive constructions
2. Discourses
3. Action orientation
4. Positionings
5. Practice
6. Subjectivity

Figure 16.3 The six stages of FDA – information adapted from Willig (2013)

The six phases of Willig's (2013) FDA model (see Figure 16.3) were applied to the data in relation to the research question:

What strategies are utilised by EC professionals to understand, cope with and engage in curriculum change?

According to Willig (2013, p. 131), the stages of FDA "allow the researcher to map some of the discursive resources used in a text and the subject positions they contain, and to explore their implications for subjectivity and practice".

For the purpose of this study, "curriculum change" was identified as the *discursive object*, and the *discursive constructions* referred to the way in which participants explicitly or implicitly spoke of this. The variations between these discursive constructions were then analysed within the broader *discourses*, while *action orientation* offered a stronger understanding of what these discursive constructions were achieving within the text in regards to how participants spoke of curriculum change. The *positionings* and *subjectivity* of participants were also examined, and, finally, *practice* and its relationship with discourse were explored.

Findings and discussion: Strategies for change

A number of coping strategies have been identified by participants as discursive constructions of curriculum change. These strategies are important for pre-service educators to consider as they enter the field, as they illustrate some of the difficulties thus far, and what has been successful in implementing curriculum change. The coping strategies identified by participants can be seen as positive (supports) and negative (stressors) (see Figure 16.4).

This figure illustrates two fundamental strategies that were identified by participants in coping with curriculum change. These strategies can be perceived as either a stressor or a support. This section focuses on excerpts regarding the role of learning and workplace in coping with curriculum change. These key strategies can provide pre-service educators with valuable insight into what to expect, and what can empower them as they enter the field.

Learning: Self-initiated or duty-bound

Two types of learning have been identified from this study. These are *self-initiated learning* (SIL) and *duty-bound learning* (DBL). SIL refers to learning that is initiated by the individual. It suggests a level of self-motivation, value for learning and new knowledge and a sense of empowerment. In contrast, DBL refers to learning that is perceived as mandatory (bound by duty), and often based on demand and expectation which can lead to a feeling of disempowerment.

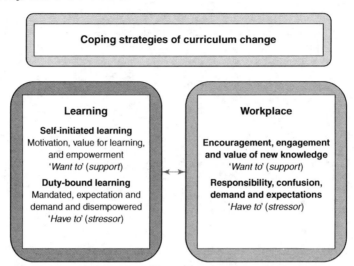

Figure 16.4 Key coping strategies of curriculum change, as identified by participants of this study

Characteristics of SIL for coping with curriculum change have been acknowledged by a number of participants. For instance, Abigail explained that she was "really *involved*" and liked to "actively participate", while demonstrating a "genuine interest and a genuine passion" to implement the frameworks effectively (Abigail, original emphasis). Adele saw herself as "really self-motivated" and "ambitious", as she proclaimed, "I want to learn more … I want to lead". This indicates that the characteristics of SIL were embedded within the subject positioning of these participants, whereby their uptake of power enabled them to better navigate the shifting discourses of curriculum change. The importance of engaging in such learning practices has been acknowledged by Mac Naughton (2005, p. 211) who proposed that EC professionals should become "critically knowing" in times of change, and reconstruct themselves "as powerful agents of equity and innovation who can practise for liberty".

SIL can be seen as a key component in developing deeper levels of understanding of changing curriculum discourses. Several participants have provided evidence of varying degrees of SIL characteristics when engaging with the new curriculum frameworks. First, Alana has suggested:

> The majority of the work that I did … in terms of my own practice and planning … was – just trying to refine it and add bits and pieces and trying to make sense of it myself.

This implies that a basic level of SIL and an internal personalisation and ownership have formed a supportive and empowering coping strategy for Alana's own professional practice. This is important for pre-service educators to understand, as the curriculum frameworks are interpretative documents that are dependent upon the subjective position and understanding of the reader (Sumsion et al., 2009). Therefore, other educators may possess diverse interpretations and understandings of these documents. Meanwhile, Abigail has offered a more assertive and externally informed SIL strategy:

> I myself started going online, and reading, and researching, and finding out all of this stuff ... But as far as *me* – it was because of my *own* research that I've learnt about it all.
>
> (Abigail, original emphasis)

This statement reflects that SIL has acted as a support for Abigail as she finally began translating the EYLF to her practice. In enhancing Abigail's understanding of the EYLF, the use of SIL ultimately led to a position of power (Foucault, 1980) and increased motivation for further learning. This was similar for Lucy, who completed her DAP-based diploma in 2009. Although the traditional discourses of DAP were embedded within her nine years of experience, Lucy was able to use SIL to better understand the new frameworks, and to inform her practice:

> Most of it was our research ... I think as I've learnt the framework and really started to implement it and feel like it's embedded, it ... gets a bit more understanding under it and it sort of has a bit of flow I think about it. It was always so forced beforehand.

This account offers a positive response to the new frameworks, and demonstrates how SIL can be used to understand the more modern and eclectic curriculum approaches in spite of the participant's prior use of historically prescriptive EC discourses, or as Foucault describes it, the "archaeology of knowledge" (O'Farrell, 2005, p. 64).

In contrast, some participants identified themselves or their colleagues as engaging in DBL. Their discussions demonstrated a lack of motivation and feelings of disempowerment. For instance, one traditionally-trained educator explained her first experience with the EYLF:

> I struggled with it. I took one look at the *huge* book and I went – "I'm not reading that".
>
> (Gabrielle, original emphasis)

This suggests a sense of resistance to changes from traditional to more contemporary discourses, and feelings of being overwhelmed. According to Foucault, "resistance to power is part of the *exercise of power*" (Kendall & Wickham, 2003, p. 50, emphasis added). Moreover, resistance is also a common emotive response to educational change (Arthur et al., 2015, p. 17; Block, 2000; Gomez, 2012; Pendergast, 2006). Although it highlights the lack of motivation associated with DBL, it also demonstrates the need for educators to take time for learning. Depending on their attitude towards this, it can be seen as SIL or DBL. In regard to characteristics of DBL, Alana has offered:

> People are having a lot of trouble because they're not wanting to learn about the Early Years Learning Framework because it seems too hard to them and because they're set in their old ways – they fight. They don't want to change, they're not interested.
>
> (Alana, sic)

Again, this lack of motivation appears to stem from resistance to change. If we think about the cycle of change (Pendergast, 2006), educators may be positioned within different stages "on the continuum from resistance to acceptance of new ideas" (Gronlund & James, 2008, pp. 21–22). Therefore, emotive responses to change are likely to occur.

It is vital for pre-service educators to acknowledge the presence of educators who engage SIL and DBL. This knowledge will assist in understanding the positions and attitudes of their colleagues towards learning and change. Furthermore, pre-service educators need to be conscious of their own attitudes to learning, as this will support them in understanding how to better empower themselves through learning to engage in future change. However, it is also necessary to examine what level of support is offered by their workplaces.

Levels of support from the professional context

A number of supports and stressors have been offered by participants regarding the level of support available from their workplaces. These excerpts illustrate the diverse approaches and contexts among different professional contexts. First, Alana has expressed the support from her service to complete a Bachelor degree:

> And our boss ... she's more than willing ... "If you want to go to it – I'll let you go". Yeah, she's very good like that ... very supportive ... she's just, "no worries ... you're improving yourself" ... And I think that's 'cause I can bring information back.
>
> (Alana, sic)

This demonstrates the value held by Alana's service to invest in their educators and the value that they attribute to new knowledge offered through the Bachelor degree. So, the service acknowledged the benefits of Alana – with the agenda of information coming back to the service – thereby developing a reciprocal relationship and shared power. It seems that this workplace realises the power of the new knowledge acquired through the Bachelor degree, because "as *knowledges* and disciplines develop they produce the experts who determine not only how we should act but also what we are" (Prado, 2000, p. 77, original emphasis).

Another sign of supportive services are the types of directors in leadership, and how they relate to the curriculum frameworks. For instance, a director named Aileen was part of the initial consultation process for the EYLF, and has continued her own studies in the field. She also acknowledged the similarities between her service's prior practice and the underpinning practices and principles of the frameworks, as "it didn't really change anything that we did here, other than how our documentation looked" (Aileen). This uptake of SIL and proactive approach appears to have assisted her understanding of these curriculum changes, thus leading her to provide a "supporting role" for her staff (Aileen) and a strategy of power (Foucault, 1980).

However, some accounts from participants have demonstrated the opposite. For example, Sonia has explained a lack of access to professional development (PDs):

> The director and the second in charge went to some [PDs] – ah, I think it was a few days where they did some seminars on it. And gave us some feedback, but we really had nothing else aside from those two books to go off and that was it [laughs].

This implies that these initial PDs were only accessible to high management-level staff, illustrating the presence and impact of positions of power (Foucault, 1980) within the service. Furthermore, this account raises possible tensions with subjectivity (Arribas-Ayllon & Walkerdine, 2017), as the knowledge attained from these PDs was reliant on the interpretation of management-level staff and subsequent translation to educators.

Another view regarding an inadequacy of support associated with the limited understanding of those in management positions was provided. In relation to this, Lucy shares the initial struggles within her service:

I think we got handed the book and they said, "this is what you have to do now". And I don't think our management, especially here, really had that overall grasp of what was happening. And maybe that aspect of long day care life, the planning side of it, is not really their strong suit. So it was really hard to get their support and that, um, was actually a real struggle for a while.

This signifies tensions regarding how the frameworks were initially dispersed, and a discourse of "not knowing" among both management and educators. Part of this sense of "not knowing" may relate to the uncertainty of whose responsibility curriculum change lies with. For example, Abigail's director had suggested that the responsibility lay with her: "She would always say to me, 'oh, you know what you're talking about. I'll let you deal with it'" (Abigail). Whereas, some services did not feel that it was mandatory to implement these documents at all until the NQF was introduced.

These excerpts offer some insight into the levels of workplace support when coping with curriculum change. As you can see, there are many issues that influence these levels of support. It is important to understand that the way in which reforms are developed and communicated to the people on the ground can greatly impact the way in which these reforms are understood, accepted and implemented. Although educators have limited power over these issues, engagement in SIL can take some power back throughout these processes. In turn, educators can share this sense of empowerment by imparting their newly-gained knowledge and understandings to others among their professional contexts.

Conclusion

From a poststructuralist viewpoint, curriculum change can be understood as a complex and fluid system that involves shifting discourses, subjective positions and power relations. This chapter offers an insight into the complex nature of curriculum change and the way in which educators are coping with these changes in ECE. It has been acknowledged that educators need to understand the ever-changing context of the field, the shifting theory and discourses and the influences that society, politics and research have in its evolution. These changes have impacted the educators in their teaching and learning. This is important for pre-service and new educators, as they need to learn to engage in teaching and learning within these new contexts, and the ever-changing landscape of the field. Furthermore, there is a need for all stakeholders in the field to understand the concepts of educational change, and the emotive responses that can occur among educators and their colleagues. As such, pre-service educators must understand these tensions and acknowledge the diverse subjective positioning of their colleagues as they enter the field.

This study has identified SIL, DBL and levels of workplace support as key coping strategies for educators for engaging in curriculum change. SIL was found to be a support for educators as they attempted to empower themselves by engaging in self-learning to enhance their understandings of curriculum changes, whereas DBL somewhat hindered this process as a stressor. Meanwhile, the level of support from the workplace was viewed as a support in some cases, and a stressor in others. It is understood that confusion and uncertainty among EC services stemmed from the inadequate information and communication during the initial introduction of these reforms. As such, it was unclear who was responsible for their implementation, and how this should be conducted and supported. Moreover, the educational values and learning dispositions of directors appeared to affect the level of support available for their educators. It is important to note the strong link between the workplace support and SIL coping strategies. Although there is often limited control over the levels of support from within the workplace, educators can influence the supportiveness of these contexts by engaging in SIL, and sharing their newfound knowledge and understandings.

It is recommended that pre-service and new educators be conscious of the processes of change and engage in SIL practices in order to keep themselves prepared for and informed of new reform initiatives. When seeking employment, new educators should be mindful of examining the teaching and learning philosophies of prospective workplaces as well as the support offered to beginning teachers, including ongoing professional development. Engagement in ongoing professional development is also advised prior to, during and following the introduction of curriculum reforms to ensure a smooth and effective transition to change. It is anticipated that the information and recommendations from this chapter can provide useful knowledge and strategies for pre-service educators as they enter the field, and for their future engagement in curriculum change.

References

ACARA (Australian Curriculum, Assessment and Reporting Authority) (2016). *Development of the Australian Curriculum*. Retrieved on October 4, 2016 from: https://www.acara.edu.au/curriculum/development-of-australian-curriculum

ACECQA (2012). *National Quality Framework*. Retrieved on May 25, 2017 from: http://acecqa.gov.au/national-quality-framework/the-national-quality-standard

ACECQA (2013). *Report on the National Quality Framework and Regulatory Burden*. Sydney, NSW: Australian Children's Education and Care Quality Authority.

Arribas-Ayllon, M., & Walkerdine, V. (2017). Foucauldian discourse analysis. In C. Willig & W. S. Rogers (Eds.), *The SAGE Handbook of Qualitative Research in Psychology* (pp. 110-123). Thousand Oaks, CA: SAGE.

Arthur, L., Beecher, B., Death, E., Dockett, S., & Farmer, S. (2015). *Programming and planning in early childhood settings*. South Melbourne, VIC: Cengage Learning Australia.

ASQA (Australian Skills Quality Authority) (2015). Report: Training for early childhood education and care in Australia. Retrieved on June 11, 2017 from: https://www.asqa.gov.au/sites/g/files/net2166/f/Strategic_Review_2015_Early_Childhood_Education_Report.pdf

Australian Government Productivity Commission (2014). *Childcare and early childhood learning Productivity Commission draft report – July 2014*. Melbourne, VIC: Commonwealth of Australia.

Block, P. (2000). *Flawless consulting: A guide to getting your expertise used*. San Francisco, CA: Jossey-Bass/Pfeiffer.

Bredekamp, S. (1987). *Developmentally appropriate practice in early childhood programs: Serving children from birth through age 8* (1st ed.). Washington, DC: National Association for the Education of Young Children.

Bryman, A. (2012). *Social research methods*. Oxford: Oxford University Press.

Copple, C., & Bredekamp, S. (Eds.) (2009). *Developmentally appropriate practice in early childhood programs: Serving children from birth through age 8* (3rd ed.). Washington, DC: National Association for the Education of Young Children.

Darling-Hammond, L. (2000). How teacher education matters. *Journal of Teacher Education, 51*(3), 166-173. DOI:https://doi.org/10.1177/0022487100051003002

DEECD & VCAA (2009). *Victorian early years learning and development framework: For all children from birth to eight years*. East Melbourne, VIC: Early Childhood Strategy Division.

DEEWR (2009). *Belonging, being and becoming: The early years learning framework for Australia*. Barton, ACT: Commonwealth of Australia.

Denzin, N. K., & Lincoln, Y. S. (2003). Introduction: The discipline and practice of qualitative research. In N. K. Denzin & Y. S. Lincoln (Eds.), *The landscape of qualitative research: Theories and issues* (2nd ed., pp. 1-46). Thousand Oaks, CA: SAGE.

DET (2016). *Victorian early years learning and development framework: For all children from birth to eight years*. East Melbourne, VIC: Department of Education and Training.

Diamond, A., & Whitington, V. (2015). Studying early brain development: Educators' reports about their learning and its applications to early childhood policies and practices. *Australasian Journal of Early Childhood*, 40(3), 11-19.

Edwards, S. (2009). *Early childhood education and care: A sociocultural approach*. Castle Hill, NSW: Pademelon Press.

Foucault, M. (1972). *The archaeology of knowledge and the discourse on language* (A. M. Sheridan Smith, tr. ed.). New York: Pantheon Books.

Foucault, M. (1980). *Power/knowledge: Selected interviews and other writings, 1972-1977* (1st American ed.). New York: Pantheon Books.

Fullan, M. (2007). *The new meaning of educational change*. New York: Teachers College Press.

Garvis, S., Pendergast, D., Twigg, D., Fluckiger, B., Kanasa, H., Phillips, C., Bishop, M., Lockett, K. & Leach, D. (2013). The Victorian Early Years Learning and Development Framework: Managing change in a complex environment. *Australasian Journal of Early Childhood*, 38(2), 86-94.

Gomez, R. E. (2012). Resistance, reproduction, both, or neither: Exploring the influence of early childhood professional development specialists on the field of early childhood education. *NHSA Dialog*, 15(1), 81-94. DOI:10.1080/15240754.2011.636487

Gorrell, P., & Hoover, J. (2009). *The coaching connection: A manager's guide to developing individual potential in the context of the organization*. New York: American Management Association.

Grant, S., Danby, S., Thorpe, K., & Theobald, M. (2016). Early childhood teachers' work in a time of change. *Australasian Journal of Early Childhood*, 41(3), 38-45.

Gronlund, G., & James, M. (2008). *Early learning standards and staff development: Best practices in the face of change*. St. Paul, MN: Redleaf Press.

Hargreaves, A. (2003). *Teaching in the knowledge society: Education in the age of insecurity*. New York: Teachers College Press.

Hughes, P. (2010). Paradigms, methods and knowledge. In G. Mac Naughton, S. A. Rolfe, & I. Siraj-Blatchford (Eds.), *Doing early childhood research: International perspectives on theory and practice* (2nd ed., pp. 35-61). Crows Nest, NSW: Allen & Unwin.

Irvine, S. & Price, J. (2014). Professional conversations: A collaborative approach to support policy implementation, professional learning and practice change in ECEC. *Australasian Journal of Early Childhood*, 39(3), 85-93.

Kendall, G., & Wickham, G. (2003). *Using Foucault's methods*. Introducing Qualitative Methods series. London: SAGE Publications.

Kilderry, A., Nolan, A., & Scott, C. (2017). 'Out of the loop': Early childhood educators gaining confidence with unfamiliar policy discourse. *Early Years: An International Research Journal*, 37(4), 341-354. DOI: 10.1080/09575146.2016.1183595

Lally, J., & Mangione, P. (2017). Caring relationships: The heart of early brain development. *Young Children*, 72(2), 17-24.

Li, M., Fox, J. L., & Grieshaber, S. (Eds.) (2017) *Contemporary issues and challenge in early childhood education in the Asia-Pacific region*. Series: New frontiers of educational research. Singapore: Springer.

Logan, H., Press, F., & Sumsion, J. (2016). The shaping of Australian early childhood education and care: What can we learn from a critical juncture? *Australasian Journal of Early Childhood*, 41(1), 64-71.

May, H. (1997). *The discovery of early childhood: The development of services for the care and education of very young children, mid eighteenth century Europe to mid twentieth century New Zealand*. Auckland, Wellington: Auckland University Press with Bridget Williams Books; New Zealand Council for Educational Research.

Mac Naughton, G. (2005). *Doing Foucault in early childhood studies: Applying post-structural ideas*. New York: Routledge.

MCEECDYA (2011). *Education and Care Services National Regulations*. Canberra, ACT: Ministerial Council for Education, Early Childhood Development and Youth Affairs.

Nagel, M. C. (2012). *In the beginning: The brain, early development and learning*. Camberwell, VIC: ACER Press.

OECD (1998). *Human capital investment: An international comparison*. Paris: OECD Publishing.

O'Farrell, C. (2005). *Michel Foucault*. London: SAGE Publications.

Pendergast, D. (2006). Fast-tracking middle schooling reform: A model for sustainability. *Australian Journal of Middle Schooling, 6*(2), 13–18.

Prado, C. G. (2000). *Starting with Foucault: An introduction to genealogy* (2nd ed.). Boulder, CO: Westview Press.

Prochner, L. W. (2009). *A history of early childhood education in Canada, Australia, and New Zealand*. Vancouver, BC: UBC Press.

Rodd, J. (2006). *Leadership in early childhood education* (3rd ed.). Crows Nest, NSW: Allen & Unwin.

Rodd, J. (2015). *Leading change in the early years: Principles and practice*. Maidenhead, Berkshire: McGraw-Hill Education; Open University Press.

Shonkoff, J. P. (2010). Building a new biodevelopmental framework to guide the future of early childhood policy. *Child Development, 81(1)*, 357–367. DOI:10.1111/j.1467-8624.2009.01399.x

Sumsion, J., Barnes, S., Cheeseman, S., Harrison, L., Kennedy, A., & Stonehouse, A. (2009). Insider Perspectives on Developing Belonging, Being & Becoming: The Early Years Learning Framework for Australia. *Australasian Journal of Early Childhood, 34*(4), 4–13.

Tayler, C. (2016). Reforming Australian early childhood education and care provision (2009–2015). *Australasian Journal of Early Childhood, 41*(2), 27–31.

UNICEF (1989). *Convention on the Rights of the Child*. S.l. United Nations Centre For Human Rights: UNICEF.

Wedell, M. (2009). *Planning for educational change: Putting people and their contexts first*. London: Continuum International Publishing Group.

Westell, M. (2016). *Supporting brain development*. Everyday learning series. Deakin West, ACT: Early Childhood Australia.

Wilks, A., Berenice, N., Chancellor, B., & Elliott, S. (2008). *Analysis of curriculum/learning frameworks for the early years (birth to age 8): April 2008*. Retrieved on December 3, 2017 from: http://www.vcaa.vic.edu.au/documents/earlyyears/analysiscurriclearnfwlitreview.pdf

Willig, C. (2013). *Introducing qualitative research in psychology* (3rd ed.). Maidenhead, England: Open University Press; McGraw-Hill Education.

17 Rights-based Indigenous education in Australia

Evidence-based policy to pedagogy

Peter Joseph Anderson and Zane Ma Rhea

Introduction

What does being a teacher in a postcolonial democracy like Australia in the 21st century mean? Given that Australia was originally the lands of Aboriginal and Torres Strait Islander nations and has only more recently been colonised and developed by Westernised, predominantly European cultural groups, this chapter aims to explore the role of education, and more specifically teachers, in Australia from this perspective. The recognition of Indigenous rights that flow from the acknowledgement that Aboriginal and Torres Strait Islanders are the First Peoples of Australia enables one to consider the roles and responsibilities of a 21st-century Australian teacher from a rights-based perspective. This perspective is guided by the role and responsibilities of education systems, as outlined under the United Nations Declaration on the Rights of Indigenous Peoples (UNDRIPs) (United Nations, 2008). Following Australia's endorsement of UNDRIPs in 2009, it is the Australian Government's intention that all teachers will have, as a minimum, a proficient level of demonstrable professional expertise in both Aboriginal and Torres Strait Islander Education and Australian Aboriginal and Torres Strait Islander Studies, and measures are being introduced in pre-service teacher education programs nationally to support this intention. In 2016, there were 394,762.5 full-time equivalent (FTE) in-school staff in Australia of whom 276,329.8 were teaching staff (ABS, 2016) and many of these teachers have had no formal professional development in the rights-based approach to the education of Indigenous children or in the methods of educating non-Indigenous Australians about Indigenous histories, languages and cultures.

A common theme raised by teachers in research conducted by Ma Rhea, Anderson and Atkinson (2012) was the inherent fear that teachers have around causing offence or lacking knowledge of a subject and the field of Indigenous education. This situation seemed to be prevalent amongst teacher educators and teachers because of their poor preparation within their previous education at school and as pre-service teachers themselves. While it may not be their fault that they lack the knowledge or skill in this space, we argue here in this chapter that unless teachers can make a shift to a rights-based approach to their teaching then they will be reproducing this fear and lack of knowledge into the future.

This chapter introduces you to schooling and its relationship with Indigenous peoples globally and the protocols of engagement with Aboriginal and Torres Strait Islander peoples. We face a complex problem in Australia in knowing how to approach education, and more specifically teaching, in the 21st century. Do we simply copy the teaching fashions of England

and the USA to ensure that our students are globally competitive? Or do we ground our pedagogical practices in Australian history and landscape, even as we ensure that we have an internationalised view of our work? What skills do teachers need to teach effectively in mainstream education in such a way that they will feel well equipped with the required knowledge and the psychological, intellectual, emotional and professional skills to teach in a way that recognises the rights of Australia's Aboriginal and Torres Strait Islander peoples?

In response to sustained work undertaken by generations of Indigenous education experts and the changing international policy landscape regarding the recognised rights of Indigenous peoples, the *Melbourne Declaration on the Educational Goals for Young Australians* began a renewed effort by the Australian Government to incorporate Indigenous histories and cultures into the Australian Curriculum. Influenced by the *Melbourne Declaration*, there are now within that Australian schooling system two guiding frameworks for changing the ways that teachers are educating Indigenous children and young adults and educating non-Indigenous children and young adults about Indigenous histories, languages and cultures. The first is the Australian Professional Standards for Teachers (APST) (AITSL, 2017). The "Standards", as they are now known, have two specific Focus Areas 1.4 and 2.4 that require teachers at the graduate level to demonstrate skills, knowledge and understanding about Aboriginal and Torres Strait Islander education and lifeways. The other is the Australian Curriculum, and its state and territory variations, that guides teachers in the development of curriculum to include Aboriginal and Torres Strait Islander content in their work (ACARA, 2017).

Problems facing the global education system

In the field of Indigenous education, there are many problems facing nation states in the modern world as they struggle to make the transition from old colonial education systems into the new postcolonial, postmodern world of international agreements and a highly globalised approach to education. There is now a growing body of evidence internationally of previously colonised nations proactively recognising the importance of the knowledge of Indigenous peoples and local communities within education (Ma Rhea, Anderson, & Atkinson, 2012). Old colonial methods and systems have significantly shaped how Indigenous education is undertaken. In the Australian example, it has only been just over 200 years since the first Native Institution was established and many of its approaches are still used to some extent today. Indigenous children are seen as being in need of civilising, often away from the influence of their families, and their knowledge is not understood for the value it could bring to the education effort (Ma Rhea, 2015).

But it is not just up to schools and teachers to change this problem. There is a distinct lack of theoretical development in the Indigenous education field and lack of resources to support education systems to preserve and maintain Indigenous systems of knowledge. This leaves schools faced with the pressure to bring Indigenous students into Westernised ways of being and thinking with no attention being given to what the child already knows. This is the case whether the child is living in an urban, rural, remote or very remote location. It is the reverse of what education theory knows to be best practice, to know the child and know how they learn. The lack of resources made available to schools and teachers to develop curriculum that is appropriate to the local area is exacerbated by the remoteness and inaccessibility of many small Indigenous populations. This mitigates against a sustained effort for research and documentation and reduces the school's accessibility to information about local initiatives in education, if they exist. The overarching problem, mentioned above, is that nations, such as Australia, are still in the grip of colonial thinking about education. We call this the colonial mindset that values particular Western industrial, scientific and technical knowledge over human lifeways knowledge. The next critical step in the development of education surely needs to be the recognition of the importance of holistic education that brings the child's world into the classroom in a respectful and culturally appropriate way. Such an approach would, by its principles, better meet the needs of not only Indigenous learners but all learners in Australian classrooms.

Starting from the right spot

What often confuses teachers and teacher educators at the outset is what language to use when they discuss, teach and research about Indigenous education. We argue that developing knowledge about this is an important first step. As a Warlpiri and Murinpatha First Nations teacher education academic, I (Anderson) argue that it is imperative to shift the attention away from learners in the first instance, to focus on teachers. As both teacher educators and researchers, we know that teachers have struggled with the challenge of indigenising their pedagogy and we suggest that this is because teachers have not had the opportunity to develop their content knowledge of the Aboriginal and Torres Strait Islander world nor their professional, pedagogical skills in this area.

Terminology and language

It is important for teachers and teacher educators to understand that the English language terminology regarding Aboriginal and Torres Strait Islander peoples is firmly rooted in a discourse of power and racial superiority informed by the anthropological gaze of early Europeans' interpretation of Aboriginal and Torres Strait Islander peoples. It is because of this colonial legacy that we would first like to make a general point about the terminology used throughout this chapter because it is important to understand the appropriate terminology and language to use. The current education system in Australia has been inherited from Australia's colonial past. It follows that the language used has also been developed from that same past. In this chapter, we suggest that we need to move beyond the colonial mindset, which shapes Australia's education engagement with its Indigenous citizens, towards a postcolonial, Indigenist mindset. This means thinking about the everyday language that we use to speak about Aboriginal and Torres Strait Islander peoples.

Internationally agreed definitions of the word "Indigenous"

The United Nations' Working Group on Indigenous Populations has been using the following definition to guide its work (United Nations, 2004, Clause 2, as cited in Cobo, 1986, pp. 379–382):

> Indigenous communities, peoples and nations are those which, having a historical continuity with pre-invasion and pre-colonial societies that developed on their territories,

consider themselves distinct from other sectors of the societies now prevailing in those territories, or parts of them. They form at present non-dominant sectors of society and are determined to preserve, develop and transmit to future generations their ancestral territories, and their ethnic identity; as the basis of their continued existence as peoples, in accordance with their own cultural patterns, social institutions and legal systems.

Summing up the deliberations of years of work, ten years later, Mrs. Erica Daes (1996a, pp. 69-71; see also Daes, 1996b), the Chairperson of the United Nations' Working Group, concluded:

In summary, the factors which modern international organisations and legal experts (including indigenous legal experts and members of the academic family) have considered relevant to understanding the concept of "indigenous" include:

- priority in time with respect to the occupation and use of a specific territory;
- the voluntary perpetuation of cultural distinctiveness, which may include aspects of language, social organisation, religion and spiritual values, modes of production, laws and institutions;
- self-identification, as well as recognition by other groups, or by State authorities, as a distinct collectivity; and
- experience of subjugation, exclusion or discrimination, whether or not these conditions persist.

The International Labour Organization's Convention No. 169 of 1989 adopted a definition that includes the rights of both Indigenous and Tribal peoples. Its Article No. 1 stipulates that it applies to peoples in countries who are regarded as Indigenous on account of their descent from the populations which inhabited the country, or a geographical region to which the country belongs, at the time of conquest or colonisation or the establishment of present state boundaries and who, irrespective of their legal status, retain some or all of their own social, economic, cultural and political institutions. Article 1(2) stipulates that *"Self-identification* (italics ours) as Indigenous or tribal shall be regarded as a fundamental criterion for determining the groups to which the provisions of this Convention apply" (ILO, 1989).

What this means for us as teachers, teacher educators and researchers is that we always capitalise the word "Indigenous" in acknowledgement that we are speaking about a distinct collectivity with *sui generis* rights who are becoming recognised in the Australian education system. The term *sui generis* is being used in the sense that Australia's Aboriginal and Torres Strait Islander peoples have cultural and intellectual property rights that exist in their own right (which also means that they were not extinguished by later legal frameworks; for further discussion, see Janke, 1998). The capitalisation of the word Indigenous also distinguishes Australia's Indigenous peoples, the Aboriginal peoples and the Torres Strait Islander peoples, from anyone who was born in Australia who is small "i" indigenous. Students will commonly say, "but I was born here so that makes me indigenous!" That is true in the small "i" indigenous sense but it does not make that person Indigenous in the sense explained in the next paragraph.

It is also necessary to understand that computing packages now have a spell check function that only recognises the small "i" indigenous, so it is something that requires attention in order to over-ride the automated system to use the capital "I". Sometimes this can be saved in a personal spell-checking system but sometimes it can not, despite international recognition of the need to capitalise this word when speaking about the Indigenous people of a country.

Who is an Indigenous Australian?

Another significant dilemma for non-Indigenous Australian teachers is knowing how to identify an Indigenous person due to the general lack of knowledge or understanding of Indigenous Australian histories, languages or cultures. For many people choosing to identify as Aboriginal or Torres Strait Islander or both Aboriginal and Torres Strait Islander it is a personal and sometimes challenging issue. That certainly has nothing to do with skin colour.

The accepted Australian Government definition (ABS, 2017) defines an Indigenous Australian person as the following:

1. of Aboriginal or Torres Strait Islander descent;
2. who identifies as an Aboriginal or Torres Strait Islander; and
3. is accepted as such by the community in which he or she lives.

For Aboriginal and Torres Strait Islander people who wish to claim ancestry, the following three key elements are applied to comprise this definition: descent; self-identification; and community acceptance (for more information, see ABS, 2017).

Historically, in Australia there has been confusion between the terms "Indigenous", "Aboriginal" and "Torres Strait Islander", and the state and territory-derived terms for Aboriginal and Torres Strait Islander peoples. The term "Indigenous", as discussed above, is a term used internationally to recognise the rights of all Indigenous peoples (see United Nations, 2008; United Nations Development Group, 2008). As a legacy of colonisation, Australia's original inhabitants were called Aborigines. By distinction, the people of the Torres Strait were known as Torres Strait Islanders. Over a number of years there have been preferences expressed by Australian Aboriginal and Torres Strait Islander peoples to be known collectively as Aboriginal and Torres Strait Islander peoples, or distinctively as Aboriginal people or Torres Strait Islander people rather than as Indigenous people.

In addition to these discussions, there has sometimes been a preference to use collective nomenclature for mainland Aboriginal people at the state and territory level. Therefore, Indigenous people of Queensland are sometimes known as Murries, in New South Wales as Kooris, in Victoria as Koories, in Tasmania as Palawa, in South Australia as Nungas and in Western Australia as Noongas.

How can this be done in a classroom? As you may already be able to see, terminology is important. There are specific rights accorded to Indigenous peoples by international law due to their distinctive identities, their deep links with their ancestral lands and their reliance on customary law and institutions (which in many cases are deeply interrelated with their surrounding natural environment), which precede the creation of nation states. Below, I (Anderson), an Indigenous teacher educator, have provided the following advice to my students on how correct language and terminology can be implemented in the classroom.

> - Know what language to use: One of the most successful ways in which to ensure correct language and terminology is for teachers and educators to model this for students and, depending on the level of the learner, specific lessons can be developed with explicit foci on terms. This can be done across the curriculum.
> - Indigenous: At the mid- to upper-primary level explanations around the differentiation of lowercase "i" and uppercase "I" can be developed into an extremely insightful lesson in raising children's awareness of First Nations peoples.
> - Koorie, Koori, Noongar, Nungar, Murri, Palawa: Depending on what state you live in, an inquiry-based lesson can be developed for all levels that investigates what the local Indigenous peoples prefer.
> - Australian Indigenous Nations names: As above, have learners identify the nation in which their school or home is located.
> - Aboriginal and Torres Strait Island people: Do not use ATSI as an abbreviation.
> - Avoid racist jokes and racist language: Learn how to help your students to respond to a racist joke in class. This will often involve teaching your students how to use appropriate language.

Before exploring the aspects of knowledge and understanding required to teach about Indigenous histories, cultures and languages and how to support reconciliation efforts by teaching non-Indigenous students about these matters, we first explain some of the history of the colonial and subsequent governments' attempts to educate Aboriginal and Torres Strait Islander children. It is important, we believe, to understand why Indigenous students, their families and their communities mistrust the Australian education system about being able to educate their children in a culturally safe manner.

Colonisation, politics and the need to "fix" Indigenous education

The past efforts to "educate" Aboriginal and Torres Strait Islander learners have left behind many traumatic experiences that are often passed down through family unwittingly in what we describe as "intergenerational educative trauma" as a result of the colonial mindset. Intergenerational educative trauma as a result of the colonial mindset provides a lens for understanding and changing the past failure in the provision of education to Aboriginal and Torres Strait Islander children. It is also important to take into consideration that because of this colonial mindset, Aboriginal and Torres Strait Islander learners more often than not occupy the educational fringes of the "other", having not truly been accepted into the centre or "center periphery" of the educational enterprise in this country.

Given the very troubled history, the education of Aboriginal peoples and Torres Strait Islander peoples as two separate entities is political by its very nature and often falls victim to the political whims of the governments of the day. Governments and their agencies frequently use Aboriginal and Torres Strait Islander education matters as vehicles for political point scoring about reactions to, and solutions for, specific elements of what that government deems as "education problems". Much of this has nothing to do with the day-to-day education of Aboriginal and Torres Strait Islander students or the concerns of parents, communities and their teachers and schools, but it is ministers and governments who provide significant financial incentives to schools to pay attention to those matters that they define as "the problem" in need of a solution. Given the seemingly endless "fixing" needed, the question posed by Aboriginal and Torres Strait Islander expert educators is: What is wrong with Indigenous education in Australia? Marika-Mununggiritj (1999, p. 2) observed that:

> Education initiatives must enhance the capacity of Indigenous peoples and local communities to engage actively in the promotion, protection and facilitation of use of their knowledge.

Following Marika-Mununggiritj, we suggest that the answer to the question of how to "fix" Indigenous education involves a twofold process encompassing: first, the need to de-stigmatise and de-problematise the Aboriginal and Torres Strait Islander learner and recognise our common humanity with the same thirst for knowledge; and second, a reconfiguration of current thinking, enactment and engagement of Aboriginal and Torres Strait Islander education at the systems level of government, by educational agencies, teachers and educational experts. In Australia, we have an educational system that continues to relegate Aboriginal and Torres Strait Islander learners to a position of being the "problem", stigmatised and pathologised through the lens of coloniality and settler society ideology. The colonial mindset is still evident at the systems level. This continued failure to recognise this fact poses a serious impedance to change in the educational outcomes and aspirations of Aboriginal and Torres Strait Islander people. A way forward, we believe, is through the adoption and enactment of a rights-based approach to the education of Aboriginal and Torres Strait Islander learners achieved through a firm understanding of the Declaration on the Rights of Indigenous Peoples (United Nations, 2008) as its guiding principle.

What can teachers do?

We propose a number of preliminary steps that need to be considered in order to learn about education from a new perspective. It is not possible in this short chapter to cover 60,000 years of Indigenous cultural knowledge but we know from our experiences of undertaking research within this field, shaping the Indigenous education units for pre-service teacher courses and providing professional development for teachers at all levels that these first steps are important.

Step One: Adopt the Declaration on the Rights of Indigenous Peoples as a guiding framework for the development of a rights-based approach to your teaching

Australia is a signatory to the Declaration on the Rights of Indigenous Peoples. Professor James Anaya, the United Nations Special Rapporteur on the Rights of Indigenous Peoples, visited Australia in August 2009. In his report, he noted that despite some recent advances, Australia's legal and policy landscape must be reformed. He recommended:

> The Commonwealth and state governments should review all legislation, policies and programs that affect Aboriginal and Torres Strait Islanders, in light of the Declaration.

> The Government should pursue constitutional or other effective legal recognition and protection of the rights of Aboriginal and Torres Strait Islander peoples in a manner that would provide long-term security of these rights.
>
> (Human Rights Council, 2010)

Article 13 and Article 14, which focus on the education rights of Australia's Indigenous peoples (United Nations, 2008), are important resources in developing an inquiry-based unit of study in a number of Humanities and Social Sciences subjects. It is first necessary to be familiar with these Articles and think about their implications for teaching practice.

Step Two: Develop education partnerships with knowledgeable Traditional Owners and other Aboriginal and Torres Strait Islander education experts

The voices and viewpoints of Aboriginal and Torres Strait Islander people must be presented in Australian classrooms. Our research has found that most non-Indigenous teachers do not know Indigenous Australians either personally or professionally, do not seek their advice when undertaking their lesson planning and do not include culturally appropriate resources. Often they will rely on the local Indigenous education worker or Indigenous student support worker to deal with issues that arise.

We argue that this is not the way to develop new pedagogies in this field because often it is not based in the development of respectful, long-term partnership between the school and the local Indigenous community. We recommend the following to teachers in Australian schools:

- Find out who the Traditional Owners are in the area where your school is located. If you cannot find this out from your mentor teacher, school or other teachers then approach your local Council and research the Recognised Aboriginal Parties (RAPs) in your local area. To start conversations with other local Aboriginal and/or Torres Strait Islander education experts you might contact the state-level Indigenous Education Consultative Body (IECB) and Local Aboriginal Education Consultative Group (LAECG) for information.
- Find out about and keep up to date with events hosted by local Aboriginal and Torres Strait Islander community organisations.
- Include dates of significance to Aboriginal and Torres Strait Islander peoples in your yearly planning processes.
- Work towards developing trusted collaborations with Indigenous people in your planning, teaching and assessing processes.

In doing so, over time, teachers will be able to develop their professional practice in a culturally appropriate manner and be able to create a powerful teaching and learning environment for all of their students.

Step Three: Find, plan and teach positive, accurate examples of Indigenous contribution to Australian society

This next step, which builds on an understanding of UNDRIPs, which should inform curriculum choices and pedagogical practice and the development of trusted relationships with knowledgeable Indigenous education experts as described above, is to consider the following:

> What can you do as a teacher or teacher educator to provide positive examples of Indigenous contribution to Australian society:
>
> *1 in how you teach (your pedagogy)?*
>
> For example, do you start the planning of your teaching with questions about how to incorporate Indigenous perspectives or is it an add-on done at the end of your planning, if at all? Do you wait until you have an Indigenous student before you consider Indigenous perspectives in your teaching? Do you think about how to teach Indigenous perspectives to non-Indigenous students in a way that supports reconciliation?
>
> *2 in what curriculum resources you choose?*
>
> For example, are the curriculum resources you have chosen been written by Indigenous knowledgeable experts? If the resource is by knowledgeable Indigenous experts but not from the community in which your school is located, how are you conveying the multicultural nature of Aboriginal and Torres Strait Islander cultures and societies?
>
> *For students at all levels, we have found the following inquiry activity prompt to be valuable:*
>
> How do you find out about Indigenous peoples and their positive contribution to Australian society?

Step Three encourages teachers to consider how to develop their pedagogical approach and curriculum choices in a way that both speaks to the rights of Aboriginal and Torres Strait Islander peoples and is clearly located in a new national understanding of what it is to live and learn in 21st-century Australia. Progressive two-way learning and both-way learning are ideas that developed during the 1980s and 1990s under the guidance of scholars such as Yunupiŋu (1994), Marika-Mununggiritj (1999) and Harris, Teasdale, and Hughes (Harris, 1990). They argued that learning about the Aboriginal and Torres Strait Islander world and the Western world is a two-way process. In the face of continual failure by non-Indigenous teachers to create learning spaces where traditionally oriented Aboriginal children could learn in the Western way without losing their cultural identity, Aboriginal and Torres Strait Islander thinkers such as Dr Yunupiŋu (1994) and Dr Marika-Mununggiritj (1999; see also Marika-Mununggiritj & Christie, 1995) began theorising how it might be possible for "both ways" learning to occur. Their "Both Ways" approach asks all teachers to consider that Aboriginal people have access to complex educational philosophy that has evolved over millennia and that only in partnership will there be a culturally safe space created for the young Aboriginal and Torres Strait Islander learner (for a fuller discussion see, for example, the Living Knowledge Project, 2008, and Ma Rhea, 2012).

A brief examination of the pedagogical considerations that arise from the education theories of Dewey and Vygotsky will allow us to consider the concept of indigenising pedagogy further. Dewey (1916, 2002) encouraged teachers to engage the curiosity appropriate to the child's developmental stage so that the student was motivated to learn what interested them, thereby encouraging their intellectual curiosity, something that would last them for their lifetime and enable them to contribute to the future development of society.

Vygotsky's (1934/1962, 1978) social cognition learning model asserts that culture is the prime determinant of individual development. He argues that humans are a species that creates culture, and every human child develops in the context of a culture. Therefore, a child's culture has a significant influence on their learning development. Of relevance to this chapter, Vygotsky posits the existence of a "zone of proximal development" for the cognitive development of the child once they have left the context of their family and immediate social environment and move into the world of the formal mainstream schooling structures.

He argues that cognitive development results from a dialectical process whereby a child learns through problem-solving experiences shared with someone else, usually a parent or teacher but sometimes a sibling or peer. This is a process of first observation, and trial and error problem solving, both pre-verbal and then verbal. Gradually this way of growing to understand the world is internalised and formalised through socialisation into the wider community and then through education. By the stage where the learner enters the school, many of their preferred ways of learning are established and it is a challenge for the teacher to invite them to learn in new and, possibly, uncomfortable and unfamiliar ways.

When the non-Indigenous teacher thinks about the education theories of Dewey and Vygotsky in relation to an Aboriginal and Torres Strait Islander student, the question immediately arises as to how much of a learner's cultural context can be understood by the teacher when the teacher is not of the same culture as the learner. How do you create a pedagogy which optimises the zone of cognitive development for the learner if the student is not from the same cultural background? How might you develop the intellectual curiosity of your students such that they can think about Aboriginal and Torres Strait Islander–settler relations in Australia in a progressive, democratic way? Einstein (n.d. [2012]) is attributed with the saying, "Problems cannot be solved at the same level of awareness that created them". Step Three also raises two important aspects to consider: first, how to teach about Indigenous histories, languages and cultures, and second, how to select culturally appropriate resources.

Teaching about Indigenous histories, languages and cultures

Teaching about Indigenous histories, languages and cultures poses a significant challenge for non-Indigenous teachers to teach respect for Aboriginal and Torres Strait Islander histories, cultures and languages if they do not start from a rights-based approach and do not know any knowledgeable Indigenous education experts. Non-Indigenous teachers cannot teach Indigenous culture and languages. Their ignorance is too great. Imagine teaching another language and culture without knowing anything about it. At best, in this situation, we teach to stereotypes and we know that in the case of Australia with its colonial past we know very little of the true history of this country, of its languages and cultures. Therefore, the only way to step forward into this work is to have a trusted partnership with Aboriginal and Torres Strait Islander people, particularly those from the local area.

Selecting culturally appropriate resources

The second matter facing teachers in Australia is to learn how to assess classroom resources, to know which websites and resources are reliable, along with understanding why they have been selected. Taking the time to source high-quality, culturally appropriate resources for use in the classroom is yet another indication of the level of respect the teacher has for Aboriginal and Torres Strait Islander Australians. If you can understand how to select culturally appropriate resources, you will then also be able to better guide your students in the classroom. With the popularity of inquiry-based teaching and learning, it becomes very important to be able to guide students in the sorts of materials they will find. There is a plethora of unsuitable, racist, stereotypical materials available on the Internet as any web search will reveal. Again, we reiterate that the only way to step forward into this work is to have trusted partnership with Aboriginal and Torres Strait Islander people, particularly those from the local area. Such people will be able to guide and support you in your work if you are able to demonstrate that you respect the rights of Indigenous people to be involved in the education of their children and of all Australian children and young adults about Indigenous histories, languages and cultures.

Conclusion

In this brief introduction to a rights-based approach to Indigenous education in Australia, we provide practical and important first steps for teachers, teacher educators and researchers to begin their journey in understanding, respecting and approaching Indigenous education. The steps provided offer approaches to help develop classroom practices. More important, we believe that by beginning on this journey teachers, teacher educators and researchers will be able to contribute to a field of teacher practice that is still in its formative period. Unlike many other aspects of the teaching profession, the field of Indigenous education is undergoing a transformation from a colonial to a rights-based approach. As yet, there is only a small but significant body of Indigenous education expertise that informs this new approach and we hope that the readers of this chapter will be part of these new approaches, informing both pedagogy and curriculum.

References

ABS (Australian Bureau of Statistics) (2016). *Staff, Australia*, 2016, cat. no. 4221.0. Retrieved on November 28, 2017 from: http://www.abs.gov.au/ausstats/abs@.nsf/mf/4221.0

ABS (Australian Bureau of Statistics) (2017). *Indigenous statistics for schools: Commonwealth definition of Aboriginal and Torres Strait Islander people*. Retrieved on November 28, 2017 from: http://www.abs.gov.au/websitedbs/cashome.nsf/4a256353001af3ed4b2562bb00121564/7464946b3f41b282ca25759f00202502!OpenDocument

ACARA (Australian Curriculum Assessment and Reporting Authority) (2017). The Australian Curriculum. Retrieved on November 28, 2017 from: https://www.australiancurriculum.edu.au/

AITSL (Australian Institute for Teaching and School Leadership) (2017). *Australian Professional Standards for Teachers*. Retrieved on November 28, 2017 from: https://www.aitsl.edu.au/teach/standards

Cobo, J. M. (1986). *Study of the problem of discrimination against Indigenous populations*. UN Doc. E/CN.4/Sub.2/1983/21/Add.8 (Last Part), paras. 379–382 (30 September, 1983). Retrieved on November 28, 2017 from: http://www.un.org/esa/socdev/unpfii/documents/MCS_xxi_xxii_e.pdf

Daes, E. (1996a). Standard setting activities: Evolution of standards concerning the rights of Indigenous peoples. Working Paper by the Chairperson-Rapporteur, Erica-Irene Daes, on the concept of

"Indigenous peoples", UN Doc. E/CN.4/Sub.2/AC.4/1996/2, paras. 69-71 (10 June, 1996). Retrieved on November 28, 2017 from: http://www.columbia.edu/itc/polisci/juviler/pdfs/united_nations.pdf

Daes, E. (1996b). Pacific workshop on the United Nations Draft Declaration on the Rights of Indigenous Peoples. Paper presented at Conference of the Indigenous Peoples of the Pacific, Suva, Fiji, September, 1996.

Dewey, J. (1916). *Democracy and education: An introduction to the philosophy of education*. New York: The Macmillan Company.

Dewey, J. (2002). *John Dewey project on progressive education*. Retrieved on October 10, 2013 from: http://www.uvm.edu/~dewey/

Einstein, A. (n.d. [2012]) *Albert Einstein quotes*. Retrieved on October 10, 2013 from: http://www.alberteinsteinsite.com/quotes/einsteinquotes.html

Harris, S. (1990). *Two-way Aboriginal schooling: Education and cultural survival*. Canberra, Australia: Aboriginal Studies Press.

Human Rights Council (2010). *Report by the Special Rapporteur on the situation of human rights and fundamental freedoms of Indigenous people, James Anaya*. Retrieved on November 28, 2017 from: http://unsr.jamesanaya.org/PDFs/Australia%20Report%20EN.pdf

ILO (International Labour Organization) (1989). *Convention No. 169 concerning Indigenous and Tribal peoples in independent countries*. Retrieved on October 10, 2013 from: http://www.unhchr.ch/html/menu3/b/62.htm

Janke, T. (1998). *Our culture, our future: Report on Australian Indigenous cultural and intellectual property right*. Canberra: Australian Institute of Aboriginal and Torres Strait Islander Studies and Aboriginal and Torres Strait Islander Commission.

Living Knowledge Project (2008). *About 'both ways' education*. Retrieved on October 10, 2013 from: http://livingknowledge.anu.edu.au/html/educators/07_bothways.htm

Ma Rhea, Z. (2012). Thinking Galtha, teaching literacy: From Aboriginal mother tongue to strangers' texts and beyond. In A. Cree (Ed.), *Aboriginal education: New pathways for teaching and learning* (pp. 24-53). Berowra, Australia: Australian Combined University Press.

Ma Rhea, Z. (2015). Unthinking the 200 year old colonial mindset: Indigenist perspectives on leading and managing Indigenous education. *International Education Journal: Comparative Perspectives*, 14(2), 90-100.

Ma Rhea, Z., Anderson, P. J., & Atkinson, B. (2012). *Improving teaching in Aboriginal and Torres Strait Islander education: National Professional Standards for Teachers Standards Focus Areas 1.4 and 2.4*. Melbourne, Victoria: Australian Institute for Teaching and School Leadership.

Marika-Mununggiritj, R. (1999). 1998 Wentworth Lecture. *Australian Aboriginal Studies*, 1, 3-9.

Marika-Mununggiritj, R., and Christie, M. J. (1995). Yolngu metaphors for learning. *International Journal of the Sociology of Language*, 113, 59-62.

United Nations (2004). The concept of Indigenous peoples: Background paper prepared by the Secretariat of the Permanent Forum on Indigenous Issues. Workshop on data collection and disaggregation for Indigenous peoples, New York, 19-21 January, 2004). Retrieved on November 28, 2017 from: http://www.un.org/esa/socdev/unpfii/documents/workshop_data_background.doc

United Nations (2008). *United Nations Declaration on the Rights of Indigenous Peoples* [UNDRIPs]. Retrieved on November 28, 2017 from: http://www.un.org/esa/socdev/unpfii/documents/DRIPS_en.pdf

United Nations Development Group (2008). Guidelines on Indigenous peoples' issues. Retrieved on November 28, 2017 from: http://www.undg.org/index.cfm?P=270

Vygotsky, L. S. (1934 [1962]). Thought and language. (E. Hanfmann & G. Vakar, Eds. and Trans.). Cambridge, MA: MIT Press. (Original work published 1934).

Vygotsky, L. S. (1978). Interaction between learning and development (M. Lopez-Morillas, Trans.). In M. Cole, V. John-Steiner, S. Scribner, & E. Souberman (Eds.), *Mind in society: The development of higher psychological processes* (pp. 79-91). Cambridge, MA: Harvard University Press.

Yunupiŋu, M. (1994). Yothu Yindi – finding balance. In *Voices from the land: 1993 Boyer Lectures* (pp. 113-120). Sydney, Australia: Australian Broadcasting Corporation.

18 Collaboration in the classroom

Jane McCormack and Michelle Smith-Tamaray

Introduction

Peering through the window or stepping across the threshold of a classroom in Australia is like entering a unique and fascinating new world. Each looks different, sounds different, feels different. In part, the difference reflects the specific content that has been studied and/or the pedagogy employed by the teacher within that particular classroom. However, the difference also reflects the uniqueness of the cohort of students within that classroom environment. Due to a range of social and political changes in the Australian education system, and in the nation more broadly across recent years, the students within Australian classrooms might now be considered the most diverse they have ever been. For instance, the numbers of children who speak English as a second or other language has increased with the arrival of more refugee and migrant families to Australia, and the range of languages spoken by these children and their families has also increased with changes in the countries from which they are arriving (e.g., Asian and African countries rather than Europe; McLeod, 2011). A less recent, but no less important change, is the inclusion of students with additional learning needs within mainstream Australian classrooms. Indeed, recent Australian research indicates that approximately one-third of primary/secondary students experience additional learning needs, with the most common being specific learning difficulties, followed by communication disorders and English as a second or other language (McLeod & McKinnon, 2007).

Diversity in the composition of Australian classrooms can be a wonderful resource for learning and teaching both academic and social skills. However, it can also present a challenge for educators in differentiating the curriculum and supporting the learning needs of each student, particularly when those students don't receive additional in-class support. The NSW Department of Education and Communities (DEC) has acknowledged that "schools and teachers are increasingly challenged by students who may present with additional learning and support needs but who do not meet the existing disability criteria for targeted services" (NSW DEC, 2012, p. 5). In such cases, collaboration between educators and other professionals can be valuable. Indeed, collaboration is valuable in the delivery of education and care to students from all backgrounds. However, in order for collaboration to be effective, educators and other professionals require knowledge about different types of collaboration, benefits of collaboration and barriers and facilitators to collaboration as well as skills in how to "do" collaboration.

This chapter explores collaboration in Australian classrooms. It is framed around a study aimed at exploring the views and experiences of early childhood educators and speech-language pathologists with regards to collaboration. These professionals play an important role in supporting that diverse group of students described earlier; in particular, students with communication disorders. The chapter commences with a description of the prevalence and impact of communication disorders to provide context to the study. A description of collaboration and communities of practice is then provided, with a review of national and international studies exploring collaborative practice with children who experience communication disorders. Despite this focus, the concepts discussed and the issues raised apply equally to collaborations aimed at supporting other learners. Following the literature review, the methods and results of the research study are presented. The chapter then concludes with a discussion of how research into collaboration, and collaboration itself, can inform learning and teaching, and a reflection on the use of evidence to guide professional practice.

What enables effective collaboration? An investigation of the views of early childhood educators and speech-language pathologists

Background

Communication is a skill that human beings utilise every day, in a range of modalities, activities, and with a range of communication partners. We do it so automatically that we sometimes forget what a complex process it is. While most children learn to communicate without any difficulties, communication (speech and/or language) disorders are still commonly experienced by preschool-aged children (Law, Boyle, Harris, Harkness, & Nye, 2000) with recent Australian research suggesting the prevalence could be up to one in five children (McLeod & Harrison, 2009). In the preschool years, children with communication disorder may experience associated difficulties with social interactions, managing frustration/behaviour and learning pre-literacy skills (McCormack, McLeod, Harrison, & McAllister, 2010; McCue-Horwitz et al., 2003). When it continues into the child's school years, communication impairment is often associated with behavioural problems (Lindsay & Dockrell, 2000), and slower progress in reading, writing and overall school achievement (McCormack, Harrison, McLeod, & McAllister, 2011; Nathan, Stackhouse, Goulandris, & Snowling, 2004). Timely and evidence-based support can address these difficulties and lead to good outcomes. However, recent research indicates that in many communities of Australia with a high proportion of children at risk of communication disorder, there is no access to specialised services (i.e., speech-language pathology) to support these additional needs (McCormack & Verdon, 2015). In other communities, there is limited access to services, so children may receive a short block of intervention or consultative rather than direct support (Verdon, Wilson, Smith-Tamaray, & McAllister, 2011). These children face dual disadvantage: (1) their additional communication needs, and (2) the lack of resources within the community to support their needs. In such communities, it is likely that educators (early childhood and/or primary teachers) will be the primary sources of communication support.

Early childhood educators (ECEs), in particular, are in a key position, given Australian government policies which require universal provision of preschool education, and given that the *Early Years Learning Framework* lists the expectation that children are "effective communicators" as one of five learning outcomes of their early childhood education (DEEWR, 2009). Collaboration between speech-language pathologists (SLPs) and ECEs is one way to ensure ECEs can provide the necessary support to children in the context of natural learning opportunities of their everyday environment.

What is collaboration?

Within the education system, we see many examples of individuals or groups working together. However, this is not necessarily collaboration. Teamwork can take many forms including: (1) communication, (2) coordination, (3) cooperation and (4) collaboration (Kinsella-Meier, & Gala, 2016). These vary according to the purpose, duration, involvement and outcomes of the team. While all may lead to more efficient work practices through information sharing and workload distribution, in the first three forms of teamwork, the duration of the partnership is typically short term and the contribution of team members/partners is largely autonomous. In contrast, *collaboration* occurs when two or more individuals or agencies work together on long-term projects to achieve complex and interdependent goals. Collaboration involves the establishment of relationships, equality of partners and shared decision making, as well as the sharing of resources, knowledge and skills to achieve common goals and enable professional growth (Friend & Cook, 2000). In this way, collaboration may be seen to align with the educational concept/learning theory known as *communities of practice* (Lave, 1991; Wenger, 1998).

What is a community of practice?

Communities of practice (CoP) have been described as groups of people who have a shared domain of interest, and who learn more about that interest through engaging in regular interactions with one another (Wenger-Traynor & Wenger-Traynor, 2015). CoP have three defining characteristics: (1) the domain; (2) the community; and (3) the practice (see Table 18.1). While earlier learning theories suggested that individuals acquire new knowledge and skills through observation (Behaviourism; Skinner) or interactions with others (Social Learning Theory; Bandura), the theory underlying CoP is that learning is a process and product of social participation when individuals with a common interest collaborate over a long period of time.

CoP belong to the realm of constructivist learning theories, which posit that knowledge is expanded and refined through linking new information with existing information (Fry, Kettridge, & Marshall, 2008). In CoP, the key way in which community members expand and refine their

Table 18.1 Characteristics of a community of practice

Characteristic	Definition
Domain	Area of interest/expertise shared by community members, and to which they are committed.
Community	Members who engage in joint activities and discussions to build relationships, learn together, help each other and share information.
Practice	As members are practitioners, they develop a shared repertoire of resources: experiences, stories, tools, ways of addressing recurring problems (i.e., a shared practice). This takes time and sustained interaction.

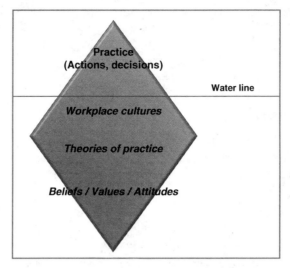

Figure 18.1 The "iceberg": Elements of professional practice (based on Fish & Coles, 1998)

knowledge is through sustained interactions with others on projects of mutual interest. Thus, CoP incorporate the notion of situated learning; the theory that individuals learn through being participants in social situations (i.e., as members of CoP). Situated learning is consistent with the idea that, "the capacity of students to learn does not simply depend upon themselves, but upon the environment in which they learn and what is regarded as valid learning" (Nillsen, 2004, p. 2). So, in CoP, members are actively involved in their own learning but also involved in the learning of one another, as they share their expertise to build another's capacity. CoP arise through a commitment to learning and growing practice-based knowledge and skills, often in order to address recurring problems or issues of importance to community members.

In order for a community of practice to be successful, there needs to be explicit recognition of the many elements that contribute to "practice" and the ways in which these elements differ from one community member to the next. The metaphor of an iceberg has previously been used to capture elements of professional practice. Fish and Coles (1998) suggested that what we notice, do or experience as "practice" (the visible tip of the iceberg) is influenced by many other elements, hiding beneath the surface (the water line). These hidden elements include workplace policies, practices, requirements and expectations; discipline knowledge, assumptions about practice, theories, evidence and frameworks; as well as personal attitudes, beliefs and values (see Figure 18.1). Once these elements have been recognised, the impact on practice needs to be acknowledged and understood. Then, any differences in practice based on these elements can be exposed and explicitly discussed in order to overcome conflicts in actions or decisions, and to enable collaboration to occur. Hence, there is the need for the practice to be sustained over time and for the community members to be committed to the process.

Barriers and facilitators to collaboration

The benefits of collaborating in a community of practice are numerous. For instance, collaboration between educators and SLPs can benefit students through ensuring a consistent approach to their care, and a more innovative approach to the provision of support which better addresses the demands of both curriculum and intervention (Baxter, Brookes, Bianchi, Rashid, & Hay, 2009; Hartas, 2004; Kersner, 1996; Kersner & Wright, 1996; McCartney, 2002). However, despite a recognition of the benefits of collaboration, it can be difficult to achieve within the classroom. Studies in Australia and overseas have identified barriers to collaboration between SLPs and educators, which can exist at several levels: individual, professional/discipline, local school setting/workplace and broader systematic issues (Glover, McCormack, & Smith-Tamaray, 2015).

SLPs are often reliant upon teachers to identify children who need additional assessment and support. They will then typically assess children's skills, diagnose difficulties and make recommendations about ongoing support/intervention. However, teachers often report feeling that they do not have the necessary skills, knowledge or expertise required to identify (Antoniazzi, Snow, & Dickson-Swift, 2010) or manage children with additional communication needs (Law et al., 2000). Many teachers suggest the training at a university level does not equip them with the knowledge and skills required to support these children (Harper & Rennie, 2009), but rather they acquire this expertise through working with SLPs, which requires time spent together allowing interactions to occur (Wright & Kersner, 1999). Thus, facilitators to good collaborative practice are time, and closer joint working, as well as a shared language and an understanding of each other's roles; elements of the practice "iceberg" that hide beneath the surface (Fish & Coles, 1998). However, SLPs are sometimes inaccessible or unable to allocate more time at schools due to logistics or limited resources (e.g., caseload constraints). In Australia, the way in which SLPs are employed (through the health system or through the education system) varies from state to state (McLeod, Press, & Phelan, 2010). This results in variation in service provision and variation in how collaboration is undertaken.

It is important to understand the barriers and facilitators to collaboration in order to create better collaborative experiences. The following section outlines an Australian study, which examined the perspectives of ECEs and SLPs with regards to effective collaborative practices when working with children who have speech and/or language difficulties (McCormack & Easton, 2013). For the purposes of this chapter, the description of results focuses on the participants' responses to the question: *What do you believe enables effective working relationships between speech pathologists and early childhood educators?*

Method

The study incorporated two stages based on a mixed methods research design. A questionnaire examining the broad perspectives and practices of SLPs and ECEs working with children with communication disorder provided initial quantitative data. A qualitative approach was then used to guide subsequent focus groups designed to provide a detailed understanding of the experiences of the two professional groups when working with these children. This chapter focuses on the results of one questionnaire item.

Participants

There were 49 paediatric SLPs from among the Speech Pathology Australia (SPA) membership who responded to the questionnaire and 51 ECEs from Early Childhood Australia (ECA).

The mean number of years spent working in early childhood settings was 10.2 for the SLPs (n = 46) and 16.2 for the ECEs (n = 31). The largest number of SLP responses was from those currently working in private practice (37.8%) or community health (24.4%), while the largest number of ECE responses was from those working in preschools (53.1%). Most participants reported working in metropolitan areas (57.1% of SLPs and 52.8% of ECEs) and small regional areas (18.4% of SLPs and 19.4% of ECEs).

Tool

Two questionnaires were developed; one for SLPs containing 50 questions and a similar questionnaire for ECEs containing 54 questions. The questionnaires requested demographic information, details about the participants' knowledge and training (relating to communication difficulties and their management as well as curriculum documents and their impact on practice), current practices when working with children with communication difficulties and with other professional groups, perceptions of need for improved services and facilitators/barriers to collaboration with other professional groups. Questions were based on a questionnaire used in previous research in the UK investigating training, confidence and practices of ECEs working with children with communication difficulties (Letts & Hall, 2003), although some modifications were made for the Australian context, drawing on other relevant research.

Procedure

Information about the research project was distributed to SLPs and ECEs via national newsletters, emailed to all members each month. The information contained a link to an online questionnaire (via Survey-Monkey), which participants were invited to complete. At the completion of the questionnaire, participants were requested to identify their willingness to contribute to subsequent focus group(s) to discuss their experiences in greater detail. Descriptive/inferential statistics were used for quantitative data to compare responses from the two professional groups and provide a context of current practice. A thematic analysis was undertaken with the open-ended responses to identify the key issues that arose from the data. First, the responses from the ECEs were read and codes were assigned to their statements. A table was created listing all of the codes that had been generated, and corresponding excerpts from the questionnaires. Next, responses from the SLPs were coded, and a table with excerpts was created for their data. The codes and excerpts from both data sets were then compared to ensure that the codes had been applied consistently within and across each data set. Following this, connections between the codes were identified and broader themes were generated to group and organise the data. In the following section, we explore the responses to the question of what enables effective working relationships.

Results

There were 19 ECEs and 27 SLPs who responded to the extended-response question regarding effective working relationships. Based on analysis of this data, four themes were found to emerge: (1) common goals/outcomes; (2) mutual respect, (3) knowledge exchange and

Collaboration in the classroom 223

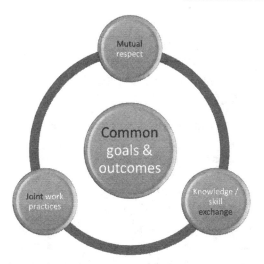

Figure 18.2 Factors that enable effective working relationships between speech pathologists and early childhood educators

(4) joint work practices. An overarching theme of "sharing" can be seen across each of these themes and relationships were found to exist among them, as illustrated in Figure 18.2.

Theme 1: Common goals/outcomes "Common understanding of the child being at the centre of what everyone is there for"

ECEs and SLPs identified that "being on the same wavelength" was important in order to work together effectively. They described this in terms of sharing a common purpose (e.g., working to support the child) as well as sharing a common knowledge, a common language, common goals, beliefs and even common models of practice (family/child-centred). This is consistent with the definition of collaboration presented earlier in this chapter; that it requires all parties to be working together for the same outcome. The other themes differed from this first one in that they described what is needed in order for the common outcome to be achieved.

Theme 2: Mutual respect "Respect for each other"

Both professional groups acknowledged a need for mutual respect if they were to work together effectively. They felt that they needed to respect each other's roles and responsibilities, expertise, perspectives, work models and environments. Furthermore, they discussed a need to "trust" one another. This suggests something more than respect. It suggests a willingness to accept the views of another as valid, and valuable, and to allow these other views to guide one's own practice when required. As one participant remarked, it means a "willingness to listen to each other and change practices according to the other's needs and child's needs". At the very core of effective collaboration, therefore, is a need to be aware of one's own beliefs, values and attitudes and the beliefs, values and attitudes of those with whom one works. Recognising how these might impact on practice can lead to improved understanding, and an openness to discussion and problem solving. However, awareness and understanding of one another's beliefs, values and attitudes can only come about through dialogue between the collaborators.

Theme 3: Knowledge exchange "Communication and information sharing"

Both professional groups described the need for communication between all parties involved in the collaboration. They identified the need for communication to be clear, regular and honest. They also emphasised the need for communication to be "open". Again, "openness" suggests more than just listening to another or talking to another. It suggests a willingness to provide information that will improve the knowledge base of the person with whom we work, and/or a willingness to act on the information we receive. As one participant commented, sharing information (about philosophical and theoretical frameworks) enables professionals to "start to speak each other's language", which in turn can lead to greater opportunities for communication and greater understanding. The communication is not one-sided, if there is mutual respect, as all collaborators recognise the potential to "learn from each other". Thus, the communication leads to a knowledge/skill exchange, rather than simply a transfer from one to another. In order for these exchanges to occur, there needs to be time and opportunities for contact between collaborators.

Theme 4: Joint work practices "Opportunities to work together and problem solve together"

SLPs and ECEs recognised that if each had more time, they would be able to liaise with one another and communicate more effectively. However, perhaps more important than time was the opportunity to have contact with one another and work together. One participant identified the need for "less restrictive working practices to enable more time to liaise". Both groups recognised the value of working in the same physical space (i.e., the setting in which children play, communicate and learn). They identified that SLPs who had practice and experience within early childhood settings were more likely to make recommendations that were "realistic", "embedded into the routines" and "accommodating of practicalities". That is, the knowledge exchange was more functional and meaningful when joint working in a shared setting occurred.

Discussion

In this research study, we explored the perspectives of two professional groups (ECEs and SLPs) who may be members of a community of practice in an education context. In practice, this community might incorporate other professionals (such as learning support officers or teaching assistants) and family members as well; however, their views were not gathered in this study. The community shared a common interest (domain) in supporting the communication and learning needs of students with communication disorders. Their practice involved ongoing interactions (via meetings, correspondence, team-teaching, training) to develop and implement resources, activities, feedback/reinforcement, strategies and learning plans for those students.

Such a community has multiple benefits. Different professionals working within the classroom bring a variety of skills to working with children in that environment. For instance, teachers have a comprehensive knowledge of the curriculum and aim to support and guide the language development of all children within their class. In contrast, SLPs have detailed knowledge of language development, language and literacy difficulties and strategies to support students at risk, and they typically work to support the children with difficulties learning language skills. These approaches are complementary, but can only work together if both parties understand each other's roles and are able to develop a shared language (Kersner, 1996; Law et al., 2000).

The metaphor of an iceberg was used earlier in this chapter to identify visible and hidden elements of professional practice. The iceberg metaphor is useful to reflect on here, as the results from the reported research suggest that a sharing of some/all of these hidden elements can lead to more effective collaborative practice. However, the research also highlighted the need for acceptance and openness to that which is shared. That is, for collaboration to be effective, there needed to be more than just an awareness of what underpins one's own (and others') practice, but also an honesty in recognising one's own strengths and limitations, respect for another's knowledge/skills, trust in each other and a commitment to working together. Thus, the foundations of effective collaboration are the core beliefs, attitudes and values we have about ourselves, our practice and the others with whom we work.

While some challenges/barriers to collaboration might be difficult or take time to overcome (e.g., government policy relating to employment of professionals or delivery of services), it is possible that other barriers (e.g., professional knowledge or personal beliefs) could be addressed sooner. For instance, educating professionals about the knowledge, skills and expertise of other team members, and providing professional development opportunities that cross professional boundaries and provide a common language and shared skill-set, could be valuable training for those working to support children with additional language/communication needs.

Conclusion

Successful inclusion of children with additional learning needs in mainstream classrooms (including children with additional language needs) may be facilitated by routine collaboration between educators and other professionals such as SLPs (Shaddock, Smyth King, & Giorcelli, 2007). Successful inclusion has obvious benefits for the children. However, the collaboration that has enabled the inclusion and support of these children has immense value for the professionals involved as well, through the development of a community of practice in which knowledge and skills are shared, which lead to improved productivity and outcomes. At the start of this chapter we explored some of the challenges to collaboration between professionals, including differences in their attitudes to practice, in their knowledge/training, in the models in which they practice and the policies guiding practice (McCartney, 2002). Next, we presented research that examined what enables effective collaborative practice from the perspective of two different professional groups (educators and SLPs). We need to use caution in interpreting the results, as they are based on responses to a single research question. However, they do provide valuable points to consider, particularly given the consistency of responses across the professional groups. Both noted the need for: an underlying, mutual respect; a willingness to share and accept professional knowledge/skills; and a sense of working together towards a common goal/outcome.

Thus, it is possible that challenges to collaboration can be overcome, at least in part, if we target these elements. For instance, different attitudes to practice may cease to be a barrier if we approach collaboration with an attitude of respect, with an awareness of the "language" spoken by our collaborators and an understanding of the theories/frameworks that guide their work. Additionally, different knowledge/skills may cease to be a barrier if we recognise the complementarity of each other's professions and approach collaboration as an opportunity to expand our knowledge/skills for the ultimate benefit of those with whom we work. But how do we do this? The theory of CoP suggests that the "community" becomes such through interaction and engagement over extended periods of time. Thus, we need to provide opportunities for communities to be established and consolidated over time. This can occur at a pre-service and in-service level. For instance, in tertiary education and health programs, pre-service students (the community) could be explicitly taught skills in collaboration and then provided with opportunities for shared practical experiences (the practice) in areas of common focus, such as supporting students with English as a second language or those with additional learning needs (the domain). Post-university, practicing professionals could be offered opportunities to engage in collaborative professional development experiences to enable the establishment of CoP based on common goals, mutual respect, knowledge exchange and joint working. There are also opportunities for joining established CoP through membership of inter-professional special interest groups (e.g., Developmental Disorders of Language and Literacy Network; http://www.cogsci.mq.edu.au/ddoll/). Collaboration is a complex process that requires roles and relationships to be reconsidered without devaluing the professional skills of either group (Hall, 2005). The more open, and willing, we are to engage in collaboration and the more practice we have at "doing" collaboration, the more effective our practice will be.

References

Antoniazzi, D., Snow, P., & Dickson-Swift, V. (2010). Teacher identification of children at risk for language impairment in the first year of school. *International Journal of Speech-Language Pathology*, *12*(3), 244–252. DOI:10.3109/17549500903104447

Baxter, S., Brookes, C., Bianchi, K., Rashid, K., & Hay, F. (2009). Speech and language therapists and teachers working together: Exploring the issues. *Child Language Teaching and Therapy*, *25*(2), 215–234.

DEEWR (Department of Education, Employment and Workplace Relations) (2009). *Belonging, being, and becoming: The early years learning framework for Australia*. Canberra: Author.

Fish, D., & Coles, C. (1998). *Developing professional judgement in health care: Learning through the critical appreciation of practice*. Boston, MA: Butterworth-Heinemann.

Friend, M., & Cook, L. (2000). *Interactions: Collaboration skills for school professionals* (3rd ed.). New York: Longman.

Fry, H., Kettridge, S., & Marshall, S. (2008). Understanding student learning. In H. Fry, S. Ketteridge, & S. Marshall (Eds.), *A Handbook for Teaching and Learning in Higher Education* (pp. 8–26). London: Routledge.

Glover, A., McCormack, J., & Smith-Tamaray, M. (2015). Collaboration between teachers and speech-language therapists: Services for primary school children with speech, language and communication needs. *Child Language Teaching and Therapy*, *31*(3), 363–382.

Hall, E. (2005). 'Joined-up working' between early years professionals and speech and language therapists: Moving beyond 'normal' roles. *Journal of Interprofessional Care, 19*, 11–21. DOI:10.1080/13561820400021759

Harper, H., & Rennie, J. (2009). 'I had to go out and get myself a book on grammar': A study of pre-service teachers' knowledge about language. *The Australian Journal of Language and Literacy, 32*, 22–37.

Hartas, D. (2004). Teacher and speech-language therapist collaboration: Being equal and achieving a common goal? *Child Language Teaching and Therapy, 20*(1), 33–54. DOI:10.1191/0265659004ct262oa

Kersner, M. (1996). Working together for children with severe learning disabilities. *Child Language Teaching and Therapy, 12*(1), 17–28.

Kersner, M., & Wright, J. A. (1996). Collaboration between teachers and speech and language therapists working with children with severe learning disabilities (SLD): Implications for professional development. *British Journal of Learning Disabilities, 24*(1), 33–37.

Kinsella-Meier, A., & Gala, N. M. (2016). Collaboration: Definitions and explorations of an essential partnership. *Odyssey: New Directions in Deaf Education, 17*, 4–9.

Lave, J. (1991). Situating learning in communities of practice. *Perspectives on Socially Shared Cognition, 2*, 63–82.

Law, J., Boyle, J., Harris, F., Harkness, A., & Nye, C. (2000). Prevalence and natural history of primary speech and language delay: Findings from a systematic review of the literature. *International Journal of Language and Communication Disorders, 35*(2), 165–188.

Letts, C., & Hall, E. (2003). Exploring early years professionals' knowledge about speech and language development and impairment. *Child Language Teaching and Therapy, 19*, 211–229.

Lindsay, G., & Dockrell, J. (2000). The behaviour and self-esteem of children with specific speech and language difficulties. *British Journal of Educational Psychology, 70*(4), 583–601.

McCartney, E. (2002). Cross-sector working: Speech and language therapists in education. *Journal of Management in Medicine, 16*(1), 67–77.

McCormack, J., & Easton, C. (2013, August). *The collaborative practices of health and education professionals in the management of children with communication difficulties.* 29th World Congress of the International Association of Logopedics and Phoniatrics, Turin, Italy.

McCormack, J., Harrison, L. J., McLeod, S., & McAllister, L. (2011). A nationally representative study of the association between communication impairment at 4–5 years and children's life activities at 7–9 years. *Journal of Speech, Language and Hearing Research, 54*(5), 1328–1348. DOI: 10.1044/1092-4388(2011/10-0155)

McCormack, J., McLeod, S., Harrison, L. J., & McAllister, L. (2010). The impact of speech impairment in early childhood: Investigating parents' and speech-language pathologists' perspectives using the ICF-CY. *Journal of Communication Disorders, 43*(5), 378–396.

McCormack, J., & Verdon, S. (2015). Mapping speech pathology services to developmentally vulnerable and at-risk communities using the Australian Early Development Index. *International Journal of Speech-Language Pathology, 17*(3), 273–286. DOI:10.3109/17549507.2015.1034175

McCue-Horwitz, S., Irwin, J. R., Brigs-Gowan, M. J., Bosson Heenan, J. M., Mendoza, J., & Carter, A. S. (2003). Language delay in a community cohort of young children. *Journal of the American Academy of Child and Adolescent Psychiatry, 42*(8), 932–940.

McLeod, S. (2011). Cultural and linguistic diversity in Australian 4- to 5-year-old children and their parents. *Journal of Clinical Practice in Speech-Language Pathology, 13*(3), 112–119.

McLeod, S., & Harrison, L. J. (2009). Epidemiology of speech and language impairment in a nationally representative sample of 4- to 5-year-old children. *Journal of Speech, Language, and Hearing Research, 52*(5), 1213–1229.

McLeod, S., & McKinnon, D. H. (2007). Prevalence of communication disorders compared with other learning needs in 14500 primary and secondary school students. *International Journal of Language and Communication Disorders, 42*(S1), 37–59.

McLeod, S., Press, F., & Phelan, C. (2010). The (in)visibility of children with communication impairment in Australian health, education, and disability legislation and policies. *Asia Pacific Journal of Speech, Language, and Hearing, 13*(1), 67–75.

Nathan, L., Stackhouse, J., Goulandris, N., & Snowling, M. (2004). Educational consequences of developmental speech disorder: Key Stage 1 National Curriculum assessment results in English and mathematics. *British Journal of Educational Psychology, 74*, 173–186.

Nillsen, R. (2004). Can the love of learning be taught? *Journal of University Teaching and Learning Practice, 1*(1), 1–9.

NSW DEC (NSW Department of Education and Communities). (2012). *Every student, every school: Learning and support.* Sydney, Australia: Author. Retrieved from: http://www.dec.nsw.gov.au/about-us/how-we-operate/national-partnerships/every-student-every-school

Shaddock, T. J., Smyth King, B., & Giorcelli, L. (2007). *Project to improve the learning outcomes of students with disabilities in the early, middle and post compulsory years of schooling.* Canberra, Australia: Australian Government Department of Education, Science and Training. Retrieved from: http://www.canberra.edu.au/researchrepository/items/1c1cba2b-42d9-248e-b79d-5e13e28c891e/1/

Verdon, S., Wilson, L., Smith-Tamaray, M., & McAllister, L. (2011). An investigation of equity of rural speech-language pathology services for children: A geographic perspective. *International Journal of Speech-Language Pathology, 13*(3), 239–250.

Wenger, E. (1998). *Communities of practice: Learning, meaning, and identity.* Cambridge, UK: Cambridge University Press.

Wenger-Trayner, E., & Wenger-Trayner, B. (2015). Introduction to communities of practice: A brief overview of the concept and its uses. Retrieved from: http://wenger-trayner.com/introduction-to-communities-of-practice/

Wright, J. A., & Kersner, M. (1999). Teachers and speech and language therapists working with children with physical disabilities: Implications for inclusive education. *British Journal of Special Education, 26*(4), 201–205.

19 Action research
A reflective tool for teaching

Louise Jenkins and Renée Crawford

Introduction: Reflective practice

Effective professional development requires teachers to be reflective about their practice, at the pre-service teacher level and as part of a life-long career practice (Clarke 1995; Cole, 1989; Wildman, Magliaro, Niles, & McLaughlin, 1990). Teachers should consistently take time to consider the impact of their work on their students and to address issues in the classroom. Credited initially to Dewey in the 1930s, the theory of reflective practice was adopted and developed by others in the 1980s, including Schön. Although Schön did not write directly about the application of the theory to teaching, it is easily applied to teachers' professional work. Dewey's theory was based on the idea that practitioners should examine what it is they do (Dewey, 1933). He suggested a systematic approach to reflection that supported the professional development of teachers with the goal of creating change in their classroom practice. In the 1980s Schön described the reflective process for professionals as having three elements: "reflection-in-action", "knowing-in-action" and "reflection-on-action" (Schön, 1983, 1987). "Reflection-in-action" is what teachers are doing as they teach, the "in the moment" reflection. It is this aspect of the reflective process that allows teachers to respond to new situations when their established responses are not effective. They then try various techniques or approaches to resolve the situation, based on what they already know and understand. "Knowing-in-action" describes the tacit knowledge which teachers have, but do not necessarily verbalise. "Reflection-on-action" incorporates the process of reflecting after the event when teachers analyse and deconstruct their work. Significant theorists in the field of reflective practice acknowledge that it is a complex process requiring application and commitment. It goes beyond merely thinking about one's work as an after-thought. Instead it involves a persistent and active consideration of beliefs and knowledge (Zeichner & Liston, 1996) and following the reflection there should be outcomes (Boud, Keogh, & Walker, 1985). For teachers the outcomes could be changes to curriculum, the implementation of a new activity, new approaches to planning for the classroom or inventive ways to manage a class. The type and range of outcomes are almost endless dependent on the school, class, students and teacher and the particular concerns or problems that have prompted the systematic reflective process.

Both Dewey and Schön encourage the systematic investigation of problem resolution through reflective practice. Dewey maintained that when teachers combine systematic reflection with their actual teaching experiences, their awareness is developed, thus supporting positive professional development. It could be argued therefore that Dewey in the 1930s was advocating for a form of evidence-based teaching (Farrell, 2012) and that Schön was encouraging this type of evidence gathering for professionals, including teachers, despite his theories not being specifically directed at teachers. In reflective practice teachers collect data about their work, reflect on the data and use the data to inform what they do in their current and future classes. Any changes they do, or do not, make to their practice are therefore evidence based. For contemporary teachers at various stages of their careers, Schön's theory of reflective practice is most applicable as part of a multi-layered process to support the provision of the evidence of the impact of their work and thereby meet the current expectations for accountability.

Action research as a methodological framework and tool for reflective practice

Due to the reflective nature of teaching and learning, action research (AR) is a valuable methodology for investigating teaching practice. The methodological framework provides educators with a way to critically analyse the issues presented in a localised context, for example, the classroom or school, with the intention that this could later be applied to a wider context such as other classes at the same level or in the same subject area. While AR is not a new approach in educational contexts, it is the contemporary discourse around evidence-based practice that has instigated a resurgence about the value of such an approach as a qualitative measure and tool for critical reflection. In essence, AR can broadly be defined as taking action based on research and researching the action taken (Crawford & Jenkins, 2015). Being a reflective practitioner is an essential part of teaching and such research can be used to demonstrate evidence of the techniques, strategies, behaviours and attitudes of professional actions taken or decisions made (Pelton, 2010). The value of such an approach compared with other research methodologies is based on the premise that local conditions vary widely and that the solutions to such educational problems cannot be found in generalised facts that take no account of local conditions. Each classroom has its own specific context, including students (age, socio-economic backgrounds, gender), teacher and subject content and, as such, finding solutions to classroom challenges requires consideration of the specific circumstances in the classroom.

The term "action research" was coined by German-American psychologist Kurt Lewin in his 1946 paper, 'Action Research and Minority Problems'. He described AR as: "a comparative research on the conditions and effects of various forms of social action and research leading to social action" (Lewin, 1946, p. 35). Lewin suggested a spiral of steps, each of which included a planning, action and fact-finding circle to investigate the result of an action. While Lewin is considered the pioneer of AR primarily associated with social change efforts, in education, some trace the conceptual roots to the progressive views of Dewey in the 1920s (Mertler, 2009; Pelton, 2010). However, it was not until Stenhouse's (1975) notion of the teacher-as-researcher that "action research" and "critical reflection" became interrelated and educational AR was considered as a process that fostered different kinds of reflection at the centre of the approach. It has since not only gained traction in the field of education, but also in a number of other professional settings such as medicine, clinical studies and government units (Noffke & Somekh, 2009). AR can be considered a qualitative measurement approach and response to evidence-based practice that can be applied to such areas as curriculum development, teaching strategies and school reform. It is proposed that the purpose of AR in educational contexts is to create an inquiry stance where questioning one's own practice becomes part of a teacher's professional work and of the culture. Many teachers may and should engage in a form of reflection as self-assessment and evaluation. However, in AR, reflection is a key component of the methodology. It is a systematically cyclical, iterative and critical approach, alternating between action and reflection, continuously refining methods and interpretations based on understandings developed in earlier cycles. While various types of AR can be used, the case study presented here was underpinned by Hendricks' (2009) AR approach.

Using Hendricks' (2009) classroom AR approach

Hendricks' (2009) classroom AR approach is used to improve classroom/tutorial practice or in the wider school/university context with the intention of changing theory and practice. This involves teacher/s in their classroom/tutorial examining issues and problems and implementing changes in order to find innovative solutions. In the case study discussed, classroom AR was considered a highly valuable approach in providing an evidence base for our teacher practice and a tool for critical reflection. The benefits of using such an approach in education have been identified by Crawford and Jenkins (2015) as a means to provide opportunities for teachers and pre-service teachers to: develop knowledge directly related to practice and focus on improving practice; promote systematic critical reflection and use of information for better decision making in the development of curriculum and pedagogy; foster openness to new ideas and encourage creativity and innovation; and encourage rethinking about how teachers' and students' work is evaluated.

Ethical and practical challenges of Action Research

AR encourages and supports beginning teachers to embed professional development in their work and experienced teachers to pursue ongoing professional development (Kane & Chimwayange, 2014). Despite the many benefits of AR, there are some identified challenges. Although AR is commonly used in small-scale studies, the method requires time and commitment for teachers to identify a problem/issue, devise a plan to address the problem/issue, gather and analyse the data and use this to inform their practice. The teacher-researcher is completing this on top of their normal teaching workload. It is imperative to structure the project carefully to balance these two commitments (Clift, Golby, & Moon, 1988; Drucker, 1994). Time management is an important consideration, which can impact on the potential research scope, quality of the data and overall project (Fraser, 1997). For pre-service teachers, teaching can be seen as something you "do", but do not necessarily "ponder" (Wideen, Mayer-Smith, & Moon, 1998), and yet quality AR requires considerable thought and a broad-based understanding of what the project is trying to achieve. Understanding the reason why you need to gather the data can support the implementation process and analysis of data (Lam, 2016). Finding time to do the necessary readings and writing can be challenging, but schools can assist by investing time in the teacher and the project (Lambirth & Cabral, 2017). AR should be incorporated in a way that avoids detracting from normal teaching work, as most teachers will prioritise their teaching over the research (Elliott, 1991).

In response to its inherent challenges, ethical issues in AR have been studied extensively (Banegas, 2015). In a tertiary context, an ethics application is normally submitted to a university ethics committee. This requires the researchers to thoroughly consider all aspects of their project as well as all ethical considerations prior to commencing. The principal, regional director or another body in charge of the school may need to be provided with an application for approval to do the project, but this will be dependent on each individual circumstance (Hendricks, 2009). Having a teacher research their own students can be problematic as "there is … little distance between the researcher and the subjects" (Crawford & Jenkins, 2015, p. 14), Essentially, the researchers are "insiders responsible to … students whose learning [they] document" (Zeni, 1998, p. 10). This insider role presents issues with bias in the data analysis as the teacher may consciously or unconsciously look for a particular outcome resulting in unsupportable classroom changes. Burgess (1985) suggests that very few educational researchers discuss the ethical questions related to their research, but the principles applied to ethics in AR require the same rigorous and systematic formulas found in other research methodologies. For example, objective data are still achievable in AR by ensuring there are multiple sources of data collection (Crawford & Jenkins, 2015; Sagor, 2000). Further, in any AR project the teacher-researchers should minimise the risk of any harm to participants. AR does not usually involve dangerous activities; however, the participants are usually under the age of 18, so consideration of potential harm is paramount.

In a preschool, primary or secondary school setting, consent forms and explanatory statements may need to be implemented. Generally, the need for these will be dependent on whether the findings from the research will be disseminated, for example, via a publication, a presentation at a school event or a conference paper (Hendricks, 2009; Mertler, 2009). Zeni (1998, p. 11) suggests that if an AR teacher's "journal remain[s] private and … videotapes aren't played, [they] can inquire with equanimity" as these are not being viewed by others or being made public. In AR though, researchers do not often work alone as they need the support of other staff or the principal, or they work collaboratively with another teacher. For this reason the data and the findings are often revealed to others. If it is ascertained that consent forms are required then these should be distributed to, and returned from, both parents and participant students. In addition, an explanatory form which outlines the project and the intended involvement of the student participants must be distributed to parents to ensure they are consenting with full knowledge of what their child will be expected to do. Consent forms should include permission for all aspects of the data collection, including the audio recording of interviews (individual and/or focus group), filming, student work samples, assessment results and teaching observations with notes. These forms should also include the right to withdraw from the project. Where appropriate, data such as classroom surveys should be made anonymous and administered by a person not involved with the class directly.

AR teacher-researchers must consider carefully issues of confidentiality and the anonymity of participants. It has been suggested though that rather than guaranteeing anonymity to participants, the most important aspect is to be honest about the level to which anonymity can be maintained as a complete assurance can sometimes not be feasible (Fraser, 1997).

Once something is seen or heard that would normally not be revealed, there is an associated risk of confidentiality being broken (Barnes, 1979). The use of pseudonyms for participants and institutions and schools does not guarantee confidentiality as general descriptors may give away a participant's identity if the school has, for example, small classes. AR teachers need to be mindful of their commitment to anonymity and confidentiality but also be realistic about the potential for this to be broken should an unforeseen circumstance occur. Therefore, application to protocols for confidentiality and anonymity needs to be meticulously planned.

Given the insider perspective, the teacher has to straddle the difficult role of planning survey and/or interview questions to which they may not like the answer or which require students to discuss uncomfortable issues. This may be particularly so if the focus of the AR is on the teacher's classroom presentation or management, or on their success in teaching a topic or unit. The quality of research is likely to be influenced by the willingness of the teacher to ask uncomfortable questions (Fraser, 1997). Where possible, data collection such as interviews should be implemented by someone other than the teacher-researcher.

Applying action research to a tertiary classroom: A case study

An AR project was developed in a tertiary music method classroom as part of a process which drew together reflective practice with AR to inform improved teaching practice for two music method lecturers. The lecturers had implemented a blended learning approach in their tertiary classroom and wanted to gather data which would support their understanding of the student experience of this new classroom environment. An AR project was implemented to enable data to be collected that would inform future practice. Whilst the project took place in a tertiary context, the AR approach used can be applied to a secondary, primary or pre-school classroom to provide demonstration of evidence-based practice. This section briefly outlines the AR design and research tools used in the case study.

Action research design

While AR designs may differ, the cycle and its processes appear to have common elements which formed the basis for the project as seen in Figure 19.1. While this project was conducted in a higher education context, it is comparable to the classroom context; therefore, the design principles can be applied to a diverse range of classroom-based educational contexts. Figure 19.1 outlines the research design and its individual processes, which has been adapted from Crawford and Jenkins (2015).

Figure 19.1 indicates two cycles representing eight phases or stages, four per cycle starting from the process of reflection. For this to be considered AR, a teacher should have at least two cycles intended in their design. Cycle 1 will inform Cycle 2 and so on (Hendricks, 2009). In Phase 1 a problem or issue is identified. A plan is then implemented which includes the identification of what data might be useful to collect, which can be in the form of both qualitative and quantitative data. The data collected are synthesised, analysed and interpreted. Findings are shared and disseminated, which then leads to the beginning of the next cycle, which will be reflective of a new understanding of the nature of the problem or issue. Figure 19.1 highlights the systematic and iterative nature of each cycle, which builds on previous knowledge, insights and understandings.

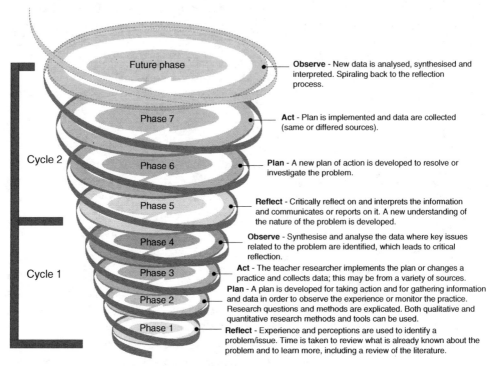

Figure 19.1 Action research design principles – outlining two cycles

In each AR cycle, two surveys were implemented to explore students' understandings and experiences of topics and learning activities designed using blended learning and how this impacted on their development. The first survey (pre) took place prior to a new topic or learning activity using the approach and the second survey (post) was administered at its conclusion.

Cycle 1 Survey 1 (pre): Prior to a new topic or learning activity

In Survey 1 the researchers explored the participants' notions of what students thought they were learning, why and how. Questions included student participants' expectations about learning, its application to practice and the profession and knowledge interest and engagement indicators. The following are example questions:

- What do you expect to learn from this topic?
- What is one thing you would like to learn from this topic?
- Why do you think you are exploring this topic?
- What is your understanding of blended learning in this context?

Cycle 1 Survey 2 (post): At the conclusion of a new topic or learning activity

Survey 2 provided data about the impact of the content taught and the blended learning approach used in the classroom. The survey was divided according to the particular aspects

Action research   235

of the teaching and learning approaches being researched and to correspond with the questions asked in the pre survey in order to measure any change in understanding or knowledge. The following are example questions:

- Did you learn what you expected to learn from this topic?
- Was this content useful and can you apply it in your own classroom?
- Has your opinion changed on why do you think you are exploring this topic?
- Has your understanding of blended learning in this context changed?
- How confident are you in applying the blended learning approach in your own classroom?

Comments were also invited to allow for a further exchange of thoughts about the changes and processes. Student participants were also asked whether they now had any issues or concerns with the content or approaches used.

Cycle 2 Surveys 1 and 2

The surveys that followed in subsequent AR cycles used a similar line of inquiry, investigating learning expectations, the value of content, application to practice and the profession and knowledge interest and engagement indicators. With each cycle new information was required in order to inform the decisions regarding teaching content and delivery. Student participants were asked to clarify their understandings and knowledge of teaching concepts and in particular blended learning. From previous student responses themes were gathered, which then could be used in future iterations of the survey to provide more accurate measurements for learning indicators such as comparing experiences of using blended learning approaches across topics and learning activities. Comparative data could then be used to inform further development of content, learning materials, teaching approaches and delivery.

Journals

The teacher-researchers kept a journal about their experience. This was a valuable process as journaling "enhances one's learning through the 'examination, clarification, and critique of pedagogical ideas and practices'" (Kaplan, Rupley, Sparks, & Holcomb, 2007, pp. 358-359, as quoted in Humble & Sharp, 2012, p. 3). Through the process of reflection, the teacher-researchers were able to examine their own work, clarify matters of concern and critique their own practices. Through these processes of examination, clarification and critique a process of metacognition took place (Humble & Sharp, 2012). The journals afforded the opportunity to become more aware of their level of knowledge and understanding prior to the project, and how this developed during the process of research and journaling. The researcher teachers focused on what they needed to do to learn new knowledge and ways they could think about this new knowledge. The written process enabled a fuller awareness of the thinking processes taking place, which was filtered back into the research regularly (Wilson & Bai, 2010) with each cycle.

De-brief meetings

Following each class, the teacher-researchers had a de-briefed meeting, either in person immediately or via email or phone. Various aspects of the class were discussed, including the joint management of class activities, student interaction with the teacher, role sharing, management of online activities and the development of resources and ideas. This allowed for a more developed awareness of the thinking processes taking place. The immediacy of the discussions about the classroom work informed the ongoing process of improvement and allowed an opportunity for a release of emotions.

Overcoming challenges

Aligning with the AR literature, the teacher-researchers faced various challenges and ethical issues as they planned and implemented their project. The research was designed to provide objective data. Triangulation and trustworthiness were achieved by using multiple data sources (Crawford & Jenkins, 2015; Sagor, 2000) as described. Ongoing challenges consisted of balancing demanding work commitments and time management with designing and implementing the AR, which required dedication when physically and mentally tired (Clift et al., 1988; Drucker, 1994; Fraser, 1997). Clarity about the purpose of the data collection (Lam, 2016) and understanding the value of the outcomes of the project helped them to overcome these challenges.

An application was submitted to the university's ethics committee under the "low risk category" and all aspects of the project were approved (Hendricks, 2009; Mertler, 2009). Surveying their own students presented an insider ethical issue for the teacher-researchers (Frazer, 2007). Given there was no financial support for the project to provide a research assistant (Lambirth & Cabral, 2017), a trusted colleague was asked to administer the survey and the teacher-researchers were not present. The student names were coded by our colleague using a class list. This allowed a number to be allocated to all surveys to maintain anonymity and enabled tracking of student progression across the data set. Although there is always a small risk that confidentiality might be breached (Barnes, 1979) it is important to adhere to ethical protocols.

Conclusion

The Australian educational system has seen a significant shift in recent times to a more managerial and accountability-driven approach. This is impacting on schools, teachers and students who are now subject to an array of accountability measures designed to inform policy, drive change and assess quality. In addition, the Australian Professional Standards for Teachers (AITSL, 2011) and the Teacher Education Ministerial Advisory Group (TEMAG, 2014) recommendations are all driving a need for teachers to regularly and efficiently implement methods in their classroom work which enable them to gather an evidence base for employment, promotion and general accountability. There is an imperative for teachers to reflect on their work and to evaluate their impact on their students.

Schön's (1983, 1987) theory of reflective practice provides an applicable and accessible way to gather data which will improve teachers' individual practice whilst enabling the construction of an evidence base for quality teaching. Through a systematic process of reflection, teachers are able to develop an awareness of their impact in the classroom and document moments of illumination and action to demonstrate improvement. An evidence base which supports notions of continuous professional development through systematic reflection can be combined with other forms of data gathering to broaden and deepen a teacher's portfolio of evidence. However, it was not until Stenhouse's (1975) notion of the teacher-as-researcher that "action research" and "critical reflection" became intertwined and considered educational AR. In the contemporary educational climate, AR has reformulated as a qualitative measurement and response to evidence-based practice.

Using AR as a tool for reflective practice provided an evidence base to enhance and extend curriculum material and cater to the differentiated classroom. This in turn informed a more sophisticated understanding of our pedagogical approach, which used blended learning, in response to the learning outcomes of the students. As a result the teacher-researchers have developed and extended their modes of delivery to provide flexible and innovative educational learning environments, which support our students' diverse knowledge, skills and abilities. We were able to consider the impact of our work in a systematic and reflective way and explore more deeply what we did, how and why.

Classroom AR has been identified as a practical tool for critical reflection and a way for teachers to approach problem resolutions about their practice and educational issues. The teacher-researchers have deconstructed the complexities of AR, including the benefits, challenges and ethical issues. AR resonates well with the overall reflective requirements of impactful teacher practice and ensures credibility and reliability when questioning pedagogy. AR is highly recommended to teachers and pre-service teachers as a reflective tool to improve and develop practice as well as providing a means to generate the necessary evidence-based data to satisfy government and industry-based accountability requirements. As part of an ongoing professional development program AR provides opportunities for development, new knowledge and a wider perspective on educational issues pertaining not only to individual classes but to whole school communities.

References

(Australian Institute for Teaching and School Leadership). (2011). *Australian Professional Standards for Teachers*. Retrieved on February 5, 2018 from: https://www.aitsl.edu.au/docs/default-source/apst-resources/australian_professional_standard_for_teachers_final.pdf

Banegas, D. (2015). A look at ethical issues in action research in education. *Argentinian Journal of Applied Linguistics*, 3(1), 58–67.

Barnes, J. A. (1979). *Who should know what?* Harmondsworth: Penguin.

Boud, D., Keogh, R., & Walker, D. (1985). *Reflection: Turning experience into learning*. London: Kogan Page.

Burgess, H. (1985). Case study and curriculum research: Some issues for teacher researchers. In R. G. Burgess (Ed.), *Issues in educational research, qualitative methods* (pp. 177–196). Lewes: Falmer Press.

Clarke, A. (1995). Professional development in practicum settings: Reflective practice under scrutiny. *Teaching and Teacher Education*, 11(3), 243–261.

Clift, P., Golby, M., & Moon, B. (1988) Educational evaluation – study guide E811. Buckingham, UK: Open University Press.

Cole, A. (1989, March). Making explicit implicit theories of teaching: Starting points in preservice programs. Paper presented at the Annual Meeting of the American Educational Research Association, San Francisco, CA.

Crawford, R., & Jenkins, L. (2015). Investigating the importance of team teaching and blended learning in tertiary music education. *Australian Journal of Music Education*, 2, 3–17.

Dewey, J. (1933). How we think: A restatement of the relation of reflective thinking to the educative process. Boston, MA: Houghton Mifflin.

Drucker, P. F. (1994). *The practice of management*. Oxford, UK: Butterworth Heinemann.

Elliott, J. (1991) *Action research for educational change.* Buckingham, UK: Open University Press.
Farrell, T. S. (2012). Reflecting on reflective practice: (Re)visiting Dewey and Schön. Invited essay. *TESOL Journal, 3*(1), 7-16. DOI:10.1002/tesj.10
Fraser, D. (1997). Ethical dilemmas and practical problems for the practitioner researcher. *Educational Action Research, 5*(1), 161-171. DOI:org/10.1080/09650799700200014
Hendricks, C. (2009). *Improving schools through action research: A comprehensive guide for educators.* Upper Saddle River, NJ: Pearson.
Humble, A. M., & Sharp, E. (2012). Shared journaling as peer support in teaching qualitative research methods. *The Qualitative Report, 17*(48), 1-19.
Kane, R. G., & Chimwayange, C. (2014). Teacher action research and student voice: Making sense of learning in secondary school. *Action Research, 12*(1) 52-77. DOI:10.1177/1476750313515282
Lam, H. C. (2016). An investigation of preschool teachers' ways of seeing action research using phenomenography. *Education Research for Policy and Practice, 15*(2) 147-162. DOI:org/10.1007/s10671-015-9187-y
Lambirth, A., & Cabral, A. (2017). Issues of agency, discipline and criticality: An interplay of challenges involved in teachers engaging in research in a performative school context. *Educational Action Research, 25*(4), 650-666. DOI:10.1080/09650792.2016.1218350
Lewin, K. (1946). Action research and minority problems. *Journal of Social Issues, 2*(4), 34-46. DOI:10.1111/j.1540-4560.1946.tb02295.x
Mertler, C. A. (2009). *Action research: Teachers as researchers in the classroom* (2nd ed.). Thousand Oaks, CA: SAGE.
Noffke, S., & Somekh, B. (Eds.) (2009). *Handbook of educational action research.* London: SAGE.
Pelton, R. P. (2010). *Action research for teacher candidates: Using classroom data to enhance instruction.* Lanham, MD: Rowman & Littlefield.
Sagor, R. (2000). *Guiding school improvement with action research.* Alexandria, VA: Association for Supervision and Curriculum Development.
Schön, D. A. (1983). *The reflective practitioner: How professionals think in action.* New York: Basic Books.
Schön, D. A. (1987). *Educating the reflective practitioner: Towards a new design for teaching and learning in the profession.* San Francisco, CA: Jossey-Bass.
Stenhouse, L. (1975). *An introduction to curriculum research and development.* London: Heinemann.
TEMAG (Teacher Education Ministerial Advisory Group) (2014). *Action now: Classroom ready teachers.* Retrieved on February 5, 2018 from: https://www.studentsfirst.gov.au/teacher-education-ministerial-advisory-group
Wideen, M., Mayer-Smith, J., & Moon, B. (1998). A critical analysis of the research on learning to teach: Making the case for an ecological perspective on inquiry. *Review of Educational Research, 68*(2), 130-178.
Wildman, T., Magliaro, S., Niles, J., & McLaughlin, R. (1990). Promoting reflection among beginning and experienced teachers. In R. Clift, R. Houston, & M. Pugach (Eds.), *Encouraging reflective practice in education* (pp. 139-162). New York: Teachers College Press.
Wilson, N. S., & Bai, H. (2010). The relationships and impact of teachers' metacognitive knowledge and pedagogical understandings of metacognition. *Metacognition and Learning, 5*(3), 269-288. DOI:10.1007/s11409-010-9062-4
Zeichner, K., & Liston, O. (1996). *Reflective teaching.* Mahwah, NJ: Lawrence Erlbaum.
Zeni, J. (1998). A guide to ethical issues and action research. *Educational Action Research, 6*(1) 9-19. DOI:10.1080/09650799800200053

20 Personal practical knowledge

Artists/researcher/teachers reflecting on their engagement in an art practice and professional work

Nish Belford

Introduction

Artists/researcher/teachers are mostly keen to maintain an art practice alongside their professional work. Although such a practice is a challenging enterprise, art educators find fascinating ways to explore, express, understand and document the significance and value of artmaking as part of their research, teaching, teacher development and personal growth. However, there are some perceived tensions in defining the dual roles of artists/researcher/teachers and, so far, the literature poorly addresses such issues from art educators' perspectives. *Personal practical knowledge* is defined as personal and professional experiences by Clandinin (1985), and it is about sharing stories that fold in details of teachers' experiences and their work as teacher educators (Ross & Chan, 2016). In this chapter, *personal practical knowledge* is used as both a theoretical framework and a "dialectic research method" (Clandinin, 1985, p. 364) in examining art educators' *narratives of experience* (Connelly & Clandinin, 1990). This chapter aimed to explore how four art educators describe their challenges and successes in maintaining an art practice alongside their professional work. Art educators share their stories and views of an art practice in offering opportunities to enhance their artistic skills, research avenues and personal, professional growth. Findings and discussions provide insight on how art educators blur boundaries between artmaking and pedagogical work and build new forms of transference from art practice and pedagogy. The importance of creative engagement and a reflexive approach to teaching and learning in the arts and the implications for maintaining an art practice in bridging creativity and reflective practice are discussed. The significance of *narrative unities* in strengthening *personal practical knowledge* as a research process with a reflexive outlook between participants and researchers is highlighted (Clandinin, 1985). In particular, the notion of *image* as embodied and enacted through an art practice is discussed.

Artists/researcher/teachers' dual roles with an art practice as part of their professional work

Engagement in artmaking is complex as it produces some interesting responses (Melcher & Bacci, 2008), including concepts and themes in communicating messages and meanings. Art is not only linked to the powerful emotions the artist wants to convey, but it extends to other dimensions such as creating a *space* to bring self-expression, authenticity, creativity and a form of appraisal and identification (Freedman, 2010; Walker, 2004). Art practice is defined as a process of conceptual and experiential inquiry which embraces inspiration, looking, questioning, making, reflective thinking and the building of meanings (Pringle, 2009). Artmaking and teaching are considered as two closely related activities (Bates, 2000; Daichendt, 2009; Hickman, 2010). However, art educators in many instances find it challenging to maintain a balance between both (Bain, 2004; Blair & Fitch, 2015; Daichendt, 2010; Imms & Ruanglertbutr, 2013; Milne 2004; Smith-Shank, 2014). The term *artists-teachers* (Adams, 2007; Anderson, 1981; Daichendt, 2009) is defined as an elitist term, often used to qualify a group or individual capable of practicing a dual career. However, within "the philosophy of teaching" (Daichendt, 2009, p. 33), *artists-teachers* are not recognised to have dual roles, although their work implicitly involves the integration of artistic experiences from their classroom practices. Such attitudes have for long created further tensions in defining their dual roles and activities.

In resolving this paradox of the artist-teacher, a/r/tography was defined as a "living practice of art, research and teaching" (Irwin & De Cosson, 2004, p. 30). The artist/researcher/teacher is defined as someone who performs within different *spaces* including the social, cultural, historical, experiential and professional contexts (Cross & Hong 2009; Danielewicz, 2014; Schutz & Zembylas, 2009; Thornton, 2011). Such definitions position artists/researcher/teachers with more possibilities and flexibility to make, create, explore, investigate, analyse and reflect on their multiple roles and activities from both personal and professional stances. This process helps them to define a professional identity while understanding varied experiences to develop their educational philosophy and pedagogy (Irwin, 2004). However, De Cosson (2002, p. 11) suggests that "for many art teachers their artist self is often neglected, hidden, even repressed, to conform to the 'norms' of being an art educator". He further explains the ambivalence art educators feel in choosing their engagement in artmaking to be considered as research, while they simply prefer labelling it as artmaking (feeling more comfortable in a familiar place), as "research is a more difficult place in which they wish to dwell" (p. 11). Anderson's (1997) case study discusses the struggle and dilemma faced by an artist/teacher in seeking excellence in both teaching and artmaking. It is important to outline that both artist and art educator share common qualities. However, there are equally many differences in perceptions and practices enacted within such dual roles. This chapter traces the stories from four art educators to extend knowledge about their art practice and professional experiences which draws upon individual actions, attitudes and circumstances.

Theoretical perspectives

Personal practical knowledge

Clandinin's (1985, 1989) influential work on *personal practical knowledge* was significant to construct meaning-giving accounts on teachers' pedagogical and curricular practices. By definition, "personal practical knowledge is the knowledge that is imbued with all experiences that make up a person's being" (Clandinin, 1985, p. 362). However, the analysis and interpretation of teachers' *personal practical knowledge* has been criticised as truncated and mainly focusing on narratives of teaching experiences from the institutional context and less onto personal and social realities (McAninch, 2005). Ross and Chan (2016) contend that *personal practical knowledge* is different from the *knowledge of teachers* gained from expert sources such as professional documents. Knowing about personal and professional experiences through stories from teachers is unique to their circumstances and contexts (Ross & Chan, 2016).

In this study, art educators' *narratives of experience* are used to learn more about their personal and social realities that inform on the implications these have for their *personal practical knowledge*. From a holistic definition of knowledge (McAninch, 2005), in this study both propositional and practical knowledge (Clandinin, 1985), including the cognitive, affective and intuitive processes involved in art practice, are examined. A focus on meaning "generated from" and "embodied in" (McAninch, 2005, p. 87) art educators' art practices and experiences is explored through their *narratives of experience* to examine the intricacies around maintaining an art practice and its implications for their research, teaching practice and training. The participants' attitudes contribute to building an *image* that entails personal beliefs, emotions and actions in contributing to knowledge as *generated from* and *embodied in* their personal and professional experience.

Since knowledge arising from "circumstances, actions and undergoing" has affective content and meanings (Clandinin, 1985, p. 362), such issues are explored from participants' stories. Personal experiences and the notion of "image" are considered as a component of *personal practical knowledge* (Clandinin, 1985, p. 363). In this chapter, the notion of *image* is examined as personal experiences art educators hold in guiding their attitudes and vision towards their future work and teaching. Clandinin (1985, p. 363) guards in defining the notion of image as part of *personal practical knowledge* while not confusing it with "image" as a "concept" and as propositional knowledge. He contends that "propositional knowledge refers only to concepts of, and their relations to practice" (Clandinin, 1985, p. 363) mostly tied to institutional practices. This chapter signals that both art and pedagogical practices from artists/researcher/teachers involve more than this. The notion of "images" is thus discussed as embodied and enacted experiences within art educators' personal and professional experiences which entails "emotionality, morality, and aesthetics" and their "affective, personally felt and believed meanings which engender enactments" (Clandinin, 1985, p. 363).

Research design

The conception of *personal practical knowledge* is based on the premise of experiential, value-laden and purposeful knowledge that is practice-oriented (Clandinin, 1985). "Practical knowledge is revealed through interpretations of practices over time and is given biographical, personal meaning through reconstructions of the teacher's narratives" (Clandinin, 1985, p. 363). *Personal practical knowledge* is viewed as tentative, subject to change and transient rather than fixed and rigid. Such characteristics led Clandinin (1985) to use *dialectic research methods* in a study to pursue an ongoing and reflexive outlook between participants' and researchers' perspectives. In this study, the concept of *image* as derived from personal and professional narratives is emphasised with participants' and the researchers' *dialectic view* (McAninch, 2005) in resolving the challenges, views and oppositions about art practice and pedagogy.

Participants' profile and data collection

Participants from four different countries including Australia, New Zealand and India participated in this study. A teacher art educator, an art educator, a graduate teacher and a pre-service teacher were invited to respond to an online semi-structured questionnaire. This study had ethics clearance and participants' consent to use their real names when reporting on the study. Narratives from four art educators including their comments on one of their artworks and their views about their personal and professional practice were used.

Data analysis and presentation

The findings and discussion are presented together with vignettes of participants' narratives. The discussion is framed as a dialogue between art educators and the researcher's interpretation using a thematic approach. This mode of discussion provided stronger and in-depth insights using "a dialectic process" (McAninch, 2005, p. 88) that involved participants' perspectives and researchers' interpretations. In other words, a *dialectic view* was significant in constructing and reconstructing *narrative unities* (McAninch, 2005). Narrative unities are useful in extending the possibilities for "imagining the living out of a narrative as well as the revision of ongoing narrative unities and the creation of new ones" (Clandinin, 1985, p. 365). Vignettes from the participants' stories were used to add to a compelling discourse about engagement in artmaking and its implications for pedagogical practices, research experiences and creative engagement. It also added much focus on the reflexive approaches to teaching and learning, and these were crucial in building *narrative unities* in this chapter.

Findings and discussions

Stories of engagement in artmaking, research and pedagogical practice

In the next sections, the findings and discussions use vignette stories from four art educators commenting on the conceptual approaches to their artworks, and their views about research, teaching experiences and teacher development. The participants respond to different aspects of their artmaking with some important links to their different roles as teacher art educator, pre-service and graduate art teacher. Their expertise in art education and teacher training equally defines their positionalities, views and engagement. In sharing their stories, they often refer to issues of nationality, ethnicity, gender and cultural identity and religious beliefs to influence the themes or messages and meanings in their artwork.

Jill Smith is a teacher educator and lecturer at the University of Auckland – Faculty of Education, School of Curriculum and Pedagogy. Jill shared her experiences in artmaking, her pedagogical work and research as thus:

> My first major encounter with art practice occurred comparatively late, partly because I was so immersed as a secondary school art teacher for 11 years, and subsequently as a pre-service art teacher educator for over 30 years. My practice is irregular in that I seek, wait for, or am motivated by significant moments which act as a catalyst for creative thinking, doing and being. I had little time to pursue my art making. In retrospect, after

Personal practical knowledge 243

completing my doctoral thesis in 2007 on the topic Art education in New Zealand: Issues of culture and diversity, I came to two significant conclusions.

In the thesis, I had included 30 pages of images by secondary school students, aged 13-14 years. The aim of the students' work (both processes and products) was to show how, and to what degree, ten secondary school visual arts teachers took into account the ethnic and cultural diversity of the students in their art programmes. The first conclusion I drew was that I had used the images merely as 'illustration,' rather than as significant 'research data.' The second conclusion was that I needed to 'visually expose' the findings of my research because this might resonate more readily with an audience. These conclusions led to my first solo exhibition, "Talking my way through culture", in 2007, a multi-media installation comprising 14 talking sticks. See Figure 20.1.

A key finding of my doctoral research was that Western art continues to dominate art programmes in New Zealand's secondary schools. To draw attention to this continued

Figure 20.1 The Ultimate Cultural Icon, 2007, timber, acrylic, slide transparency mounts, archival photographic paper, 1240 x 55mm

reverence for Western 'high art' I used an image of Leonardo da Vinci's Mona Lisa, and 79 other artists' representations of Leonardo's painting, as the focus for the talking stick called The Ultimate Cultural Icon. This supreme exemplar of high culture (high Renaissance perfection and the Western art canon) has been reified in art and art historical discourse and held up by art historians, theorists, critics and the public at large as the ultimate cultural icon. To illustrate how the Mona Lisa has been 'projected' continuously over the centuries I 'captured' the images in transparency mounts.

Kanchan Chander has been an art educator in College of Arts in New Delhi, India, and she has studied printmaking at École Nationale des Beaux-Arts, Paris, France. She shares her perspectives on artmaking and teaching:

I find time to devote to my art practice almost every day. I am inspired by Indian miniature paintings to create my own creative and contemporary compositions either in prints or paintings. I focus on the use of colours that add to distorted proportions, intricate foliage from miniature paintings that are predominant in my works. In using mixed media, I work a lot with found materials.

My approach guides my students to incorporate Miniature Indian paintings in their compositions in a creative way although their works are contemporary. I realised that such an approach started to get into my creative endeavours while making my own art like paintings and prints. As for colour combinations, distorted proportions and intricate representation of foliage inspired from Miniature paintings became predominant features in my own works. It is an interesting process to observe how my students incorporate such ideas as inspired by my own works and they trace their own careers as established artists and as teachers. See Figure 20.2.

Devi – Mother Goddesses have been my subject for long. I portray motherhood, sensuality, fertility, the sensitivity of a woman. The floral patterns at the back and on her body, are symbolic of fertility and femininity. The goddess has more than two hands as a multitasker, handling juggling the world inside and outside. The blue dots are symbolizing the river Yamuna flowing.

I have been working on the 'Devi' series from the past few decades. Presently I am presenting her as the new Avatar – 'Devi Nouveau' – she is a symbol of empowerment, compassion, motherhood, sensitivity and sensuousness, fertility and she represents the women of today. She can perform the task of a plumber, carpenter, technician, a mother, housewife, and colleague. She manages all this very beautifully … Like Rabindranath Tagore called her – "the incarnation of tolerance".

My dual role as an artist and art educator or to say my role as a multi-tasker makes me express powerful themes, colour combinations. This intertwines with my role as a mother and a daughter which empowers me to invest such strong emotions in my work.

Karyn is a pre-service art teacher in Melbourne. She shares her perspectives about artmaking and teaching where she mentions:

I had a part-time artist career until 2014, which stopped when I began the Master of Teaching. Earlier in my career, I was also involved with the artist collective known as DAMP, here in Melbourne. I have also taken quite a few private portrait commissions.

Personal practical knowledge 245

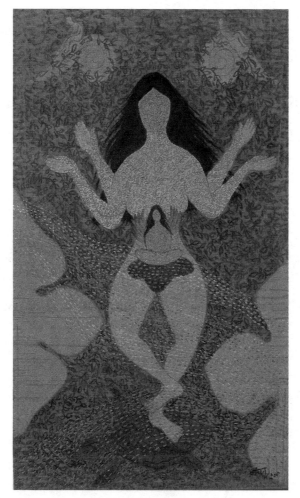

Figure 20.2 Devi – acrylic on canvas, 3 x 5 feet

Talking about her regularity of practice and artmaking she explains:

> Zilch in the last 18 months except for four commissions, which is not zilch, but it is for other people – not for my practice. I usually work in watercolour and pencil on paper in making portraits, both 'loose' and 'tight' in technique. See Figure 20.3.

> I investigate the use of watercolour as an equivalent to the blur in painting. Academic and writer Rosemary Hawker has written about Gerhard Richter's use of the blur in his paintings … this blurring shows nothing yet at the same time it generates a play between what is visible and what cannot be shown.

> How are mothers and related subjects represented by the media and by history? Depicted are a variety of people whose actions have helped shape our opinions around mothering. We are 'haunted' by them. The title refers to the phrase "In the Pink", meaning in perfect condition. We usually associate it with good health, but in earlier times it was used to describe excellence. Pink is the stereotypical colour that 'screams' female, but it is also the colour of human scars, the underside of our hands and feet and our 'insides.'

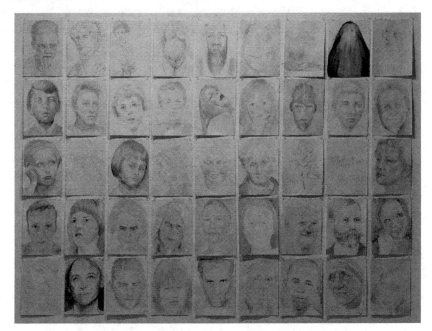

Figure 20.3 In the Pink, 2013-2014, watercolour, coloured pencil and pencil on paper, 198 x 268cm overall

> I have had very little involvement in Art education, a semester at TAFE teaching drawing to mostly mature age students, and my placement experience in secondary school, which was vastly different from TAFE. I am going to say at this stage I will keep my artistic practice and teaching experience separate because I need to make my own work. My art practice will not be my teaching. In education, it is all about the students, and I am not going to give my art practice over to that.

Maya is a new graduate teacher in Melbourne, Victoria - she has worked in the film industry professionally for over ten years, both in Australia and overseas. She explains her art journey and teacher development as:

> Alongside my professional career, I have worked at developing my skills in drawing, painting, and sculpture and animation. My experience in Art education is presently limited to 25 days teaching placement undertaken as part of my teaching qualification.

Maya mentions that she has slowed down a lot on her artistic practice since having a baby, two years ago, and hence she has not submitted any of her recent works; yet she has responded to the other questions.

Art educators blurring the boundaries between artmaking and pedagogical work

Art educators describe the different complexities around their multiple roles, contexts and circumstances in which they perform, which has implications for their artistic practice, teaching, research or learning experiences. For Kanchan, the themes she explores have major relevance to her culture and beliefs, as she explains:

My empathy towards women would not have been so strongly felt if I was born elsewhere. Delhi is the cultural hub of India and now of Asia and it has a lot to offer regarding inspiration and connectivity.

Kanchan's art practice focuses around her beliefs and interests and what she does influences what she teaches, including themes, ideologies and the medium and forms of expressions and representations. Her approach resonates with what Ball (1990, p. 54) explains: "the artist in me is the internal private self who strives to remain creative, autonomous and individual".

Jill's work echoes the opportunities to use her creative engagement and artwork as visual and image-based research and how her approach potentially reinforces her beliefs, cultural belonging and identity. Her work is an example of how to make visible and strengthen other forms of social and cultural knowledge and semiotics, and how to challenge and contradict the paradox and "politics of representation in art education" which is still highly dominated by Western art (Desai, 2014, pp. 347-348).

For the graduate and pre-service teacher, there is some hesitation to identify a resonance or merging of art practice with their teaching. Adams (2007, p. 267) situates "transformative identity" of beginning teachers to experienced teachers, and he explains the process where teacher identity emerges from the former identity as an artist, however "not without the attendant struggle of what the former might come to mean in practice". Such a struggle can happen as teachers trail for "an ideal practice to which they must conform; encouraging them to reject or deny the subjectivity of both teacher and learner", which can result in "threatened artist identities" (Adams, 2007, p. 269). As Adams (2007) states, there is scope for seeking out ways to engage in critical practices as artists within the teaching and learning fields in schools. For pre-service and graduate art teachers, although they acknowledge the value of maintaining an artistic practice, they define it as distinct, difficult and challenging to strike a balance. Even though there can be opportunities to merge both, they seem ambivalent towards such experiences that can significantly support them to "model, explore and create a place for their overlapping identities" (Page, 2012, p. 71). Building confidence in defining self-identities and professional identities (Lim, 2006) is crucial for pre-service and graduate teachers to bridge innovation and creativity alongside critical pedagogy in their future teaching career. Artmaking, as other art educators assert (Adams, 2007; Daichendt, 2009; Desai, 2014; Hall, 2010; Irwin & O'Donoghue, 2012; Pringle, 2009; Thornton, 2011), can empower artist teachers to embody, negotiate and sustain an art practice while being invested in teaching and critical pedagogy.

Ways art educators build new forms of transference from art practice to pedagogy

Coming from the varied length of experience in art education, participants conveyed their views of and connections with artmaking, teaching, research and learning. This section is a discussion of their perspectives on the intersection of artistic practice and pedagogy while drawing on vignettes of their experiences and views.

Jill's response was:

> My art practice is comparatively recent. The A/R/T journey has enriched that dimension. My art practice is not an isolated or independent action. It is influenced by my

engagement in an approach that I call A/R/T in which art practice, research, and teaching inform, interact and interconnect in an ever-continuing cycle. Each entity is underpinned by differing, yet complimentary, theoretical frameworks brought together in a personal reconceptualization. There is a strong connection between my practice, research, and teaching. Each informs the other, and all are used in my pedagogical practices in pre-service teacher education and postgraduate courses. Using research evidence, and having this reconceptualised as art practice, lends veracity to pedagogy. The impact of the 'visual' is critical for reinforcing knowledge and understandings.

Kanchan shared her views as thus:

> There is a connection in the way I inspire my students ... Quite often they get influenced by my way of working ... And at other times my discussions with them gives way to new inspirations and ideas in my work ... They are helpful in getting me becoming more savvy with latest technologies.

Pre-service and graduate art teachers' responses

Talking about how her artmaking informs new forms of transference from her art practice to teaching, Karyn replied:

> I will have to wait and see what happens. This area is new to me so something may evolve ... My experience here is quite limited; I think my art practice is going to inform my teaching.

Whereas, Maya explained:

> As I am not teaching yet, this is difficult to answer. However, I can see that there would be overlaps. I would use my creative ideas and research in my teaching. I would probably also be exposed to different art practices and be influenced by them. I would also need to acquire new skills in mediums I have limited experience in.

Participants commented on their motivations, choices, connections and the implications an artistic practice has for their professional practice. For Jill, as a teacher art educator, she has far more opportunities to make significance of her multiple roles and to make use of her knowledge and skills of artmaking through research and critical reflection. Whereas, Kanchan is more gripped by her art practice that keeps her abreast and close to learning and critical reflection and mutual sharing and enrichment of ideas with her students. Kanchan's experiences resonate with what Milne (2004) calls upon as issues of trust, vulnerability, censorship and power relations that can emerge between educators and students, however, as Kanchan mentions her experience more as empowerment to her artmaking and reflexive practice.

For pre-service teacher Karyn and graduate teacher Maya, being at an early stage of their career they are still hesitant to explore the overlapping roles and significance of art practice and pedagogy. However, both of them are positive about how their different roles might unfold and empower them in their future teaching career. As Eisner (1991) describes, it is important for art educators to understand how artistic practice and pedagogy overlap and to identify the complexities around them. Ball (1990, p. 54) contends that "it is not possible to separate the artist" within from the art teacher "without". In other words, she finds a paradox in fulfilling both roles and in explaining the contrasts between the skills needed within such dual roles. Similarly, Thornton (2011) discusses the two concepts of the artist-teacher: first, "as an individual who practices making art and is dedicated to both activities as a practitioner" (p. 37); second, the art teacher who is "dedicated to the artistic development of the students" and "does not necessarily practice as an artist"(p. 34). Thornton (2011) suggests that there is no evidence that the abilities of an art teacher rely heavily on the premises of being an artist. However, there are divergent views on this issue as examined through the literature (Daichendt, 2010; Graham & Zwirn, 2010; Hall, 2010; Hoekstra, 2015; Imms & Ruanglertbutr, 2012; McDougall, 2011) and as supported by the participants' views.

The participants' views differed from their positionalities, experiences and involvement in art education. Although their perspectives suggest the challenges of dual roles, they refer insightfully to their artistic practice as part of their personal and professional growth and teacher development. Indeed, a teacher has the legitimacy of choice in deciding to engage in an art practice, and, as Karyn describes, she is looking forward to keeping her artistic practice separate from her teaching. Although there are divergent views on this issue, artists-teachers' art practice does contribute to professional development, creativity and innovation in art education and this is important towards reinforcing a more conducive art curriculum in school systems (Adams, 2007; Page, 2012; Thornton, 2011) and to support a better advocacy for the arts. The dual roles and identities of art educators need to remain unthreatened (Schutz & Mikyoung, 2014; Thornton, 2011) to provide them with a scope for "critical pedagogy" and a strong footing to maintain their "critical practices as artists" (Adams, 2007, p. 271). "Discourses and practices of liberation that overlap between the world of arts and Art Education" (Thornton, 2011, p. 35) are vital for such initiatives and, as Jill reiterates, her research findings were "reconceptualised as art practice" which "lends veracity to pedagogy".

Art educators' creative engagement contributing to their reflexive approaches to teaching and learning

There are different definitions of creativity that surface in the literature which drift in varying ways (Merrotsy, 2017). Csikszentmihalyi (1994) states "the concept of creativity cannot be studied or measured without addressing the parameters of the cultural symbol system" (as cited in Beattie, 2000, p. 179). The creative activity takes place within "social roles and norms that regulate the given creative activity" (as cited in Beattie, 2000, p. 179). Artists/researcher/teachers input a lot of time towards recollecting and reflecting on their creative process which is part of an interaction between the three-fold concepts of field, domain and the individual. The *field* is probably the most affluent concept that affects artists' work, and it is defined by both "the social and cultural aspects" of their craft and profession (Feldman, Csikszentmihalyi, & Gardner, 1994, p. 16). In the visual arts, the field will include artists, art curators, art critics, art educators, art galleries, government agencies and other stakeholders that are concerned with culture. In short, the field includes the structures of knowledge and inquiry and the "knowledgeable others" (Gardner, 1995, p. 15) who act as gatekeepers of the domain in influencing artists/researcher/teachers' creative endeavours (Beattie, 2000). The participants shared their views about developing and building confidence in their self-expression and creativity which provide some insights into their work and the implications for their empowerment in teaching, reflection, research and collaborative work.

Jill reiterates her views:

> I use my A/R/T approach to encourage my students, and other Arts staff, to be reflexive educators and practitioners. By modeling this approach, I can convince the people I work with to engage in creative practices in their research, art making, and teaching. My current A/R/T practices are vastly different from when I became a secondary school art teacher in 1969, and a secondary sector art teacher educator in 1980. Changes over time in the social, political, economic, and educational environment have demanded constant appraisal and re-appraisal of my art practices in the context of a contemporary, multicultural, image-saturated, globalised world.

Similarly, Kanchan reflects on her personal experiences with the themes and medium as part of her creative process and how she provides scaffoldings for her students to conceptualise and execute their ideas.

Karyn shared her views:

> Wow, easy, 100% without a doubt, we are trained as critical and creative thinkers and researchers. I really think artists see the world differently and unfortunately those that have not had artistic training do not get it! I would like to know how to say this in a very polite way to the world, but cannot think how it does not sound patronising. I think it is very important to develop and extend skills to negotiate and articulate my professional work, but it does not necessarily involve a reappraisal of my own practice, which is ongoing at any rate. So my answer would be not important at all.

Maya's response was:

> If the teacher is an active participant in art-making – constantly learning and creating new work, it would probably make it more natural for them to be able to relate to the learning process of the student. I would hope this would encourage students to take ownership of their own work, as being taught by someone who is passionate about their craft is often contagious.

Through art, the reflexive process is valuable and significant and, for an artist, reflection is central to the creative process. The participants describe how their art practice is focused on their interests, attitudes and beliefs and a creative engagement is about extending their knowledge, artistic skills and research. Jill finds a reflexive approach in her practice to empower her professional work successfully, and her research inspires her students to be proactive in research and creative endeavours. Maya thinks more about extending creative autonomy and ownership to her students, conversely to some artist teachers who impose their ideas on their students, as expressed by Thornton (2011). Getzels and Csíkszentmihályi (1976) consider creativity in the arts as a process in which the artist discovers a problem as they engage and create an artwork and *not a priori* (Beattie, 2000). Karyn advocates such ideas by saying that "artists see the world differently", where she also acknowledges the creative process in artmaking and how artists also work around their interests and abilities. However, Karyn also has her idiosyncratic views about situating the artist, the teacher and creative engagement. In her opinion, teacher training in arts education in both the UK and Australia does not demand extensive art skills or knowledge and the requisites of being an artist. Consequently, art teachers have different attitudes and dispositions towards defining creative engagement and teaching practices. Her response entails some poignant reflection as proposed by Csikszentmihalyi (1988, p. 325) on "what is creativity?" and "where is creativity?". These questions provide appropriate lenses to examine how creativity is part of art education (Beattie, 2000) where unfortunately many art activities in the school context are regularly taught from a "cookie-cutter" (Dinham, 2017, p. 45) learning approach. Art educators need more autonomy to engage in similar questioning and shifting of their positionalities with the flexibility to think about the arts through their teaching and learning. This process encourages creativity and authentic art learning experiences in schools as advocated by other art educators (Desai, 2014; Dinham, 2017; Ogier, 2017; Roy, Baker, & Hamilton, 2015).

In defining the *creativity paradigm* during the artmaking process, art educators like Irwin and De Cosson (2004) and Sullivan (2007) believe that artists pose and solve problems while making and perceiving art (Irwin & Chalmers, 2007). Artists ask critical questions that represent and encode messages and meanings relating to personal and social, cultural or current political and globalised issues and changes that prompt critical thinking. Irwin, Kind, and Springgay (2005) write about the need for art educators to engage in ongoing reflective and reflexive practice-based inquiry. A reflective practice needs to be *a dialogue of thinking* and doing through which one becomes more skilful (Schon, 1987). Smith (1998) advocates that reflecting during teaching improves ways teachers reflect upon their actions, thoughts and practices concurrently and, after review, it enables them to change and positively construct their knowledge and improve their practice. As a teacher educator, Loughran (2002) focused on modelling reflexive practice as a method in which he valued what was implicit to his student teachers' conception of reflection and this was interwoven with their understanding of reflection on their terms. Milne (2004), as a teacher art educator, extends her views on the importance of finding time to reflect and make art as a useful tool in building a deeper understanding of her pedagogical practices. Such perspectives resonate with some of the participants' views and the reflexive approach they undertake through artmaking and teaching, which in many ways is vital in valuing their work and in making meaningful connections to pedagogical approaches and practices.

Conclusion and the implications of this study

The conclusion summarises the importance of an art practice as part of artists/researcher/teachers' *personal practical knowledge* from two perspectives: first, the notion of *image* as embodied and enacted through personal and professional art practice and, second, the contribution of *narrative unities* in sharing participants' stories from a dialectic research method. Finally, the implications of this study are discussed in ways an ongoing art practice from artists/researcher/teachers builds knowledge and artistic skills. It provides evidence for future art educators to reflect on the importance of promoting creativity and a reflexive practice through the teaching and learning of the arts.

Personal practical knowledge – the notion of image as embodied and enacted within artists/researcher/teachers' personal and professional experiences

The participants' *narratives of experience* shed light on the different meanings they generate and construct from their embodied and enacted actions, attitudes and views. Knowledge arising from the participants' circumstances and the context of their art practice are vivid examples of "expressions of images in practice" (Clandinin, 1985, p. 382). Their experiences suggest their actions as *embodied* with the personal value they place on an art practice that offers reflection from many stances (their aspirations, emotions, disempowerments and fears) while investing in a reflective approach in their pedagogical practice. Clandinin (1985) describes the notion of *images* to draw upon the emotional, affective, aesthetic and moral dimensions that create meaningful and useful patterns generated from a *minded practice*. This chapter examined how art educators understand such *minded practices* with *images* from personal and professional experiences that guide them to make sense of their work and in sharing their stories it creates an insight for others.

Personal practical knowledge – "narrative unities" contributing to a dialectic process of research

A theory of *personal practical knowledge* as asserted by Clandinin and Connelly (1987, p. 482) is "made up of participants' rhythms, images, personal philosophy and as based on narrative unities in participants' experience". In this chapter, a *dialectic process* enabled both the participants and the researcher to construct and reconstruct (McAninch, 2005) "meaning-giving accounts" (Clandinin, 1985, p. 365) from *narrative unities* that provide an understanding of experiential knowledge. This study points out the significance of *narrative unities* in providing a reflexive outlook on the ongoing and continuous process of artmaking as part of art educators' personal and professional experience. It also suggests that reflexive practice is a large part of "living out of one's narrative unities"(Clandinin, 1985, p. 365) and if shared from a *dialectic view* it provides an experiential and practical understanding with more diverse and authentic examples of personal and professional experiences. This chapter is only one attempt in strengthening *personal practical knowledge* as a research process that is "experiential and holistic" (Ross & Chan, 2016, p. 10) by focusing on experiences merged from personal and professional work.

Concluding remarks

This chapter aimed at providing insights on how artists/researcher/teachers share *narratives of experience* on art practice and the implications for their personal and professional growth. There are several implications of this study that provides evidence for art educators, pre-service and graduate teachers to consider how maintaining an art practice is significant in building art knowledge and skills while enhancing their confidence to teach. Participants' stories contribute to an understanding of how they value their art practice and professional work (Hames, 2015).

Artists/researcher/teachers need to be mindful that in choosing dual roles and in particular in becoming an art educator they have moved from one field of practice (art, craft, design) to another (that is, pedagogy) (Addison, Burgess, Steers, & Trowell, 2010). It is important that artists/researcher/teachers signal and communicate the value and vital contribution of an art practice in defining their dual roles and its significance in a reflexive approach to pedagogy. As Loughran (2002, p. 17) suggests:

reflection is to be valued by student-teachers as a worthwhile attribute for their professional development, and they must experience it as a logical consequence of learning to teach; not as a generalist process skill but as an appropriate tool for unpacking and learning from the uncertainties of practice.

This line of thought equally applies to pre-service art teachers, if they are encouraged and willing to develop *personal practical knowledge* from an art practice and as an embedded experience through their teacher development. Such competencies should be encouraged through teacher training models which unfortunately often focus on more procedural and technical aspects of teacher training, due to time constraints on developing more hands-on work through artmaking. Pre-service teachers often find it challenging to maintain an art practice as an artist/researcher/teacher, alongside some of their distinctive views and attitudes towards it. However, focusing on the positives of a *minded practice* that reinforces the notion of *image* as *embodied* and *enacted* through attitudes on personal and professional practice is important. As future art educators, they need the skills and an art knowledge, which they can foster through engagement in artmaking, and this experience can also empower the cognitive, social, emotional and moral demands for teaching in the arts (Wetzel, Hoffman, & Maloch, 2017).

This discussion on how artists/researcher/teachers blur boundaries between artmaking and pedagogical work and reflect on creative engagement in building a reflexive practice to teaching and learning of the arts adds knowledge to the field of research in art education. It signals pathways for art educators to powerfully approach and nurture teacher and professional growth while enhancing a professional identity in the face of challenges and adversities within art education. For instance, creativity is being "squeezed out of schools", and UK-based research shows a decline of arts subjects offered in public schools with fewer specialist art teachers and less time devoted to arts in the curriculum (Ricci, 2015, para. 1). Such reverberations are felt across different countries including Australia where pressures of cuts in educational research funding (Gardner, 2016), overcrowded curricula and the lip service given to the arts in the curriculum (Department of Education and Training, 2014) are blamed for a weakened focus on the arts. Art educators need to pay more attention to nurturing their image, art knowledge and skills to foster creativity. "Creativity is reflexive" and it involves "critical reflection" in looking at one's own art practice and teaching (Freedman, 2010, p. 10). In the educational context, it is important to extend beyond what is taught and explored as artmaking. This approach refers to a form of creative leadership where art educators need to show how new ideas and skills, research initiatives and sharing of experiences convey new meanings and messages from personal stories, insights, values and beliefs to embrace professionalism (Milne 2004; Walker, 2004).

References

Adams, J. (2007). Artists becoming teachers: Expressions of identity transformation in a virtual forum. *International Journal of Art & Design Education*, 26(3), 264–273. DOI:10.1111/j.1476-8070.2007.00537.x

Addison, N., Burgess, L., Steers, J., & Trowell, J. (2010). *Understanding art education: Engaging reflexively with practice*. London: Routledge.

Anderson, C. H. (1981). The identity crisis of the art educator: Artist? Teacher? Both? *Art Education*, 34(4), 45–46.

Anderson, R. (1997). A case study of the artist as teacher through the video work of Martha Davis. *Studies in Art Education, 39*(1), 37–56. DOI:10.1080/00393541.1997.11650017

Bain, C. (2004). Today's student teachers: Prepared to teach versus suited to teach? *Art Education, 57*(3), 42–47.

Bates, J. K. (2000). *Becoming an art teacher*. Belmont, CA: Wadsworth/Thomson Learning.

Ball, L. (1990). What role: Artist or teacher? *Art Education, 43*(1), 54–59.

Beattie, D. K. (2000). Creativity in art: The feasibility of assessing current conceptions in the school context. *Assessment in Education: Principles, Policy & Practice, 7*(2), 175–192. DOI:10.1080/713613331

Blair, L., & Fitch, S. (2015). Threshold concepts in art education: Negotiating the ambiguity in pre-service teacher identity formation. *International Journal of Education through Art, 11*(1), 91–102. DOI:10.1386/eta.11.1.91_1

Clandinin, D. J. (1985). Personal practical knowledge: A study of teachers' classroom images. *Curriculum Inquiry, 15*(4), 361–385. DOI:10.2307/1179683

Clandinin, D. J. (1989). Developing rhythm in teaching: The narrative study of a beginning teacher's personal practical knowledge of classrooms. *Curriculum Inquiry, 19*(2), 121–141. DOI:10.2307/1179405

Clandinin, D. J., & Connelly, F. M. (1987). Teachers' personal knowledge: What counts as 'personal' in studies of the personal. *Journal of Curriculum Studies, 19*(6), 487–500. DOI:10.1080/0022027870190602

Connelly, F. M., & Clandinin, D. J. (1990). Stories of experience and narrative inquiry. *Educational Researcher, 19*(5), 2–14.

Cross, D. I., & Hong, J. Y. (2009). Beliefs and professional identity: Critical constructs in examining the impact of reform on the emotional experiences of teachers. In P. A. Schutz & M. Zembylas (Eds.), *Advances in teacher emotion research: The impact on teachers' lives* (pp. 273–296). New York: Springer Publishing.

Csikszentmihalyi, M. (1988). Society, culture, and person: A systems view of creativity. In R. J. Sternberg (Ed.), *The nature of creativity* (pp. 325–339). Cambridge, UK: Cambridge University Press.

Csikszentmihalyi, M. (1994). The domain of creativity. In D. H. Feldman, M. Csikszentmihalyi, & H. Gardner (Eds.), *Changing the world: A framework for the study of creativity* (pp. 135–158). Westport, CT: Praeger.

Daichendt, G. J. (2009). Redefining the artist teacher. *Art Education, 62*(5), 33–38.

Daichendt, G. J. (2010). *Artist-teacher: A philosophy for creating and teaching*. Bristol, UK: Intellect.

Danielewicz, J. (2014). *Teaching selves: Identity, pedagogy, and teacher education*. New York: State University of New York Press.

De Cosson, A. (2002). The hermeneutic dialogic: Finding patterns amid the aporia of the artist/researcher/teacher. *Alberta Journal of Educational Research, 48*(3), 1–31.

Department of Education and Training (2014). Review of the Australian Curriculum – final report. Canberra: Retrieved on October 17, 2017 from: https://docs.education.gov.au/documents/review-australian-curriculum-final-report

Desai, D. (2014). 'Make an invisible artwork': Instructions for a pedagogy of visibility/invisibility. *Visual Inquiry: Learning & Teaching Art, 3*(3), 347–357. DOI:10.1386/vi.3.3.347_1

Dinham, J. (2017). *Delivering authentic arts education* (3rd ed.). Victoria, Australia: Cengage Learning Australia.

Eisner, E. W. (1991). What the arts taught me about education. *Art Education, 44*(5), 10–19.

Feldman, D. H., Csikszentmihalyi, M., & Gardner, H. (1994). *Changing the world: A framework for the study of creativity*. Westport, CT: Praeger.

Freedman, K. (2010). Rethinking creativity: A definition to support contemporary practice. *Art Education, 63*(2), 8–15.

Gardner, H. (1995). Creating creativity. *The Times Educational Supplement*, January 6, 15.

Gardner, M. (2016). *Innovation in learning and teaching is too important to cut*. Retrieved on October 15, 2017 from: http://theconversation.com/innovation-in-learning-and-teaching-is-too-important-to-cut-58629

Getzels, J. W., & Csíkszentmihályi, M. (1976). *The creative vision: A longitudinal study of problem finding in art*. New York: Wiley.

Graham, M. A., & Zwirn, S. G. (2010). How being a teaching artist can influence K-12 art education. *Studies in Art Education, 51*(3), 219–232.

Hall, J. (2010). Making art, teaching art, learning art: Exploring the concept of the artist teacher. *International Journal of Art & Design Education, 29*(2), 103–110. DOI:10.1111/j.1476-8070.2010.01636.x

Hames, H. (2015). Embodied subjectivity: The impact of reflexive engagement with personal narrative upon the values of trainee primary art teachers. *International Journal of Education through Art, 11*(1), 103–116. DOI:10.1386/eta.11.1.103_1

Hickman, R. (2010). *Why we make art and why it is taught*. Chicago, IL: Intellect.

Hoekstra, M. (2015). The problematic nature of the artist teacher concept and implications for pedagogical practice. *International Journal of Art & Design Education, 34*(3), 349–357. DOI:10.1111/jade.12090

Imms, W., & Ruanglertbutr, P. (2012). Can early career teachers be artists as well? *Canadian Review of Art Education, 39*(1), 7–23.

Imms, W., & Ruanglertbutr, P. (2013). The teacher as an art maker: What do pre-service teachers identify as the issues? *Australian Art Education, 35*(1/2), 81–92.

Irwin, R. (2004). *Artist portfolio: A/r/t as metissage in the borderlands*. Retrieved on November 12, 2016 from: http://www.curricstudies.educ.ubc.ca/wusers/IrwinRita/portfolio.html

Irwin, R., & Chalmers, F. G. (2007). Experiencing the visual and visualizing experiences. In L. Bresler (Ed.), *International handbook of research in arts education* (pp. 179–196). Dordrecht, the Netherlands: Springer.

Irwin, R., & De Cosson, A. (2004). *a/r/tography: Rendering through arts-based living inquiry*. Vancouver, Canada: Pacific Educational Press.

Irwin, R. L., Kind, S. W., & Springgay, S. (2005). A/r/tography as living inquiry through art and text. *Qualitative Inquiry, 11*(6), 897–912. DOI:10.1177/1077800405280696

Irwin, R. L., & O'Donoghue, D. (2012). Encountering pedagogy through relational art practices. *International Journal of Art & Design Education, 31*(3), 221–236. DOI:10.1111/j.1476-8070.2012.01760.x

Lim, E.-H. M. (2006). Influences of studio practice on art teachers' professional identities. *Marilyn Zurmuehlin Working Papers in Art Education (1)*.

Loughran, J. J. (2002). *Developing reflective practice: Learning about teaching and learning through modelling*. Hoboken, NJ: Taylor & Francis.

McAninch, A. (2005). What do critical ethnographies of schooling tell us about teacher knowledge. In J. Raths (Ed.), *What counts as knowledge in teacher education: Volume 5* (pp. 85–102). Greenwich, CT: Information Age Publishing.

McDougall, H. (2011). Artist-teacher: A philosophy for creating and teaching. *International Journal of Art & Design Education, 30*(2), 328–328. DOI:10.1111/j.1476-8070.2011.01698.x

Melcher, D., & Bacci, F. (2008). The visual system as a constraint on the survival and success of specific artworks. *Spatial Vision, 21*(3–5), 347–362.

Merrotsy, P. (2017). *Pedagogy for creative problem solving*. London: Routledge.

Milne, W. M. (2004). The use of reflective artmaking in pre-service education. *Mentoring & Tutoring: Partnership in Learning, 12*(1), 37–52. DOI:10.1080/1361126042000183057

Ogier, S. (2017). *Teaching primary art and design*. UK: SAGE Publications.

Page, T. (2012). A shared place of discovery and creativity: Practices of contemporary art and design pedagogy. *International Journal of Art & Design Education, 31*(1), 67–77. DOI:10.1111/j.1476-8070.2012.01732.x

Pringle, E. (2009). The artist-led pedagogic process in the contemporary art gallery: Developing a meaning-making framework. *International Journal of Art & Design Education, 28*(2), 174–182. DOI:10.1111/j.1476-8070.2009.01604.x

Ricci, C. (2015). Research shows cutting arts education a loss to all: Teaching of the arts is sometimes viewed as an optional extra, but some of the most successful educational systems see it as essential, *The Age*. Retrieved on November 15, 2017 from: http://www.theage.com.au/national/education/research-shows-cutting-arts-education-a-loss-to-all-20150302-13sszl.html

Ross, V., & Chan, E. (2016). Personal practical knowledge of teacher educators. In J. Loughran & M. L. Hamilton (Eds.), *International handbook of teacher education: Volume 2* (pp. 3–33). Singapore: Springer.

Roy, D., Baker, W., & Hamilton, A. (2015). *Teaching the arts: Early childhood and primary education*. Melbourne: Australia: Cambridge University Press.

Schön, D. A. (1987). *Educating the reflective practitioner: Toward a new design for teaching and learning in the professions*. San Francisco, CA: Jossey-Bass.

Schutz, P. A., & Mikyoung, L. (2014). Teacher emotion, emotional labor and teacher identity. *Utrecht Studies in Language & Communication, 27*, 169–186.

Schutz, P. A., & Zembylas, M. (Eds.) (2009). *Advances in teacher emotion research: The impact on teachers' lives*. New York: Springer.

Smith-Shank, D. L. (2014). Dragons and art education: Pre-service elementary teachers' memories of early art experiences. *International Journal of Education through Art, 10*(2), 149–162. DOI:10.1386/eta.10.2.149_1

Smith, J. (1998). Qualitative focus groups of study of crystalizing and flow experience in educators' professional development. Unpublished doctoral dissertation, Indiana University of Pennsylvania.

Sullivan, G. (2007). Creativity *as* research practice in the visual arts. In L. Bresler (Ed.), *International handbook of research in arts education* (pp. 1181–1198). Dordrecht, the Netherlands: Springer.

Thornton, A. (2011). Being an artist-teacher: A liberating identity? *International Journal of Art & Design Education, 30*(1), 31–36. DOI:10.1111/j.1476-8070.2011.01684.x

Walker, S. (2004). Understanding the artmaking process: Reflective practice. *Art Education, 57*(3), 5–12.

Wetzel, M. M., Hoffman, J. V., & Maloch, B. (2017). *Mentoring preservice teachers through practice: A framework for coaching with CARE.* New York: Routledge.

21 Evidence-based learning and teaching

Unlocking successful pedagogy

Melissa Barnes, Sivanes Phillipson and Maria Gindidis

Learning and teaching internationally and in Australia have hinged on teacher experience and knowledge that are known to impact on educational outcomes (Hattie, 2009). Hattie's meta-analyses of 800 pieces of research around achievement showcases the need to use research evidence to inform teaching practices that result in academic success. Furthermore, Hattie (2012) also concluded that good teaching requires continued evaluation of learning and teaching practices in order to make a meaningful difference to student achievement.

In Australia, the declines in student achievement in comparison with other countries have generated an increasing sense of "urgency" (Ingvarson et al., 2014, p. 2) to enhance the quality of its teachers. The argument is that there is a clear link between teacher quality and student achievement (Hattie, 2009, 2012), and that enhancing the teaching profession through raising standards will help to reverse the decline in student achievement. In defining teacher quality, countries such as Australia look to the "systems" (Ingvarson et al., 2014, p. 4) within Singapore, Hong Kong and Finland as exemplars for the recruitment, education and graduation of professional teachers.

Not all teachers make a difference to student achievement. Although the link between quality teaching and student achievement is well established, Loughran (2010) alludes the attributes of quality teaching to premises of reflective practices. Loughran presents expert teachers as those who are learners from their own teaching as well as those who see learning through the eyes of their students. These attributes are important because they provide benchmarks for both the design of teacher education programs as well as their ongoing professional development.

With increasing pressure from international testing and comparisons (OECD, 2014), the importance of expert pedagogy based on existing research becomes more prevalent. With this issue in mind, this book's broad aim is to marry theory and practice through authentic classroom research that addresses issues surrounding current learning and teaching practices. By exploring research surrounding learning and teaching in the Australian context, the chapters in the book articulate a range of practices that present fundamental elements needed for successful pedagogy across streams, paradigms and subject matters. These elements can be seen as four major approaches that teachers (beginning and experienced) can use to achieve success in learning and teaching in the Australian classroom. These approaches are *reflective practice, professional learning, giving students more voice* and *new pedagogies*. Each of these important approaches for learning and teaching is discussed in relation to the three main sections of the book – understanding learning and learners; encouraging learning through pedagogy; navigating structures and tools.

Reflective practice

According to Loughran (2010), expert teachers think deeply about their teaching and how students learn. This statement suggests that teachers who are successful base their practice on an understanding of how students behave, manage and process information and engage in ongoing professional learning. This thought process that involves reflecting on one's own practices and the outcome of those practices is widely known as reflective practice. "The goal of reflective practice is self-discovery and growth, as well as the expansion of one's knowledge" (Pretorius & Ford, 2016, p. 241), a clear reference to how reflective practice improves one's learning and teaching. Reflective practice, hence, is both a "review" of what has been done and "projection" of what needs to done better for success in learning and teaching (Gaye, 2010, p. 5).

A number of the chapters in this book took to reflective practice as a main premise of their paradigm for learning and teaching. For example, Adams (Chapter 3) and Sellings (Chapter 10) put forward that as part of learning and teaching, teachers need to document how formative assessment (as/for) can transform learning and also guide teaching. This process, of course, requires teacher reflection over the practices that they employ throughout the learning and teaching that happen within and outside the classroom.

Several chapters in this book used teacher inquiry, or the process of action research, as a vehicle for meaningful reflection to provoke insights to improve current learning and teaching practices. Barnes (Chapter 4) and Jenkins and Crawford (Chapter 19) discuss the cycles of action research in a secondary classroom setting and a tertiary setting, respectively, in order to explore how to not only better support students' learning but to improve their approaches to teaching. A number of studies used reflection, as a method, through reflective journals and interviews, to explore the beliefs, attitudes and experiences of teachers (e.g., Gindidis [Chapter 5]; Lyons [Chapter 6]; Janssen, O'Connor, and Phillipson [Chapter 12], and Belford [Chapter 20]), with Rimes, Gilkes, and Thorpe (Chapter 9) arguing that the process of children reflecting on and documenting their own learning processes is a powerful tool.

Professional learning

In addition to reflective practice being a powerful tool, for both teachers and students, the overall findings from this book suggest that targeted and meaningful professional learning is another needed approach for a successful classroom. Not surprisingly, the connection between reflective practice and professional learning is strong as reflective practice is an important component of the learning process. DeLuca, Bolden, and Chan (2017) argue that more recently professional learning (or development) advocates context-embedded and data-driven learning that focuses on teachers identifying problems of their own practice. They argue that professional learning not only provokes teacher reflection which then can result in action, but that this type of reflection, when done within a collaborative learning environment, promotes educator growth and development and overall school improvement.

In the case of both Education for Sustainability (EfS) and Indigenous education, Barnes, Moore, and Almeida (Chapter 15) and Anderson and Ma Rhea (Chapter 17), respectively, argue that there is a need for teachers to understand more about these topics both conceptually and in practice. In addition, Kewalramani, Phillipson, & Belford (Chapter 8) and McCormack and Smith-Tamaray (Chapter 18) suggest that teachers require more awareness of the diverse nature of student needs which requires collaboration between teachers and other professionals (e.g., career counsellors and speech-language pathologists). Finally, Gindidis (Chapter 5) argues that there is a need for understanding and knowledge, particularly in the case of pre-service teachers, regarding concepts relating to information-processing theory and its role in learning.

Giving students more voice

Toshalis and Nakkula (2012) suggest that if we can empower youth to express their ideas and opinions, they will have a much more positive educational experience. In other words, if they feel that they have voice and as if they have a stake in the outcomes, they are more likely to be engaged in the learning process. They argue that there is an intrinsic link between engagement, motivation and student voice and that the more voice a student has in the classroom, the more motivated and engaged they are in learning. Furthermore, Crosswell (2009, p. 69) argues that enhancing student voice is an important component of a democratic classroom, which entails "the vital and dynamic process of a learning community that recognises and validates the individuality and responsibility of each participant".

This notion that children and students engage in learning when they are active participants is evidenced by several of the studies presented in this book. In an early childhood setting, Moore (Chapter 7) and Rimes, Gilkes, and Thorpe (Chapter 9) argue for children to tell their stories and share and document their learning as this allows them to be active and participatory citizens. From a secondary and middle years perspective, both Barnes (Chapter 4) and Lyons (Chapter 6) argue the role of allowing for more student voice and ownership, particularly when using digital technologies.

New pedagogies

The final approach to a successful classroom, as indicated from the chapters in this book, is allowing for new and varied pedagogies. While there is not one defined "best" pedagogical approach which will in turn transform teaching and learning, it is the process of considering and conceptualising new ways to approach learning that can often provide unexpected results. At times, educators fall into habitual patterns of thinking and, therefore, reflective practice and professional learning provide an opportunity to turn newfound knowledge into action. The experimentation of new pedagogies is one way for educators to learn more about their teaching approaches while also exploring the varied ways in which children and students learn.

As demonstrated in this book, Cheeseman (Chapter 2) found that the use of one-on-one conversations between teachers and students promotes learning in mathematics. In contrast to the one-on-one work, Janssen, O'Connor, and Phillipson (Chapter 12) found that when placing students in groups, there needs to be group differentiation due to the mix of group productivity. In addition, Sellings (Chapter 10) found that the use of student-generated representations allowed for better understanding of assessment of student learning.

Moving forward: Knowledge to action

According to Dewey (1925), experience is the very way in which humans are connected with, are part of and are involved in *the world*. Dewey's transactional understanding of experience provides a framework in which knowing is no longer about a mind looking at the material world and registering what goes on in it, a view to which Dewey referred as the *spectator theory of knowledge*. Dewey's *transactional theory of knowing* was not about a world *out there*, but the *relationship* between our actions and their consequences. Knowing can help attain better control over our actions. "Where there is the possibility of control", Dewey observed, "knowledge is the sole agency of its realization" (Dewey, 1925, p. 29).

It is important to note that for Dewey "control" did not mean complete mastery, but the ability to intelligently plan and direct our actions. This ability is most important in those situations in which we are not sure how to act.

The reason Dewey's transactional theory of knowing is important to this discussion is that it provides a framework for understanding the role that knowledge plays in action.

Using Dewey's practical epistemology, classroom-based research cannot supply us with rules for action but only with hypotheses for intelligent problem solving. Research can only tell us what has worked in a particular situation, not what will work in any future situation. The role of the teacher in this process is not to translate general rules into particular lines of action. It is rather to use research findings to make one's problem solving more intelligent. Dewey's practical epistemology challenges the idea of evidence-based education in two ways: it challenges the way in which evidence-based education thinks about what research can achieve in relation to educational practice, and it challenges the technocratic model in which it is assumed that teaching can and should be restrained to technical questions about *what works*. Dewey's work helps us to see that questions in classroom-based research are serious research questions in their own right, questions that need to be part of a full, free and open debate among all those with a stake in education.

The authors in this book take a critical look at the idea of evidence-based practice and the ways in which it has been promoted and implemented in the field of education. Whilst there is scope for improvement of the ways in which educational research and educational practice communicate and interact, pre-service teachers need to be aware that evidence-based education can sometimes advocate a technocratic model in which it is assumed that the only relevant research questions are questions about the effectiveness of educational means and techniques. The tension as to what counts as "effective" crucially depends on judgements about what is educationally desirable. Evidence-based education needs to offer opportunities for educational practitioners to make such judgements in a way that is sensitive to and relevant for their own contextualised settings.

References

Crosswell, L. (2009). Student relationships: Democratic classrooms. In J. Millwater & D. Beitel (Eds.), *Transitioning to the real world of education* (pp. 69–96). Frenchs Forest, NSW: Pearson Education Australia.

DeLuca, C., Bolden, B., & Chan, J. (2017). Systematic professional learning through collaborative inquiry: Examining teachers' perspectives. *Teaching and Teacher Education, 67*(1), 67–78.

Dewey, J. (1925). *Experience and nature*. Chicago, IL: Open Court Publishing.

Gaye, T. (2010). *Teaching and learning through reflective practice: A practical guide for positive action.* (2nd ed). London: Taylor & Francis.

Hattie, J. (2009). *Visible learning: A synthesis of over 800 meta-analyses relating to achievement.* London: Routledge.

Hattie, J. (2012). *Visible learning for teachers: Maximizing impact on learning.* Oxford, UK: Routledge.

Ingvarson, L., Reid, K., Buckley, S., Kleinhenz, E., Masters, G., & Rowley, G. (2014). *Best practice teacher education programs and Australia's own programs.* Canberra: Department of Education.

Loughran, J. (2010). *What expert teachers do.* Oxford, UK: Routledge.

OECD (2014). *PISA 2012 results: What students know and can do - student performance in mathematics, reading and science.* 1, Revised edition, February 2014. Retrieved on October 1, 2017 from: https://www.oecd.org/pisa/keyfindings/pisa-2012-results-volume-I.pdf. DOI:http://dx.doi.org/10.1787/9789264201118-en

Pretorius, L., & Ford, A. (2016). Reflection for learning: Teaching reflective practice at the beginning of university study. *International Journal of Teaching and Learning in Higher Education, 28*(2), 241-253.

Toshalis, E., & Nakkula, M. (2012). Motivation, engagement, and student voice. *The Education Digest, 1*(1), 29-35.

Index

Aboriginal and Torres Strait Islander peoples *see* rights-based Indigenous education
accountability in Australian education system 236
action research: case study 233-236; definition 230; design principles 38-39, 233-234; ethical and practical challenges 231-233; Hendricks' (2009) classroom AR approach 231; and reflective practice 229-231; *see also* language development through online communities (study); small-group learning (study) active listening in Reggio Emilia approach 74, 101, 103-105, 110-111
additional learning needs students 217; *see also* collaboration in the classroom (study)
Adelman, Clem 38
Anaya, James 211-212
anonymity and action research 232-233
anti-malaria drug developed at Sydney Grammar School 169
artist/researcher/teacher (a/r/tography), definition 240; *see also* personal practical knowledge (study)
artist-teacher, definition 240
art practice, definition 240
arts as an undervalued curriculum area 253
assessment: for, of and as 26-27, 31, 33-34; formative 26, 113, 114, 120, 121, 123, 152; self 123; summative 114
Assessment as Learning (AaL) approach *see* Student-Directed Assessment (SDA) process (study) assessment of student-generated representations to explore theory-practice connections (study): implications and conclusions 120-121; literature review 113-116; methodology 116-117; results and discussion 118-120
Australian Curriculum 179-181, 190, 206
Australian Curriculum and creativity: creative thinking focus 156-158; reasons for emphasis on creativity 155-156; study of English teachers' perceptions of creativity 158-164
Australian Institute for Teaching and School Leadership (AITSL) standards 171, 172
Australian Professional Standards for Teachers (APST) 206, 236

Bandura, Albert
Behaviourism 168
Biffle, Chris 49-51, 57
Bloom's taxonomy 157-158, 161, 162, 163
"Both Ways" approach 213
brain-based learning and neuroscience 48-49
brainstorming 157
Bronfenbrenner's ecological model 83-84, 92

Capability Approach 85
career counselling process *see* student experiences of career counselling process (study)
Chander, Kanchan 244, 246-247, 248, 250
"child as citizen" concept 100
childhood: identity construction in 21st century 68; knowledge of place 73-74, 79; and technology 61-62; understandings of 72
citizenship in Reggio Emilia approach 100, 101, 103, 111
Clandinin, Jean 87, 239, 240-241, 252
Clark, Alison 74
"class on the stage" problem 15

264 Index

classroom environment and mathematical thinking *see* mathematical thinking and classroom environment (study)
Clements, Douglas H. 26
cognitive learning theory 49
cognitive load theory (CLT) 50
Coles, Colin 220
collaboration in the classroom (study): barriers and facilitators to collaboration 220-221, 223; collaboration defined 219; communication disorders as background 218-219; Communities of Practice (CoP) 219-221, 226; methodology 221-222; results and discussion 222-225; student diversity 217
collaborative learning, teaching and assessment in early years mathematics assessment (study): assessment 26-27; background 25; findings and discussion 28-32; implications 32-34; learning about mathematics 26; methodology 27-28; theoretical basis 27; *see also* mathematical thinking and classroom environment (study)
collaborative learning *see* small-group learning (study)
colonial mindset and Indigenous education 206, 207, 210-211
common goals/outcomes in collaboration 223, 226
communication disorders 218-219; *see also* collaboration in the classroom (study)
Communities of Practice (CoP) 35-36, 37-38, 42, 45, 219-221, 226
competence as a learner 125, 132-134
complementary accounts methodology 12
confidentiality and action research 232-233
conjecturing in mathematics 22
consent and action research 232
constructionism 169
constructivism 168-169, 219; *see also* social constructivism
content knowledge understanding aided by digital technologies 171-172
Convention on the Rights of the Child (UN) 71, 191
conversational interactions in mathematics 11, 21-22, 29-30
cooperative learning *see* small-group learning (study)
coping strategies of curriculum change 197-201
creative thinking 156-158, 161-162, 163, 164

creativity and Australian Curriculum *see* Australian Curriculum and creativity
creativity and digital technologies 173
creativity paradigm 251
critical filter for neuromyths 57
critical practices 247, 249
critical reflection 230, 237, 248, 253
critical thinking 173, 250, 251
culturally appropriate resources for rights-based Indigenous education 215
curriculum reform *see* early childhood curriculum reform (study)

Daes, Erica 208
Davis, Brent 11
de Bono's lateral thinking 157, 161-162, 163
democracy in Reggio Emilia approach 100, 101, 103, 105, 108, 110, 111
dendritic growth 48-49
developmental psychology 72
Devi (Mother Goddesses) 244, 245
Dewey, John 213-214, 229-230, 260
dialectic research methods 241, 242, 252
digital equity 45
digital literacy 166-167; *see also* digital technology and learning (study)
digital native 167
digital technology and learning (study): literature review 166-167; methodology 170-171; results and discussion 171-174; theoretical basis 167-170
DiSessa, Andrea 115, 116-117
diversity of students 217
documentation in Reggio Emilia approach 101, 102, 103-105, 106-110, 111
dogs in mathematics classroom 13-15
duty-bound learning (DBL) 197-200, 201

early childhood curriculum reform (study): changing discourses and evolving influences of society, politics and research 191-193; educational change 194-195; methodology 195-197; shifting theories of early childhood education 193; strategies for change 197-201
early childhood educator and speech-language pathologist collaboration *see* collaboration in the classroom (study)
Early Numeracy Research Project (ENRP) 9, 10

Early Years Learning Framework: Being, Belonging, Becoming (EYLF) 190, 191-192, 219
ecological model (Bronfenbrenner) 83-84, 92
economically disadvantaged students 84-85, 86-94
economic productivity and human capital 191, 192
Edmodo *see* language development through online communities (study)
educational change in early childhood education 194-195
education for sustainability (EfS) (study): EfS in Australian Curriculum 179-181; implications 188; methodology 183-184; National Solar Schools Program as background 182-183, 186; results and discussion 185-188; systems thinking 181-182, 185
effective mathematics teachers *see* mathematical thinking and classroom environment (study)
Elliot, John 38
engagement and Whole Brain Teaching method 56-57
English as a second or other language 217
English teachers' perceptions of creativity (study) 158-164
ethical challenges of action research 232-233
evaluative listening 11
exclusion strategies in young children's play 78-79
exit slips 113, 114, 120, 121
expectations by teachers of mathematics students 22
experiential learning theory 169-171

Facebook 63-68
field, domain and the individual interactions 249
Fish, Della 220
forethought phase of Student-Directed Assessment process 125, 126-127, 128-31, 134, 135, 136
formative assessment 26, 113, 114, 120, 121, 123, 152
Foucault, Michel 195-196, 199
Foundation for Young Australians (FYA) 167
Freeman's teacher-researcher cycle 38-39, 45, 237

game-based learning 168-169
Geake, John 57

General capabilities: critical and creative thinking (ACARA) 156, 157
group work *see* small-group learning (study)

habituation and Whole Brain Teaching method 51
Hedegaard's three-stage data analysis approach 28
Hendricks' (2009) classroom AR approach 231
hermeneutic listening 11
hermeneutic phenomenology 102
higher order thinking 139, 166, 167
holistic approach in education 207
human capital and economic productivity 191, 192
hundred languages of children 110
hypothetical learning trajectories 26

"iceberg" of professional practice 220, 221, 225
identity and art educators 247
identity construction in 21st century childhood 68
ill-structured tasks 138-139
image in personal practical knowledge 241, 251-252, 253
imaginative play places 76-79
Indian miniature paintings 244
Indigenous, definitions 207-209
Indigenous Australian, definition 209
Indigenous education experts 212, 214
Indigenous education *see* rights-based Indigenous education
information and communication technologies *see* digital technology and learning (study)
information-processing model *versus* Whole Brain Teaching method 49-51, 56
instructional talk in mathematics 11
InterCultural Education Today (ICET) 39-40
interdependence in small-group learning 139, 141
intergenerational educative trauma 210
international educational assessment 1-2
International Labour Organization Convention No. 169 of 1989 208
Interpretative Phenomenological Analysis (IPA) 51-53
interpretive listening 11
intrapersonal factors in social cognitive theory 124, 125, 127, 132, 135, 136

Japanese exchange students *see* language development through online communities (study)

joint work practices in collaboration 224
justification in mathematics 22

Karyn (pre-service art teacher) 244-246, 248, 249, 250-251
knowing-in-action 229
knowledge exchange in collaboration 224, 225, 226
Kolb's experiential learning cycle 169-171

language development through online communities (study): Communities of Practice (CoP) 35- 36; Edmodo as an online learning community 37-38; implications 45-46; methodology 38-1; results and discussion 41-44; social media tools 36-37 lateral thinking (de Bono) 157, 161-162, 163
Lave, Jean 35-36
learners' perspectives in mathematics 11-12
learning actions in social cognitive theory 124, 128, 129, 134, 136
Lewin, Kurt 230 listening in mathematics 11
listening to voices of young children in educational settings: adult assumptions about 71; children's knowledge of place 73-74, 79; research studies 74-80; shifts in 72-73
literacy, definitions 60-1
literacy and numeracy skills testing 128, 180, 187
literacy in and for 21st century (study): literature review 60-62; methodology 62-63; phenomenological narrative 63-68
long-term memory and Whole Brain Teaching method 50-51
low socio-economic background students 84-85, 86-94

Malaguzzi, Loris 100 Marika-Mununggiritj, Dr 212, 213
mathematical communication 11 mathematical representations 114-115
mathematical thinking and classroom environment (study): background 9; implications and recommendations 21-23; literature review 10-12; methodology 12; results and discussion 13-21; theoretical basis 10; *see also* collaborative learning, teaching and assessment in early years mathematics (study)
Maya (new graduate art teacher) 246, 248, 250

Melbourne Declaration on Educational Goals for Young Australians 155, 164, 179, 206
memory and Whole Brain Teaching method 50-51
metacognition 26, 31
migrant students 217
mirror neurons 50
Mishra and Koehler's TPACK model 167-168
more capable/significant other 27, 29, 30, 33, 83, 84, 92, 93-94, 169
Mosaic Approach 74
Moss, Peter 74
multimodal representations 114-115
multiple representations 114
mutual respect in collaboration 223-224, 226

narrative inquiry approach 76-77, 87, 158-162
narratives of experience 241, 251-2
narrative unities 242, 252
National Assessment Program - Literacy and Numeracy (NAPLAN) 128, 180, 187
National Assessment Program (NAP) ICT 167
National Conservation Strategy for Australia 179
National Quality Framework (NQF) 192
National Solar Schools Program (NSSP) 182-183, 186
national testing 61
neurofacts 49
neuromyths 49, 51, 57
neurons 48-49, 50
neuroscience and brain-based learning 48-49
neuro-scientific research and early childhood education 191
new literacies 166, 167
new pedagogies 257, 259
New Zealand secondary school art programmes 243-244
Northfield, Jeff xii
numeracy *see* collaborative learning, teaching and assessment in early years mathematics (study); mathematical thinking and classroom environment (study)
numeracy skills testing 128, 180, 187

observational learning 50
online learning communities 35-37; *see also* language development through online communities
Organisation for Economic Co-operation (OECD) 1, 156, 162, 163

Papert, Seymour 169
parent-school partnerships *see* student experiences of career counselling process (study)
partially productive groups 147-149, 152
pedagogical documentation 27, 33
performance phase of Student-Directed Assessment process 125, 126-7, 128, 131
personal practical knowledge (study): art educators' dual artmaking and teaching roles 239-240, 246-249, 252-253; conclusion and implications 251-252; creative engagement and reflexive approaches to teaching and learning 249-251, 252, 253; findings and discussion 242-6; research design 241-2; theoretical basis 239, 240-241
perspectives of learners in mathematics 11-12
phenomenology in classroom research 51-53, 62, 63-68, 102
Piaget, Jean 50, 72, 168, 169
place, children's knowledge of 73-74, 79
play places 73-80
point-of-need teaching 134
politics and Indigenous education 210-211
poststructuralism 195-196
Prensky, Marc 167
productive groups 146-147, 152
Productive Pedagogies framework 139, 143
professional development/learning 200, 202, 257, 258-259
Programme for International Student Assessment (PISA) 1-2
propositional knowledge 241 provocations in lateral thinking 157

qualifications of early childhood educators 192-193
quality of teachers 1-2, 257
questioning in mathematics 11

reasoning in mathematics 22
reflection-in-action 229
reflection-on-action 229
reflective practice 53, 229-231, 251, 253, 257, 258
reflexive approaches in art teaching and learning 249-251, 252, 253
refugee students 217

Reggio Emilia classroom practices (study): discussion 103-110; key features of Reggio-inspired educators 99; methodology 102-103; philosophy and principles of Reggio Emilia approach 74, 100-111
representational competence 115-116
representations in science and mathematics 114-115; *see also* assessment of student-generated representations to explore theory-practice connections (study)
respect in collaboration 223-224, 226
rights-based Indigenous education: appropriate terminology and language use 207-210; colonisation, politics and need to "fix" Indigenous education 210-211; problems facing global education system 206-207; steps to aid teachers' learning about 211-215; teachers' lack of knowledge and skills in 205-206, 207

Sarama, Julie 26
scaffolding: collaborative learning, teaching and assessment in early years mathematics 32, 33-34; constructionism 169; language development through online communities 41-42, 45; small-group learning 144, 145, 148, 149, 150, 151, 152, 153; Student-Directed Assessment (SDA) process 124, 125, 126, 128, 136 Schön, Donald 53, 229-230, 236-237
science studies *see* assessment of student-generated representations to explore theory-practice connections (study)
second language acquisition *see* Whole Brain Teaching (WBT) method (study)
"secret places" of children 73, 74-76, 77-80
self-assessment 123
self-efficacy as a learner 125
self-initiated learning (SIL) 197-200, 201, 202
self-reflection phase of Student-Directed Assessment process 125, 126-127, 128
self-regulated learning (SRL) processes 123, 129, 132, 134, 136
Sen, Amartya 85
short-term memory and Whole Brain Teaching method 50
Shulman's model of pedagogical and content knowledge 168
significant/more capable other 27, 29, 30, 33, 83, 84, 92, 93-94, 169

268 Index

situated learning 220
situational/social factors in social cognitive theory 124, 125, 127-128, 129, 132, 134-135, 136
Skinner, B.F. 168
small-group learning (study): background 142; definition and implementation of small-group learning 138-139; discussion 151-153; methodology 142-143; pedagogical processes and productivity 139-142, 146-151; results 144-146 smart meter websites *see* education for sustainability (EfS) (study)
Smith, Jill 242-244, 247-248, 249, 250
social cognitive theory 124, 125, 127-128, 129, 132, 134-136
social constructivism 10, 36; *see also* constructivism
social media tools 36-37; *see also* language development through online communities (study); literacy in and for 21st century (study)
social relationships within online and physical worlds 67-68
social skills and small-group learning 140
sociology of childhood 72
spectator theory of knowledge 260
speech-language pathologists (SLPs) *see* collaboration in the classroom (study)
standardised national testing 61
Stenhouse, Lawrence 38, 230, 237
Student-Directed Assessment (SDA) process (study): Assessment as Learning approach and self-regulated learning processes 123, 129, 132, 134, 136; competence and self-efficacy 125; methodology 125-128; results and discussion 128-135; SDA defined 125; social cognitive theory 124, 125, 127-128, 129, 132, 134-136; writing as a goal-directed cognitive process 125
student experiences of career counselling process (study): findings 87-92; implications 94; lessons learnt from student narratives 92-94; research design 86-87; student perceptions about parental role in subject choice thinking 84-85; student perceptions about school career counselling process 85-86; theoretical basis 83-84
student voice 257, 259
subject choices in secondary schooling *see* student experiences of career counselling process (study)

summative assessment 114
supervisory regulations and young children's sense of place 74, 80
sustainability *see* education for sustainability (EfS) (study)
Sydney Grammar School students' anti-malaria drug 169
systems thinking 181-182, 185

tasks for mathematical thinking 22-23
Teacher Education Ministerial Advisory Group 236
teacher quality 1-2, 257
teacher-researcher cycle 38-9, 45, 237
teachers' situational influence on learning 134-135
teaching up in small-group learning 152
Technological Pedagogical Content Knowledge (TPACK) model 167-168
technology and childhood 61-62
theory-practice connections in science *see* assessment of student-generated representations to explore theory-practice connections (study)
"think slow" approach 157, 162
time management challenges of action research 231-232
Traditional Owners 212
training of early childhood educators 192-193
transactional theory of knowing 260
transferrable skills 167, 172-173
transformative identity of beginning art educators 247

United Nations: Convention on the Rights of the Child 71, 191; Decade of Education for Sustainable Development 181; Declaration on the Rights of Indigenous Peoples (UNDRIPs) 205, 211-212; Educational, Scientific and Cultural Organization (UNESCO) 181; Working Group on Indigenous Populations 207-208
unproductive groups 149-150, 152

Victorian Curriculum 155, 156, 157
Victorian early childhood curriculum reform *see* early childhood curriculum reform (study)
Victorian Early Years Learning and Development Framework (VEYLDF) 190, 191-192
vocabulary competence 132-134
voice of students 257, 259

Vygotsky's sociocultural theory: and Communities of Practice (CoP) 35; and digital technology and learning 168; more capable/significant other 27, 29, 30, 33, 83, 84, 92, 93-94, 169; zone of proximal development 10, 27, 31, 33, 113, 134, 169, 214

Web 1.0 36
Web 2.0 36
Wenger, Etienne 35-36
Western art in New Zealand secondary school art programmes 243-244
"what can be" thinking 157, 161
"what is" thinking 157, 162
Whole Brain Teaching (WBT) method (study): findings 54-56; implications 56-57; methodology 51-54; neuroscience and brain-based learning 48-49; WBT *versus* information-processing model 49-51, 56
Willig's Foucauldian Discourse Analysis (FDA) model 196-197
workplace support during curriculum change 200-201, 202
World Wide Web 36
writing competence 132-134
writing for Student-Directed Assessment process 125-135

Yardley's evaluative criteria for qualitative research 53
Yunupiŋu, Dr 213

zone of proximal development (ZPD) 10, 27, 31, 33, 113, 134, 169, 214

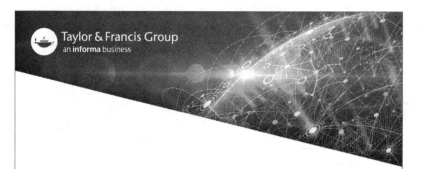